THE MONOTHEISTS

THE MONOTHEISTS

JEWS, CHRISTIANS, AND MUSLIMS IN CONFLICT AND COMPETITION

VOLUME I

The Peoples of God

F. E. Peters

Princeton University Press **Princeton and Oxford**

In the United Kingdom: Princeton University Press, 3 Market Place, Woodstock,
Oxfordshire OX20 1SY

Library of Congress Cataloging-in-Publication Data
Peters, F. E. (Francis E.)
The monotheists : Jews, Christians, and Muslims in conflict and competition / F. E. Peters.
p. cm.
Includes bibliographical references and index.
Contents: v. 1. The peoples of God—v. 2. The words and will of God.
ISBN 0-691-11460-9 (v. 1 : alk. paper)—ISBN 0-691-11461-7 (v. 2 : alk. paper)
1. Judaism—Relations—Christianity—History. 2. Christianity and other
religions—Judaism—History. 3. Judaism—Relations—Islam—History. 4.
Islam—Relations—Judaism—History. 5. Islam—Relations—Christianity—History. 6.
Christianity and other religions—Islam—History. I. Title.
BM535 .P32 2003
291.1'72—dc21   2002042462

British Library Cataloging-in-Publication Data is available

This book has been composed in Janson

Printed on acid-free paper. ∞

www.pupress.princeton.edu

Printed in the United States of America

1 3 5 7 9 10 8 6 4 2

For

Peter Paul Peters,

good man, great son

Contents

②

but
cumulative
and
dialectical

③

Preface

IN 1982 I WROTE a small book called *Children of Abraham*. In it I attempted to put the three monotheistic faith communities of Jews, Christians, and Muslims in a comparative context. The work was undertaken before the appearance of my annotated collection of texts, *Judaism, Christianity, and Islam: The Classical Texts and Their Interpretation*, and my repeated use of this latter book in the classroom. I have taught a course on the combustible mix of Jews, Christians, and Muslims in every academic orbit for more than twenty years, and have lectured on one or another aspect of the subject in a variety of venues across the country. I have learned a great deal not only from my own research and study but from listening to student and audience reactions, and even on occasion from listening to myself since I too have had the not uncommon teaching experience of hearing myself say things I didn't realize I knew or understood. I have tried to put something of what I have learned into this new book.

Another fruit of the classroom experience is my attempt here to be somewhat fuller in my explanations. My first essay was much too condensed in its matter, too telegraphic in its style. The present effort may still suffer some of those same ills because the complexity of this subject has managed to stay well ahead of my understanding of it. The reader must just be patient: I shall do better the next time.

I have also become more venturesome and extended the time frame of the story, as far as Christianity is concerned, to somewhere beyond the Reformation. A similar decisive moment does not occur in Judaism until the nineteenth century, and I have had something to say at least about Hasidism. One of Islam's defining experiences seems to be occurring in the very immediate present, but I have done no more than touch on it.

For all that, this remains an introduction rather than a history, a guide to some of the notions and practices shared by the three monotheistic communities, notions that have also been sources of contention among them. The hard realities of politics and economics are never very far removed from this probe into issues, ideas, and institutions. Who was in charge or who possessed the power at this time or in this place is always a basic ingredient mixed into the relations, and the perceptions, of Jews, Christians, and Muslims. Sometimes these are explicit and apparent in the text; at other times they glare darkly from between the lines. But they are always there.

The intent of this work is not to make peace or to stir up war, or even ill feelings, among the three religious communities, but simply to lay out their common roots, their evolution over time, and what I see as their striking resemblances and their equally striking differences. I am not so foolish, however, as to think this is a value-free exercise. Comparisons can of course be read as invidious; certain resemblances can be parsed as reductive, or relativizing, particularly among believers who are characterized by their conviction of their own unique destiny, as these three certainly are. But this same approach can also broaden understanding in quite remarkable ways. It is a little like experiencing one's own personality in one's offspring, where traits may appear far less endearing and charming than we imagine them in ourselves. It is one of the more salutary effects of forcing these three particular siblings to pose, however briefly, for a family portrait.

A caution for the reader: As everyone since Thales has discovered, it is considerably easier to talk about complex phenomena if we essentialize or reify them into a single, and relatively simple, "thing." It is difficult to imagine more complex phenomena than the three "things" here called—not for the first time, of course—Judaism, Christianity, and Islam. We know but sometimes forget that there really are no such "things." There are only Jews, Christians, and Muslims, billions of them, whose common marks we try to make sense of here. They have collected themselves in communities and answer to those names, and a book like this is an attempt to answer why. It is assuredly easier to get and compare the answers if we attend to what is called the "high tradition," the thoughtful literary works of educated Jews, Christians, and Muslims who, like us, are looking for the forests, instead of scrutinizing the scattered records carved on the individual trees. The latter records are assuredly there, thin in some times and places, thick in others, telling which Jews were mixing their milk with their mutton and which not, how many Christians were sleeping in on Sunday mornings, and why this Muslim woman wore a veil and that one chose not to. The argument can be made that *this* is really what those three "religions" are all about, and not what Maimonides or Augustine or Ibn Khaldun thought they were. Perhaps, but these forests, for all their subversive nonexistence, are not yet so clearly charted that we can all fall to counting trees. Hence, this essentialist guide to three very thickly wooded, and essential, patches of the human experience.

Each of these volumes has been indexed separately in the hope of saving the reader some thumb-wrenching acrobatics, and there are abundant cross-references to carry one back and forth between the two. Finally, some paragraphs of these volumes, notably those having to do with Islam, have appeared in somewhat different form, and in a quite different context, in my work *Islam: A Guide for Jews and Christians* (Princeton, 2003).

In my earlier work I gave abundant thanks to my academic colleagues for their help and inspiration. The gratitude is still academic, but this time it is for all the winning young men and women who have paid quite extraordinary sums of money to sit on the other side of the desk and listen, after a fashion, to what I have had to say. They may not have always understood what the gentleman leaning on the podium and rattling on about Rambam and plenary indulgences was exactly up to, but they listened, most of them, and they talked back on occasion, some of them, though always in good humor. They likely taught me a great deal more than I taught them, and I take this occasion to thank them all for giving me a couple precious months of their lives.

Introduction

FROM WHAT WE READ in the recorded history of his devotees, the god ⟶ C: | sent
who created the universe had shown some earlier, generally benevolent interest in what he had brought into being. Then, at a given moment in historical ⟶ election:
time, he addressed himself to one Abram, the sheikh of an extended family of
Near Eastern sheep nomads who were camping in what is today called the
Negev. Worship me, the god said, and I will make you and yours a great people. It was not a unique or a solitary voice: we know from plentiful evidence
that there were other, many other, gods on that landscape and in the minds of
Abram's contemporaries. Abram, however, limited his worship to this one deity, and the god in turn granted his favor to Abram, or Abraham, as he was
henceforward called.

The story continues—in the Bible and in the countless books that derive
from it—with an account of how Abraham's descendants, the "Sons of Israel,"
were drawn into Egypt, where there were gods in great abundance, figured in
almost every form of human and beast. The Israelites eventually escaped under
divine guidance and the shrewd and courageous leadership of Moses. On their
long trek across Sinai, their god, who revealed that his name was Yahweh, unfolded his will to Moses and the Israelites. From atop a mountain in Sinai, he
unmistakably asserted what was already perhaps implicit in the dialogue with
Abraham: I am your Lord; you will worship no other but me.

This was an assertion of divine primacy; the god was *primus inter impares*,
though in this instance Yahweh did not explain in what his primacy consisted, ∨
whether the other deities were his offspring, his consorts, his messengers, or
perhaps just too minor to matter. He simply ignored them, though his wor- ∨
shipers assuredly did not on occasion. What was truly revolutionary in the
covenant offered to Abraham, and then in more detail to Moses, was its exclusivity clause. The tribe of Israel was to worship no other god, to pay no
dues, to give no respect, honor, or even acknowledgment to the deities of other
peoples. This appears to us, who define monotheism as the denial of belief in
any god save one, as at best henotheism, the recognition of a primary god

above all others. But it is in practice, true monotheism. Where it really counted, in sacrifice and invocation, the Israelites were required to behave as if there were only one god. It would take centuries for that radical liturgical disregard of the other gods to be fully conceptualized into a denial of their very existence, a process immeasurably aided by the fact that this god, astonishingly, had no image or effigy. Boldly, Yahweh could only be imagined.

Yahweh would have it no other way. He was, in his own words, a "jealous god" whose very first commandment to Moses on Sinai had to do with his own exclusive rights to the gifts and rituals that were the dues of a god. Jealous and phobic: in the biblical account that sets the tone and terms for all who subsequently worshiped him, Yahweh demanded that all forms of "impurity" be kept at a very safe distance from him, away from his throne and his house, away from his city, away from his land. We are puzzled by the exact nature of this terrifying impurity that runs broadly and somewhat erratically through Yahweh's own creation, which he had earlier praised as "good." But the "abomination of abominations," the Mother of all Impurities, was an altar set up to one of those other gods in Yahweh's own Jerusalem sanctuary. Finally, and with extraordinary consequence, what was abominable to Yahweh was also to be abominable to the Israelites, who thus became morally identified with their god.

These are the beginnings of monotheism, a way of acting toward, thinking about, and, eventually, of believing in this deity known as (but not readily called) Yahweh by the Israelites, as God the Father by others, and as Allah by still others. Whatever the name, he is the same God worshiped by Jews, Christians, and Muslims as the creator and sustainer of the universe, the supreme and unique Deity from whom all proceeds and in whom all ends. Why there are three distinct communities of his believers and how and why they worship and think about him (and one another) as they do is the subject of the following pages.

The three communities have had a long, complex, and profoundly imbricated history, and I have here divided it, to grant some intermission, into two volumes. The first, *The Peoples of God*, describes how the three communities came about, evolved, identified and organized themselves. The first volume has a great deal to do with externals of community formation, whereas the second, *The Words and Will of God*, is given over to what might be called the internal or spiritual life of the monotheists, the working out of God's will in the lives, hearts, and minds of his believers. Running through both volumes is the enormously interesting and increasingly vital question of how Jews, Christians, and Muslims have dealt with one another. In another book I used the metaphor of the family to describe that relationship—these are the "Children of Abraham"—and the figure is still useful in understanding them, as I attempt to spell out in the end thoughts of each volume.

details

Before we begin, some simple cautionary remarks may be in order. Whatever may be thought of it, Christianity is by now common intellectual and spiritual coin in the West, and Judaism only somewhat less so. But for many Western readers, "Islam" and "Muslims" are still exotic or even somewhat baffling terms and concepts. The notions surrounding Islam will be unfolded in detail in the pages that follow, but a few sentences on the terms themselves will help at the very outset. "Islam" is an Arabic term that broadly means "submission," in this context, submission to God; thus, a "Muslim," a derivative from the same root, is "someone who has submitted." Though "Islam" and "Muslim"—as well as "Quran"—are all Arabic in origin, not all Muslims are Arabs by a long shot, and a great many Turks, Iranians, and Afghans, and millions and millions of Pakistanis, Indians, and Indonesians are properly upset when they are thought to be Arabs because they are Muslims. If all Muslims are not Arabs, neither are all Arabs Muslims. Many Palestinian Arabs are Christians, for example, and so too are very many Lebanese Arabs. Christians too can be of any ethnicity, and how the Jews identify themselves will emerge as we go along.

The reader will already perhaps have noted a discrepancy between an anticipated "Moslem" and the somewhat less familiar spelling of "Muslim." There is much of the same ahead. The more common Englished "Koran" will appear in these pages as "Quran," and even though I have used only one of them, there are almost as many English versions of "Muhammad" in circulation as there are of "Hanukkah." The reason is that both Arabic and Hebrew use their own, non-Latin scripts, and they do not normally insert vowels in writing their words. Thus, when these words are transcribed into a Latin script that must represent both the consonants and English vowel sounds, some transcriptions reflect what is written and others what is heard. In any event, I have tried to be both consistent and helpful rather than baffling or just downright quirky. But, as the Muslims say, God knows best.

To pass from simple orthography onto the more slippery terrain of the theology of names, which the monotheists take extremely seriously, as already noted, the name of our subject deity will here be referred to throughout simply as "God"—with apologies to those who prefer an even more reverential but somewhat distracting "G-d." And no effort will be made to conceal God's unmistakable—to his earliest devotees—masculine gender, even after worshipers came to believe he had no body at all.

As some will doubtless note, the punctilious rubric "is understood" or "is believed," or the less polite and more pointed "says you," will be omitted throughout—though the reader may supply it as liberally as is thought necessary. The descriptive and argumentative statements in the text will be presented, unless otherwise noted, as they are accepted and understood by the monotheist community in question.

The present work is more about faith than about history, more about the faith communities than about the various tribes of historians who have studied them. At stake here is not what *really* happened, even if that were possible to ascertain, but rather what Jews, Christians, and Muslims *believe* happened. I do not forswear analysis; indeed, there is a good deal of it here. But it will be used principally to elicit the similarities and differences among the three faiths and so render their comparison intelligible, not, in the manner of the critical historian, to weigh and verify or discard. Some things are ignored here from economy or perhaps simple inadvertence; nothing is discarded. The contents of every page of this book, like every line of the Scriptures and traditions on which they are based, have been the subject of intense critical scrutiny and equally intense argument among historians who are believers, nonbelievers who are historians, and generations of believers caught between the two.

Finally, in everything that follows, "Bible" always means the Hebrew or Jewish Bible. Although the Christians certainly reckon their own Scriptures as part of the Bible, these will always be called here the "New Testament" or the "Gospels." "Old Testament," which is an argument rather than just a name, will be reserved for the quite different version of the Jewish Scriptures preferred and used by the Christians.

Note: It is my unhappy but inevitable duty to say something about calendars since they have been the source of both mischief and misunderstanding. Jews, Christians, and Muslims reckon time in different ways, so here all years will be recorded as B.C.E. (before the common era) and C.E. (common era). A distinction must be made between *where* people begin counting time and *how* they count it. The Jews begin with Creation, which they put at 3760 B.C.E., and count straight onward without a break. Thus, our portentous year 2000 fell quite innocuously across the years 5760–5761 in the Hebrew calendar. Christians too begin with Creation, except their traditional date for that event is 4004 B.C.E. They count downward from there to the end of 1 B.C., when they reverse at this watershed year of Christ's birth (A.D., *anno Domini*), which marks the beginning of the Christian era. Thenceforward they begin numbering upward toward the end of the world, the day or the hour of which no one knows. For Muslims, the years from Creation to the Hegira, Muhammad's migration from Mecca to Medina, in 622 C.E. are simply lumped together as "the era of ignorance" (*al-jahiliyya*). In 622 begins the Muslim era proper, generally designated by A.H., *anno Hegirae*, "year of the Hegira."

How the three communities count is another matter. Jews and Muslims use lunar calendars made up of 12 months of 29+ days for a total of 354 days. This puts the lunar year 11 days behind the solar cycle of our

> (*continued*)
>
> calendar. Jews address the discrepancy (and thus keep their festivals in step with the seasons) by intercalation, the practice of adding an extra month seven times in every cycle of 19 years and adding a single day at other shorter intervals. The Quran (9:36–37) strictly forbade Muslims to intercalate (as they had in pre-Islamic days), and so their lunar year falls 11 days behind the solar cycle each year. By their reckoning, the solar year 2000 C.E. spanned the lunar years 1421–1422 A.H. Christians follow the solar calendar commonly used in the West.

I

The Covenant: From Israelite to Jew

A Prologue on Earth

The Bible starts not with the Covenant but with Creation, the absolute beginning of time. It is a complex account that fills the first chapter of the Bible's first book, appositely called Genesis, and spills over into the succeeding chapter, where the narrative picks up and follows the story of the first man and woman, Adam and Eve. The Christians read the same Bible, of course, though they called it the Old Testament, and they often interpret it quite differently from the Jews who wrote it. But the third set of monotheists, the Muslims, have their own separate version of those primordial events in a complementary Scripture called the Quran, which they likewise venerate as the Word of God. The Quran's account of Creation, although similar to that of the Bible in intent and some detail—both insist on an omnipotent creation from nothing, for example, and on the Creator's fashioning of humankind—is not laid out in the linear narrative fashion of Genesis (or of the Bible as a whole). The Quran is the collection of revelations given by God to Muhammad over the last twenty-two years of his life. They are divided into 114 suras or chapters, but some of the suras almost certainly contain more than one revelation. The Muslims' Scripture, then, is a collection of "occasional" revelations rather than a single narrative or story, and so the events of God's creation are introduced in the Quran at various appropriate points—appropriate to God's purpose of warning and instructing—rather than at the outset on the linear model of Genesis. Where Creation events are cited in the Quran, they are generally in résumé form and presented as moral examples, to underline God's power, for instance, or his goodness.

The Quran's Account of Early Humanity

Adam and Eve—Eve, Hawwa in Arabic, is never mentioned by name in the Quran (cf. 2:35)—are also given a somewhat different treatment in the Muslim Scripture. The Bible tells a deftly crafted story of the first couple's temptation, fall, and banishment from Eden (Gen. 2:15–24), a tale from which Christian theologians like Augustine later fashioned the powerful doctrine of Original Sin (see II/5). The Quran is well aware of that back story (2:35–39; 7:19–25), though no mention is made of Eve's role in the fall. Rather, the villain of the tale is Iblis (< Gk. *diabolos*), the angel who refused to bow down before Adam at God's command and was banished from heaven with whomever of the angels chose to follow him (2:34; 7:11–18). Then, as Shaytan (< Gk. *satanas* < Heb. *satan*), he seduces both Adam and Eve to eat the fruit of the forbidden tree (2:36; 7:20).

Among the other pre-Abraham patriarchs in Genesis, the Quran takes some note of the briefly mentioned Enoch (Gen. 5:23–24), who, after a lifetime of 365 years, "having walked with God was seen no more because God had taken him away"—that is, if the prophet Idris of Quran 21:85 is to be identified with him, as is commonly done. But this is small note indeed when compared to the veritable library of works attributed to the gone but assuredly not forgotten Enoch by the Jews of late Second Temple times and the early Christians who grew up in their midst. Of far greater interest to the Quran is Noah (Gen. 6:9–9:27), who is mentioned often in the Muslims' Book; indeed, all of Quran 71 is devoted to him. An account of the Flood is given in more than one place, and the main, and nonbiblical, thrust of the story is clear from the theme's lengthy treatment in Quran 11:25–48. Noah was, like Muhammad, a messenger (*rasul*), sent to a people who rejected him and who were consequently punished with the Flood. Noah was one of the prophets from whom God took his covenant (Quran 33:7), yet the Bible's description of its terms (Gen. 9:8–17) and the other dietary and criminal laws laid down for Noah and his descendants (9:1–7) are nowhere mentioned in the Quran. The matter of Genesis, then, is familiar terrain to both Jews (with the Christians reading over their shoulder) and Muslims. How not, thought the Muslims, since the same God had revealed his truth to all three "Peoples of the Book," *his* Book.

History Begins

The history proper of the three great monotheistic communities begins late in chapter 11 of Genesis. There we are introduced to Abram, as he is then named, whom God summons to a special relationship with himself. A promise is made, a promise repeated numerous times under differing circumstances in the subsequent chapters of Genesis. Abram is first bidden to leave Haran—he had already emigrated from his native Iraq ("Ur of the Chaldees")—to a place that God would indicate. The place is Canaan, and Abram passes through several of its holy places—holy even before Abram's arrival—like Shechem, Bethel, and later Hebron. Interwoven with these movements are two divine promises: "I will make you a great nation" (12:2) and "I give this land to your descendants" (12:7). Just before Abram's arrival at Hebron, the promise is expanded:

> Raise your eyes and look into the distance from the place where you are, north and south, east and west. All the land you can see I will give to you and your descendants for ever. I will make your descendants as countless as the dust of the earth; if anyone could count the dust upon the ground, then he could count your descendants. Now go through the length and breadth of the land, for I give it to you. (13:14–17)

There follows (14:18–20) the curious incident of Melchizedek, whose name may be a title ("My king (is) Zadek/Justice") and who is described here as king of Salem and a "priest of God Most High." He pronounces a blessing on Abram and in turn is given a tithed share of Abram's war booty. The historical and textual significance of the brief passage is complex, but what concerns us here is its religious development. Melchizedek reappears in Psalm 110:4 where the Davidic king of Jerusalem (as the "Salem" of Genesis was later sometimes understood) is declared to be "a priest forever in the succession of Melchizedek." His appearance in this context may have been intended as a bolster to David's monarchy, but its long-term effect was to introduce Melchizedek into the messianic complexes of late Second Temple Judaism. Christians read the Bible differently, as will be seen. Melchizedek was taken up, in any event, by the Christian author of The Letter to the Hebrews, where Psalm 110 is invoked to illustrate the transfer of the Jewish priesthood from the "succession of Aaron" to that of Melchizedek, who, it is said, "owed his priesthood not to a system of earth-bound rules but to the power of a life that cannot be destroyed" (Heb. 7:16). Thus the high priesthood of Jesus and, subsequently, the Christian sacerdotal system were grounded and validated in the appearance of the mysterious Melchizedek in the fourteenth chapter of Genesis.

Faith and Act

Like the authors of the Bible, monotheists past and present see Abraham—as he finally came to be called—from the perspective of his worship of their god, who was, of course, the Only God. But if we regard Abraham in his own context, though obviously through the focusing (or distorting) lens of the biblical account, we can see that he is actually first identified as someone who worshiped this god rather than that, a choice the Quran's complementary narrative of the same events makes particularly clear, and, more importantly, worshiped *only* this god. We must think that at least some of Abraham's ancestors or relatives had worshiped this god too—Yahweh, to give him his later

self-identification—but what made Abraham notable was his *exclusive* worship of
Yahweh. This was the reason Yahweh chose to reward him with the Covenant.

Was it, however, Abraham's worship of Yahweh or his belief in this deity
that rendered him pleasing to God? His faith or his acts? Paul answered this
question for his fellow Jews in the first century, and Martin Luther posed it
afresh to his church in the sixteenth. It was belief, Luther responded with
Paul: Abraham's faith had made him "righteous" in God's eyes (see II/5).
Luther's answer has generally prevailed in the Christian tradition, which
thinks of religion chiefly in terms of faith. The ancients, however, had a somewhat different view. While religion certainly included what we would call interior states, like fear of God's justice or trust in his mercy, it was more often
judged in terms of practice, more specifically, of ritual practice or worship. It
was never a question of Abraham's believing in Yahweh, as in "Do you believe
in God?"—there were very few atheists in the ancient or, indeed, the premodern world—so much as his putting trust in Yahweh and showing it by performing acts of worship, like sacrifice, to acknowledge that trust, or, to use a
later Muslim term, that submission (*islam*).

When the promise was first made to him, the man still known as Abram was
past seventy-five years of age and had no children; indeed, when God later appears to him "in a vision" (Gen. 15:1), Abram points out that his sole heir is a
certain Eliezer of Damascus, possibly an adopted slave. God assures him that
there will be an heir of his own line, "a child of your own body," and once
again there is a promise to the still nomadic Abram and his descendants of a
land, here defined in enlarged fashion to embrace all the territory "from the
River of Egypt to the Great River, the river Euphrates" (15:18).

A Holy Land

This last literary tracing of the Promised Land represents, in what was even
then a rhetorical exaggeration, the extent of the kingdom later ruled over by
Solomon (so 1 Kings 4:21), a matter of interest to the biblical historian perhaps, but not for the Jewish believer who read it as one definition of the land
owned by God—and thus sanctified—and now shared with his favored people. This holy land, Eretz Israel, as it will later be called, eventually came into
the possession of Abraham's descendants—these events are chiefly described
in the Book of Joshua—and then the consequences of dwelling in that land
first fell into place. Many of the regulations, those governing agricultural
tithes, for example, which were later given to Moses in the Torah (see II/4)
could—and can—be fulfilled only within the boundaries of the Land of Israel.
Thus the boundaries of that land had to be accurately drawn for purposes of
precise observance of the Law. We do not know how early that task began, but
it was certainly taken seriously in early rabbinic times.

The connection of the Land and the Law had as its obvious corollary the notion that perfect observance was possible only within the Land of Israel, whence flowed the obligation of return (*aliya*, literally, "going up") to that Holy Land. The obligation to return to the Promised Land increasingly informed Jewish sensibilities as the number of Jews living "abroad" in the so-called Diaspora (see below) grew over the centuries. This amalgam of spiritual nostalgia and desire for strict observance of the Law constituted a kind of spiritual Zionism—Zion is one of the names of the temple mount in Jerusalem—which most Jews in most places embraced over the centuries, and led eventually to its modern, more nationalistic counterpart, political Zionism (see I/6).

Both Christians and Muslims view the same land as holy, though for quite different reasons. Very early on Christians had begun to disassociate themselves not only from the main body of Jews but also from the Jewish Holy Land in general and their Holy City, Jerusalem, in particular. The Muslims, who see no visions of a "heavenly Jerusalem," have no particular religious claims on that land, though they do on certain of its holy places, and, what is quite a different matter, some Arabs of the region obviously have a political claim on Palestine. Neither Christianity nor Islam fosters the notion of a "return" to their Palestinian holy land, however—not, at least, in the sense of a migration. What was generated instead was, first, a powerful desire to visit the places esteemed holy in that land—the practice we call "pilgrimage"—and second, the more overtly political wish to control those same places. In Western Christendom this impulse led in the eleventh century to the first of the Christian holy wars against Islam, the Crusades (see I/8), and in Islam, to a powerful Counter-Crusade under the famous hero Salah al-Din (Saladin), who in 1187 retook Jerusalem and Palestine from the Frankish Christian crusaders. Both these events have colored European thinking about Palestine and Muslim thinking about Christian Europe's designs on it down to modern times, and from the late nineteenth century the Jewish political movement called Zionism has both used and resisted those impulses.

Hagar and Ishmael

It is his wife Sarai who in the opening verses of Genesis 16 suggests to Abram that perhaps he can and should father a son with her Egyptian slave-girl, Hagar. So indeed he does. There is quickly, and perhaps inevitably, a falling-out between the two women. Hagar flees and returns only after a divine apparition promises that her son will have many descendants, though he himself will ever be an outcast. At his birth this first son is called Ishmael; Abram is by then eighty-six years old (16:10–16). Some thirteen years later, the Lord appears once more to Abram. He repeats the promise of numerous heirs and a land to

possess, but now the promise is connected with a reciprocal act on Abram's 2ⁿᵈ
part: as a sign of the covenant, he must <u>circumcise</u> all the males of his house- visit
hold, kin and foreigner alike, the newborn on the eighth day. It is on this occasion too that, in an act symbolizing the transformation of their state—it
happens often in these three communities—Abram's name is changed to
Abraham and Sarai's to Sarah. Abraham is puzzled, however. He and his wife
are far beyond parenthood; perhaps it is Ishmael, after all, who will inherit the
promise. No, the Lord insists, Ishmael will be the father of a great nation, but
it is the son of Abraham and Sarah who will inherit. Abraham has himself,
Ishmael, and the other males of his household, kin and slaves, circumcised
without further comment (Gen. 17).

The promise will be offered once again by God before it is finally fulfilled 3ʳᵈ
in Isaac's birth. It next arises during a mysterious visit of "three men" to Abra- visit
ham's camp at Mamre by Hebron. Abraham responds with a hospitality that
makes him into the Bible's paradigm of generosity, the "friend of God," as he
will be known to Jews, Christians, and Muslims. One of the "strangers," who
becomes, in the midst of the following exchange, the Lord, assures Sarah she
will have a child; she laughs (18:1–15). There follow the extended incidents of
the destruction of Sodom and Gomorrah, and not until the beginning of
Genesis 21 is Isaac, the heir to the Covenant, born to Sarah. Sarah and Hagar
are still at odds, however, and it is at Sarah's insistence that Hagar and her son
Ishmael are driven out of Abraham's camp near Beersheba to wander in the
desert, where the child would surely have died had not God heard Hagar's
prayer and caused the miraculous appearance of a well. "God was with the
child," the account concludes, "and he grew up and lived in the wilderness of
Pharan" (21:20–21).

This is almost the last we hear of Ishmael in the Bible. Ishmael himself
marries an Egyptian wife (21:20–21), and one of his daughters marries Esau
(25:13–15), from whom the Edomites—later the Idumeans—of the Negev are
descended. In Genesis 25:9 Ishmael is somewhat unaccountably present with
Isaac to bury Abraham at Hebron, and there is a list of his sons in Genesis
25:12–18. They dwell somewhere to the east of the Israelites.

Ishmaelites and Arabs

Although at his death, at age 137 (Gen. 25:17), Ishmael disappears from the
Bible, he remained in the consciousness of the Jews. We cannot follow the full
gestation of the story, but we can read its denouement. The source of Genesis may have thought the Edomites of the Negev, one of Israel's inveterate
enemies, were the nation descended from Ishmael, but a later generation of
Jews thought otherwise. The second-century B.C.E. *Book of Jubilees*, which is
largely a retelling of Genesis from a slightly different perspective, informs

us that Abraham before his death summoned all his sons and grandchildren, including Ishmael and his twelve offspring, and bade them to continue to observe circumcision, to avoid ritual uncleanness and marriage with the Canaanites. Then, at the end of the same passage, a crucial identification is made, though almost certainly not for the first time. The sons of Ishmael, and their cousins, the offspring of Abraham and another wife, Keturah, with whom they intermarried, did indeed become a great nation, as God had promised: they were the Arabs. Abraham sends Ishmael and his offspring to settle "between Pharan and the borders of Babylon, in all the land to the East, facing the desert. And these mingled with each other, and they were called Arabs and Ishmaelites" (20:11–13).

Both the name and the identification stuck, first among the Jews—the historian Josephus discusses this at length in speaking of the Nabateans, Israel's Arab neighbors east of the Jordan (*Antiquities* 1.12.2–4)—and then among the Christians of the Middle East. For these latter, the Arabs were either Ishmaelites or Saracens. The latter word is of unknown origin, but the Middle Eastern Christians of the pre-Islamic era parsed it in biblical terms: "Saracen" came from "Sarah" and the Greek "kene," "empty" or "void," thus "Sara-is-barren." When Sozomen wrote his *Church History* in 440 C.E., he pointed to the obvious similarities between Arab and Jewish customs, like circumcision and refraining from pork. True, the Ishmaelite Arabs had been corrupted by their long association with the pagans who surrounded them, but, adds Sozomen, "many still live in the Jewish fashion."

None of this had anything to do with Islam. The identification of the Arabs as Ishmaelites was strictly ethnic—everyone knew the Arabs were polytheists—based on a similarity of customs. One not, apparently, aware of the identification was Muhammad. Ishmael appears several times in the Quran, first as a somewhat indistinct Hebrew prophet, and then, in later chapters, as Abraham's son. Quite remarkably, he and Abraham are said to have built the Kaaba, the sacred shrine building that stood in Muhammad's day—as it does today—in the midst of Mecca (2:125–127). The Quran offers no explanation for this extraordinary information, and so we can only assume that it was known and accepted as true not only by Muhammad but, even more astonishingly, by his listeners.

Muhammad strongly emphasized that the Islam being promulgated in the Quran was nothing other than the "religion of Abraham" (see I/3) and that the earlier activity of Abraham—and Ishmael—in Mecca was crucial to this *origins* enterprise. But nowhere is it suggested or even hinted that Muhammad was aware that Ishmael was widely recognized elsewhere as the Arabs' ancestor. Nor is it ever asserted that Islam's claim to be the new version of the true faith was based on the Arabs' blood descent from Abraham through Ishmael, as the Jews' was by their descent through Isaac and Jacob. Muslims are *not*, in any event, the "Children of Ishmael."

Abraham in Mecca

The Quran pays far greater attention than the Bible to the story of Abraham's "conversion" from his father's paganism to worship of the One True God (6:74–79), but then it passes directly to the patriarch's activities in Mecca. There is no mention of Hagar or Sarah, nor of the Bible's elaborate stories of the births of Ishmael and Isaac. It was left for the later Muslim tradition to spell out the details of how Abraham and Ishmael got from Palestine to Mecca. There are numerous differing accounts of the Abraham epic in the Muslim historians of the ninth and tenth centuries, who by then had access, through Jewish (and Christian) converts to Islam, to a great deal of postbiblical legend of the type known in Hebrew as *haggadah* (see II/2). According to one common version, Sarah in her rage has Hagar circumcised before banishing her and her son. Abraham himself escorted Hagar and Ishmael to Mecca, and the latter had then to be old enough to assist his father in building the Kaaba.

But there are other versions of the story. Hagar and Ishmael wander off to Mecca while the latter is still an infant. Then Genesis 21:15–19, the travails of mother and child in exile near Beersheba, is integrated into the story, though now transferred to Mecca and its vicinity. This explains some of the practices of the Muslim pilgrimage or hajj. Only later did Abraham come to Mecca in search of his son, and on that occasion, when Ishmael was grown up, they built the Kaaba together and Abraham instituted the practices of the hajj (Quran 22:26) (see II/6).

At the end of these tales Abraham returns to Palestine, where the rest of his biblical career unfolds. But Ishmael and his sons—Ishmael marries a local Arab princess in the Muslim stories—remain behind in Mecca, where they worship God and rule the town for a generation until they are overwhelmed, politically and religiously, by the pagan Arabs who surround them.

Hebron

Hebron looms large in the story of Abraham. Originally there were three distinct localities in this settlement nineteen miles south of Jerusalem: the town of Hebron, the nearby village of Mamre where Abraham greeted his guests beneath the oak, and the cave called Machpelah, where were thought to be buried not only Abraham and Sarah but Isaac, Jacob, and their wives (save Rachel). Adam's grave site was also shown nearby. Hebron must have become an important cult and pilgrimage center since there was a grandiose sanctuary built over the graves, probably by Herod, which still stands. The Christian emperor Constantine constructed a basilica at Abraham's oak at Mamre, on a site where already, on the testimony of a contemporary witness, Jews, Christians, and pagans held festivals together. Jews and Christians also worshiped together in the great tomb building—which the Christians seem to have converted into a church, St. Abram's—though they were separated, we are told, by a screen. With the seventh-century arrival of the Muslims, whose devotion to Abraham, the friend of God, was no less than that of the Jews and Christians, Hebron became further magnified. Muslim legend soon made Solomon the builder of the great sanctuary, which was quickly turned into a mosque. By the tenth century there was at Hebron, much in the tradition of the generous Abraham, a hostel and soup kitchen for the care and feeding of pilgrims, which was supported by one of Islam's oldest pious foundations (*waqf*: see II/4, II/8).

Isaac and the Covenant

The Bible makes perfectly clear that the Israelites, later called Jews, are the Chosen People, and why not, since they wrote it. Why, then, do the Christians and Muslims think *they* are? First, recall that the Christians were themselves Jews, and that when they claimed they were Abraham's heirs they were earmarking themselves, like other Jewish sects, as the one faithful remnant among God's own. They were following Abraham in faith in their conviction that Jesus was the promised Messiah, an argument spelled out at some length in Paul's Letter to the Romans. There were also plentiful suggestions scattered through the Bible that God was more than a little displeased with his people. There were even hints, like those dropped in Jeremiah 31, that the Covenant might be renegotiated, which is, the Christians claimed, exactly what happened. Finally, the Christians also maintained that this was a New Covenant for an eschatological moment in the history of Israel, one that justified the Gentiles' (the goyim, or non-Jews) being drawn into "the Kingdom," to use Jesus' own preferred image for the End Time (see I/2). Faith, then, was at the base of the Christians' claim, faith in Jesus, not mere obedience of the Law. That is the background of the debate about the commanded, then aborted, sacrifice—usually referred to in Hebrew as the "binding" (*aqedah*)—of Isaac, Abraham's son, in Genesis 22, whether it was, as the Christians maintained, a model act of faith or, as the Jews countered, a manifestation of Abraham's obedience, a fidelity that won him God's Covenant.

The same incident of a human sacrifice demanded of Abraham is described in the Quran (37:101–107). In the immediately preceding verses (83–100) Abraham argues with his father and his people about their idolatry. When Abraham insults their gods, they say, "Build for him a building and fling him in the red-hot fire. And they designed a trap for them but We [that is, God, who often refers to himself by the plural pronoun in the Quran] . . . made them the undermost." Then, without transition, the text turns to a new topic, Abraham's unnamed son: "We gave him glad tidings of a son. And when he was old enough to work with

him, he . . . [presumably Abraham; the Quran is not always generous in identifying its pronouns] said: 'O dear son, I have seen in a dream that I must sacrifice
you. So look, what do you think?' He said: 'O my father, do that which you are
commanded. God willing, you will find me steadfast.'" And then, "when they
had both submitted (*aslama*)," God tells Abraham that it was merely a test, and
concludes, "And We ransomed him with a momentous victim."

The entire incident is a good example of the Quran's allusive style. The
story is filled with spaces and moves uncertainly to its point—"Thus do We
reward the good"—stripping all the biblical details of time and place, the
journey, the servants, the fuel, the altar, the ram caught in the thicket, while
adding the dream vision and his son's urging Abraham to do what he had to
do. As it stands, the story is comprehensible, but only barely so, and only if we
assume that the listeners already had, as we do, some idea what was being
talked about. Two points are worth noting, however. First, the text does not
say which son was being sacrificed, and the earliest Muslim commentators
were uncertain whether it was Isaac, as in the Bible, or Ishmael, as his importance in the Muslim Abraham tradition seemed to require. Second, the
Quran, unlike the Bible's account but in agreement with many later Jewish
treatments of the subject, makes that son, whether Isaac or Ishmael, both
aware and approving of Abraham's willingness to sacrifice his own child at
God's command. His self-sacrifice was voluntary.

Claims and Counterclaims

The promises of God's Covenant were made not merely to Abraham but to
his descendants as well, and among those descendants emerged a theme that
would later be of great interest to the Christians in their claim to the
covenanted inheritance. In the Bible that inheritance passes over the firstborn
to the benefit of a younger brother, from Ishmael to Isaac in the first generation, and then, in the next, from Esau to his younger brother Jacob. Thus, the
Christians argued in their typical figurative reading of Scripture (see II/2), the
Bible foreshadows the displacement of the firstborn Israel and their replacement by the latter-day faithful, the followers of Jesus the Messiah.

The Muslim claim feeds off two traditions. The first is that the call to Islam
is one of successive revelations sent by God to humans, each in effect replac-
ing an earlier, imperfectly observed revelation (see II/1). In that sense Islam
supersedes both Christianity and Judaism. But it is also more pristine than either in that it returns to the religion of Abraham, whose traces were still to be
found in Mecca in Muhammad's day. As we have seen, the Quran (2:125–127)
notes that the Meccan Kaaba was built by Abraham and Ishmael. Abraham
also originally instituted, again at God's command, the hajj, which Muhammad purified and restored to its proper perspective among the believers

Muslim bracket

(see II/6). All this occurred long before the Torah was given to Moses or the gift of prophecy was bestowed on Jesus, and so, though Muhammad is the "seal of the prophets" (Quran 33:40) in the sense that none will come after him, his message has a certain primacy in that it goes directly back, by both its content and its historic Meccan affiliation, to the oldest form of monotheism.

M
B
A

Jacob's Dream at Bethel

The Bible dwells at length on Jacob, Abraham's grandson. We are told (Gen. 28:1–23) that he had a dream vision, a not uncommon event in the ancient world. In it Jacob saw a stairway reaching to heaven and "angels going up and down." At this time in this same place the Covenant was renewed "by the Lord standing beside him," an event Jacob commemorates—"This is none other than the house of God," he exclaimed (28:17)—by calling the place Bethel and setting up a stone pillar and anointing it. We are reminded of other stones: the black one in Mecca installed in one corner of the Bayt Allah, the "House of God," as the Kaaba is called, and the other great stone, sacred to Muslims, as once it apparently had been to the Jews, that sits enshrined on the temple mount in Jerusalem under the Dome of the Rock.

The dream at Bethel was not the only epiphany or theophany granted to Jacob. Once, when he was about to ford a stream, he engaged in a wrestling match with a stranger who changed his name to "Israel" and whom Jacob identified as God himself: "I have seen a divine being face to face and yet my life has been preserved," he later fearfully recollected (32:30).

Jacob, now Israel, had twelve sons—whose descendants would constitute the Twelve Tribes of Israel—and the ongoing narrative in Genesis carries them and their descendants into Egypt and eventually into bondage to the Pharaoh. At this point Moses, the Israelite with the curious Egyptian name, enters the narrative (Exod. 2). His life and role as a prophet of Israel, and the expectation that there would be another like him (Deut. 18:15), powerfully ∨ influenced the shaping of the stories of both Jesus and Muhammad, and Moses' name is invoked often in both the New Testament and the Quran. In Exodus and the following biblical books Moses is presented as a political and social leader, the one who overmastered the Pharaoh. This incident is given extensive treatment in more than one place in the Quran (7:103–136, e.g.), and "Pharaoh" (Firawn) became the archetypal villain of Muslim lore as well ∨ *nb.* as the modern paradigm of the tyrant. After a series of trials commemorated in the Jewish celebration of Passover (see II/6), Moses brought the people called Israel out of Egypt. This Exodus or going-out became an emblematic ⌐ event for Jews and, in a different interpretation (e.g., 1 Cor. 10:1–11), for the Christians, just as the Hegira, Muhammad's removal from Mecca to Medina, did for the Muslims (see I/3). Moses preserved the community's integrity and ⌐

purpose as he guided them for forty long years across the wilderness of Sinai. Furthermore, Moses was the prophet "whom the Lord knew face to face" (Deut. 34:10) and who brought down from Sinai a law both moral (see II/4) and ceremonial (see II/6).

The Name(s) and Nature of God

In Exodus 3:14 Moses boldly asks God his name and the response is (in Hebrew) *ehyeh* ("I am") *asher* ("who" or "that which"), whose meaning—"I am who I am"? "What I am"? "What I will be"?—is by no means clear. The Israelites called him something very similar, Yahweh, which shows up as early as Genesis 2:4. Here God is called Yahweh Elohim, perhaps "the divine Yahweh," but the two names often appear apart as individual names of God, with Yahweh usually translated into English as "Lord" and the plural Elohim as "God." Early on, the name ceased being pronounced out of reverence (or fear—the ancients believed names represented the actual essences of things). When the Hebrew consonants YHWH appeared in a text, either they were pronounced with different vowels (which is where our "Jehovah" comes from) or a completely different appellation, such as Adonai, "My Lord," was substituted, as was the simple *shem* (divine name), customs that still prevail.

God is chiefly called Allah in the Arabic Quran, though Muslims later counted ninety-nine appellations for the deity in that book. The phenomenon gave rise to various practices and beliefs in Islamic circles. Allah (a contraction of *al-ilah*, "the god") was well known in Mecca and to the Arabs generally before Islam. Muhammad thought of him—and preached him—as the same God worshiped by the Jews and Christians. Some Muslims prefer to leave the name untranslated in English, but that practice gives the impression of Allah's being alien or exotic instead of the same deity referred to by most English speakers as "God" (capitalized), the Divine Creator and Final Judge of monotheism.

Though the God of the three monotheistic communities is clearly understood to be the same deity, he has not had quite the same history. The earliest Christians, many of them Gentiles with no Jewish background, read their Bible in a Greek translation, the famous version called the Septuagint (see II/1), where "Yahweh" is rendered as *Kyrios*, "Lord," and "Elohim" as *theos*, the latter word freighted with the baggage of Hellenic paganism. Moreover, if the Bible is read not as an account of the salvation of Israel, which is how both Jews and Christians understand it, but as a long history of Yahweh, it is clear the Book's central figure has a richly detailed and complex "personality" that emerges in his many encounters with his creation. The Christians' "God the Father" suffered further mutations from the Yahweh prototype at the hands of the Church's exegetes and theologians. A preferred Christian approach to

> **Note:** Whereas Jews shied away from using any of the names of God available from Scripture and increasingly resorted to circumlocutions like *ha-qodesh barukh hu* ("The Holy One, Blessed be He"), Muslims followed the Quran's lead that God's were "the most beautiful names" (*al-asma al-husna*; 7:180, etc.) and developed numerous cult practices, devotional, mystical, and magical, around the quranic names. Most directly, God's names could be recited as a form of prayer, sometimes counted out by means of a *subha*, thirty-three or ninety-nine beads strung out in the form of a chaplet—the Eastern Christian prayer rope (see II/9) and Western Christian rosary were modeled on the Muslims' subha—though among more profane Muslims this handheld prayer calculator eventually degenerated into the omnipresent Middle Eastern worry beads. Sufis incorporated the litany of divine names into their regular *dhikr*s, or group "séances" (see II/9), and mystics eagerly sought out the unique "true" name of God, assumed to be one among the canonical ninety-nine, that would reveal his inner being. Finally, the most beautiful names, because of their formulaic nature, were frequently used on amulets and in other forms of apotropaic magic.

Jewish Scripture was a typological reading (see II/2), a searching of what came increasingly to be called the "Old Testament" for foreshadowings (Gk. *typoi*, "archetypes") of personalities and events in the life of Jesus and the Church. The present became privileged at the expense of the past, the Church at the expense of Israel, the God of prophecy at the expense of the God of history, and it was certainly within the folds of the latter that Yahweh's identity lay. The Jews read the Bible as explanation, the Christians, increasingly, as verification.

Christian theology too worked its own reconfiguration of the biblical portrait of Yahweh. Jesus' progressive emergence, from John's Gospel onward, as the Son of God cast Yahweh not merely as Creator, which is our initial view of the deity in Genesis, but as the Father of the Christ, a role ever more heavily and exclusively underlined in the theological controversies of the third and fourth centuries, where "the Father" becomes but one person among the three of the Trinity. And if the theology of Nicaea declared that all three persons that constitute the Godhead are equal ("consubstantial", see II/7), Christian cult and piety declared quite otherwise. It is the eucharistic Jesus who represents the Godhead on the altars of Christendom, on the walls of its churches, and in the prayers of Christians. Yahweh, now solely Pater Omnipotens in the Christian dispensation, retreats to a shadowy heavenly home: "who art in heaven . . ."

The Quran's Allah is the same Creator God who covenanted with Abraham and dispatched the prophets to their tasks, and although he is perhaps more dominantly central to the Quran than Yahweh to the Bible, he is not portrayed in the same manner as his biblical prototype. The Allah of the Quran is at once more powerful yet unmistakably more remote than Yahweh. Allah controls all, but from a distance; he is a universal deity quite unlike the Yahweh who in the early books of the Bible follows close on every step of the Israelites. Allah had his own history, which we can to some extent construct from the cult of the deity of that name who in pre-Islamic days was worshiped all across the Fertile Crescent and Arabia by the polytheistic Arabs. Though both the Quran and its Meccan audience knew at least part of that history, very little of it is laid out in the Quran. Later Islamic generations, who cared nothing about Allah's pre-Islamic career, had the quranic portrait of their God filled out by Muslim authors, many of them converts from Judaism or Christianity, who were well aware of Yahweh's biblical history, but the Muslims' notion of God, though in its main lines identical with the Bible's, has very different nuances of detail.

The Builder Kings

The "five pieces" (*Penta-teuche*) that make up the Torah portion of the Bible end with Moses' death. The books that follow, from Joshua down to the end of Chronicles, carry us through the history of the Israelites from their occupation of the land of Canaan to their own conquest by the Babylonians in 597 B.C.E. The focus of the narrative rests heavily on the history of the Israelite monarchy, how the original loose confederation of the Twelve Tribes yielded to a reluctantly God-granted monarchy bestowed first on Saul, then on David—the "anointed one" (*mashiah* in Hebrew)—and guaranteed to his descendants forever (2 Sam. 7:16). In the long view, David's most important act may have been the conquest of the Jebusite stronghold of Jerusalem, an event traditionally dated to 996 B.C.E.

The Israelites got what territory in Canaan they could manage to hold by force of arms. It expanded and shrank under different political circumstances, as it still does. But it was theirs, as God had promised. God had not signaled Jerusalem in that promise; its prominence was a later idea—David's, according to the Book of Samuel—and on the testimony of that same biblical source, he took it by force from the Jebusites (2 Sam. 5:6–10) and then simply bought its chief holy place from the Canaanite owner (2 Sam. 24:18–25). David chose the city as the capital of the unified Israelites. That made it a political center, but Jerusalem began its career as a holy city when David first brought into the city the portable ark-throne of the once nomadic Israelites (2 Sam. 6:1–19), and his son Solomon enshrined it permanently in the grandiose temple he built atop Mount Moriah. Thus, the God of Abraham, Isaac, and Jacob, and, of course, of Jesus and Muhammad, established his presence in Jerusalem and was worshiped there. And not too long after Solomon, only there. After

621 B.C.E. all Jewish liturgical acts of the first order, that is, sacrificial worship, took place in the Jerusalem temple and nowhere else. A Jew might live in someone else's country, but he could truly worship God only atop Mount Moriah in Jerusalem.

There were three successive Jewish temples in that place—the Jewish tradition prefers to count only two; Herod, the builder of the third, is not a beloved figure in Jewish history—though not continuously. The first, Solomon's, was sacked in 597 and destroyed ten years later by the Babylonians. Its expensive magnificence, even its dimensions, are spelled out only in the Books of Kings and Chronicles. It seems a dream house, the stuff of later generations' nostalgia for a past architectural glory that distance and loss had rendered schematic. With its successor, that built by the Jews who returned from exile in Babylon in 525 B.C.E., we do not even possess the dream. That the restored temple stood where Solomon's had, atop the same mount, we can be certain. For the rest, Ezra and Nehemiah's silence is eloquent: God's house was in that generation a modest dwelling.

The third temple was anything but modest. It was the grandest structure conceived by Judaism's greatest builder, Herod, surnamed the Great. Begun in 20 B.C.E., it took more than half a century to build, and it is not difficult to understand why. The entire mountain top had to be flattened, planed down at its northern reaches, and filled in on its southern side, where immense stones were fit in place to support that end of the mile-square platform, which is still seated there in all its impressive monumentalism. The Western Wall, the principal Jewish holy place in contemporary Jerusalem, is an exposed stretch of this platform near its southwest corner. Atop the platform was the temple complex itself, with its monumental gateways, its royal stoa, its graduated courts, and the Holy of Holies at the center. The temple was constructed so carefully and in such a ritually impeccable manner around the earlier and smaller edifice that at no time, the historian Josephus (d. ca. 100 C.E.) assures us, were the cult and sacrifices interrupted. Herod's temple was, in size and circumstance, the largest sacred building in the ancient world.

The Temple as Haram

The banishment of the unfit *pro fano* "outside the shrine," the process of limiting access to a place, is what we may call "haramization," and it is a telltale sign that we are in the presence of the holy. A boundary was set about Mount Sinai, where the presence of God was made manifest, and those who violated it were subject to death (Exod. 19:12–13). Touching or even seeing holy objects—how much more the face of God (33:20)—was forbidden, and Moses, who spent a great deal of time in the Lord's presence, had to veil his shining face after each dangerous encounter (34:33–35).

Moses had experienced a recurring theophany, which often plays a role in the consecration of a place. Some of the earliest biblical theophanies are associated with specific places—Abraham's meeting with the three strangers at Mamre, Moses' encounter with the Lord on Sinai, and Jacob's at Bethel—but somewhat oddly, Israel's most important theophany was not site-tied in the ordinary sense. The God of premonarchical Israel had signaled his unmistakable presence through cloud and fire, either at the mobile "Tent of Meeting," where Moses and others encountered him in scenes reminiscent of Sinai (Num. 7:89)—though now institutionalized in format—or at the mobile tabernacle of the Ark, whose progress God guided across the wilderness (Exod. 40:36–40). But once the Lord became permanently housed, first at Shiloh and then, finally, in Jerusalem, those visible theophanies ceased, though not the conviction that the Glory of the Lord dwelled within.

Solomon's temple was explicitly built and furnished to house the deity. In an "epic passage" in 1 Kings, Solomon cries out, "O Lord, who has set the sun in the heaven but has chosen to dwell in thick darkness, here have I built You a lofty house, a habitation for You to occupy forever" (8:12–13). The holiness proceeded from within, from "the resident deity," Yahweh, who alone was holy, and who was protected by a series of curtains, gates, or baffles that constituted what has been called a "graduated taboo." Both the architecture and the taboos had as their objective keeping impurity at a safe physical distance from the abode of the deity, just as the various rites of expiation served as a spiritual prophylaxis or inoculation against the approach of impurity.

The Israelites of David's and Solomon's day, and likely earlier ones as well, regarded the tabernacle or temple as a holy and purified place and attempted to preserve that quality both through ritual as well as by limiting profane physical access to its holiest parts. Only the ritually pure, that is, the priests, might touch, see, or approach the sanctuary's holy areas, all others—"others" in its earliest definition included only the Levites and the Israelites—were kept at a distance (2 Chron. 29:16). In architectural terms, this limitation of access was expressed by the discrimination between the sacred building and its surrounding court.

Temple and court seem to have been the only distinctions in Solomon's temple. The priests alone were permitted access to the temple's interior; all others—apparently without further discrimination—could enter its courtyard. Solomon's temple appears to have had but a single surrounding temple courtyard. A second "greater" courtyard also enclosed not only the temple but the king's throne room and his very secular palaces (1 Kings 7:9,12). Protection of the sacred from the profane appears to have been enforced with severity. The biblical tradition emphasized that God himself might strike the interloper down dead—witness the frequent invocation of the phrase "lest he [i.e., the ritual trespasser] meet death," and, in a phrase that strongly suggests that the Levitical guards enforced the ban on the Lord's behalf, "he [i.e., the trespasser] shall be put to death."

In Ezekiel's visionary temple a new distinction was introduced, in imagination, if not in fact. There were now two exterior courtyards surrounding the temple: an inner court reserved for the priests and an outer one where access was permitted to Levites and others (Ezek. 44:15–19, etc.). Thus by Ezekiel's time the notion of an inner "court of the priests" had emerged, and likely the exclusion of nonpriests from that inner court was operative in the second temple. By the Herodian era, however, perhaps due to the Pharisaic ascendancy in Hasmonaean times, the temple's taboo zones had been further extended. The "Israelites" who had shared Ezekiel's outer court with the Levites were now further distinguished: Israelite women were segregated into a zone one degree more remote from the high sanctity of the Holy of Holies. Beyond them, however, we encounter an apparent anomaly, the "court of the gentiles," an invitation to, it would seem, or at least an accommodation with, the unclean, though accompanied by a grave warning. In Ezekiel's program uncircumcised foreigners were banned from the sanctuary altogether, and according to Isaiah and Joel, they would not even have been permitted inside Jerusalem (Ezek. 44:9; Isa. 52:1; Joel 4:17).

Herod, as we know, was fastidious about his version of the Jerusalem temple, if about little else. The temple precincts were patrolled by guards both day and night, and other wardens were stationed at the gates. They kept the unfit out of the areas inappropriate to them—a delicate task, and we are not at all sure how it was accomplished. But the king also appears to have accepted the inevitable magnetism of this, the largest sacred edifice in the ancient world, to the Gentiles—the era was generally one of growing Gentile interest in matters Jewish—and to have attempted to regulate their access to Israel's sacrosanct shrine. According to Josephus, signs posted on the balustrade of the outer court in Herod's temple expressly forbade the unclean—in this instance non-Jews—to come closer under the explicit threat of death (*Jewish War* 5.193).

The Sanctity of Jerusalem

By the seventh century B.C.E. Jerusalem possessed in its temple Israel's sole certified holy place, though it is difficult to believe that the earlier sacred locales, high places, and tomb cult sites, like that of Abraham and his family at Hebron, lost either their cultus or their allure at Josiah's decision to centralize formal liturgical worship in the capital. Josiah's act was essentially political; it gave the Jerusalem temple a monopoly on divine worship, which may have enhanced the city's prestige but did not alter its status. Other events were at work, however. The Northern Kingdom fell to the Assyrians in 721 B.C.E., and the passage of substantial elements of both Israelite population and Israelite territory—and its minor cult centers—into the domains of pagan rulers, and then the eventual erection of a rival temple on Mount Gerizim in Samaria focused Jewish piety even more closely on Jerusalem. We can read in the prophets that Jerusalem was the symbol and center of their concerns for Israel. Yahweh would again choose Jerusalem (Zech. 2:12): it is to Jerusalem and its temple that "the glory of the Lord" will return at its restoration (Ezek. 43:4–6) (see II/6).

The rise of the Pharisaic party and its program of ritual purity, and, above all, the destruction of Herod's temple in 70 C.E. finally shifted emphasis away from God's sanctifying presence to the holiness of ritual purity, even with respect to places. Mishnah Kelim 1:6–9 provides us with a holiness map of Eretz Israel. There we learn that all the land of Israel is holy, that the walled cities within it are holier than the countryside, and that "within the wall (of Jerusalem) is more holy than they"—that is, than Israel's other walled cities (1:8). The only reason offered by the Mishnah for Jerusalem's special status vis-à-vis Israel's other walled cities is that "they eat there the lesser holy things and the second tithe," which was not done elsewhere.

But there is more. From David's day Jerusalem was the national capital of the Jewish people, and its temple was the sole place for the sacrificial worship of the One True God. The Jews have always regarded themselves as a single historical people, and so they alone, not the Christians or the Muslims, were capable of possessing—and actually did possess—a national capital. No Christian pope or Muslim caliph, both of whom are quite different from a national king to begin with, ever had Jerusalem as his seat. Jerusalem has had Christian and Muslim governors, and even a few ephemeral Christian kings during the Crusades, but that was either sectarian sovereignty or rule by delegated authority.

Jewish sovereignty over Jerusalem did not last very long: from David's day to the Babylonian conquest in 597 B.C.E., and then again from the Maccabean war of independence in the early 160s B.C.E. to the Roman takeover of their Judaean puppet in 6 C.E., when Jesus was perhaps ten years old. In 66 C.E. a Jewish insurrection against the Romans broke out across Palestine and was not quenched until Jerusalem had been taken and sacked and its temple destroyed in 70 C.E., never to be rebuilt. The Romans' grip was firm. There was another unsuccessful Jewish revolt led by the messianic Bar Kokhba in 132–135 C.E., but the Romans held Jerusalem, though they never chose to rule even Judaea from it—Herod's more Gentile city of Caesarea-by-the-Sea was a far more congenial place—for six and a half uninterrupted centuries. What the Romans thought of Jerusalem—which was not much—is inconsequential to our purposes, but for three of those six and a half centuries, the Roman sovereigns of Jerusalem were also Christians, and what _they_ thought and did was important in the long run.

Jerusalem had quite a different status for the new Christian community than it had for the Jews. Paul, in a famous passage in Galatians (4:21–27), drew a sharp distinction between Hagar and Sarah, two women who stood for two covenants. Hagar represented the Torah covenant and "the Jerusalem of today"; Sarah, in contrast, was "our mother" and "the heavenly Jerusalem." A heavenly Jerusalem was not a new notion—it appears in the Apocrypha, most graphically perhaps in 4 Ezra 10:40–55—but in Paul's use the contrast, and the judgment, regarding the earthly and the heavenly city had profound consequences in the Christian tradition. When Paul wrote, the city was intact and the temple still stood, but after 70 C.E. Christian exegesis was confronted with an altogether different state of affairs.

"This is an allegory," Paul had announced at the beginning of the Galatians passage, and the Christian exegetes understood it as such. Though there were other interpretations of the text, Origen (d. ca. 254 C.E.) projected Paul's distinction back onto the Bible's, particularly the prophets' references to Jerusalem, and forward to the Christians' own hope of a restoration: it was not the Jerusalem of Origen's day of which they were speaking, but a new heavenly city. As Origen put it in *Against Celsus* (7.28): "Moses taught that God promised a holy land . . . to those who lived according to his law. And the good land was not, as some think, the earthly land of Judaea." That much must have been clear to Origen's Christian contemporaries. Rebellious Jerusalem was destroyed by the Romans not once but twice—the second time in 135 C.E.—and then quickly rebuilt by Hadrian as a spanking new—and ostentatiously pagan—metropolis of Roman Judaea, a province from which the Jews were henceforth banned. Jerusalem once again had holy places, but they were now of the pagan variety. On the main forum in the Upper City was a temple of Venus, and perhaps another to the tutelary deity of the new Jerusalem, Jupiter Capitolinus. Although there were no Jews in the city, there was a small Christian community, now no longer Jewish Christians, however, but solely the Gentile variety acceptable to the Romans and becoming increasingly dominant throughout the churches (Eusebius, *Church History* 3.5–5).

The new Aelia Capitolina, as Hadrian called his city, must have been attractive, as we can infer from his contemporary project at nearby Gerasa/Jerash, but it could hardly have enjoyed any great prosperity beyond imperial subsidy. From David's day down to the Roman apocalypse, the chief industry, employer, and money- and goods-magnet of Jerusalem had been the temple. Without it, and without the Jews who were banned in 135, Jerusalem would doubtless soon have sunk to the status of an inglorious, and overdressed, provincial town had it not attracted the pious attention of another, now Christian, emperor, Constantine. In the fourth century the newly converted Constantine initiated a deliberate plan to convert Palestine, or at least those parts of it connected with Jesus, into a Christian Holy Land (see II/6)—but not on a Jewish model. Christian Palestine was rendered holy by its association with Jesus and his immediate followers, a site-tied association formalized through the enshrinement of those sites by architectural embellishment and soon ratified by the growing practice of pilgrimage.

> **Note:** We have a rare and remarkable picture of Jerusalem's enshrined
> Christian holy places in the mosaic floor map in the sanctuary of a church
> in Madeba, Jordan. The date is sometime about 580 C.E., and the well-
> preserved Jerusalem cartouche on the map shows the walled city of the
> sixth century with its churches and shrines highlighted in gold. Con-
> stantine's church, called the Anastasis or Resurrection, shines like a
> medallion from the midst of the city. Unhighlighted, unmarked, and al-
> most unidentifiable is the site of the temple on the city's southeastern
> side (the upper right, slightly distressed part of the cartouche). Judaism's
> holiest of holy places, "God's holy mountain," was, as evidenced by the
> map's ambiguous iconographical vacuum and the eyewitness testimony
> of Christian pilgrims who visited the site, nothing more than a field of
> ruins during the entire period from the Roman destruction down to the
> Muslim rebuilding projects in the seventh century. There were some
> Jewish pilgrims, a few hardy souls—it must have been a dangerous en-
> terprise under any circumstances, Roman or Christian—who bought or
> stole their way into the forbidden Jerusalem and up onto the temple
> mount. The observant and well-informed Jerome knew they came on
> the Ninth of Ab, the anniversary of the destruction of both temples, "a
> piteous crowd, woebegone women and old men weighed down in rags
> and years." Jerome was not only observant; he was also a theologian:
> "... all of them showing forth in their clothes and bodies the wrath of
> God" (*On Zephaniah* 1.15–16).

In the mid–seventh century the Muslims took Jerusalem, together with
much else around the Mediterranean, almost effortlessly and without blood-
shed. They left the Christians pretty much as they were, but the city's new
Muslim masters seem to have struck up what appears to us an odd symbiotic
relationship with the Jews. The Jewish community was permitted to return to
Jerusalem, which they did, soon moving the yeshiva that directed Jewish legal
and religious affairs from Tiberias, where it had been for more than five centuries, back to Jerusalem. Furthermore, the Muslims built their first place of
prayer in the city not in or by one of the Christian churches or shrines but
atop the temple mount, a place ignored and neglected by the Christians but
obviously still important to the Jews. Indeed, the Jews may have been permitted to pray once again on the mount itself. Within a generation the Muslims
had greatly enhanced their first crude mosque and constructed within that
same Herodian enclosure a magnificent domed shrine over the rock said to
have been the temple's foundation stone. This Noble Sanctuary, or Haram al-
Sharif as the Muslims call the Herodian platform, with the Dome of the Rock
and the Aqsa mosque placed atop, not only dominates Jerusalem's cityscape to
this day; it is probably the single most impressive architectural expression of
Islamic sanctity.

Why did the Muslims choose that place? If we jump forward from the seventh to perhaps the eighth or ninth century, there are answers in abundance, since by then the Muslim traditions on the subject were well established. The Haram, it was said, was holy for two reasons. There were its biblical associations, which, by reason of the Quran's certifying them as God's true revelation, became Muslim sacred associations as well. The temple of Solomon, one of the Quran's most tantalizing and mysterious figures, stood there. Before Solomon, David had prayed at the site, Jacob had had his vision of God there, and Abraham was bade to sacrifice Isaac there. But if the Haram is biblical and so Muslim, it is also "Muhammadan," that is, connected with the life of the Prophet. "By night," sura 17 of the Quran begins, "God carried His servant from the holy sanctuary [of Mecca] to the distant shrine (*al-masjid al-aqsa*)." The Quran says no more about this "Night Journey" or the location of the distant shrine but the Muslim tradition identified it with Jerusalem, more precisely, with the temple mount. From this same spot, the tradition continues, the Prophet was taken up to the highest heaven and granted a supernal vision.

Both the biblical and the Muhammadan associations are sorted out around various places atop the Herodian platform, chiefly clustered about the Dome of the Rock. The mosque built there at Umar's command in 638 and rebuilt more splendidly later that same century is called al-Aqsa, the Distant Shrine, with direct reference to Quran 17:1. Jesus traditions too were connected with the temple mount, an association the Christians themselves never chose to make, even though the Gospels put Jesus in Herod's still unfinished temple on more than one occasion. Finally and predictably, since such motifs collect about every holy place, cosmological themes appear. The rock beneath the dome is not merely the foundation stone of the temple; it marks the very navel of the earth.

Thus Jerusalem became a Muslim holy city by reason of its Muslim holy place, though for the next four centuries it remained overwhelmingly Christian in its demography. Around the Haram al-Sharif grew a Muslim population whose interest in living there was part administrative and part simple piety. A modest Jewish community lived somewhere in the southeast corner, rabbis many of them, who enjoyed the prestige of constituting the principal yeshiva of the Jewish world but who otherwise shared little of their coreligionists' prosperity in Islamic urban centers like Fustat/Cairo or Baghdad. The reason was not oppression; it was simply that Jerusalem was not very prosperous. The city was of secondary political and administrative importance. It had little share in the burgeoning trade and commerce that was beginning to enrich other cities in the Abode of Islam. Jerusalem remained what it had been since the second century: a provincial backwater that now possessed major Christian and Muslim shrines and a Zionist recollection of a Jewish one. Pilgrims still came and went, more and more of them Western Christians.

Jerusalem's modern history germinated and was hatched in Europe. The actual eleventh-century Palestinian city was, as has been remarked, neither prosperous nor a very safe place to live. Palestine was often overrun by armies heading elsewhere, with the additional hazard that when the dust cleared, the predatory Bedouin who infested the area often moved in to pick over the bones. The Muslims did not often visit Jerusalem in those days; indeed, they could scarcely defend the place. When tyranny descended on the land, usually all three communities shared the oppression. For the Muslims that oppression was largely economic; for the Jews, and particularly the far more visible Christians, it frequently cast itself in religious raiment. Al-Hakim, the eleventh-century Ismaili ruler of Egypt whose memory is fragrant in no one's annals, Muslim, Jewish, or Christian, and who was disturbed, if not entirely deranged, senselessly and maliciously destroyed the Church of the Holy Sepulcher in 1009 and so unwittingly set in train events that had their immediate consequence in the Crusades and other long-term hostilities still unfolding to this day.

A Troubled Legacy

Solomon was David's astonishingly successful son, and his fame lives on not only in Jewish legend but in Islam's as well. He is portrayed as a prophet and wonder-worker in the Quran and later as a magician extraordinaire. But at his death, both the father's and the son's legacy almost immediately began to unravel. The northern kingdom, called Israel, drew apart from the south, dominated by Judah; paganism became rampant and the kings vile. There were few bright spots. King Josiah was one, and it was to him that copy of the Torah newly discovered in the House of the Lord was brought. The king interpreted this as a summons to reform. Among the reforms was the centralization, in 621 B.C.E., of all sacrificial ritual in Jerusalem. Yahweh's priests were drawn into the capital and the local shrines were closed down.

The times were as evil as the people—evil is never accidental in the Bible. The eighth-century B.C.E. in the Middle East was dominated by two superpowers, Egypt and Assyria, and Israel lay like a doormat across the land bridge between them. War swirled across and through the two troubled Israelite monarchies. In 721 B.C.E. Israel succumbed to the Assyrians, who carried off to points uncertain whatever was left of ten of the original Twelve Tribes and put in their place new, non-Israelite colonists (2 Kings 17:24–41). The break between Judah and Israel was now complete. The Judaeans, who assembled our Bible and so could privilege themselves in the account, regarded the northerners, the "Samaritans"—the area was named after the city of Samaria built as the northern capital in the ninth century (1 Kings 16:24)—as inauthentic heirs of Abraham and their rival temple on Mount Gerizim above the town of Shechem as an abomination.

The Samaritan Schism

This was a major schism in the Israelite community—the only comparable break was the later one with the Christians, who, unlike the Samaritans, got to present their case to a larger audience—and it can be read as essentially a political event, the conversion into religious language of the long-standing tension between northern and southern Israel. The northerners were simply resisting the hereditary claims of the Davidic monarchy and the centralization of worship in Jerusalem. During the Exile the Jewish community had lost its connection with the land and was now trying to reconstitute itself on ethnic criteria—criteria that the northerners, by reason of their intermarriage with Assyrian colonists, could not meet. The rupture was never healed. The Samaritans, in many ways as determined to survive as the Judaeans, dwindled down by degrees into modern times as a tiny remnant.

In the eighth century Jerusalem managed to hold off the Assyrians with gold, silver, and the considerable assistance of Yahweh—it was his last reported direct intervention on behalf of his Chosen People (2 Kings 19:32–37)—but when the Assyrians were replaced by the Babylonians in Iraq, the energetic new dynasty swept Judah too into its empire. The political realities of the era might appear to make the conquest inevitable, but the Judaeans had far more reliable warnings. A series of prophets, most notably Isaiah, Jeremiah, and Ezekiel, foresaw what was coming and its cause: the repeated infidelities of God's Elect.

The Voice of the Prophets

In the sixth and seventh centuries B.C.E. Judaea lay like some antique Belgium wedged helplessly between a larger and stronger Germany and France, a tiny and troubled kingdom full athwart the narrow land bridge that connected an old power at one end of the Fertile Crescent, Egypt, and the organized, militaristic, and aggressive new superpowers on the other, Assyria and then Babylonia. In the Bible's providential terms, God had once intervened to preserve the Judaean kingdom from the Assyrians—although, as we have seen, he declined to do the same for the kings of Israel in Samaria. But neither God nor promised ransom intervened to save Judaea from the Babylonians of Iraq. Judaea was not wealthy enough to prompt a superpower attack for its own sake, but it was always worthwhile to stop and shake out the loose change from a temple or two en route to richer prizes. The Babylonians took and looted Jerusalem and its temple in 597 B.C.E.—carrying off the Ark of the Covenant among other things—and led off into Babylonia for their own use Judaea's upper social and economic classes. They too were a form of booty.

n.b .

We know little about what happened to the Jews in what is today called Iraq. There is a great deal of self-recrimination in the prophets over the sins of Israel that provoked a national catastrophe, but no descriptions have survived of how the exiles dealt with a life of relative (we think) servitude without king, polity, or temple. Their numbers were probably not very large, and Judaeans do not seem to have suffered unduly in their new home—many of them chose not to return to Eretz Israel in the years after 520 B.C.E. and the Jewish community in "Babylonia" enjoyed a spiritual and intellectual prestige that endured for many centuries (see II/3). But as an event, the Exile (*galut, golah*), and this one in particular, looms as large as the Exodus in Jewish consciousness, chiefly as the prototype of the extended exile that Jews suffered after the destruction of first their state and then their holy city by the Romans in 70 C.E.

The exile to Babylonia was merely the terrible climax of a long series of political blows that had fallen on Israel almost uninterruptedly since Solomon's death. First, there was the division of the northern kingdom of Israel from the southern one of Judaea and the eventual loss of identity of ten of the traditional Twelve Tribes. That was followed by malevolent and mischievous kings north and south whose harems introduced alien gods into the land and into the temple itself. God's lash fell on Judah in the form of Assyrian and Babylonian warlords. The Judaeans' political responses to these political challenges were increasingly ineffectual, but out of the Israelites' spiritual resources came another, and different, response: the voice of the prophets.

There had long been prophets in Israel; on occasion they even appear to have been organized into fraternities or guilds. Individual prophets like Samuel and Nathan had played an important role in guiding the kingdom in its early days, but in this time of trouble a new, more powerful breed of prophets—whose extraordinary influence later reached deep into Christianity where they seemed to speak to attentive Christian ears of a New Covenant and a New Redeemer, and who then still later provided Muhammad with the paradigm of his own calling in Islam—began to speak. Their voices sounded more loudly perhaps for a people served by increasingly impotent political rulers and a temple priesthood ever more silent in the face of disaster. These prophets were towering figures, preserved in all their terrible grandeur in the Bible. The chief among them—Isaiah, Jeremiah, and Ezekiel—pointed a path out of the darkness of contemporary Israelite history to a light on the other side.

n.b.

A Harsh Theodicy and an Uncertain Future

The prophets did not disguise the woes of the present; indeed, they seem to have delighted in describing the terrors that beset Israel and to promise even greater ones to come. But they also offered an explanation, a theodicy (Gk. *theos* + *dike*, "justice") "justifying the ways of God to man." In the world of

prophets

the Israelites, where God is all good and all just and has, moreover, a guiding care, or providence, for his creation, such suffering cried out for explanation. Why, as the prophet Habakkuk asked when the Assyrians and the Babylonians were taking out their wrath on a hapless Israel, why does "law become ineffective and justice defeated? The wicked hem in the righteous and justice is perverted?" (1:3–4). Either God has nothing to do with it, a position the twentieth-century Holocaust drove some Jews to embrace, or else it is God's will, directed in anger against his Chosen People. Israel had a choice, Deuteronomy had explained, between a blessing and a curse: "the blessing if you obey the commandments of the Lord your God which I gave you this day; the curse if you do not obey the commandments of the Lord your God but turn from the way I command you and go after other gods" (11:26–28).

Though the Book of Job does not share it—the righteous suffer for their own good, not as a punishment—the opinion that sin begets suffering prevailed among the prophets who set it before Israel's eyes with a new and terrible vigor: Israel's woes were due to her sins. As the prophets viewed history in the light of their divinely inspired intuition, Israel's unfaithfulness had brought on the present calamities. In the sexual imagery that abounds, it is Israel the whore who leaps, all fantastic and sorrowful, from the prophetic page.

- Te. past

This is a diagnosis of the past, but these prophets' visions extend to the future as well. The God of Israel, the Israelites are told, is the God of all humankind, a universal God. The resounding point was not either philosophical or theological, although later it was fruitfully developed along both those parallel paths (see II/7), but *political*. The God who was presently punishing Israel for her sins—the image of Israel, wife of Yahweh, also comes easily to the prophets— was also the God of the Egyptians, the Assyrians, and the Babylonians who were tormenting her. The Lord would restore order; he would bring down her enemies and restore Israel. And why should God show such consideration? The Covenant, the prophets insisted, the Covenant God had made with Israel through Abraham was still in force and God would remain faithful to his part of the contract, even though the Israelites repeatedly failed in theirs.

-Te-Future

God's RULE

The prophets' meditations on the Exile were part of the Israelites' struggles to reconcile their experience with God's undoubted justice. The field of discourse was limited, however. God's justice had to be satisfied in the present— the wicked are struck down on the spot, like the Sodomites—or else in the discernible historical future. "I am a jealous God," the Lord announced to Moses, "punishing the children for the sins of the parents to the third and fourth generation of those who reject Me" (Exod. 20:5). Although this was a hard saying with deep resonances in popular Jewish religious culture—"Who sinned, this man or his parents?" Jesus was asked by his disciples of a man born blind (John 9:1)—it might appear to some to solve the problem of redressing evil and provide, in a somewhat clumsy, mechanical way, an answer to why the wicked prosper.

But this explanation was not for everyone. Jeremiah (31:29–30) and Ezekiel (1:14) both rejected the easy aphoristic theodicy of "the parents have eaten sour grapes and their children's teeth are set on edge." But there were other remedies almost ready to hand. The pre-Exile Israelites had no strong sense of an Afterlife, but on their return to Judaea, the notion of at least some form of personal survival began to unfold and, with it, the possibility that divine justice might be satisfied in some other way. The righteous would be rewarded and the wicked punished in the Afterlife (see II/10).

For all their lacerating criticism, the prophets supplied Israel with hope of salvation from the present and of redemption from their woes. They held out the vision of a new and better future for God's Chosen People, better because it would be a New Covenant for the new age, a covenant based not only on sacrifices and ordinances, as in the past, but on the spirit, the Torah within. "This is the covenant which I will make with Israel in those days, says the Lord. I will put My Torah within them, and I will write it upon their hearts" (Jer. 31:31–32).

To our proleptic ears, the words are already full of consequence. Salvation, redemption, and a New Covenant would continue to be meditated on after the immediate but defining crisis of the Exile had passed, and the Israelites, now the "Jews," would pass into a new world whose problems and prospects would seem as bleak and threatening as the one they had left.

Judaea and Ioudaioi

The Iranians under Cyrus overthrew the Babylonians in 539 B.C.E., and sometime afterward those Israelites who wished were permitted to return to Judaea, where they resettled and rewalled Jerusalem, rebuilt the temple, and attempted to restore Jewish observance in the land, as the Books of Ezra and Nehemiah describe. A new chapter in the history of the Jewish community had begun. Two obscure centuries of restoration and growth under Persian sovereignty (ca. 530–330) were followed in quick succession by a cultural, religious, and political confrontation with the Greeks (330–167), a war of national liberation that led to the restoration of a long-defunct Jewish monarchy (164), and finally, in 6 C.E., the annexation of what was left of Jewish Palestine to the powerful Roman Empire, under whose sovereignty it remained for six centuries. Politically the community now constituted nothing more than a tiny province named Judaea (Jerusalem and its surrounding areas) within the enormous Persian empire, and the people began to be called "Judaeans" (Gk. *Ioudaioi*; Lat. *Ioudaei*), from which our word "Jew" derives, though they themselves continued to use Benei Israel, the tribe or descendants of Israel, or simply "Israelites."

Judaea after the Exile differed from what it had been before, and so too did the world around it. The older parochial empires had disappeared and new

ecumenical political forms prevailed, accompanied by new social and economic institutions and a quickening of the intellectual life in the Near East.
Judaism too was different, as we can see with the historian's hindsight. It both
clashed and blended with the new world about it, and though it had done this
from the beginning, the results were now deeper, more volatile, and far more
visible.

Pre-Exilic Judaism had been, perhaps, farther up the ladder of religious
evolution than the faith of the Philistines, Canaanites, and Phoenicians, and
so could resist or assimilate those competitors with relative ease. But the
Greeks were not Canaanites and Caesar Augustus was not Hiram of Tyre or
even Ashurbanipal. Judaism's new rivals were at once more attractive and
threatening, and possessed intellectual and spiritual resources little understood in parochial Judaea. Judaism did not simply react. It first refracted the
incandescent energies of the new age and then slowly brought them into
focus in a form that has survived with vigor into our own day.

In the course of that difficult process of self-transformation, Judaism
proved remarkably fertile in new perspectives, some of which were finally rejected but proved nonetheless to have a vitality of their own. Christianity immediately and Islam somewhat more obliquely appear in certain lights like
Jewish reform movements. At the very least they are growths from the same
stock—post-Exilic Judaism—in a generative process that has no parallel in the
varieties of human religious experience.

The biblical books of Ezra and Nehemiah portray a Jewish community already facing both temple and Torah. Ezra himself, who was the chief architect
of the post-Exilic restoration, is the perfect type of his age: he was both a
priest (*kohen*) and a scribe (*sofer*). The latter was already a new office and function in Israel, a man learned in the Scriptures, a teacher certainly, and possibly
a judge on matters of the Law.

Though the older priestly and the new clerical Judaism were united in
Ezra's person and philosophy, that cohesion was not permanent. With the inroads of Hellenism and the affluence it brought to the urban centers of the
Near East, we can observe the natural evolution of the Jewish priesthood's upper levels into a class of power and privilege drawn into the cultural and political orbit of the new Greek rulers of Palestine, whether they governed from
Alexandria in Egypt or Antioch in Syria.

The Passage of Power and Prestige

In the Judaism of temple times there had been two poles of community authority, generally to be found on the eastern and western hills of Jerusalem. On
the former was the temple, after 621 B.C.E. the unique locus of sacrifice, and so
of the formal worship of God among the Jews. The priests, a hereditary caste

of males descended from Aaron (see II/6), controlled the temple and its ritual, and, if we read the evidence right, they were also the chief interpreters of God's law. The historical books of the Bible, primarily emphasize the other source of power and prestige in Israel, that often found on the western hill in Jerusalem: the king and his court. A king ruled in Israel, if not by divine right, then at least with divine approval, which had been explicitly bestowed on David and his descendants (see I/6). After David, however, or perhaps Solomon, we are more often confronted by the sovereign's power rather than his prestige, much less any signs of divine approval. Indeed, the Israelite kings' moral failings often provide the texts for prophetic chastisements through those same biblical books.

The Bible's prophets, who are sometimes organized in shadowy confraternities but more often represented as specially gifted individuals, do not constitute anything like a class; they appear and disappear with circumstances. Kingship and the priesthood, in contrast, are permanent features of temple Judaism and we can take some measure of the influence of each of these dominant institutions. After the Exile, another class seems to emerge, the already noted scribes (*soferim*), of which Ezra was one. The post-Exilic scribes were almost certainly experts in Torah—who perhaps learned or practiced their expertise in another apparent Exilic institution, the synagogue (see II/6)—and were possibly another product, or a symptom, of a shift of emphasis from ritual to Torah piety during the years in remote Babylon. The shift, if it occurred, was not yet radical since on their return to Eretz Israel, the Jews immediately rebuilt the temple and resumed public sacrifice. But the soferim were thereafter a constant, though indistinct, part of the Jewish cultural and political landscape.

By the first century B.C.E., both kingship and the priesthood had become somewhat problematic in Palestine. After a long vassalage to the Persians and the Greeks, the Jews had managed, through the Maccabees, to restore their independence in Eretz Israel in 164 B.C.E., but once the Maccabees, who as freedom fighters were national heroes, assumed the kingship under their dynastic name of the Hasmonaeans, their luster began to dim. In some way the Hasmonaeans were as Hellenized as the Greek kings they had replaced, and during their tenure profound sectarian divisions appeared among the Jews. One of the divisive issues was certainly the Hasmonaeans' decidedly un-Davidic kingship; another was the priesthood. The Hasmonaean ruler Jonathan had assumed the high priesthood in 152 B.C.E., though not until Aristobulus (d. 103 B.C.E.) did a Hasmonaean formally declare himself both king and high priest of Israel, a dual claim none had ever made before. From 76 to 67 the widowed queen Salome was "king" of Israel; she could not, however, serve as high priest, and thus that office once again became a political pawn. It was doubtless these developments that rendered the priesthood increasingly troublesome for a group like the Essenes, who, like others, had problems with the politicized, Hellenized, and occasionally venal priesthood that served the temple in Jerusalem. In the end the Hasmonaeans were replaced by the house of Herod, and the opposition to Israel's rulers, political and religious, became even more fierce, inflamed by overt signs of class warfare.

Deeper distinctions of class are not the only visible changes in the post-Exilic Jewish community in Judaea. The sources that cover the two centuries reveal a surprisingly sectarian landscape. There are no apparent sects in pre-Exilic Judaism, but on the return from Babylonia proliferate a wide variety of groups who appear to us now as parties, now as genuine sects. The Exile experience had cast doubts on the legitimacy of the priesthoods and some of the temple practices, dividing the community, as was the even more profound issue of Jewish identity. Everyone knew *who* was a Jew—someone born of a Jewish mother. But what might further be required by way of belief, practice, or observance were questions that troubled many in the days of the second temple.

Second Temple Sectarianism

The "Israelites" of the Bible are clearly the same people as the "Jews" who appear in the literature of Second Temple times. They worship the same God in the same place and in the same way. They follow the same Law of Moses. The Israelites are clearly reckoned by the Jews as their own past. But they are also strikingly different. The biblical Children of Israel present themselves as a single people, with political differences perhaps, most notably in the era after Solomon, but ideologically united. If there were dissidents, like the Samaritans, they were obviously marginalized. In post-Exilic times there are, however, no master narratives like the Pentateuch or Kings to keep intact the portrait of One God and One People. We have instead a great mass of special pleading on behalf of groups that have usually been qualified as "sects." Second Temple Judaism seems, if nothing else, sectarian.

The characterization may be misleading. A sect is generally understood to be a small organized group that distinguishes itself in some way from a larger parent religious body and asserts that it alone, or it especially, represents the true ideals of the larger group because it alone, or it especially, understands God's will. The sect usually possesses identity markers in the form of teachings, rituals, or lifestyle. All these qualities are arguably present among the groups in which Jews sorted themselves in Second Temple times; what is missing is the center, the "larger parent religious body" from which the sects had separated themselves. Where, indeed, lies Jewish "orthodoxy" in the centuries between the first destruction of the Jerusalem temple in 587 B.C.E. and its second, and final, destruction in 70 C.E.?

According to Josephus, Jews of that era were divided into three (or perhaps four) main "schools": Pharisees, Sadducees, Essenes, and Zealots. The word he uses for these schools is *haeresis*, and though later in Christian circles the term developed a strongly pejorative flavor as "heresy," Josephus here probably intended only to remind his Gentile readers, gently and favorably, of Greek philosophical schools. There is, in any event, no "center" in Josephus's Jewish landscape, no suggestion that these are deviations from a norm, a standard or "normative" Judaism.

We once knew about the varieties of post-Exilic Judaism only from these (sometimes hostile) descriptions in Josephus and others, less schematized, in the New Testament. Now, however, with the discovery of the Dead Sea Scrolls near Qumran, we have what appears to be the Essenes' library and, at Qumran itself, the remains of one of their closed settlements.

Some of the Jewish groups described or mentioned in the sources seem like little more than political parties. Such are the Zealots, a group of revolutionary priests involved in the insurrection of 66–70 C.E., and their extremist core, the Sicarii; likewise the Herodians, a group of Pharisees who apparently made their peace with the house of Herod. There were several similar though unnamed movements—their identity comes principally from their leader—many of them in Galilee, which in the years following the Roman takeover of the land responded to a "prophetic" summons and took some form of action against the Roman administration. These were movements of the moment, charismatic rather than ideological in their inspiration. The Roman reaction was rapid and sharp, however, and these groups of religio-social protest had a brief life indeed.

We cannot be sure exactly where the Pharisees came from. They may have been a somewhat later version of the hasidim or even a party among the scribes. When first identified by name, they are both a party and a sect in that they had a distinct religious position and were at the same time deeply engaged in political activity under the Hasmonaeans. Or so we suppose. We are not on very firm ground here, since we must rely for our information on the self-serving narrative of the Books of Maccabees and on the historical works of the Pharisee Josephus, who was writing with a special purpose of his own for a Roman audience. Josephus's *Jewish War* and *Jewish Antiquities* remain, however, our best sources for the period.

The authors of the Books of Maccabees were appealing to the sympathy and support of Jews outside Palestine as surely as Josephus was attempting to explain the somewhat arcane practices and convictions of his coreligionists to a baffled audience of Gentiles, and so neither was much concerned with either historical or theological accuracy when it came to the Pharisees. The Gospels likewise present a number of vignettes, generally unflattering, of Pharisees engaged in controversy with Jesus. The overall result is, not surprisingly, a confused and often contradictory portrait of the group. Making sense of this mélange has exercised both Jewish and Christian scholars, with sometimes astonishing results. The Pharisees have been regarded as everything from hidebound and frigid legalists to Jewish revivalists and social reformers.

However they are interpreted, the Pharisees appear in our sources as staunch upholders of the Torah, lay experts in the Law, whose particular characteristic is their conviction that their own tradition—the "tradition of the elders" or, "the fathers"—was as authentic and as binding as the Torah (see II/3). Consequently, they were scrupulous in their observance, particularly of the laws of ritual purity. That observance effectively separated them—their name seems to mean "Separatists"—not only from any form of social contact with the Gentiles, the goyim, but even from notable segments of the Jewish population. Yet, as Josephus claims, they had widespread support. They were active in Palestine from the second century B.C.E. to the first C.E., and though early on they were deeply involved in Hasmonaean politics, under Herod they appear to have adopted a passive and even pacifist stance.

Linked by both Josephus and the Gospels to the Pharisees are the Sadducees. Their name may have come from Zadok, a high priest at the time of David (1 Kings 1:26)—the priestly hierarchy at Qumran was also known as "the Sons of Zadok"—and it seems plausible to identify the Sadducees as supporters of, if not identical with, the priesthood that presided over the Jewish temple liturgies in Jerusalem. They were almost certainly defenders of the legitimacy of the Hasmonaean high priesthood, but Josephus was far more concerned to show their legal and theological positions vis-à-vis the Pharisees. The Sadducees were, by his testimony, literal interpreters of the Law who rejected all Pharisaic appeals to the traditions of the fathers, and so could be at the same time stricter in their exegesis of scriptural prescriptions and more permissive where the Torah had not explicitly spoken. They were unwilling, for example, to accept, as the Pharisees did, the notion of an Afterlife, since it had little or no scriptural attestation.

This portrait of the Sadducees is not a very full likeness, since none of their own writings is preserved, and after the destruction of the temple in 70 C.E. they had no spiritual progeny in Judaism, save possibly the Karaites, a sect that arose in the eighth century under Islam and that shared the Sadducees' repudiation of an oral tradition. The same judgment of ignorance once prevailed with respect to a third group linked by Josephus (but strangely absent from the Gospels) to the Pharisees and Sadducees, the Essenes. They are portrayed, in Josephus's usual shorthand fashion, as an ascetic congregation who had separated themselves from the main body of the Jews. They lived in communities and possessed goods in common. More recently, however, the Essenes of Josephus, Philo, and others have been tentatively identified with a group about which we know a great deal, the sectaries at Qumran.

Since 1947, when their center and writings were discovered at the northwest corner of the Dead Sea, the community at Qumran is better known by direct and contemporary evidence than any other Jewish religious group of its day. Their own writings have been published and translated, and their habitat and way of life intensively studied. They were in fact much as Josephus described them, a highly organized community (*yahad*) who lived a life of strict asceticism, some of them celibates, apart from the rest of the Jews. But what is now clear is the context of this life. The Essenes were priestly dissenters who rejected the authority of the Hasmonaean high priesthood in Jerusalem, and so did not participate directly in the temple liturgy. Instead, they awaited their vindication through a messianic return and a climactic and victorious war against the forces of evil. In the meantime, the community lived in a state of severe ritual purity and spiritual readiness for the eschatological battle that lay ahead. They were a purified people of a New Covenant who were elected for survival in wicked days. They practiced frequent ablutions in expectation of the coming End Time and its two Messiahs, one an Aaronic or priestly Messiah who would guide the group in religious matters, and the other a Davidic or kingly Messiah who would govern them politically. The Qumran Essenes were a highly organized and tightly controlled sect.

One of the issues that divided these three Jewish groups, as it inevitably must all forms of monotheism, was that of free will and predestination, how to vindicate human freedom in the face of the providential plan of an omnipotent God. Josephus tried to explain, though he may have framed his answers somewhat more philosophically than the parties themselves. The Sadducees, according to Josephus, believed absolutely in human freedom of choice and human responsibility for good and evil, while at the other extreme the Essenes believed that all was in the Lord's hands. The Pharisees apparently tried to adopt a middle position whereby human free will interacted—it would take considerably more subtle philosophical language to explain that part—with God's providence.

Two other Jewish sectarian movements unnoted by Josephus (though he did avert to their founders) were also in the early first century C.E. trying to define what a Jew was or was supposed to be. These were the followers of John the Baptist and, as an offshoot of those Baptizers, the members of the Jesus movement (see I/2).

The cataclysm of 70 C.E., when the Romans took Jerusalem after a long siege and destroyed the temple, marked the end of most of these groups. The Essenes, Sadducees, and all the little-known movements that opposed Rome disappeared from the Jewish landscape. The Baptizers dissolved even earlier, when their leader John was executed by Herod Antipas, Herod's son and the ruler of Galilee from 4 B.C.E. to 39 C.E. Only the Pharisees and the followers of Jesus of Nazareth survived. Neither group was much involved in anti-Roman politics and both managed to get out of the city before the end. The Pharisaic leadership reorganized themselves in Galilee, where, as seems likely, they eventually emerged as the rabbis (see II/4). The Jesus movement sought refuge in Pella across the Jordan, and, as will be seen, eventually separated from its parent body and passed from a Jewish sect to a distinct religious community.

Although all these groups present in the Jewish community after the Exile have many of the characteristics of sects—their closed nature, their insistence that they alone or they especially represent the true Israel or know what constitutes the true Israelite—they fail one major criterion, as has been remarked: the existence of a parent or normative group against which they can be measured. Though the later rabbis claimed that the Pharisees, and later themselves, constituted an authentic and unbroken link back to the Torah, there is clearly no such thing as "normative" or "orthodox" Judaism in the long centuries that stretch from Babylon to the final triumph of rabbinic Judaism after 200 C.E. We have instead a community attempting to redefine itself against the loss of homeland and of national sovereignty, the disruption of a monarchical tradition, and a new and problematic priesthood in the new but unimpressive temple in Jerusalem. Each of the so-called sects represents a proposed cure to the spiritual and national malaise of this Jewish age of anxiety.

These were not all the Jews, however. One estimate has these sectarian groups representing no more than 10 percent of the total population of Palestine. Invisible behind them were an overwhelming number of Judaeans, the "silent majority" of men and women who shared an ill-defined but firmly held "consensual Judaism" (see I/5).

Words and the Word of Wisdom

The Bible's view of the supernatural world is straightforward. God alone existed before the creation of the world: no helpers, adjuncts, or "associates," as the Muslims dismissively called them, were present at the inception of the universe, and all other supernatural claimants are rejected as false gods. God has his angels, who served chiefly as messengers, never as surrogates, and Yahweh intervened often and personally in the affairs of humankind. After the Exile, the cosmic landscape, where once Yahweh had reigned serenely unchallenged in his solitary majesty, underwent gradual change. God no longer micromanages his creation; the angels have been distinguished, organized, and assigned specific duties by rank, possibly on the analogy of a royal court. God reigned in heaven in exactly the same remote and hieratic style as contemporary eastern sovereigns. But the universe itself is now filled with new moral powers, forces of good and evil, the latter led by Satan, the "Prince of Darkness" (see below), while near to God stand new figures, no mere spear-carriers or messengers but personifications of God's wisdom, of his spirit and his word.

Wisdom in the Bible begins with the words of the wise, the counsels of sages that appear throughout late books like Proverbs, Job, and Qohelet (Ecclesiastes), and, among the Apocrypha, quite explicitly in works like the

Wisdom of Jesus ben Sira (Ecclesiasticus) and the Wisdom of Solomon.
These post-Exilic wise men counseled a somewhat worldly wisdom of self-
control, honesty, and hard work, remote from any consideration of the
Covenant of Abraham or the Mosaic Law. This later Jewish wisdom literature
has numerous parallels throughout the Middle East, and Jesus' own teachings
show many of the traits of the traditional sage (so Matt. 6:19–27); indeed, his
wisdom is said (Luke 11:31) to be greater than Solomon's, the Jewish sage par
excellence.

But wisdom takes another turning in the Bible. Wisdom (*hokmah*) belongs
properly to God (Job 28), but in Proverbs 1:20 ff., and often in Jewish religious literature thereafter this divine attribute appears personified as a female.
God's "darling and delight," is "at His side every day," "playing in His presence," she was created before the universe itself (Prov. 8:22), and indeed
served as his agent in Creation. The theme is expanded and at the same time
localized in Ecclesiasticus. Wisdom's earthly home is only in Israel (24:8),
where she is identified with the Torah (24:23), an association worked out in
some detail in the book called Baruch. Indeed, in post–200 C.E. rabbinic Judaism, the personification of the Torah will largely replace Wisdom. In the
Wisdom of Solomon, which was probably written by an Alexandrian Jew soon
after 100 B.C.E., the praise of Wisdom takes on an unmistakably Hellenic tone
when "Solomon" begins to speak in the undisguised accents of a Greek
philosopher (7:15–30). Wisdom is described, in contemporary Hellenic cre-
ational terms, as an emanation from the glory of God: "She is the brightness
that streams from everlasting light, the flawless mirror of the active power of
God and the image of His goodness" (Prov. 7:26). Solomon seeks her as his
own bride, since "she is initiated into the knowledge that belongs to God, and
she decides for Him what He shall do" (8:4).

A Cure for Transcendence?

Though it is not always clear whence these various notions about God entered post-Exilic Jewish consciousness, it is more easily surmised why they became so popular. The most powerful intellectual current operating like a field
of force around Second Temple Judaism was undoubtedly Hellenism, and the
theologians among the Greeks had arrived at a remarkable consensus on
God's transcendence or "otherness." For the Jews, as for most other peoples,
the deity is more knowing, more powerful, and more ubiquitous than humankind, but the Greeks had come to define their divine First Principle in far
more absolute terms: God, the cause and end of all things, enjoyed a remote,
solitary, and unique existence outside the universe as eternal, immaterial, un-
moving, and unmoved Being. This portrait of God caused many problems for
Jews, Christians, and Muslims alike, particularly in the matter of creation and

providence (see II/10), but its chief lineaments became in effect the outlines of the way these groups began to think about God, even though their Scripture and their piety might suggest otherwise on occasion. The God of the Peoples of the Book was in the end recognized as an omniscient, omnipotent Being of pure spirit.

Jews found among other peoples, and perhaps within their own religious sensibilities, effective ways of coping with the shift of Yahweh from the hands-on, interventionist deity of the Bible to the more august, and more remote, Supreme Being of the post-Exilic Middle East. The intermediate figures of Second Temple Judaism are, in a sense, a response to God's growing transcendence, ways of establishing connections with the Absolute, through intermediaries of some sort, in order to fathom God's will, effect God's purpose, or explain the existence of good and evil in a world increasingly distant from its source. For the rest, the language shied off from the direct gaze the Bible seems to direct toward God. Among Second Temple Jews, Yahweh began to be called by his epithets of majesty—"the Eternal One," "the Holy One," even simply "the Name"—as more and more his actual name was avoided. The Septuagint, for example, translates "Yahweh" simply as Kyrios, "Lord." Elsewhere the "hereness" of God is replaced by his "presence" (Heb. *shekinah*, literally "dwelling"): it is not God but God's presence that is in the temple or otherwise manifested on earth. Similarly, in the targums, the Aramaic translations of the Bible, it is no longer said that "God speaks" but rather "His speaking speaks" or "His word (*memra*) speaks."

In this intellectual and religious climate the richly personified Wisdom becomes one of God's agents or surrogates. The transfer of both quality and function from God to his agent protects God's transcendence, even at the cost of progressively denuding the deity itself. This is, in fact, the beginning of the mystics' *via negativa*, the manner of approaching God from the rear, so to speak, by progressively denying him the limiting attributes that characterize humankind. It was under this same impulse that Hellenized Jewish intellectuals like Philo of Alexandria (d. ca. 50 C.E.) began the project of rereading the Bible in the light of the new theology (see II/2, II/7).

The Harvest of Hellenism

Philo is a new figure on the Jewish landscape, or rather, the best-known example of a new type of intellectualism that was making a profound impact on the upper classes of the Middle East since the late fourth century B.C.E. Alexander the Great had driven the Persian armies out of their conquests (including Judaea) and even their own Iranian homeland in the 330s B.C.E., and in his wake the Middle East entered an extraordinary new age. Some Jews had found the rituals of paganism alluring, to say nothing of the possibility of benefit from laying a side bet on another god or goddess; the Bible had to warn constantly against such temptations. But the attractions of Hellenism, which began to manifest themselves in the Near East in the aftermath of Alexander's conquests, were more fundamentally threatening.

There are various types of "Hellenism," which may be useful to introduce schematically here:

Political Hellenism   At its heart was the Greek ideal of political autonomy: the conviction that humans—providing they were men, free, and of a certain wealth—were capable of governing themselves in their own settlements. By the third century B.C.E. in the Middle East, this meant living under the general sovereignty of a Greek or Greek-origin king— the Ptolemies in Egypt, the Seleucids in Syria, both of whom ruled Palestine in turn—while at the same time enjoying the autonomy of a citizen (*polites*) in the new type of city-state (*polis*) that had originated in Greece but was being planted all around the Mediterranean. The most brilliant polis was Alexandria in Egypt, where Philo learned his Hellenism. The chief institutions of political Hellenism were the *boule*, a council or senate of "elders," the *ekklesia*, or popular assembly of all the citizens, and assorted municipal officials that every polis possessed.

Religious Hellenism   The religious side of Hellenism, or rather, the religious side of political Hellenism, meant paying appropriate reverence to the gods, whether traditional-local, civic, or "manufactured," like the kings and emperors who claimed and received divine honors. Descriptively, this was polytheism (shading off among the intelligentsia into henotheism, the worship of a single supreme god); judgmentally, from the monotheistic perspective, it was variously regarded as idolatry, paganism, heathenism, associationism, or unbelief. Its chief institutions, again with notable political overtones, were the temples and the state-endowed priesthoods that served in them.

Cultural Hellenism   The Hellenes' name for culture was *paidaia*. It spoke Greek—the word "barbarian" came from the mimicking of people who could not speak Greek properly—and its chief institutions were the *gymnasion* and the *skole*. Like our own sense of "culture," it embraced not only formal studies—rhetoric (our humanities), philosophy, law, and medicine were all popular subjects of higher education in antiquity—but also certain characteristic styles in dress (or undress; the Greeks pioneered nudity in the Middle East), entertainment, food, language, and more.

Intellectual Hellenism   From the beginning, the Greeks entertained a certain view of the gods, their nature and work, and of the world and of humans, their powers and perfection. Over time, this complex portrait was modified and refined among the intellectuals known as philosophers, and it was the Greeks' systematic *philosophia*, particularly the branch called *theologia*, that took God—most of the *philosophoi* were at least henotheists who held for the existence of a single Supreme Being—as its special subject of investigation. It was philosophia, with both its methods and its findings, that confronted first Philo in Alexandria and then every thoughtful monotheist, Jewish, Christian, or Muslim, who came after him.

One of the main propositions of Hellenic philosophia was that humans have the unaided intellectual capacity to understand, on the basis of the available empirical evidence, (1) the existence and nature of God; (2) humans' position in the universe; and (3) the moral imperatives that flow from (1) and (2). These propositions challenge the very need of revelation, and one of the revelational communities' responses has been that God uses revelation to make his truths understood to those who lack the time, education, or ability to become philosophers. Thus the truths of science and revelation are essentially the same (as allegorical exegesis shows; see II/2). The latter differ only in that they are expressed in concrete terms and material images to make them available to everyone.

The other proposition of philosophical Hellenism that challenged the revealed religions is that God had no special or individual care for his creation (see II/7). As already noted in connection with the problem of theodicy, God was thought to have a general providence that governs the world and ensures that certain ends are programmed into creation; or, to put it another way, that things act according to their natures, the motherboard of each species. But intelligent creatures also have the ability to choose to act against their natures, hence the moral necessity of understanding who and what we are and acting morally—that is, according to nature. The study of the natures of things reveals the natural law, which is, then, an authoritative guide to the morality of human acts (see II/5).

The new city-states built by Alexander and his successors throughout the Middle East were the primary carriers of Hellenism. Hellenism's worldview offered a modern and scientific interpretation of the universe, while its intellectual premises, its elegant reasoning, and its civic institutions (citizens, elected officials, popular assemblies, schools, and theaters) turned many Jewish heads (to say nothing of later Christian and Muslim ones) at home in Palestine and in the Diaspora.

Jews in Diaspora

Alexander's conquests carried Hellenism into the orbit of Palestinian Judaism, but even earlier Jews had been moving out of Palestine into the orbit of Hellenism in what is called the Diaspora. The Greek word *diaspora* means "dispersal" or "scattering," and it is used of Jews living outside Palestine. It is difficult to know when that first occurred, but its conditions were certainly put in place when the Judaeans were carried off to Babylonia. In that instance they had no choice, and what they experienced was exile (*galut*) rather than diaspora. But when Cyrus released them, not all the Jews returned to Judaea. Those who remained behind constituted—and continued to constitute over many centuries—a genuine Diaspora community. The phenomenon of voluntary dispersal was hastened by Alexander's converting the eastern Mediterranean and the Middle East into a single cosmopolitan community. All ethnic groups dispersed more widely and freely in search of better land, better wages, a different life, or were carried there as slaves or prisoners, and the Jews were no exception. From the second century onward there were large Jewish communities scattered all around the Mediterranean, all to a degree assimilated to the contemporary Hellenism, at least in language and lifestyle, while continuing to identify themselves—most of them—as Jews. They came up to Jerusalem in increasing numbers to celebrate the great pilgrimage feasts of Pesach (Passover), Shabuoth ("Weeks") and Sukkoth ("Tabernacles") (see II/6), and they were an important source of tithing income for the Jerusalem temple from the Exile onward. We can read their works, written in Greek, or written for their benefit, such as the Books of Maccabees, whose intent was to persuade the Diaspora Jews of the legitimacy and authenticity of the new Hasmonaean dynasty in Eretz Israel. We can also measure something of their assimilation in the remains of the synagogues that served as their prayer and study halls and community centers.

There was also resistance to fashioning a Hellenized version of the Jew, if not of Judaism. A new leadership arose out of the lower priesthoods and from among those whom the class distinctions of Hellenism had disinherited in their native land. The Maccabees extended social and economic distress into the incendiary area of religion: they equated Hellenism with godlessness, and so brought into their camp all those pious groups (*hasidim*) and clerics of the Law who were genuinely outraged by the new, alien, and irreligious style of the Jewish upper classes.

The Jewish revolt against the Greek Seleucids of Syria was a stunning political success—it reconstituted a nominally independent Jewish state in Judaea that lasted until 6 C.E., when the Romans simply annexed Judaea—but its sequel brought to the surface new factional strains in the community. The Maccabees' coalition disintegrated over the twin issues of the Maccabees'—or Hasmonaeans, as they were called in their new dynastic role—own progressive Hellenization and their legitimacy as high priests in the restored kingdom.

The Word of God

The Maccabees were conducting one form of cultural war in Judaea, but there was another, quieter front in the same struggle in Alexandria, where a large Jewish population was being exposed to many of the same notions and styles troubling the Judaeans. Alexandrian Jews had their religio-political problems—it was scarcely possible to worship both the political gods of the state and Yahweh, as several discovered—but many accommodated to the style without embracing altogether the substance of Hellenism. Philo, as we have seen, was one, and he attempted to explore just how much of Hellenism was both useful and safe for a Jew.

Logos (pl. *logoi*) is a richly connotative term in Greek. It means word, speech, reason, definition, and, finally, a scientific accounting as opposed to a mere narrative unfolding (*mythos*; see II/7). Early on Greek thinkers had used it to describe the organizing principle of reality, hidden from ordinary sight but discernible by the intelligence. The Stoic philosophers of the Hellenistic era revived that sense of the word. For them, logos was the creative force in the universe, creative in the fashion of sperm—the expression "spermatic logoi" was current among them—and pervasive throughout nature. Indeed, logos was sometimes identified with the nature of things, and as such provided the ground for the Stoics' theory of natural law (see II/5) and the moral imperative to "live according to nature."

Philo was aware of these developments within Stoicism, as well as their distinction—logos was speech as well as reason—between interior logos or thought, and exterior logos or speech. For Philo, then, who already knew a developing Jewish tradition emphasizing God's word (*memra*) as something outside him, it must have been an easy transition to apply the Stoic logos to the God of Israel. In the first instance Logos is the Divine Reason that embraces all the "Forms" (*eide*; also *logoi*) that served as the templates of Creation. For Plato and others these had always been external to the Creator, in the manner of blueprints; Philo is the first we know to have made the prototypes of Creation the actual ideas of God. This Logos that exists in God's mind as thought is then externalized to form the intelligible universe apprehensible only to the intellect. This intelligible world is transcendent—that is, it stands outside our world—and it is in some sense God, according to Philo, but it is not *the* God; rather, it may be called "the elder son of God."

The creation account in Genesis 1:26 is doubled by another in 2:4ff. This curious fact gave Philo ample opportunity, and perhaps even an invitation, to introduce the two Platonic worlds, the intelligible and the sensible, into his reading of Scripture. With the creation of the visible world, the Logos begins to play an immanent role: it shapes creation and at the same time holds it together and organizes it. The Logos is the "seal of creation," the "bond of the universe," and its fate. Even more boldly, Philo calls the Logos the first-born Son of the uncreated Father, the "second God," and the "man of God." Some mistakenly think that the Logos is God, but it is only the image of God.

Personification and Hypostatization

This is bold language, and we cannot be certain whether Philo derived it directly and solely from Greek Platonists and Stoics. The worldview and cosmology is certainly Greek, but much the same language and many of the same notions that Philo applies to the Logos, particularly in his more metaphorical flights, had already been used among the Jews when speaking of God's Wisdom, and the inner resonances of Philo's thinking about the Logos may well have come from those Jewish sources. The same is true of the Christians who followed close on Philo. Though he had more of a Pharisaic training, Paul lived as a Jew in the same highly Hellenized world as Philo, at about the same time, and so too did John, whose Gospel opens with a hymn to Logos that almost certainly predates the Gospel itself (John 1–16; vv. 6–9, 13, and 15 are probably later additions). This early Christian hymn echoes some of the same Logos language as Philo and many of the same ways of speaking that had been used of God's Wisdom. John's prologue is addressed more to Logos as speech than as reason and has none of Philo's philosophical underpinning; it seems more likely to have come directly from Jewish rather than Greek ways of thinking. Though Wisdom too "tented" among men, John's "enfleshment" of the Logos in a human person (v. 14) has no parallel in either Philo or Jewish wisdom literature.

There is every evidence, then, that Jews of the era after the Exile had few problems personifying many of the attributes of God, his Wisdom, his Word, his Spirit, and even to engender them: the Logos was male, Sophia unmistak-ably female. The difficulty appeared with the growth of self-consciousness about that process, which likely came through philosophical channels and was perhaps prompted by Christian thinking on the subject. The Greek technical philosophical term *hypostasis* means a real or existent being, and thus to hypo-statize is to convert a name or a notion, in this case an attribute, into an existing reality. The term and the process mark a crucial fault line between Second Tem-ple Judaism and its Christian offspring. Few Jews of late antiquity would have trouble accepting the notion that God had a "Wisdom" that was somehow distinct from him, or a "Word" or a "Spirit," and that the first might be called his "daughter" and the second his "son." The issue here was "somehow distinct." Were Jews moving down the road to hypostatizing God's attributes or were they merely pushing metaphors to their limits? Some seemed willing to push very far indeed, though it is worth noting—and this may be critical—there is

no evidence whatsoever that any of these personifications—or any other of the "intermediaries" of Second Temple Judaism—was the object of a religious cult, that any Jew ever offered sacrifices or prayers to them, or that any rituals were performed in their name. Nor is there reason to think that any historical person was identified with these personifications (or hypostases) in the way Jesus of Nazareth was, as we have just seen, in the prologue of the Gospel of John.

Satan from Prince of Darkness to Desert Demon

If Wisdom and the Word are transparently personifications of divine attributes, the fully developed figure of Satan appears more like an intruder. The Hebrew word *satan* may mean "adversary" and is rendered in Greek by *diabolos*, the "slanderer." Satan may be in the first instance a characterization rather than a name, but in any event he—or it—is not terribly consequential in the Bible (see 1 Chron. 21:1). His profile as a person does grow somewhat clearer, however, in passages like Zechariah 3:1–2 and Job 1–2, where he appears like a kind of prosecuting angel in God's heavenly court, though not yet as God's adversary. Sometime in the post-Exilic period, Satan becomes more personified and far more potent as the embodiment of evil, possibly as a result of Jewish contact in Babylon with Iranian dualism and its belief in two gods—a god of light, Ahura Mazda, and a god of darkness, Ahriman, who was responsible for the evil in this world. In that same vein, Satan becomes identified among the Jews (already in Wisdom 2:24) with the "crafty" serpent that tempted Eve in Genesis 3:1–5.

Satan is powerfully present in the New Testament, from his temptation of Jesus early on his mission (Matt 4:1–11) and his guiding role in the events of the Passion (Luke 13:27, 22:3), down to his final defeat in the End Time (Rev. 20:2–3, 8, 10). Here too he is a fallen angel, willfully disobedient and yet preternaturally powerful.

The Quran knows Satan under both his Hebrew name (Ar. *Shaytan*), which is used as a personal name and, in the plural, as a generic description of "demons" or jinn (so Quran 6:71, etc.), and his Greek one (Gr. *diabolos* > Ar. *Iblis*). The natural history of Satan/Iblis is as complex and confused in the Quran as in the Jewish and Christian sources. He is both a fallen angel cast from heaven for refusing to bow down to Adam—hence Quran 7:11–18 and others—and at the same time one of the jinn, although angels and jinn appear to have entered the quranic world through quite different portals. The quranic Satan is otherwise much like his Christian counterpart: he has been permitted by God to tempt humankind through lies and misrepresentations.

The Quran provides a great deal of instruction about angels, much of it similar to Jewish and Christian beliefs about such preternatural beings.

They are, for example, God's creatures who serve his winged messengers (15:8; 35:1), as individual guardians of humans (13:11; 82:10–12), and as singers of God's praises around his heavenly throne (40:7; 42:5). Gabriel and Michael are identified by name (2:97–98). How many of these notions the Meccans were already familiar with or shared is difficult to ascertain. But Muhammad and his compatriots parted company on some subjects related to angels. Indeed, there may have been some confusion between the "daughters of Allah," the local Meccan goddesses, and angels (cf. Quran 21:26) since the same derisive argument about God's having daughters (and not sons) is common to both (Quran 37:149–150). Elsewhere the Quraysh are quite explicitly accused of worshiping angels, and in the form of women (43:19).

Close to the quranic angels stood the more native jinn, spirits familiar to the pre-Islamic Arabs. Jinn were thought to haunt dark and desolate places in the desert, and though the mischievous and dangerous jinn were the subject of considerable apprehension, they were not normally the objects of the kind of cult associated with the gods. They are fully integrated into quranic theology—on one occasion (46:29–32; 72:1–19) they overheard the Quran being revealed, as they had earlier heard the Torah, and were converted to Islam—but once again they are merely creatures, Muhammad insists against the Quraysh, who worshiped them (6:100). The Quran fitfully attempted to combine the two, God's biblical angels and the folk demons of Arabia, though not always successfully or consistently.

Apocalypticism: Unveiling the End

Apokalypsis in Greek means "unveiling," and in Second Temple Judaism a vision of the End Time was unveiled in a number of striking literary works. As commonly used in English, "apocalypse" and "apocalyptic" refer to both the eschatological scene (and its emotional overtones) and the literary form in which it was presented. A full-blown example stands as the last book in the New Testament, the Apocalypse or Revelation of John. When that work was written, sometime around the turn into the second Christian century, Jewish interest in both the genre and its message was perhaps flagging, as was the Christians', who had appropriated it from their spiritual antecedents.

The contents of the apocalyptic vision are briefly described. History was coming to an end. God was on the point of intervening in the world he had created. A new age was approaching, born in chaos and confusion, but finding its fulfillment in the final triumph of God's Kingdom. The scene was vivid, dramatic, and powerful, and the message, in the end, reassuring: the wicked of the world would be cast down, the True Remnant saved. The apocalypses put forward a vision of the future provided by some privileged agent who is the reputed author of the work. This is usually a figure from the venerable

past like Adam, Enoch, the Patriarchs generally, Baruch or Ezra, but there are exceptions: Daniel is a contemporary in the book called after him and Jesus provides the apocalyptic vision in Mark 13 and its parallels. The authors have been initiated into the secrets of Creation and propose in the work at hand to "unveil" these for the instruction and benefit of the believers. Behind this premise is the existence of heavenly books or tablets on which all of history—in this instance the events of the future End Time (see II/10)—are recorded and to which the visionary has access.

A Message of Hope

We have preserved Jewish apocalypses for a span of about two and a half centuries, roughly from 165 B.C.E., when Daniel, the only such work included in the biblical canon, was written, down to about 100 C.E., the probable date of composition of the apocalypses attributed to Abraham, Moses, and Baruch. It was, most obviously, a time of troubles for the Jews confronted by the religious and moral challenge of Hellenism and the overwhelming political presence first of Greek kings and then of Roman emperors. The apocalypses are smashing tales in their own right, filled with sound and fury, catastrophes of all descriptions, exotic beasts, and esoteric lore. But they had a message for the powerless and the downtrodden as well. The troubles of this time and age, which seem insoluble in that context, are transferred to a cosmic arena—the classical Hebrew prophets had cast their visions in the plane of history—where the great eschatological drama will be played out, with God and his agents triumphant in the end. God's Chosen should not lose hope, even in the face of insuperable odds; the day was drawing near when they would be sustained and validated by God's own forceful, and final, intervention in history.

There is no sign that apocalypticism was a movement in any formal sense. It was a spirit that manifested itself broadly in the population, inciting some to fearful or expectant contemplation and a few perhaps to action, those engaged in "hurrying the End" (see II/10). The Essenes at Qumran seem suffused by it; the Pharisees, in contrast, appear hardly moved at all. Jesus and his followers were fully caught up in its grip. But Christians, as has been remarked, ceased writing in the apocalyptic genre early in the new era as the expectation of Christ's Second Coming, and the inauguration of the full messianic age, slipped ever more deeply into the future. Yet apocalypticism remained profoundly influential on Christian thinking. Christians continued to view history in cosmic terms: human progress operated under God's providential hand, and, since the Incarnation, was moving inexorably toward a triumphant end. At the Final Judgment, whose hour no person knew, the Church Militant would join the Church Triumphant in the enjoyment of the vision of God.

Second Temple Messianism

Jewish expectations of the decisive future come in diverse shapes and forms. For some there would be a straightforward, though triumphant, kingdom in Israel. Others anticipated utopian versions of this world, or wholly new and different worlds, or simply a kind of general and unspecified spiritual fulfillment. One feature of many of these visions of the End Time was the presence of a supernatural figure who would be instrumental in restoring Israel. That figure is commonly referred to as a messiah, an "anointed one." We know where the word came from: *mashiah* is used nearly forty times in the Hebrew Bible, referring once to the shah Cyrus, twice to the patriarchs, six times to the high priest, and twenty-nine times to Israelite kings, chiefly Saul and David (see I/6). In postbiblical writing it refers, however, to an anticipated, not a past, personage. It is difficult to be precise about that figure since, if the New Testament is excluded, the thirty-odd references to a messiah in the preserved Jewish literature from 200 B.C.E. to 100 C.E.—chiefly in Apocrypha like Enoch and the Psalms of Solomon; Philo and Josephus do not use the term— offer no clear profile of the person and no single notion of his role.

The idea of a messiah was not central to Jewish thinking in Second Temple times. The Jews, as a whole, do not seem to have been waiting for a messiah, not, at least, in the profoundly eschatological sense that the Christians came to understand the term. Some Jews, perhaps many Jews, were likely expecting, or hoping for, the restoration of the Davidic kingly line, which God had promised would rule Israel forever. What cannot be precisely measured is the degree to which it was thought that restoration would be historical or utopian, whether it would come about by force or the onset of the End Time. The radicals who brought down the catastrophe of 70 C.E. seem to have entertained both hopes, history hastening eschatology; but there was no place for a messiah in their plans.

The Son of Man

The visionary style was not new in Israel. The great canonical prophets collected into the Bible favored it, and Ezekiel in particular became a paradigm for those who thirsted to catch some sight of the supernatural (see II/9). But Jewish writing of the post-Exilic era, the works that circulated under the names of Ezra and Baruch of the recent past (Jer. 36:4–8) and Enoch of remote, patriarchal antiquity (Gen. 5:17–24; cf. Wisdom 4:10–15 for his post-Exilic "resurrection") peered into a far more transcendental future than their predecessors. They were witnesses to a new age, a terrible and glorious era, a trial and a fulfillment for Israel on a level very remote from merely human history.

The starting point for this burst of visionary excitement was, however, a biblical book, likely the latest included in the canon (see II/2), and known as the Book of Daniel. It was composed toward the second quarter of the second century B.C.E., so late, in fact, that sections of it were no longer composed in the now colloquially obsolete Hebrew of the Jews but in the contemporary Jewish vernacular, Aramaic.

The setting of Daniel is supposedly the period of the Exile in Babylon, but the actual time, as the narrative constantly testifies, is the second century B.C.E. during the Greek occupation of Palestine. Daniel, one of those in "Babylon," has a dream; his book recounts the vision that occurred to him.

> **Note:** The ancients believed that communications from the supernatural took place in the dream state, and among the Greeks and Romans it was common religious to spend the night within a temple precinct—this practice was called incubation—in the hope that such would occur. Jacob's vision of the Lord, for example, took place in a dream (Gen. 28:12), and dreaming is explicitly connected with visions in Joel 2:28, a text cited by Peter to his fellow Jews in Acts 2:17. Matthew's account of Jesus' birth includes a number of visionary dreams. Evidence relating to Muhammad is sometimes conflicting, but at least some of his revelations seem to have occurred in a dream state, and according to one standard account, he was sleeping in a sacred space next to the Kaaba when his famous Night Journey to Jerusalem took place (see I/3).

Daniel's vision includes a complex political parable. Of concern here, however, is the messianic figure, or what is sometimes taken as such, referred to as "one like a son of man" who comes before the "elder of Days," that is, God, and "to him is given domain and glory and kingdom" (Dan. 7:13–14). But both the title and ascription are somewhat more doubtful than the later Christian reading of the text assumed. The phrase "son of man" is not necessarily the title Son of Man. It may be no more than a simple descriptive phrase meaning merely "a human," and so here "someone like a human." He was not, in any event, Daniel's messiah; in his account the messiah is slain after a fierce battle (9:26), and there is no clue in the text as to his actual identity.

That was not the end of the phrase's career, of course. Somewhere between Daniel's "son of man" and the occurrence of that same phrase in the Gospel of Mark, apparently as a messianic title, lie the Jewish sensibilities that produced, sometime toward the end of the first century C.E., the anonymous work called 2 Esdras and the other called Enoch. In both works there are portraits of a messiah, and in both he is referred to, in addition to other ascriptions, as "Son of Man." In Enoch he was created before the universe, and at the End Time he will sit on the throne of glory. Here we are in the presence of an unmistakably supernatural figure, and though we cannot reconstruct the stages whereby the author of Enoch came to promote Daniel's "son of man" to a transcendental status, it is clear that Mark, and the Christian tradition that followed him, read Jesus back into the Book of Daniel through the lens of works like Esdras and Enoch.

2

The Good News of Jesus

THE CHRISTIANS' HOPE OF SALVATION is based, as Paul put it, on "faith in Christ Jesus," and, more precisely, on the conviction that this same Jesus of Nazareth was raised by God from the dead, since, "without the resurrection, our faith is nothing" (1 Cor. 15:14). The Christian debate over the nature, source, and effects of that saving grace has been long and often acrimonious—so acrimonious that it created a major schism in Western Christianity that separated Catholics and Protestants in the sixteenth-century (see I/6) and keeps them apart until the present. But all agree that, however they are read, the foundation of the Christian's faith is to be found in the body of documents called the New Testament.

The Dossier on Jesus

The New Testament took its final comprehensive form a century or even more after Jesus' death, but the four biographical-type works that call themselves the "Good News (Gk. *euangelion*; Lat. *evangelium*) of Jesus the Messiah" and lie at the heart of the collection were composed somewhat closer to Jesus' own lifetime, by one common estimate between 70 and 100 C.E. "Good News" is not a familiar literary genre from antiquity; the works seem in fact most closely to resemble what the Greeks called *Bioi*, "Lives," which is a literary form similar to but not identical with what we call biography. We classify biography as a subgenre of history, whereas the ancients thought of the "Life" (*Bios*) rather as an example of ethical writing. The objective was not so much to give a factual account of an individual's lifetime as to display his or her character through a judicious choice of anecdotes, which seems a fair, if somewhat broad, characterization of the Gospels.

The presence of these four Bioi at the head of the New Testament leads us to suppose that the Christians of that generation thought it important to know something of the events of Jesus' life, his teachings, his miracles, and particularly, given the space and emphasis devoted to them in the Gospels, the circumstances of his arrest, trials, and execution. If, however, we try to discover what the original focus on Jesus was by consulting Paul, whose letters—which are also included in the New Testament—were written in the 50s of the first century and so are the earliest preserved testimony to the new faith and Jesus' role in it, the historical ground shifts precipitously. Paul makes little direct mention of the teachings, miracles, or events of Jesus' life generally—it would be quite impossible to reconstruct these on Paul's evidence—but it may be a mistake to conclude that neither he nor the contemporary Christian communities to whom his letters were addressed considered these subjects of significance. They had already had, as Paul himself says, the "good news" preached to them, probably in a form not very different from our four preserved Gospel examples. Paul was not introducing Jesus to the Christians but composing a kind of midrash or explanation, not on a fixed text but on the meaning of events they all firmly believed had occurred.

The Historical Jesus and the Christ of History

Whatever Paul's take on Jesus—which the early Church obviously approved by bracketing his letters with the Gospels—the New Testament opens with four documents, each of which claims to be a narrative of events that actually occurred, in short, a kind of history. Hence, the life of Jesus, the "historical Jesus" as he would be more self-consciously referred to in modern times, was of crucial importance to the Christians from the beginning, an importance that manifested itself in a number of different categories. Jesus' reported miracles were thought to be proofs of his messianic claims, or of his authority, or even of his relationship with the deity he often called "Father," or, far more familiarly, "Abba," almost "Poppa". His teachings became the basis of Christian ethics and his life generally a paradigm of Christian virtue. His enactments, like the Eucharist and baptism, became the basic institutions of the new Christian society, whereas his call and dispatch of followers were the foundations of a hierarchical authority for that society. His death was regarded as the sacrificial act that redeemed humankind from the sin incurred by Adam and enabled salvation. Finally, his resurrection from the dead provided proof of Jesus' supernatural nature and unmistakably identified him as God's Beloved Son.

   All these events are described or mentioned in the Gospels at the heart of the Christians' Holy Scripture. But their interpretation likewise forms a solemn part of the Christians' belief system as it expanded from Paul through the teachings of the early Fathers (see II/2), through the pronouncements of the bishops and Church councils (see I/6). All are part of the enlarged portrait of the "Christ of history," to use another modern term.

The separation of the historical Jesus, the man of Nazareth, from the Christ of history, the object of Christian belief and adoration, is the work of nineteenth- and twentieth-century historical criticism. Traditional belief held from the beginning that the two were identical, that the selfsame individual was, in Paul's terms, "Jesus Christ." For Paul the title Christ (Gk. *Christos* < Heb. *Mashiah*, "anointed") is already part of Jesus' name: Jesus is the Christ and the Christ is Jesus. The authors of the Gospels surely felt the same, though perhaps not quite so insistently as the more theologically oriented Paul. Their works all begin with the title that is a proclamation: "The Good News of Jesus the Messiah."

The Gospels

The four Gospels included in the New Testament—and thus judged canonical (see II/1)—represent a choice. The early churches elected these four out of what we know were a large number of accounts of Jesus in circulation in early Christian communities. Left out of the New Testament were, whatever accounts might have predated the canonical Gospels, whether they were, as some surmise, narratives in Aramaic that lay behind our Greek Gospels or perhaps collections of Jesus' sayings like the one dubbed "Q" (German *Quelle*, "source") that both Matthew and Luke seem to have drawn on for two hundred-odd verses where they are in almost identical agreement but that do not come from Mark. The churches also left aside other works proposing to be the "Good News of Jesus" and generally attributed to some other member of the Twelve, like Thomas or Peter, or other or slightly later followers, including James, Barnabas (see below), and even Mary. The authors of some of these other "apocryphal" gospels—literally "hidden" but perhaps more accurately rendered as "sequestered"—obviously knew the four canonical Gospels and intended nothing other than to fill in some of the gaps in these accounts. There was the long period of Jesus' childhood, for example, or the careers of one or another of the figures left tantalizingly vague, such as Mary Magdalen, whom Jesus exorcised (Luke 8:2) and who then became part of his circle (Mark, 15:40; 16:1 ff.), or Joseph of Arimathea, who provided Jesus' tomb (Mark, 15:46 and parallels). Other works were written to advance a particular theological point, like those that have Jesus issue secret teachings or a hidden wisdom, which was precisely the point of the later movements termed "Gnostic" (see II/9).

Modern historians are still engaged in trying to discern what, if any, authentic historical recollections might also be contained amid the storytelling and theological argumentation of these other gospels, but Jesus' early followers long ago made up their minds on what was wheat and what was chaff. In the early Churches' view the four Gospels attributed to Matthew, Mark, Luke, and John were the most reliable testimonies to the Messiah, not necessarily the most historical—that is the quarry of more modern searchers in quest of "only" the historical Jesus—but the most authentic in a spiritual sense. Spiritual in this context is not divorced from the historical, of course; the Christians were committed to the historical "reality" of Jesus of Nazareth, his birth, life, and death in Herodian-Roman Palestine. But their faith involved something more, a conviction that these four accounts were written under the inspiration and guidance of the Holy Spirit and so were inerrant sources.

The four Gospel narratives are not identical; they differ on a great many details. That problem, which properly exercises historians, aroused interest but caused little disturbance for Christians who skillfully wove the four narratives into a single harmonious whole for diverse purposes: to celebrate Jesus' life in the liturgy, to meditate on it in piety, to study it theologically, or simply to construct a *Life of Christ* in the manner of a biography.

> **Note:** Although they successfully harmonized the four Gospels, Christians declined to combine them into a single authoritative text. Such a project was undertaken by a Syrian churchman named Tatian (ca. 160 C.E.), and his *Diatessaron*, or "One-through-Four," had an extensive but brief vogue in Christian circles. In the end it never displaced the four canonical Gospels.

The traditional order of the canonical Gospels is Matthew, Mark, Luke, and John. One reason, historical rather than theological, for the Church's confidence in the four canonical Gospels is that it identified their human authors either with members of Jesus' own circle of Twelve (Matthew, John) or with their followers (Mark of Peter, Luke of Paul, an apostolic claimant). But the evidence seems persuasive that Mark, the shortest account, was also the earliest, and that Matthew and Luke had a copy of Mark before them when they wrote their Gospels. All three cover the life of Jesus following the same order of events and so are called the synoptic Gospels. John is the odd man out; he does not include everything the others do and he adds a great deal, notably long continuous discourses of Jesus, whereas the others mostly cite Jesus' words in characteristic aphoristic form.

Luke and History

A brief look at the Gospel attributed to Luke may illustrate how the process of modern historical criticism operates. Luke, whom tradition makes a physician, was a Greek Gentile convert (Col. 4:11, 14) and, together with Paul—the "we" that begins at Acts 16:10—visited the congregations in Macedonia.

He is the most formal of the evangelists and the most professedly historicist in his work. Luke's Gospel is the first part of what was conceived as a two-part work, with the Acts of the Apostles constituting volume 2, as its preface indicates (Acts 1:1–2). Luke clearly intended to write history in a sense close to what we understand by that term. Thus he announces at the very beginning of his Gospel that it is to be an "orderly account" based on reports of "those who were from the very beginning eyewitnesses," in order that Theophilos, the otherwise unknown dedicatee (or perhaps patron) of the work "may know the truth about the things of which you have been informed" (1:1–4). True to his word, Luke sets the action in a time and a place: John the Baptist (and so Jesus) makes his appearance "in the fifteenth year of Tiberius Caesar, when Pontius Pilate was governor of Judaea, Herod tetrarch of Galilee, his brother Philip prince of Iturea and Trachonitis, and Lysanias prince of Abilene, during the high-priesthood of Annas and Caiphas" (3:1–3). Jesus at the time was "about thirty years of age" (3:23).

For all these indications that we are in the presence of secular history, this Gospel is no less than the others a sacred history, except here perhaps on a grander scale. Luke locates Jesus' life not only in the past, the history of Israel that predated it, but also in the reign of the Holy Spirit that began on Shabuoth (Pentecost) at the opening of the second volume of Luke's account, the Acts of the Apostles, and continues to manifest itself through the pages of that work. Nor is Jesus just a man, though Herod, Philip, Pilate, and all the secondary characters in this historical drama are: he is the Messiah and, increasingly in Luke, the Son of God.

Luke's special importance to modern scholarship is not only that he is trying to write history, or better, to present sacred history in the more acceptable—to the Gentiles—garb of secular history, but that he alone shows us what he did with the received tradition about Jesus and to some extent why. Luke provides us with what has been called "two glorious moments in New Testament criticism." Most scholars accept that Luke wrote his Gospel with Mark before him as one of the unnamed earlier "narratives" of Luke 1:1. Thus we can detect rather precisely Luke's editorial retouching of Mark's narrative, as well as compare him to Matthew, who also edited Mark's account.

> **Note:** Luke and Matthew did not merely rewrite Mark. They had other sources on Jesus as well. They both used the aforementioned "Q," which Mark did not. Furthermore, additional information shows up only in Luke, just as there is information that appears only in Matthew.

Luke provides greater insight into the developing Jesus tradition in Acts, a synopsis of what he knew about the subsequent history of the movement eventually called Christianity. He knew how the Jesus story turned out, at *n\o* *ʌ*

least in the short term. Luke knew, for instance, that neither the Second Coming of Jesus nor the End Time connected with it had yet taken place a half century after Jesus' death and resurrection, whereas Paul, for example, still thought it soon would a half century earlier. Luke was aware that the Jesus movement was becoming institutionalized as a long-time operation (the phase called by some modern scholars Early Catholicism). Finally, Luke also saw that the so-called Christians—first identified as such in Acts 11:26—were increasingly drawn from among the Gentiles, resulting in a deepening chasm between followers of Jesus and their Jewish coreligionists, and a rising tide of hostility on both sides. All this is amply documented in Acts and has not unnaturally been projected backward into Jesus' lifetime. Luke knows far more than Jesus' contemporaries and he uses that knowledge throughout his Gospel. But unlike Mark, Matthew, or John, he allows the modern reader to chart exactly how much he does know (and what he thinks about it) and so trace its editorial influence back into the Gospel.

Jesus: A Life

Mark's Gospel begins at the commencement of Jesus' public ministry, as does John's, after the opening prologue-hymn. But Matthew starts with a genealogy of Jesus stretching back to Abraham (1:1–17)—Luke's, which occurs a little later in his narrative (3:21–38), goes back to Adam. Both Matthew and Luke—though not Mark or John—provide circumstantial details on Jesus' birth and early childhood (Matt. 1:18–2:23; Luke 2:1–52). They locate his birth in Bethlehem, David's town just south of Jerusalem, and tell of the miraculous events surrounding it, including the story of the three kings; of Herod's attempts at discovering the newborn Messiah and his massacre of all the infants of Bethlehem to ensure the child's destruction; of Mary and Joseph's flight with their child to Egypt to avoid the catastrophe; and finally, of Jesus' unremarkable youth in Nazareth, a quiet village in Galilee.

Galilee was the northernmost of the three provinces of Herod the Great's kingdom—at his death in 4 B.C.E., the likely date of Jesus' birth, the Romans split them up among his sons—and the most recently added to Jewish sovereignty. Galilee also had the most mixed population and, on Josephus's testimony, some of the most politically and socially troublesome. Nazareth was the most anonymous of its small villages, unknown to both the Bible and Josephus. If we follow Mark's account (1:2–11), Jesus appears, quite without fanfare, from Nazareth to present himself at the Jordan for baptism by a certain John, an ascetic Jew who was preaching repentance in the face of the coming end of the world. John, who is mentioned in Josephus as well as in the Gospels, for all his importance in this initial moment of the Jesus movement, is an opaque figure: an erratic loner, a charismatic with a Galilean following, an eschatological doomcrier who used the Jewish purification ritual, "baptism" or immersion, as a symbolic act to signal the forgiveness of an already repented sin, and who, on the testimony of the Gospels, acknowledged Jesus as the Messiah.

Born Again

Jews "baptized" themselves to wash away the pollution of ritual defilement, after sex, for example, or after menstruation. But Gentiles were baptized by Jews as part of their conversion ceremony. And John? There had long been debate over what made a Jew. Who was a Jew was clear enough: a descendant of Abraham traced through the maternal line. Was something more required or, as the Christians were later to claim, something else? John might have been preaching either. It was he who claimed that "God could raise up children of Abraham from these stones" (Matt. 3:9), apparently scoffing at the idea that one could inherit the Promise simply by an accident of birth. Yet he was preaching a conversion ritual to his fellow Jews, perhaps to remind them that by their repentance they might become "born-again Jews" or perhaps simply "true Jews."

This was the spiritual background of Jesus and his first followers. The Gospels themselves are clearly puzzled that the Messiah was the disciple of another preacher, but the fact is evident. Jesus too preached the imminent end of the world, and his circle, and perhaps Jesus himself (so John 4:1), used the baptism ritual. John came to a violent end. He was arrested by Herod's son, Herod Antipas, and executed, for personal reasons according to the Gospels, for political ones according to Josephus; possibly for both.

The Ministry

Still following the Synoptics, immediately after his baptism by John, or rather, after a series of temptations by Satan and the selection or "call" of his inner circle of "the Twelve"—their exact number seems far more important than their names, which vary among the Gospels—Jesus began his ministry in Galilee. It is described starkly by Mark: "The time has arrived. The Kingdom of God is upon you. Repent and believe the Good News" (1:14). The "Kingdom of God" was likely the eschatological reign of God of the Baptist's preaching, and it was rapidly approaching (see II/10). Jesus did not behave much like John, however. Jesus worked wonders—chiefly casting out demons and healing the sick (Mark 1:32, etc.), both conditions attributable, in the Jewish view, to moral as much as physical causes. "Who sinned, this man or his parents?" onlookers asked of a blind man Jesus had cured (John 9:2). Neither exorcisms nor cures were unheard of in that day and age, and even Jesus' raising the dead back to life (Matt. 9:18–26) left witnesses in awe but not in disbelief. He also taught, often in synagogues, sometimes in the open or in public places in Galilee villages. He implicitly avoided large and gentilized cities like Sepphoris and Tiberias and explicitly his hometown of Nazareth, whose disbelief he found invincible (Mark 6:5).

It is difficult to characterize Jesus' teaching. He preferred a rather unusual form of instruction, the "curve ball" (Gk. *parabole*) called in English a parable (Mark 4:10–12). In it some scene from everyday life is briefly sketched and the listener is expected to draw his own, not necessarily obvious, conclusions from the acts and events described. There is a distinct social cast to much of Jesus' teaching by parable and preaching, particularly as recorded (recreated?) by Luke; concerns for the poor, the helpless, and the hapless—traditional Jewish virtues, though not always practiced in Jesus' milieu—are deeply expressed, as is a profound compassion for society's sinners and outcasts. But there are no attacks on the authorities, either Herodian or Roman, or, in fact, Jewish. The Gospels have their arguments, to be sure, but they are between Jesus and various (other) sectaries, chiefly the Pharisees (see I/1), the guardians of strict observance (Matt. 23:1–33, etc.). Jesus was not against observance, it is clear, nor even strict observance of the Mosaic Law. He observed the Law himself, not as strictly as the Pharisees would have wished perhaps, but it seems fair to call him an observant Jew of that time and place. What he quarreled with was the Pharisaic disdain for the "unclean," which was quite simply the state of the ordinary Jew, and the overwhelming of the spirit of the Law by its letter. "The Sabbath was made for man and not man for the Sabbath" was one of his more notable sayings in this regard (Mark 2:27).

> **Note:** Jesus' language to and on the Pharisees is remarkably strong in the Gospels, and in some places the severest judgments—the Gospels', not Jesus'—are broadened to an indictment of "the Jews" generally. The Gospels were written in an era when the separation of Jesus' followers from the rest of the Jews was beginning to cause grief to both parties. The language in the Gospels may not represent that of Jesus, in whose mouth such a condemnation of the Jews sounds absurd, but may reflect the growing antagonism between Christians and Jews in the 80s and 90s of the first century, when the Christians were increasingly Gentile and the Jewish leadership was becoming overwhelmingly Pharisaic. The same is true of the Gospels' apparent injunctions to go forth and preach to the Gentiles. These too may reflect a later generation of Christians' realization that the future of the movement lay not with the Jews but with the Gentiles. These are a modern historian's thoughts, however. Christians, as has been remarked, regarded the Gospels as absolutely

> (*continued*)
>
> authentic and inerrant, though more and more even traditional believers are willing to grant some space to human conditioning in the composition of the New Testament. That is, the authors had their say as well as the Holy Spirit, and whereas the latter always got it right, the former may not have on occasion.

Jesus' teaching has been described as an "intensified ethic." Just as the Pharisees took biblical observance and intensified it in the face of the rising attraction of Hellenic gentility, so Jesus raised the intensity of standard Jewish ethical teaching in the face of an impending End Time. His was an apocalyptic ethic for *la courte durée*.

The Last Days

Hovering over the accounts of Jesus' ministry is a sense of providential doom, of a divine plan headed for a fierce denouement in Jerusalem. Jesus may have visited the city on feast days but it was certainly not the focus of his preaching or other activities. God was leading Jesus to his foreordained end in the heart of Judaism.

The Gospels, which up to this point give only the most general indications of time ("Then . . ." "On the next day . . ." "It was the Sabbath . . ."), now carry the reader on a precise, day-by-day—sometimes hour-by-hour—chronology through Jesus' last days. They start in triumph. The time is just before Passover, probably in the year 30 C.E. Jesus approaches Jerusalem from the Mount of Olives and a spontaneous demonstration breaks out: he is hailed as "Son of David" and "king" (Mark 11:1–10 and parallels). He goes into the temple and in the portico causes a public commotion by overturning the tables of the money changers—the temple tax had to be paid in temple coinage, not Roman—and the booths of the sellers of small unblemished animals for sacrifice, both legal and necessary activities (Mark 11:15–19 and parallels). The Gospels say this aroused the priests' ire, and some modern scholars have seen this ostensible attack on the temple and its institutions as the most plausible explanation for Jesus' arrest and eventual execution. For their part, the Gospels constantly allege a plot against Jesus by the Jewish authorities (Mark 11:18), that is, the temple priesthood—the Pharisees, Jesus' Galilean antagonists, largely disappear from the narrative in these last days—but in the end God's plan, not man's work, leads to Jesus' death and so there is no very clear delineation of human motives.

On Thursday of the last week of Jesus' life an evening meal, possibly a Passover seder (Mark 14:12–25 and parallels), takes place. The Christians call it the Last Supper and it is the setting for an extraordinary scene in which

Jesus identifies for the Twelve the bread and wine before them as his body and blood and bids his followers to "take and eat." This marks the institution of the Eucharist, an act whose commemoration constitutes the primary liturgical act of Christianity (see II/6). At its completion Jesus and the Twelve—all save one, Judas, "who was to betray him"—go out into the night to a garden place called Gethsemane in the Kidron Valley on Jerusalem's eastern side. There Jesus draws apart to pray and, on the Gospels' own testimony, experiences doubts about what he is to undergo. Abruptly a group of temple priests and police appear. With them is Judas, who identifies Jesus. There is the briefest of struggles and Jesus is led away to the house of Caiaphas, the high priest, and subjected to an inquiry at the hands of the high priest and the Sanhedrin, the chief judicial body of the Jews (see II/4). It is difficult to discern whether this was a genuine trial or whether such took place early the next morning (so Luke 22:66–71), Friday, which, according to the Synoptics, was the first day of Passover. Jesus is asked, Did he threaten to destroy the temple? Was he the Messiah? The Son of God? He does not deny: neither does he forthrightly confirm any of the allegations.

Jesus is then taken to Pilate, the Roman prefect of Judaea, who is in Jerusalem during the always potentially dangerous period of Passover. This was done, we are told, because the Jews did not have the power to inflict capital punishment (John 18:31). Although this appears to be true, it still does not explain why the temple authorities were so bent on having Jesus put to death in the first place, and the Gospels, which are caught midway between their theology of God's plan and their half-formed desire to write history, provide no satisfactory answer. Pilate seems somewhat more forthright. His interrogation of Jesus is openly political—"Are you the king of the Jews?"—even though there is much more secondary chitchat—"What is the truth?"—than seems plausible between a short-tempered Roman autocrat and one more Jewish troublemaker. We can understand, in any event, that Pilate might easily be convinced by the Jewish authorities, who were generally compliant in such matters, that he had a potential or actual political insurrectionist on his hands and that it would be best to get rid of him. The Gospels add some grace notes, however: Pilate—and hence the Romans generally?—is made to seem reluctant to condemn to death a man he himself regards as blameless. The Gospels present Pilate as a somewhat unwilling tool of an intractable Jewish enmity toward Jesus (Matt. 27:15–26).

Jesus is led through the streets of Jerusalem to the place of his execution—we are given the name, Golgotha, the "place of the skull"—outside the city's walls. He is to die by crucifixion, suspension from a wooden cross until death by either suffocation or shock occurs. Two others are executed with him (Matt. 27:38). These are transparently political prisoners: the Greek word *lestes* applied to them is commonly translated as "thief" but is much closer to "bandit" and served as a contemporary code word for "political terrorist".

The indictment posted on Jesus' cross, "King of the Jews," also underscores that Jesus was being executed for a political crime (Matt. 27:37).

It was noon that same Passover Friday. Jesus hung on the cross for three hours until finally pronounced dead—there may have been a coup de grâce with a lance to hurry his expiring. At the end few were left to mourn him; all his followers seem to have scattered. The body was removed from the cross and buried in a newly hewn-out tomb chamber nearby, all before the sunset that would mark the beginning of the Sabbath (Mark 15:42–47).

The End and the Beginning

The Gospels were face to face with an enormous paradox. The man his followers thought was the Messiah of Israel had died an ignominious public death, and the Gospels do not attempt to conceal the fact that the event had shattered those followers' expectations. Some scattered in despair; others sat in stunned grieving over their dashed hopes. And yet within twenty-odd years, perhaps sooner, that despair had given way to a kind of exaltation: it was *because* the Messiah had died on the cross that all humankind was saved. Jesus was none other than the foreshadowed "suffering Messiah" of Isaiah 53, the "oppressed servant" who had "given himself as a sacrifice for sin."

Between the crucifixion and the later readjustment of messianic expectations occurred the extraordinary event of the resurrection. It was an event without witnesses, however. What the Gospels, Acts, and Paul present instead is the undoubted testimony of an empty tomb on the first day of the week (our Sunday), when first some of his women followers and then, as the news spread, a few of the Twelve went out to see for themselves. Not long after, Jesus himself began to appear to various of his followers. The earliest confirmation is Paul's statement in 1 Corinthians 15:3–7, written in the late 50s, that, according to "the tradition I had received, . . . he [Jesus] appeared to Cephas [as Paul almost always calls Peter], and afterward to the Twelve. Then he appeared to over five hundred of our brothers at once, most of whom are still alive, though some have died. Then he appeared to James and afterward to all the apostles." Paul quickly proceeds to put himself in the same privileged group (1 Cor. 15:80), though his apparition occurred some three years after Jesus' death, on the road to Damascus (Gal. 1:16; Acts 9:3–7). Paul's was a vision; when Jesus appeared to the Apostles and others immediately after his resurrection, it was in flesh. He actually shared food and drink with them, it is carefully explained (Luke 24:41–43).

The postresurrection narratives, all quite brief, are somewhat awkwardly appended to our present Gospels (Mark 16:9–19; cf. John 21:1–25), which in their original form quite possibly ended with Jesus' death and the discovery of the empty tomb. There are also broad discrepancies, whether the appearances took place in Galilee or Jerusalem, for example, and who precisely witnessed them. But Paul's testimony on the risen Jesus is early, certainly pre-Gospel, and forcefully asserted. The conviction remained strong thereafter: Jesus had been raised from the dead. The Messiah lived.

Jesus the Messiah

Although he uses the title repeatedly, Paul does not much concern himself with unpacking the literal significance of *Christos*. That is not surprising since his attention was increasingly focused on explaining to his young congregations the larger—that is, the non-Jewish—implications of their new faith. The Gospels were apparently produced by and for a markedly more Jewish milieu than the Pauline letters and so they argue in some detail the scriptural support for Jesus' messiahship. Matthew in particular attempts to build a strong case. The pertinent scriptural sources have been collected, and Jesus is shown in each case to have fulfilled the prophetic words regarding the Messiah—even to the point of indicating, as Luke also does, that Jesus must have been born in Bethlehem, David's own city, and so a persuasive messianic birthplace, even though all the other Gospel evidence points to his having been born and raised in Nazareth.

The fulfillment of prophecy is only one of the many argumentative themes running through the Gospels. Jesus' identity and mission are also signaled from on high. His birth and infancy are surrounded by supernatural signs and portents—the Muslim biographies of Muhammad adduce comparable birth and infancy evidence to argue a similar case of divine mission. At Jesus' baptism by John, God's own voice is heard proclaiming that "this is My beloved son" (Matt. 3:17; somewhat differently in Mark 1:11), and at one point in his life Jesus is "transfigured": his divinity is publicly revealed in a "manifestation" (*epiphany*, *theophany*) in the company of Moses and Elijah before the startled eyes of three of his disciples (Matt. 17:1–8) (see II/9). In the Gospels, even the Gentiles, unclean Romans, and a despicable Samaritan woman acknowledge his supernatural status. Only his own followers seem to have had doubts. In one famous scene Peter confesses that Jesus is indeed the Messiah (Mark 8:29), and although after his death all his other disciples came to the same conclusion, they were not nearly so certain during his lifetime. Jesus did not much assist them: he appears at the time notoriously reluctant to state his claims openly and unequivocally.

Jesus in the Quran

Jesus (Isa ibn Miryam) is spoken of often in the Quran, some thirty-five times in all, though never in an extended or consecutive account, since he was, like the other prophets, being cited merely as an example. The Quran sometimes echoes the canonical Gospel accounts and in other places diverges from them quite remarkably. We are told, for example, that Mary, who is identified as the daughter of Imran—which is also the name of Moses' father and suggests to some, chiefly Christian polemicists, that the Quran has confused the two Marys, the mother of Jesus and the sister of Moses—enjoyed the protection of God. Zachariah, the father of John the Baptist, whom the Quran also regards as a prophet and speaks of at some length, was chosen to be her guardian—Mary's father is called Joachim in the Christian Apocrypha—and she lived in the temple, where God miraculously provided food for her (3:33–37, 44).

The Gospels' annunciation scene appears twice in the Quran. Once, it is described briefly and to the point (3:42–47). An unnamed angel comes from God and tells Mary that she has been chosen—"God has made you pure and exalted above other women"—to bear the Messiah. She protests: "How can I bear a child when no man has touched me?" None ever will; there is no Joseph in the quranic narratives, though the Quran elsewhere angrily dismisses a Jewish calumny (4:156) that Jesus was illegitimate. The angel replies: "God creates whom He will. When He desires a thing He need only say 'be' and it is." Among the things the angel then predicts of the still unborn Jesus is that he will preach from his cradle, which may be an echo of the Gospels' portrait of the child Jesus teaching in the temple.

The second account is in the sura named "Mary" (19:16–22) and it is more circumstantial. God sends to Mary his spirit "in the semblance of a full-grown [*or* perfect] man" who makes the announcement of her pregnancy. It is not said how this takes place, but the Quran is steadfast that Jesus is in no sense the "son of God." Elsewhere, however, it is twice remarked that God "breathed into Mary of His Spirit" (21:91; 66:12). The account of Jesus' birth (19:22–35) bears little resemblance to that described in the canonical Gospels. Mary retires to a far-off place. When she feels her first labor pains she lies down by a palm tree and cries out in despair. God consoles her and miraculously provides water to drink and dates to eat. Mary is instructed to speak to no one. Her own people accuse her of unchastity, and when she keeps silent the infant Jesus defends her from his cradle (19:26–33), finishing with, "May peace be upon me when I am raised to life."

Jesus' life and teachings are not described in any detail in the Quran, although he too was instructed to pray and give alms to the poor (19:31). The same covenant was made with him as with the other prophets (33:7), and of course with Muhammad as well (42:13). It is predicted that Jesus will provide signs for his mission by healing the blind and the leper and make come alive birds he has made from clay—a vivid story that also occurs in the Infancy Gospel of Thomas. When again a sign was demanded of him, God sent down from heaven a table spread with food (5:112–115), an event some Muslims (and non-Muslims) have seen as a reference to the eucharistic Last Supper and others to the miraculous feeding of the multitudes. Jesus will confirm the truth of the Torah and make lawful some of the things forbidden to the Jews (3:50–51; 5:46; 61:6). His message was chiefly that of monotheism, a double of Muhammad's own: worship the One True God and eschew polytheism. Indeed, he predicted Muhammad's coming: "I am God's messenger to you, . . . announcing the good news of the messenger who will come after me, bearing the name Ahmad" (61:6).

Note: Once Muslims came in contact with Christians, they had to meet the challenge of finding Jesus' prediction of the coming of "Ahmad" (i.e., Muhammad) in the Christians' own Scripture, and in the Jewish as well since Jesus' messianic case was made by reading him out of the Bible. The challenge was sometimes met by finding texts that might serve. Muhammad's first preserved biographer Ibn Ishaq (d. 768) thought that John 15:23 ff., with its promise of a Paraclete—with some vowel changes *parakletos* can become *periklytos*, close enough to the Arabic "Ahmad" to be plausible—filled the bill. Isaiah 21:6–9, the call of the watchman announcing the fall of Babylon to newcomers on "a column of camels," was also occasionally cited from the Bible. The other method was to finesse the entire question by pointing out that the Peoples of the Book had tampered with their Scriptures, including, of course, removing all references to the coming of the prophet Muhammad.

The Quran departs most markedly from the canonical Gospel accounts in its version of Jesus' last days. In 3:54–55 it is said that the unbelievers schemed against Jesus but that God had a better scheme: "I am gathering you up [*or* causing you to die?]," God says, "and causing you to ascend to Me." Elsewhere the Quran declares that God has set a seal on the Jews' disbelief, "so that they believe not, save a few" (4:155). It then continues: "And because of their disbelief and because of their terrible calumny against Mary and because of their saying that they killed the Messiah, Jesus, son of Mary—they did not kill him nor did they crucify him but he was counterfeited for them [*or* it just seemed so to them]. . . . They did not kill him certainly; rather, God raised him to Himself" (4:156–158). But all the Jews will believe in him before his actual death, and on the Day of Judgment he (Jesus) will be a witness against them (4:159).

This is a difficult passage—one of many such in the Quran—but the traditional Muslim interpretation was that Jesus did not die on the cross, that a substitute died in his place—there were many candidates, from Judas to Simon of Cyrene, the hapless bystander of Mark 15:21—and that God took him up to heaven while still alive. According to these same commentators, Jesus must eventually return—by an almost common consent it will be at the End Time—and suffer mortal death. More recently, however, other possible meanings of the text have been explored, meanings somewhat more in line with the Gospel accounts of Jesus' death, though certainly not of his resurrection.

In the end, then, Jesus was, despite his miraculous birth, a human prophet like God's other messengers (Quran 5:75), who ate earthly food like other men (25:22). He denied that he ever asked anyone to worship him (or his mother) as gods (5:116–117). Christians are wrong in making Jesus God (5:72) and part of a Trinity. He was only a messenger (4:17; 5:72).

The Jewish and the Muslim Jesus

One almost contemporary Jewish source seems to have taken note of Jesus. In his *Jewish Antiquities*, Josephus, who wrote after the destruction of Jerusalem in 70 C.E., covers most of the events that took place in Palestine during Jesus' lifetime. In the Greek manuscripts of that work there occurs in book 17 a passage concerning Jesus. It calls him a wise man, "if indeed one ought to call him a man," and later baldly states that after his execution "he was restored to life" and that he was in fact the Messiah. It is apparent that some gross Christian retouching has taken place, but there is a fairly widespread conviction that the *entire* passage is not a forgery and that Josephus did mention Jesus in his history.

After Josephus, however, Jewish writers fall generally silent on the subject of Jesus. But they are not entirely mute. Some of the rabbinic authorities seem to have averted indirectly but disparagingly to the Jesus whose reputed acts in the first century were, by the fifth and sixth, changing the world in which they and every other Jew lived. In the twelfth century, particularly in Spain, Christians began to be made aware by new Jewish converts of the contents of the rabbinic writings and the hostile remarks about Jesus to be found there. These dangerous texts were later excised from the rabbinic corpus but enough traces survive to give some idea of their tone and contents. Jesus is identified as Ben Stada or Ben Pandera—more fully as Jeshua ben Pandera. He was thought to have been the illegitimate son of Pandera (a Roman soldier?) or a certain Stada, and his mother was a married woman, Miriam, a "dresser of women's hair."

Rabbinic references to Jesus are invariably oblique and occur chiefly in the context of the mishnaic Sanhedrin treatise dealing with judicial matters. The texts agree that he was tried before a Jewish court, found guilty, and put to death, either by stoning or hanging, "because he has practiced sorcery and enticed Israel to apostasy." Interestingly, there is no suggestion of Roman intervention or responsibility. The reluctance of the Jews living in a Christian world to discuss Jesus is understandable, but when many of them passed from Christian to Muslim sovereignty, the climate was no more encouraging. The Muslims too venerated Jesus (though they never worshiped him) and, as we have just seen, the Quran severely chastises the Jews (4:156–158) for attempting, unsuccessfully, to put Jesus to death.

The Quran's extraordinary regard for Jesus, "the Messiah," as it often styles him, is unmistakable and it is echoed throughout the history of Muslim piety—and that, incredibly, in the face of his supreme exaltation by Christians. The Muslims condemned the Christians' worship of Jesus but their disdain never spilled over onto the object of that worship. Casting free of its quranic moorings (which had already moved away from the Jesus of the canonical Gospels and set its bearings toward the Apocrypha), the Muslim tradition, which was still adding new stories as late as the eighteenth century, shaped a Jesus in the form of a wandering ascetic much given to aphoristic utterance. "The world is a bridge," the Muslim Jesus says. "Cross the bridge but do not build on it." Yet that was by no means the end of it. The stories about Jesus became more elaborate and detailed as the pious tradition surrounding him evolved. Jesus the ascetic was enlarged into Jesus the mystic. Jesus the miracle worker was not neglected, but there was also Jesus the social reformer and Jesus the ethical model. The portrait of Jesus became in the end as broad as it was varied, serving as a magnet for religious and spiritual sensibilities now Christian, now Muslim, now Buddhist in the porous environment that was medieval Islam.

Note: Reports on Jesus float in the Muslim tradition chiefly as detached sayings, ands there was little interest in fashioning them into a connected narrative that would approximate a biography. Much later, however, such a biography-gospel treatment did surface in Muslim circles in the form of the Gospel of Barnabas, the latter the companion of Paul mentioned in Acts 13:2 ff. and the author of an early Christian letter. This gospel turned up in an Italian translation in the early eighteenth century, reputedly purloined from the papal library under Sixtus V. (r. 1585–1590). The text was finally published in 1907 and almost immediately caught the attention of Muslim modernists like Rashid Rida in Egypt since the Jesus of this gospel acted and sounded very much like the Jesus of the Quran. An Arabic translation was published in Cairo in 1908 and is still cited by Muslims on occasion as a verification of the Quran's account of Jesus. But an examination of both the manuscript's physical evidence and its contents has convinced most that there was no original in Greek or any other language and that the Italian text was a forgery done sometime between the fourteenth and sixteenth centuries, possibly by a Christian cleric converted to Islam.

The Kingdom

It is difficult to know what Jesus' contemporaries made of what they were hearing and seeing in Galilee and Judaea in the years between 27 or 28 and 30 C.E. At one point, Mark (8:28) offers a menu of contemporary guesses as to Jesus' identity: he was a prophet, some thought, or Elijah, even John the Baptist come back to life. We know that his own relatives occasionally thought him daft, that the Jewish priests regarded him as a blasphemer and perhaps a sorcerer, and that the Romans guessed he was politically dangerous and executed him. His teaching had its radical edge—his notion that sin could be forgiven without recourse to prescribed temple ritual was extremely bold—but by and large it belongs to a familiar "spiritualizing" current present in post-Exilic Judaism. Nor was his wonder-working unknown or unheard of in that Jewish Palestinian milieu. Perhaps most striking was Jesus' eschatological message. The Gospels reveal, with only slight embarrassment, that Jesus and his first followers came forth from the baptist movement of John, an ascetic revivalist who was preaching repentance for sin in the face of an impending End of Days. Jesus' own message was much the same: "The Kingdom is at hand," and he was, or would be, its initiator.

His followers later calculated that Jesus' death was to have brought on the End Time. This latter notion came gradually, with the passage of time and the absence of apocalypse—an absence remarked on by the Jews skeptical of Jesus' claims—to be understood not as an end but as the beginning of a new era. It was, the Christians began to explain to themselves, the Second Coming, the Parousia, that would mark the actual End Time (see II/10). The result was that the communities of the Jesus movement, which were progressively distancing themselves from their Jewish congregations (see I/5), had to fashion an ongoing form of the Christian life. Thus, the teachings of Jesus and the early forms of worship, now detached from their Jewish context, were formalized and institutionalized to create the system called Christianity. Jesus' message became the possession of the Church.

After the Crucifixion

The Christian reader of the New Testament turns immediately from John's Gospel to the Acts of the Apostles, actually a narrative designed by Luke to follow as a sequel to his Gospel. Acts traces the development of the communities of Jesus' followers from shortly after his death in 30 to sometime near 60 C.E., when Paul arrived in Rome. The story in Acts begins with Jesus' bodily ascension into heaven (1:9–11) and then turns to the activities of his followers. The Twelve (Judas, the Apostle who betrayed Jesus, is dead; another is chosen in his place) are somewhat dispiritedly collected in Jerusalem for

Shabuoth when they experience the coming on them of the Holy Spirit (of God). This stirs them to fervor in preaching the new cause, soon to be dubbed Christianity (2:1–13). A tension, cultural certainly and possibly religious as well, also develops in the Jesus community in Jerusalem—all of them Jews, of course—between the Hebrew speakers and the Greek speakers (6:1–6). There is even more tension when a fire-breathing Diaspora Jew named Saul is converted to the cause.

But Acts is an afterthought, written from the perspective of the 80s. For a nearer view of what happened after Jesus' death, or rather, what his followers began to think about it, we must turn to the letters Paul wrote to Christian communities (*ekklesiai*) in the 50s, some twenty-five years after Jesus' death and well before the composition of the Gospels and Acts.

> **Note:** The New Testament includes fourteen letters bearing Paul's name. Modern scholarship judges only seven of these as actually from his pen: 1 Thessalonians, 1 and 2 Corinthians, Philippians, Philemon, Galatians, and Romans. The other seven (2 Thessalonians, Ephesians, Colossians, Titus, 1 and 2 Timothy, Hebrews) were probably written in the next generation by authorities who thought of themselves as standing close to Paul in their theology, which they do in varying degrees.

Saul / Paul

Paul, or Saul, as he was originally called, was a Diaspora Jew on a Jerusalem fellowship, a contemporary of Philo, and, like his Alexandrian counterpart, profoundly Hellenized. He was also far more radical. Philo was a sober and clear-minded academic, a man who seems hardly to have left his study, though he did on occasion write a broadside in defense of his fellow Jews. Paul, in contrast, had a brilliant mind, contorted more than clear, whose thoughts impatiently outran the language at times; he was an intellectually assimilated orthodox rabbi suddenly seized of a new idea, a *big* new idea. His letters were directed to various Christian communities around the eastern Mediterranean: they address what was on the minds of those communities and, more often and unmistakably, what was on Paul's mind.

Paul was not shy about presenting his credentials. He was a Jew by birth, a citizen of "no mean city"—Tarsus, in modern Turkey—and a Roman citizen as well (Acts 22:27), who had gone to Jerusalem to study with the leading Pharisees of his day (22:3). He became aware of the Jesus movement there sometime about 33 C.E. and read it as a danger to Judaism as he understood it. Did he think, and were Jesus' followers actually preaching, that the Messiah's coming freed them from the Torah's obligations? Whatever the basis of his fear, he began to "persecute" them, though precisely how he does not say. On his own initiative he sought to extend his personal vendetta to Damascus—we have no idea why—and it was on his way there that Jesus appeared to him and constituted him an Apostle (Acts 22:4–11), equal in authority to the others in Jerusalem, Paul argued, the "pillars," as he called them (Gal. 2:9). He was chosen particularly to carry the Good News to the Gentiles (Gal. 1:15).

Paul's Jesus

It is tempting to derive a portrait of the historical Jesus from the Gospels and to leave Paul to explain the theological Christ. Even historians who know better and who understand perfectly well that the Pauline letters were written well before the canonical Gospels do the same since the Gospels appear to be historical in their approach and the letters theological. The Church recognized no such distinction: the two sets of documents stand on equal footing in the New Testament, are thought to be equally inspired, equally reliable testimonies to Jesus Christ, the one and indivisible man-God who redeemed humankind.

We cannot know the full extent of Paul's knowledge of the details of Jesus' life, though there is no reason to think that he knew any less than the readers of the Gospels knew; indeed, he may have known a great deal more. But he had no need to display it since he was writing to Christians who had already had the Good News preached to them and so Paul was painting in finer, more calculated strokes on a far broader canvas.

Writing only a quarter century after Jesus' death, Paul reflects a very different understanding of Jesus and of his vision than that expressed by the Twelve and, in fact, by Jesus himself as he is presented in the Gospels. In those days Jesus' followers thought, with frequent and powerful misgivings, that he was precisely the Messiah of the Jews. We do not have the complete profile of what a messiah might be expected to be, but before his death in 30 C.E., Jesus did not act or preach like any of the envisioned Jewish messiahs. He was a mild—mildly ascetical, mildly reforming—preacher-healer from a backward village with no strongly enunciated political program and only the sketchiest vision of the End Time (Mark 13 and parallels). What so convinced his followers that he was in fact the Messiah? There is little doubt: it was his resurrection. It persuaded the Twelve, who suddenly turned toward aggressively spreading the Good News. And it convinced Paul, once Saul. Moreover, Paul began to comprehend the real meaning of Jesus' death. That emblematic death on the cross was not merely the fulfillment of prophecy, in this case of the "suffering servant" prophecies inscribed in Isaiah and the Psalms, but it was in fact the crucial deed of Jesus' life: his death was a sacrifice—a common notion not only in Israel but throughout the ancient world—and was, in Jewish terms, an atonement for the sins of humankind. Paul puts it as succinctly as it can be: "Christ died for our sins according to the Scriptures." He explains: In the fullness of time, and according to God's plan (1 Cor. 2:17), Jesus descended to earth, died on the cross, was raised from death by the Father, and ascended to heaven. Paul provides a swift thumbnail portrait of this great act, perhaps a fragment of an early hymn, a true Christian relic that antedates even the letter to the Philippians in which it occurs (2:6–10):

> He was in the form of God, yet he laid no claim to equality with God, but made himself nothing, assuming the form of a slave. Bearing the human likeness, sharing the human lot, he humbled himself and was obedient, even to the point of death, death on a cross. Therefore God raised him to the heights and bestowed on him the name above all names, that at the name of Jesus all knees should bow—in heaven, on earth and in the depths—and every tongue acclaim, "Jesus Christ is Lord," to the glory of God the Father.

The Resurrection

This parsing of the crucifixion gave new meaning to Jesus' death, a meaning that had escaped, at least at first, his closest followers but has remained one of the two foundation stones of Christian belief in him. The other is the resurrection. Like the crucifixion, but more easily than that terrible event, the resurrection fit into the traditional messianic schema: it was God's own verification of Jesus' messianic claim and status. But for the early Christians, including Paul, it was considerably more. "Paul," he wrote in the opening of Romans, "a servant of Christ Jesus . . . set apart for the service of his 'good news'":

> This "good news" God announced beforehand in Sacred Scriptures through His prophets. It is about His Son: on the human level he was descended from David, but on the level of the spirit—the Holy Spirit— he was proclaimed Son of God by an act of power that raised him from the dead. (1:1–4)

In short, the resurrection verified Jesus' status as Son of God, a Christological title that, in the Gentile world (as attested, for example, in the Gospel of Luke), eventually displaced the more Jewish messianic title of Son of Man (as attested by the Gospel of Mark). Paul pushes the conclusion a step further:

> If there is no resurrection, then Christ was not raised. And if Christ was not raised, our gospel is null and void, and so too is your faith. . . . If Christ was not raised, your faith has nothing to it and you are still in

your old state of sin. It follows also that those who have died within Christ's fellowship are utterly lost. If it was for this life only that Christ has given hope, we of all people are most to be pitied. But the truth is, Christ was raised to life—the first fruits of the harvest of the dead. For since it was a man who brought death into the world, a man also brought resurrection of the dead. As in Adam all die, so in Christ all will be brought to life. (1 Cor. 15:13–22)

The Gospels' presentation of the resurrected Jesus is almost homely. To substantiate his reality he is described eating and drinking with his followers and even inviting one of them, Thomas, to place his hand in the wound in his side (John 20:27). But whereas the Twelve and other witnesses had experienced Jesus in the flesh, Paul's encounter with his Savior was entirely spiritual. This is probably why Paul's notion of Jesus' resurrected body, a view shared by the early Christian believers, for whom Jesus' resurrection was the powerful paradigm of their own, was not of flesh but of spirit. Among the post-Exilic Jews there was a growing belief in the resurrection of the body (Dan. 12:2; 2 Macc. 7). The Pharisees in particular—and Paul had been one of their number—believed in the body's physical resurrection after death (Acts 23:8), as did Muhammad. The notion, as we shall see, was greeted with derision by his compatriots. The Christian Church generally would later affirm that belief in a corporeal resurrection, but not Paul. The resurrected believer, he asserts, will meet Jesus "in the air" (1 Thess. 4:17).

In Paul the apocalyptic struggle is likewise transformed. At the heart of Paul's letters is no mere Galilean Jesus; this is a cosmic Christ, the preexistent Son of God "through whom all things are" (1 Cor. 8:6), and whose crucifixion too takes on an elemental significance. Jesus' death redeemed humankind, and he accomplished this by becoming hostage to, and being crucified by, not the Jews or the Romans, as variously in the Gospels, but by the "Archons of the Age." These are not human agents but cosmic powers operating on a cosmic landscape, enormous elemental spirits (Gk. *stoicheia*, "elements"). This age, Paul explains, is evil (Gal. 1:4), ruled by Satan (2 Cor. 2:10; 4:4). The universe is dominated by these cosmic and astral powers (Gal. 4:3–9; 1 Cor. 15:24; Rom. 8:38–39). The gods of the pagans are real: they are demons, "feeble elemental spirits" who also tempt the believers (1 Cor. 10:20; Gal. 4:8–9). The death of the human Jesus would not have affected this powerful array (1 Cor. 15:12–19); it was Christ's subsequent exaltation as Son of God that broke their grip.

Paul's grand cosmic vision of Jesus' sacrifice had no long future in Christianity. Christians preferred to read the crucifixion as an act of moral rather than cosmic redemption, and the Archons of the Age soon passed out of Christian consciousness.

Christology

What made Paul anathema to many of his fellow Jewish Christians was his apparently radical Christology, the name used to designate the titles of majesty assigned to Jesus by himself or his followers and their consequences for his person and role. "Low Christology" emphasizes Jesus' humanity and accords him exalted titles that do not necessarily imply divinity—for example, Messiah, Rabbi, Prophet, High Priest, Savior, Master—whereas "high Christology" accords Jesus some degree, and eventually the highest degree, of divinity. Thus the passage from low to high Christology charts and measures the trajectory of the historical Jesus into the Christ of history. In 30 C.E. a Jewish man named Jesus, abandoned by all his followers and, as he thought, by his God, was executed as a criminal outside Jerusalem. Within thirty years he was being proclaimed as the redeemer of humankind: within seventy he was declared to have been with his Father from all eternity. Within three hundred, his followers formally announced that he was "of the same substance as the Father," and again in 451 C.E. that he was "true God and true man" (see II/7).

Jesus' original Christological titles (and claims?) were all Jewish and make sense only in that same context: Messiah, Son of Man, and Son of God. All three are intelligible in a Jewish matrix, and though it may be debated whether Jesus qualified for them, there is nothing non- or even anti-Jewish in such claims, including Son of God. The attributions "Son of God," "Word (Logos) of God," "Wisdom (Sophia) of God," all understood in some personified sense, were current in Second Temple Judaism (see I/1). The Gospels devote most of their attention to the claim of messiahship, which they attempt to demonstrate quite specifically from Jesus' fulfillment of the messianic predictions found in Scripture. The other two titles are more often asserted than demonstrated—Jesus' miracles do not seem to be used to prove his claims—though the resurrection might be considered a general proof.

Ebionites and Docetists

After Paul and the Gospels, Christian writings swell from a thin and often enigmatic trickle to the broad historical narrative of Eusebius's fourth-century *Church History*. The Church as an institution produced its own documents. With this literary material at hand and with considerable help from more recent archaeology, it is possible for the modern historian to write a consecutive and detailed history of the Christian community and its spread across the inhabited world.

Christians' attempt to explain to themselves precisely who and what Jesus was continued well into the fifth century when an agreement of sorts was reached on the subject. The fifth-century debate tended to thrust the "humanizers" (Nestorians) and the "divinizers" (Monophysites) to the margins of the community (see II/7), but a similar division had already occurred among Jesus' earliest followers when they attempted to explain how Jesus of Nazareth, the undoubtedly human man of the synoptic Gospels, could also be the preexistent Son of God identified by John and Paul. The humanizers here were, quite naturally, some of the Jewish Christians, people who believed from the outset that the Messiah would be, in Daniel's terms, "like a son of man." Paul's high Christology they found offensive, as they did Paul himself, whose views of the obsolescent Torah and superseded Judaism must have been deeply repugnant. Some among them even believed that Jesus had an earthly, not a "ghostly," father, the shadowy Joseph of the Gospels—Luke actually traces Jesus' genealogy back to Adam through Joseph—and though God may have "exalted" him through his resurrection, Jesus of Nazareth, the Messiah of Israel, was a mortal man.

These views were eventually rejected in the rapidly evolving dogmatics of the early Christian movement. They survived, and we know of them only through their inclusion in various inventories of heresies what were judged, deviant opinions about Jesus and his message. There their champions are generally (though not exclusively) called "Ebionites," a word of unknown origin. Being characterized are transparently the last, despised remnants of the original Jewish Christians, pushed beyond the tolerated limits of belief by swelling Gentile sensibilities or dragged there by their own misunderstanding.

> **Note:** Muhammad and the Quran's own Christology seems to belong somewhere on this spectrum of belief, and there has been speculation (among non-Muslims, needless to say) that it may in fact have derived from some marginal Arabian version of early Jewish Christianity.

The other extreme in early Christology may be termed Docetism (Gk. *dokein*, "to seem"), another appellation derived from the early Christian catalogers of heresy. The Docetists held that Jesus' human nature was an "appearance," a position that sounds not too remote from that of Paul, who said Christ had appeared "in the form of a slave" and "in the human likeness" (Phil. 2:7–8). By the first century certain Hellenized intellectuals found it inconceivable that God should be material or corporeal. That was precisely what they had rejected in their own struggle against anthropomorphism and their allegorizing of their own myths (see II/2). Docetism is, then, the furthest reach of Gentile Christian belief about Jesus: incapable of coming to terms with Jesus' humanity, Docetists ended by declaring it an illusion.

The Apostle of the Gentiles

One of the more persistent, if more submerged, themes of the New Testament is that of the persecution of Jesus' followers by Jewish authorities, whether of the temple or the synagogue. The Gospels predict that the Christians will be attacked by the Jews and driven from the synagogues (John 9:22); Paul describes how he himself was the object of frequent physical assaults by synagogue authorities (2 Cor. 11:24–25). Stephen was stoned to death by a Jewish mob (Acts 7:54–60) and a "great persecution" followed (8:1–2). James, Jesus' brother and head of the Jerusalem church, was arrested and executed on the authority of the high priest Ananas and the Sanhedrin for violating Jewish law (Josephus, *Antiquities* 20.9.1).

Though Acts in particular may have exaggerated the violence, it seems certain that there were grave problems between Jesus' followers and their Jewish coreligionists from the beginning. Why? Early on the repeated proclamation that this executed criminal was the promised Messiah may have been considered blasphemy. Perhaps the concern was political: a messianic movement could be dangerous in those tumultuous Roman times and should be suppressed. Or finally, the tension may have sprung naturally from the conviction that the Jesus movement would, or *was*—depending on the time—undermining the authority of the Law. All these motifs are plausible, given the state of the sources and our understanding of the eras, but the undermining of the Torah asserts itself most insistently, particularly if we view it through the well-documented pronouncements of Paul, the self-proclaimed Apostle of the Gentiles.

In the first century, the Jews, even the Jews of Palestine, lived in a Gentile-dominated world, as they mostly do today. Gentile thinking, Gentile expression, Gentile fashion and aspiration, all under the encompassing name of Hellenism, had deeply penetrated the Jewish community, without subverting Jewish monotheism—the influence here may well have been in the other direction, from the Jews on the Hellenes—whether expressed in belief or ritual. Many upper-class Jews assimilated, some reluctantly, some greedily, to the dominant Hellenism, but, more interestingly, many Gentiles began to express an interest in Judaism. The Jews, for their part, were open to proselytizing. The literature of the day attests to the existence of "God-fearers" and other Gentiles at the margins of Jewish religious society, and, particularly in the Diaspora, the presence of interested or curious Gentiles in the synagogue services.

Paul, though probably of strict observance himself, came from this Diaspora world of familiar Gentile presence. Once converted to the Jesus fellowship, he preached the Crucified and Risen Christ in those same Diaspora synagogues, keeping a careful distance between himself and the "Jewish"

Christian authorities in Jerusalem, where many priests were being drawn into the new movement (Acts 6:7), as well as some Pharisees (Acts 15:5). By Paul's account, he himself did not decide to embark on a mission to the Gentiles; rather, he was called to it. "I had been entrusted to take the Good News to the Gentiles as surely as Peter had been entrusted to take it to the Jews; for the same God who was at work in Peter's mission to the Jews was also at work in mine to the Gentiles" (Gal. 2:7–8). He responded with a vengeance, preaching indefatigably in the mixed Jewish-Gentile congregations in the Diaspora and accepted those who responded, including the Gentiles, for baptism, the initiatory rite for entry into the Christian community. The question must soon have arisen as to whether these latter had also to become Jews, and if so, in what sense?

Paul's answer to the first and essential question was "no." Christians were, after all, a privileged community poised on the brink of the End Time, awaiting the imminent return of Jesus that would signal its beginning. Jewish accounts of the End Time were filled with predictions of the "ingathering" of the Gentiles into Israel, either as people brought finally into submission or as willing participants in the Kingdom. Paul must have understood the latter as what was actually happening: the Gentiles were, under his ministry, knocking at the door of the Kingdom, and Paul, his eye on the approaching End, was eager to let them in.

The other brethren in Jerusalem were not so enthusiastic. Paul was told to come and explain himself to the "mother" *ekklesia*. He came and pleaded his case at what has been called the first Council of the Church. James, Peter, and the others took counsel and made their decision, which James, the "brother of the Lord," announced: "My judgment therefore is that we should impose no irksome restrictions on those of the Gentiles who are turning to God" (Acts 15:19). There were, however, some restrictions—refraining from things polluted by contact with idols, from fornication, and from blood (15:20). Whatever their intent and details, Paul seems to have ignored them in his instructions to his Gentile converts.

Note: These restrictions may have been some version of the Noahic or Noahide Laws, seven regulations constituting a kind of Covenant-before-the-fact concluded with Noah after the Flood (Gen. 9:1–7). They were understood by Jews as pertaining to all humanity, unlike the Torah, which was intended solely for the Chosen People. In medieval times rabbinic scholarship regarded these instructions as little more than an interesting topic of discussion, but in the modern era, some, like the Lubavitcher Habad (see II/10), have begun proselytizing for their observance in the Gentile world.

The tensions between the "Church from the Gentiles" and the "Church from the Circumcision," as the Jewish congregations of Christians were occasionally called, is everywhere evident in Paul's letters as he struggled to explain to the new converts (and perhaps to himself) historical Israel's role in the mixed congregations of the Diaspora. What concerns us here, however, is the main body of Jews who neither accepted the recently exalted Jesus as their Messiah nor even attended the imminent arrival of the End Time. For them, acceptance of these Gentiles into Jewish communities without benefit of circumcision or even the slightest degree of Torah observance must have been a growing source of aggravation. It is perhaps there that we can discover the true grounds for the swelling Jewish animus against the Christians toward the end of the first century C.E. (when the Gospels were being written) and that led to the complete separation of the two communities at the beginning of the second (see I/5).

Paul and Judaism

The heart of Paul's complex and troubled thinking about the Law, Jews, and Gentiles can be found in his Letter to the Romans, with additional interesting comments in the one to the Galatians (see II/4). In his view, God was and is the God of all humankind, Jew and Gentile alike. All human beings lived under sin, but because of their righteousness the Jews were singled out for a special Covenant whose sign and seal was the Law and circumcision. Nevertheless, righteousness preceded the Covenant and circumcision, as is clear from the case of Abraham, who figures in much the same way in Muhammad's argument to the same point. The Jews had a written Law as a consequence of the Covenant; the Gentiles had the Law inscribed in their hearts. Now, however, with the coming of Jesus, whose death redeemed humankind—the image is from the Roman institution of slavery—from the bondage of sin, the question of the Mosaic Law was not so much abrogated as rendered moot. The Christian assembly was now "the Israel of God" (Gal. 6:16). Henceforward Jews and Gentiles alike will gain acquittal (the famous Pauline "justification") at the bar of divine justice by pleading their faith in Christ. The Mosaic Law had paradoxically formalized sin; humanity was now free of sin and, consequentially, of the Law.

If this is a Jew's meditation on Judaism's past, other elements of Paul's thought appear far less familiar. First, it should be recalled that Paul is the rarest of creatures for the historian, a Pharisee of the Diaspora. Hellenized Jews are familiar figures and Palestinian Pharisaism is tolerably well known. But the combination is novel for us. Thus, when we speak of Paul's cosmic version of the Messiah as the Son of God, present with the Father at Creation, who descended from the heavenly world of eternity to take flesh in the historical present, though we can locate it comfortably within neither Jewish nor Hellenistic speculation, we may simply be ignorant of how the Hellenized Jewish Diaspora, or some members or it, thought about the Messiah to come.

Paul never repudiated his own or others' Jewishness. He preached Jesus the Christ in synagogues all over the eastern Mediterranean, northward to Syria, Anatolia, Greece, and eventually Rome. In accord with his principles, he also preached publicly and willingly, to Gentiles. Missing in this religious geography, particularly as it is presented in the Acts of the Apostles, is the spreading of the Good News to the southwest, to wit, the founding of Christian centers among the many Jewish communities of Egypt. This might have been the primary mission field of the Judeo-Christians, which would explain somewhat the silence of Acts and our historic uncertainty about Christian origins in Egypt.

Jewish Christianity

Paul never repudiated his own or others' Jewishness, but his single-minded focus was on the Gentile Church, as was that of his disciple Luke, the author of Acts. Consequently we are singularly ill informed about what happened to those other early Christians who were born of Israel and who continued to live under the Torah as well as the law of Christ. Only by reading between the lines of Acts and Paul's letters, and then turning to Eusebius (d. ca. 340) and other later authorities on church history can we begin dimly to discern the sad history of what is now called Jewish Christianity or Judeo-Christianity.

Both names are modern ascriptions. The ancient authors rather recognized what they called the Church from the Circumcision, a community of Jesus' followers centered at Jerusalem, composed and governed from Jesus' death to 70 C.E. by what Eusebius named "practicing Hebrews," that is, circumcised Jews who continued to observe both the liturgical practices and Torah ideals of contemporary Judaism. These Jews had problems, however. They first arose in connection with granting the "Hellenists" a share in the administration of the community's welfare system—there was no question of permitting them to preach the Word. The Hellenists were Greek- rather than Aramaic-speaking Jews, possibly Jews of the Diaspora who had resettled in Palestine. But in the story of one of them, Stephen, we can discern a more fundamental difference than that of language. Stephen had publicly argued against both the temple and the oral tradition, and his apologia in Acts is remarkable in that it is a Jewish, not a Christian, attack on Jewish traditions. Stephen was executed, and the Hellenists were forced to leave Jerusalem; the "Hebrew" Christians seem to have suffered no harm from the incident.

The immunity from trouble of some Jews who accepted Jesus' messiahship was doubtless by reason of their reverence for both temple and Torah—and somewhat more besides, if James, Jesus' brother and the first head of the

Jerusalem community, was at all typical. James, like most of his overseer successors at Jerusalem "from among the Hebrews," owed his position at least in part to his family connection with Jesus. But he was also a Jew of not only strict but ascetical observance, and he was revered by the Jews, Christians, and non-Christians alike as a zaddik, a holy man.

The "Hebrew" succession at the head of the Jerusalem assembly of Jesus' followers lasted until 135 C.E., when the community was dispersed by Hadrian's anti-Jewish pogrom, and thereafter the Jerusalem church was governed by bishops "from the Gentiles." What happened to them after that is difficult to say. By 135 the body of Christians was chiefly composed of Gentile converts, and the Judeo-Christians, those who viewed Jesus as a strictly Jewish Messiah whose coming abrogated neither the Law nor ritual observance, were thrust to the fringes of the Christian movement, where their history and teachings must be painfully excavated from under judgments of heresy and apostasy.

Some of those judgments may indeed be true, as the forces of action and reaction pushed the Jewish Christians into more and more extreme forms of belief and practice. As a result, we can attempt cautiously to reconstruct their system of beliefs from what early authorities tell us about certain marginal Christians sects like the already described Ebionites, who might well be descendants of the Jerusalem Church from the Circumcision. This is possible, but it is equally plausible that they grew out of far more esoteric forms of Judaism, and that their rejection by the Great Church may have been a result of that latter influence rather than a more general turning from Christianity's Jewish antecedents.

Thus it is difficult to speak of Jewish Christianity as if it were a single, unitary phenomenon. All Christianity is in some sense Jewish Christianity in its acceptance and affirmation of the Jewish Scriptures and Jesus as a Messiah, a claim and a title that make no sense outside a Jewish context. Instead the specific forms of Jewish Christianity are what reflect on ethnic origins—like Eusebius's "Hebrews"—and on doctrinal positions—Ebionites, Elkasaites, and the terms favored by Jewish writers, *notzrim* and, possibly, *minim* (see I/5).

The pursuit of the Jewish Christians is an exercise in both history, with archaeology playing an increasingly important role, and the reconstruction of a theology. What can be pieced together is the portrait of a community, or communities, that was deeply committed to an apocalyptic and eventually, in some quarters, a Gnostic view of history, and a severe asceticism; that stressed the human, Davidic descent of Jesus; that had its own canon of Scripture; that placed a liturgical emphasis on baptism and celebrated the Resurrection on Passover; that cherished the ideal of ritual purity; and that had a deep-seated hostility toward Paul.

The Jewish Christian attitude toward Paul arose with the question of admitting Gentiles into the Christian community. According to Acts, the issue may have first presented itself in the Hellenists' proselytizing among the

"God-fearers," a somewhat shadowy Gentile group on the fringes of Judaism. Association with them, and a fortiori with absolute Gentiles, clearly violated the community sense of Christian *haburah* (brotherhood) and its attendant notions of ritual purity. The issue came to a head in Jerusalem in 48–49 C.E. By then Paul, once a Pharisee of Tarsus and now a new Christian who had been openly preaching the Good News to Gentiles, was at the center of the controversy. Some at Jerusalem, described as believers of the Pharisaic party (Acts 15:5), insisted that those new converts be circumcised and bound to observance of the Mosaic Law. The resolution of the dispute, which had been put before James and the Apostles, was, as already noted, a compromise. Paul was permitted to preach to the Gentiles, and his converts would be bound to a modified version—certainly not the Pharisaic ideal—of the Law. Christianity, it appeared, was for the Gentiles as well as the Jews.

Paul left behind a body of letters that were incorporated into the canon of the New Testament, and they provide an extraordinary glimpse of early Christian thought in the intelligence of a deeply original thinker whose own personality shines through almost every line he has written. It was Paul's Jesus who became the Church's Christ, and it was Paul's attitude toward the Torah and the Jewish past that shaped Christianity's own.

Judaizers

Both Jews and Jewish Christians may have thought Paul was speaking to them, and though much of what he said pertained to them in one fashion or another, it is not at all certain he was addressing them directly in his letters. His letters were written to Christian communities where the majority were likely baptized Gentiles. The urgent question for him, and for them, may well have been that of "Judaizing," the natural impulse of Gentile Christians, most of whom at this early stage had likely been attracted in the first instance to Judaism—there was as yet no such thing as "Christianity"—and now, caught up in a Jewish messianic movement, wished to draw closer to what they surely regarded as the parent body. It was no easy matter explaining to them that in the urgency of the times this was not necessary, and even more difficult to make them understand that at base it was wrong. They had been saved by Christ's death and resurrection at the very threshold of the End Time, and indeed, as part of the plan for the End Time. The New Covenant was precisely for them, so that all humankind might be eligible for salvation, not merely the Jews, who had been granted theirs through the Torah. In the end both Jews and Gentiles will be redeemed (Rom. 11:26).

If Paul's intent was in fact to reject Judaizing by his Gentile converts while at the same time affirming Torah and Judaism, it must be judged a failure. The Jews either did not understand or did not accept the distinction, and perhaps the Gentile Christians rejected it as well. The option became, as time passed, to be either a Jew, which meant rejecting Jesus' messianic claims, or a Christian, which meant rejecting the Torah and, in the end, the Jews themselves. Debate turned into polemic, and then, as the number of Christians steadily mounted and their power grew accordingly, the Jews lapsed into a dense and prudent silence on the subject. The triumphant Christians began to construct their own post-Pauline theology of Judaism and proceeded to remove most of the many traces of its Jewish past from what was now known purely and simply as Christianity. At the end of the first Christian century, Ignatius (d. 107 C.E.), bishop of Antioch, a large ancient metropolis with a considerable Jewish—and Christian—population, was referring to the Jews' "worn out tales," and the anonymous "Letter to Diognetus," written in 124 C.E., explains at length to a pagan why Christians do not share the "nonsensical" beliefs and "fussy practices" of the Jews without once revealing that these objectionable beliefs and practices came from a book that the Christians too regarded as divinely revealed.

Paul: Jerusalem to Rome

Paul spent most of his missionary career traveling among the Greek Christian communities in the eastern Mediterranean. We cannot always tell whether they were mixed synagogue communities of Jews and Gentiles or whether, in some cases, Jesus' followers had already formed themselves into separate congregations. Paul's correspondents had a variety of problems, ranging from worries about the coming End to the conflicting claims of rival preachers of the Word, to matters of sexual behavior and the role of women in the new communities. Paul had to address them all in his letters and to explain, not always very patiently, the profound significance of the new thing in which they all believed. He was much troubled by his own demons, inevitably and invariably by his wrestling with the hopeless question of where he stood with regard to his own and his people's past, and by almost constant conflicts with the Jewish congregations where he traveled, and where his reputation often preceded him.

Paul had been summoned to Jerusalem early on, as we have seen, probably in 49 C.E., to answer for his actions in the Diaspora. When he next visited the city, sometime before 60, once more bringing alms for the perpetually impoverished mother church, the Gentile issue rose again. The Apostles there told him, almost defensively, according to Acts 21:20, that their own efforts at convincing their fellow Jews, "all of them staunch upholders of the Law," were going very well, but that the news that the notorious Paul was in the city was bound to make their work difficult. Paul agreed to a public relations gesture, the performance of some supererogatory religious acts in the temple to demonstrate that he was in fact a practicing Jew. The tactic backfired. No sooner was Paul in the temple than he was identified by some Jews from the

Diaspora who knew all about his "Gentile mission." Rumor quickly spread that he had brought a Gentile into the temple and he was set upon by an outraged mob. He was barely saved by some Roman troops—the Roman guard post of Fortress Antonia in the northwest corner of the temple precinct was fully manned on holy days—but then, being Paul, he got leave to say a few parting words to his tormentors. His remarks began innocently enough—he flourished his Jewish credentials once again—but as soon as he began to describe his call to the Gentiles, new violence broke out (Acts 21:37–22:22). Once inside, and on the point of being flogged—Roman justice was not always nice, but it could be rapid on occasion—he revealed to the sergeant commanding that he was a Roman citizen.

The news may have come as a relief to the garrison commander. It meant that Paul could be packed off to another jurisdiction, in this case the Jewish Sanhedrin. There was a trial of sorts (Acts 22:30–23:10), with more inflammatory oratory and, according to Acts, a conspiracy to assassinate him (23:12–15). The Roman commander had had enough. He sent Paul under heavy military escort to Caesarea-by-the-Sea and to Felix, the Roman governor of Judaea. There was a hearing: the high priest and his lawyer were the plaintiffs, Paul the defendant, and Felix, "who was well informed about the new way," the judge. This time there was no speedy decision. It served Felix best to do nothing and Paul remained in prison for two years. When Felix's term was up, he was replaced by a new governor, Festus, who soon had his fill of his troublesome prisoner—at one point, during one of Paul's "explanations," he cried out, "You are raving! Too much study has driven you mad!" (Acts 26:24). Paul eventually ended the governor's misery by appealing his case, as was his right as a Roman citizen, to the emperor (25:11–12).

Acts ends with a circumstantial description of Paul's voyage to Rome. He was placed under house arrest there while awaiting a hearing on his case. "He stayed there two full years at his own expense, with a welcome for all who came to him; he proclaimed the Kingdom of God and taught the facts about the Lord Jesus Christ quite openly and without hindrance" (28:30–31) are its final words. We are not told, though the author surely knew, that Peter, with whom Paul had not had an entirely friendly relationship (Gal. 2:11), was the head of the church there and that both men were put to death by the Roman authorities, likely in 62 C.E. That same year James, Jesus' brother and the head of the Jerusalem church, was executed in the holy city.

The Great War and Its Aftermath

For documents supposedly written shortly after the cataclysmic events of 70 C.E., the Gospels show remarkably little trace of what must have been for all Jews, followers of Jesus or not, a shattering blow to the entire religious, social, and economic life of Palestine: the Roman siege and capture of Jerusalem with the concomitant destruction of the temple. The Christians had their own particular reason to reflect on the event since Jesus is credited with predicting its destruction some forty years earlier, and we know from the Gospels that his followers had not forgotten the fateful prediction. Some of those disciples were living in the city when the Jewish insurrection against Rome began in 66 C.E. All we know of them comes from much later sources like the fourth-century church historian Eusebius. We are told there of the Jesus community managing to escape from the city before the catastrophe of 70 C.E. and relocating at the city of Pella on the other side of the Jordan, but we cannot be sure of its truth. All that is certain is that when Christians resettled in Jerusalem, they were, all of them, now of the Church from the Gentiles.

We possess a graphic account of Jerusalem and its destruction by the Romans in *The Jewish War* by the Jewish historian Josephus (d. ca. 100). At the outbreak of the revolt he had commanded some of the insurrectionists' forces in Galilee, but he had become convinced that the entire venture was both foolish and suicidal and gone over to the Roman side. Josephus tells us that many like-minded Jews managed to escape Jerusalem before its final siege and destruction. He does not, however, mention the most famous of them, Yohanan ben Zakkai, the leader of the Pharisaic party who was smuggled out of the besieged city in a coffin. Yohanan later reconstituted the party, and particularly its teaching tradition at Yabneh (or Jamnia) near the coast of Palestine and so provided a spiritual and intellectual bridge between the temple Judaism that was no more, and the Pharisee-inspired and Pharisee-shaped Torah Judaism that found its voice in the Mishnah some 130 years after the events of 70 (see I/4).

Yohanan had seen enough in his own lifetime to be wary of all types of extreme behavior or fanatic appeals. One of the cautionary sayings attributed to him is "If you have a sapling in your hand, and it is said to you, 'Behold, there is the Messiah,' continue with your planting, and then afterward go out and receive him." This was probably sound advice, given recent events in the community, but it went unheeded by Yohanan's premier student, the man later known as Rabbi Akiba (d. ca. 135). Akiba's reputation as a religious scholar is beyond dispute—both Mishnah and Talmud are filled with religious rulings by him and stories about him—but they are somewhat overshadowed by an act of staggering imprudence. The chief religious authority of his time, Akiba recognized the messiahship of the insurrectionist Bar Kokhba, who in 132–135 brought Roman vengeance down a second time on the Jews of Palestine. The Bar Kokhba revolt marked the painful end of messianic speculation among most Jews but it also marked the cessation of Jewish life in Judaea and particularly in Jerusalem whence the Jews were banned by the Romans and did not return until readmitted by the Muslims who took the city in 635.

Earthly Messiahs

Interspersed in Josephus's circumstantial description of the events that led up to the Jewish insurrection of 66 and the Romans' fierce response between 66 and 70 appear numerous figures who do not easily fit into our tentatively constructed models of a biblical messiah but were examples of a related type, human agents of God's will with respect to the Jewish people. Leaving aside the simply politically ambitious like the Judas and the Simeon who coveted Herod's crown (Josephus, *Antiquities* 17.10.5–6), the profiles of the others range widely from a Samaritan agitator on Mount Gerizim (*Ant.* 18.3.1), self-proclaimed prophets like Theudas (*Ant.* 20.5.1 and Acts 5:27), and "the Egyptian" who led thirty thousand men to the Mount of Olives for an attack on Jerusalem (*Jewish War* 2.13.5) to the chaotically obsessive Jesus, son of Ananas, who for seven years and five months daily cried out, "Woe, woe to Jerusalem" until he was killed in the Roman siege of that city (*War* 6.6.3). Jesus of Nazareth was one of that company (*Ant.* 18.3. 3), and he fits no more comfortably than the others into the older messianic mold. Jesus' reluctance to press his own messianic claims is notorious (Mark 3:11–12 etc.), but if he did not aggressively press his own case as Messiah, the Gospels did it for him. Matthew in particular goes to some lengths to demonstrate that Jesus was the expected Messiah by reason of his fulfillment of the biblical prophecies on the subject (see II/2). Matthew already assumes a well-defined messianic prototype built on scriptural texts and into which Jesus comfortably fits. Whether such a prototype predated Jesus' career or whether the cloth was cut to suit the wearer we cannot tell.

Jewish messianism did not disappear with Jesus' death in 30 C.E. or with the Roman destruction of Jerusalem forty years later. Indeed, the Jews rose once again against the Romans sometime around 132. Their leader in arms on this occasion, a certain Bar Kosiba, appears to have made a public messianic claim to be God's agent for the restoration of Israel—his sobriquet, Bar Kokhba, or "Son of the Star," has just such implications—and, as we have seen, even to have been validated as such by the era's preeminent religious authority, Rabbi Akiba. With the bloody failure of this final gesture of Jewish defiance, however, and the extraordinary success of the movement of the once Jewish Messiah and now Christian Savior Jesus of Nazareth, the Jews generally lost their appetite for revolutionary redeemers. Though there were occasional apocalyptic frissons, at the sudden rise of Islam, for example, and there is the Quran's assertion that the Jews of that day thought Ezra was the Messiah (9:30), the Jewish clergy attempted to cultivate a posture of political quietism in the scattered communities that now lived in the sometimes hostile and never entirely friendly worlds of Christendom and Islamdom.

Later Jewish Messiahs

Jewish postbiblical messianism has been characterized by two types. The first is utopian and looks toward the disruption of the current historical process in the name of an End Time (see II/10) from whose chaos the messianic figure who will accomplish the redemption will emerge. The vision is apocalyptic and highly political. The other type has been called restorative. It yearns for a pristine Judaism, when the community was united in the Holy Land in the worship of the One True God. Or perhaps it anticipates something even more primeval, *tikkun*, the aboriginal harmony of humankind.

> **Note:** The *tikkun*, a notion that found enlarged meaning among the adepts of Kabbalah (see II/9), is not very remote from the Quran's vision of *fitra* (3:29), a state of harmony that existed in Eden between God and his human "deputy" (*khalifa*), Adam. Islam is an approximation of that state by reason of its being the religion of Abraham, which was itself a later manifestation of what might be called the "religion of Adam," that is, the *fitra*.

That pristine state is not achieved, however, through the travails of an apocalyptic End Time but though a messianic enlightenment. Such restorative messianism may be represented by the Spanish mystic Abraham Abulafia, who, after dwelling and teaching in both the eastern and western estates of Judaism, attempted to see Pope Nicholas III in Rome on the eve of Rosh Hashanah of the year 1280. The pope died before his determined Jewish visitor could get to him; Abulafia was seized by Franciscan monks but finally released. He retreated to Sicily, where he taught Kabbala in his own school. Abulafia's attempt at a papal summit may have been, as some claim, nothing more than a quixotic attempt at an unlikely conversion, but it has been argued that the attempted meeting owes more to Abulafia's vision of his own prophetic (or messianic) mission to effect the tikkun, here in concert with Christendom's chief representative.

Though his mystical writings were highly influential, Abulafia's zealous gesture had little impact on his fellow Jews. A more apocalyptic impulse is evident in the events of the last decade of the fifteenth century. The expulsion of the Jews from Spain in 1492 and their scattering across the Muslim, mostly Ottoman, Mediterranean created a crisis in religious thinking. For some, the event was a catastrophe, another implacable punishment for sin. Others, however, reverted to another Jewish way of coming to terms with historical misfortune: this was the opening and highly significant step into the "time of troubles" that by all accounts must precede the End Time. At Safad in Palestine, the principal herald of this apocalyptic scenario was Isaac Abrabanel (d. 1508), the same highly placed Jew who persuaded Ferdinand and Isabella to postpone the Jewish expulsion from Spain for a few days so that it would fall on the ninth of the Jewish month of Ab and so correspond precisely with the anniversary of the destruction of the Jerusalem temple. It comes as no surprise that the apocalyptically minded Abrabanel was the author of tracts called *Fountains of Deliverance, Announcing Deliverance*, and, most provocatively, *The Deliverance of the Anointed One.* The "Anointed One" was of course the Messiah, by then a standard element in the great drama of the End Time. Abrabanel calculated that the messianic era would begin in 1503, when Israel would triumph and all Jews would live together in Eretz Israel under the Messiah.

It was not so, but in the manner of many disappointed messianic forecasts, the date was recalculated, this time by a Jerusalem Kabbalist who moved the "breaking in" of the new era to 1534 and the actual appearance of the Messiah to 1530. Provocateurs, agitators, and would-be messiahs rapidly appeared on the troubled landscape, which, as 1530 came and went, suddenly flattened back into the dolors of everyday life, though not quite to what it had been before. Messianism was by then deeply embedded in Jewish religious life and merely awaited another spark to fan the embers back into flame.

Sabbatai Zvi

The spark was this time supplied by Sabbatai Zvi (d. 1676), though in tinder prepared by the Kabbalists. He was born in Smyrna, studied Talmud and Kabbalah in Jerusalem, and then in 1665 in Gaza proclaimed himself the awaited Messiah. By all accounts he was an odd and erratic man and his pronouncement was met with little but disdain. That suddenly changed when a certain Nathan, a gifted theologian and mystic who did have a local reputation in Gaza as a prophet, claimed to have had a vision of Sabbatai as the Messiah. The Messiah had found his Paul and Sabbatai's claims spread with astonishing speed across the Jewish Diaspora (see I/7). Within a year there were believers as far afield among the Sephardim as Persia and the Yemen and in the Ashkenazi world from Russia and Poland, which had recently experienced a bloody pogrom-massacre of Jews, to as far away as England, and, more consequentially, to the ears of the Ottoman sultan. The sultan offered the Messiah the usual blasphemer's courtesy of death or conversion. Sabbatai chose Islam, and far from sounding the death-knell of the movement, Sabbatai's conversion seemed to strengthen some of his followers, who in any event managed to integrate it into their new faith. As one of them wrote, "The Torah as it is now observed will not exist in the Messianic Age." It was more than a slogan. For some of the Sabbatians, the Torah's most serious prohibitions, those against incest, for example, became the legal cornerstones of the new messianic fellowship.

Many of Sabbatai's followers eventually fell away, but those who did not survived in the West by going underground, by becoming "a Church within a Church." In the Muslim world, in contrast, the opportunity of following the Messiah's example and becoming Muslims was an attractive possibility. Those who did became known in the Ottoman Empire as the Dönmeh, nominal Muslims who continued to observe at least some Jewish practices. Thus there came into existence in the Ottoman lands a Jewish community parallel to the earlier *conversos* of Spain (see I/5), families that had converted under duress to another faith and whose sincerity continued to be doubted by their new core-ligionists. Indeed, Abraham Miguel Cardoza (d. 1706), born of a converso family in Spain, was drawn into the ranks of the earliest Sabbatians after he formally returned to Judaism in Venice in 1648, and used the Messiah's example to justify the conversion of Spanish Jews to Christianity during the century before 1492.

3

Muhammad the Prophet of God

FROM THE CHRISTIAN PERSPECTIVE, Jesus is God's revelation, and the meaning of that revelation unfolds in the events of his life as described in the Gospels. His followers accept only the Gospels that the Church as a whole had received as authentic and believed were inspired: the four canonical Gospels are consequently regarded as veridical accounts of the great work of redemption. That work unfolded in early first-century Palestine, in temple Judaism, and under Roman sovereignty. The Christian, then, is committed to history, in particular to the historicity of the life of Jesus of Nazareth and the authenticity, both historical and spiritual, of the Gospel accounts of it. "I believe in Jesus Christ," the earliest Christian creeds solemnly intone, "born of the Virgin Mary, suffered under Pontius Pilate, crucified, died and was buried. And on the third day he rose again . . ."

Muhammad's life bears no such theological weight for Muslims. The Quran is the revelation, not Muhammad, who was merely its messenger, the mortal who delivered God's warnings and promises to audiences in western Arabia early in the seventh century C.E. Events reflect the difference in the Muslim and Christian perspectives: it was the Quran that was collected and preserved from the outset (see II/1), not the life of the man who delivered it. People recalled Muhammad, of course, but no one thought to compose those recollections into a formal *Life* until well after his death, and once done, no one version ever gained canonical standing or even remotely approached the status of revelation.

> **Note:** It is customary among Muslims that whenever the name of Muhammad is mentioned in speech or writing, it is immediately followed by a "blessing" (*tasliyya*): *salla Allahu alayhi wa sallam* (May God bless him and give him peace). In writing the formula is often abbreviated. The custom will not be followed here.

The Muhammad of History

A *Life of the Prophet* was eventually composed by his followers. Not only do we possess various biographies of Muhammad that purport to go back to the recollection of his contemporaries; we also have an enormous mass of free-floating, discrete reports thought to contain his sayings on assorted topics from prayer to table etiquette. The reasons for this proliferation of information are not surprising. Throughout the Quran Muhammad is made to insist that he is merely a man (18:10)—his critics expected something more considerable of a divine messenger (6:37) and were understandably surprised when he turned out to be someone they knew from the market—but for his followers he was indeed the best of men since he had been chosen to deliver God's message of salvation. But more importantly, Muhammad was in his own person the most perfect embodiment of that message: he was the Muslim paradigm, as the Quran itself announces (33:21). That fact alone would explain the growing Muslim interest in the Prophet's life, but there is more. People remembered, of course, some of the things this remarkable man had said and done during his lifetime, and those recollections were handed down from one generation to the next. Eventually the reports of these recollections became a determining precedent in Islamic law (see II/3), and so it became important to verify the many statements in circulation that purported to describe what soon was called generally "the customary behavior (*sunna*) of the Prophet." An important branch of Islamic historiography was born.

When God Speaks

Other motives urged the Muslim to become a historian in the matter of Muhammad. The Quran is, in many instances, an opaque document. It has almost nothing direct to say of either Muhammad or Mecca, for example, or indeed of contemporary events generally, and its teachings are most often delivered without discernible context. Only very rarely are we told what particular circumstances provoked or the reason behind this or that prescription or prohibition, and so the believer is often hard-pressed to understand the practical application of that same divine command. Context is immeasurably important in moral matters, and the Quran provides little or none. Muslims turned for that context to the life of Muhammad, for there, if anywhere, were the settings for the revelations that issued from his mouth over twenty-two years and that are preserved in the Quran. These circumstances came to be called by Muslim exegetes and lawyers the "occasions of revelation," and they were another powerful incentive for assembling the known facts of Muhammad's life in the form of a biography. Not unexpectedly, then, the preserved biographies of the Prophet do note the historic occasion when this or that revelation was "sent down."

Hagiography and History

We have before us, then, a life, or rather a number of relatively early lives of Muhammad. As time passed those lives not only multiplied but, as happened with the lives of Jesus, they also expanded to include more and more material as both piety and theology added their own glosses to what had once been substantially recollection. It is easy enough for the historian to dismiss these later, overblown treatments of the life of the Prophet as hagiography of the type that surrounds many Christian saints. More pertinent is to ask how much of the traditional and standard *Life*—as it will often be referred to here—the one composed by Ibn Ishaq (d. 768) and known to us chiefly in the edition of Ibn Hisham (d. 833)—is made of the same stuff of piety and legend. Muslims in any event accept it is history, just as they accept the larger, more generously enhanced stories and tales of the Prophet that followed as a proper matter for contemplation and imitation.

Mecca and Its Gods

When the later Muslim sources speak of Mecca, they conjure up a vision of that seventh-century settlement as a thriving mercantile center that controlled a lucrative international trade in luxury goods flowing from east Asia to Roman consumers around the Mediterranean. There is not much evidence that this was the case, or even that such trade existed in that era, much less that the mud-brick-housed traders in Mecca either controlled or even profited from it. The nearer reality is that the Meccans used the annual truce-protected pilgrimage to do some trading with the Bedouin and even to enlist the latter to supply transport and protection for a modest trade network that the Quraysh, the paramount tribe of Mecca, were building in the Hejaz, the northwestern two-thirds of the Arabian hinterland facing onto the Red Sea.

The Quran gives an impressionistic overview of how the gods of pagan Mecca were worshiped in the days before Islam. The chief liturgy was doubtless sacrifice, of both animals and cereals, and the rites—a common one was divination—were performed at the Kaaba and several other places in the vicinity, notably at the ancient spring called Zamzam. Pilgrimage to Mecca by the surrounding tribes was a popular—and seasonal—practice, and included ritual processions or circumambulation (*tawaf*) around the Kaaba and a similar rite between the two hills of Safa and Marwa next to the Kaaba sanctuary.

There was prayer in the pagan era, but it is characterized in the Quran as "whistling and clapping of hands" (8:35). One form of prayer has been preserved. When Muslim pilgrims approached the sanctuary on pilgrimage, they cried out again and again a formulaic salutation beginning "We are here, O Allah, we are here." This is the so-called *talbiya*, which, like most else connected with the pilgrimage, antedated Islam and survived into it.

Allah was worshiped at Mecca before Islam, as the Quran, which calls him "the Lord of this house" (i.e., the Kaaba), makes clear (106:3). So too was a male deity named Hubal, whose idol in human form—Allah had no idol— seems to have been placed inside the Kaaba. The Quran makes no mention of Hubal but it does speak of three other deities of the many worshiped at Mecca in pre-Islamic days: Manat, al-Uzza, and al-Lat, collectively called the "daughters of Allah" by the Quraysh. We do not know their stories since one of the characteristics of Arab paganism as it has come down to us is the absence of a mythology, narratives that might serve to explain the origin or history of the gods. These Meccan deities were manifestly cult objects and we have only the cult descriptions, and an occasional appellative, to instruct us about them. Thus we have no idea why the Quraysh should have assigned them their filial roles, save perhaps simply to introduce some order into the large and somewhat chaotic Meccan pantheon. Nothing we know suggests that Allah was otherwise thought to have had daughters, or that the three goddesses possessed any family relationship. They often swapped characteristics and shared shrines, but Manat, al-Uzza, and al-Lat were quite discrete divinities, and the best examples, by all accounts, of the personified worship of heavenly bodies.

The Meccan Haram

Islam's premier sanctuary, the cubical Kaaba and its surrounding *temenos*, or sacred enclosure, set in the midst of Mecca, long antedated Muhammad's seventh-century promulgation of the Quran. Its origins are lost to us—the presence of a sacred spring, the Zamzam, located nearby perhaps explains it— and gone too are whatever myths the local Arabs recounted to explain its presence in their midst. There are reports of animal sacrifice outside ancient Mecca's only stone construction, but most traces of the Meccan cult were swept away by Islam or integrated into a new founding myth that traced the Kaaba and its surviving rituals back to Abraham and his son Ishmael's residence in Mecca (Quran 2:125–127). The Meccan Kaaba was not Mecca's only pre-Islamic sacred place; there were additional shrine sites within the town's temenos and others scattered in the environs. We know of them chiefly because Muhammad sanctioned their continued (though somewhat modified) use for Muslims in the complex of site- and time-tied ritual practices known as "the pilgrimage" (*hajj*) par excellence (Quran 2:196 ff.) that climaxed not at the Kaaba in Mecca but in the "standing" on the hill known as Arafat eleven miles outside Mecca.

We cannot speak uniquely of the Kaaba, however. There are three religiously defined and connected areas in Mecca and its environs. First is the just noted Bayt Allah, the *templum* that still stands at the center of the modern city: cubical in shape, windowless, with access through a door that in historical times was, and remains, some six feet or so above ground and could be approached only by means of a mobile stairway rolled up to it for that purpose. Second is the area immediately surrounding the Kaaba. This was not properly a temenos in that originally it was not defined in any sense other than as an open space: the walls of the surrounding dwellings provided its only definition. Under Islamic auspices the area was enlarged and later enclosed by a columned and gated arcade, which effectively converted it from an open into a constructed space. Finally, there is the larger district of Mecca. In this instance there were markers, sacred stones that, like the Greek *hermes*, were both boundary signs and objects of veneration; from very early times they defined the sacred territory of Mecca.

As for the matter of access, it is perhaps more illuminating to proceed in the opposite direction, from the periphery to the center. The city-territory of Mecca, today marked by large signs in Arabic and English on the Saudi thruways banned to all non-Muslims, shows no evidence of having been so restricted in late paganism or early Islam. But there are other indications that the entire territory of Mecca did in fact constitute a haram, the "secure sanctuary" of the Quran (28:57). The sacred stones at its limits have already been remarked; and within it no trees or shrubs were to be cut down, no wild animals hunted, no blood spilled in violence. Indeed, no profane soil should be mixed with that of the haram.

> **Note:** Efforts were made as early as the second caliph, Umar (r. 634–644), to extend the haram to all of Arabia. In the nineteenth century the principle yielded to commercial concerns—Jidda had become an important international port—and in the early twentieth to military ones. Today entry to the kingdom of Saudi Arabia is strictly controlled but it is by no means prohibited to non-Muslims, save, of course, the two *haramayn* of Mecca and Medina.

The narrow Meccan temenos—there is a more extended zone of taboo surrounding the town—is known as "the taboo shrine" (*al-masjid al-haram*) or simply as the Haram. It had all the familiar characteristics of a holy place, offering the privilege of immune sanctuary and banning the ritually impure. The actual Kaaba, in contrast, despite its resemblance in shape and function to the Jerusalem Holy of Holies—even before Islam it was regarded as the

Bayt Allah, the House of God (Quran 106:3)—was not governed by the same severe access taboos as the Jerusalem "house" of Yahweh, where only the high priest was permitted entry and that but once a year.

The Kaaba

Not much history can be concluded from the present Kaaba in Mecca, which substantially dates from a ground-up rebuilding in 1629. From the many literary descriptions we possess, the seventeenth-century reconstruction seems to have differed little from the building that stood there all through the medieval era and back to the late seventh century. In 683, however, the Kaaba had been rebuilt on ideological grounds. The rebel Ibn al-Zubayr (d. 692), who then held Mecca against the Umayyad caliphal government, reconstructed it, we are informed, as it was in Abraham's day. The original building was joined to the shoulder-high semicircular wall, the *hijr*, at the northwest face—how or to what purpose we are not told—and had two ground-level doors, "one toward the east for people to enter and one toward the west for people to exit." This tradition goes back to Muhammad, on the authority of his wife Aisha. The Prophet was recalling the rebuilding of the Kaaba in his own day, sometime about 605, a project in which he cooperated but did not approve, since it distorted Abraham's original building. The reason the Quraysh closed one door and lifted the other well above ground level was, according to the same tradition from Muhammad, "to make sure that no one but whom they [that is, the Quraysh] wished would enter it." The clear implication was that the Kaaba was intended to be open to all but that access was, in Muhammad's time, controlled, not by any notions of purity or holiness, but by the will of the Quraysh, who had "guardianship" of the building.

There was, and is, no prohibition against entering the Kaaba, and no particular merit—or danger—in praying within it. Quite to the contrary, the most primitive cult traditions associated with the building have the Meccans and their pilgrim guests behaving much like the perfidious Ephraimites who "mumbled their prayers" and kissed their calf-idols, as other idolaters kissed the image of Baal (Hos. 13:2; 1 Kings 19:18). Before Islam, and even after, the devotees at Mecca were not kept away from the Kaaba, as the Israelites were from Sinai or the inner temple precincts: rather they attempted to establish as close contact as possible. They clung to the building's drapes, pressed themselves against its walls, and touched and kissed the Black Stone embedded in one of its corners. The Israelites feared impurity by contagion; the pre-Islamic Arabs of Mecca, like many others early and late, were more interested in the contagion of holiness.

There was, then, nothing *haram* about "Allah's House" in Mecca (see I/1). Even after Muhammad had effected his "high god" revolution there, and created an analogy whereby the Kaaba should have exactly corresponded to the Holy of Holies in temple Jerusalem—an analogy strongly urged by Muhammad's changing his prayer direction from Jerusalem to the Meccan Kaaba during his early days at Medina—the old rituals continued to be followed. Muhammad's close associate, and the second caliph of Islam, Umar ibn al-Khattab, apparently had a more perfectly formed Muslim conscience than Muhammad himself when he remarked, "If I had not seen the Prophet kissing it [that is, the Black Stone], I would never have kissed it again." The Islamic revolution was one of concept, not of cult.

Muhammad: A Life

The traditional accounts date Muhammad's birth in Mecca to 570, which seems somewhat too early, but, as in the case of Jesus, the exact year is of no great consequence. Of greater importance was that Muhammad was orphaned at a young age, to which the Quran itself seems to allude in one of its rare personal asides (93:6), and the Book more than once urges a merciful justice toward such bereaved children. Otherwise Muhammad seems to have had an unremarkable youth, this young man of the Banu Hashim, a not particularly notable clan of the paramount Meccan tribe of Quraysh. Mecca was a mercantile town as much as it was a shrine settlement, and although the Islamic tradition has kept Muhammad at a very safe distance from Mecca's polytheism even before his prophetic call, he was involved on what seems a minor scale in Mecca's commerce. This occurred through his marriage to Khadija, a previously wed woman of some means with a stake in Meccan trade. They had several children together—only the daughters survived into adulthood—and she was his only wife until her death in 619.

Sometime in his adulthood—the traditional date is 610—Muhammad received his first revelation. This might be the two visions described somewhat obliquely in Quran 53:1–18 (see II/9), but the biographical tradition thought otherwise. It describes a far more graphic scene in a cave near Mecca, a struggle with the angel Gabriel, and finally the revelation of Quran 96:1–5 or, according to others, the opening verses of sura 74. We really cannot say what happened; all we are sure of is that no verses in the Quran explain to the Meccans that they were about to hear the newly revealed words of God. Whatever that earliest revelation, Muhammad was apparently uncertain of the source of this voice in his head, or perhaps of what he was expected to do in consequence. Only after psychological support from Khadija and help from one of her relatives who knew something about Judaism and Christianity did Muhammad

have the courage to venture into the public places of Mecca and announce this
message whose name was Islam.

The Message of Islam

We have some idea, as we shall see, which are the earliest suras or chapters in
the Quran, and from them we can form a substantial notion of what that original message was. Originally, it must be recalled, Muhammad's mission was to
turn the Meccans from their cultic polytheism to the worship of the One God
and to reform their corrupt morality. Later in the Quran, after he was the
head of a growing Muslim community in Medina, the point of the message is
somewhat different: it is directed to believers, no longer to pagans, and its objective is to reinforce and instruct them in their faith.

What God required of the Meccans, the Quran instructed, was "submission" (Ar. *islam*; one who has so submitted is a *muslim*) to God, *the* God, who
is none other than the High God Allah worshiped at Mecca; the "Lord of this
house," the Quran calls him, referring to the Kaaba or central shrine of
Mecca. Muhammad had no need to introduce the Meccans to Allah: they already worshiped him, and in moments of crisis, they even conceded that he
was in fact *the* God. The trouble was, they worshiped other gods as well, and
that is one of the central aims of the Meccan preaching: to make the Quraysh
and the other Meccans surrender their attachment to other deities, the idols
and empty names they associated with the One True God.

This was the theological or cultic point of the early preaching, but Islam
was far more than an acceptance of monotheism. The Quran called on the
Meccans to change their moral ways. A look at the very earliest suras shows
that the reformation was overwhelmingly social in its emphases. The Quran
would eventually go on to speak of many things, but the original message was
narrowly targeted: it is good to feed the poor and take care of the needy; it is
evil to accumulate wealth for one's own behalf.

> As for the orphan, be not overbearing; and as for the beggar, scold not;
> and as for the goodness of your Lord, speak of it. (93:9–11)

> Woe to every maligner and scoffer; whoever gathers wealth and counts
> it over, thinking that his wealth will perpetuate him! (104:1–3)

> So as for him who gives and shows piety, and counts true the best re-
> ward, We shall assist him to ease. But as for him who is niggardly, and
> prides himself in wealth, and counts false the best reward, We shall as-
> sist him to difficulty, nor will his wealth profit him when he perishes.
> (92:5–11)

He used not to believe the Almighty, nor did he urge the feeding of the poor; so on this day [the Day of Judgment] he has not here a friend. (69:33–35)

Little of the night did they usually slumber, and in the mornings they asked forgiveness, and from their wealth was a share assigned to the beggar and the outcast. (5:17–19)

The message got scant hearing from the Quraysh, whether they thought monotheism would lessen Mecca's appeal as a pilgrimage center (surely one of the gravest miscalculations in the history of commerce) or because they did not relish Muhammad's brand of social and economic reform. The early suras reflect the criticism directed back at the messenger. The heat of the quranic preaching begins to rise in reaction. There are fierce denunciations of the scoffers and unbelievers: for them is reserved a fiery hell, just as the believers would have reserved for them a true paradise of peace and pleasurable repose. At this point both the language and the imagery suddenly become familiar to the Jewish or the Christian reader. The promised paradise is called the "Garden of Eden" (Jannat Adan) and the threatened hell, "Gehenna" (Jahannam). The Quran early on unveils, in bits and pieces, its eschatological vision (see II/10), not to stress its absolute imminence, as in the New Testament, but to warn the unbeliever that the price of doubt is high and the rewards of submission great. Though it has its own particular details, the Quran's version of the End is obviously different from anything we encounter among the pre-Islamic Arabs and noticeably similar to that current among the Jews and Christians. Moreover, in the face of that same opposition, the Quran begins to unfold its own elaborate history of prophecy. Muhammad, the Meccans were told, was not the first prophet sent to humankind, though assuredly he was the last.

Sacred History

The Quran is profoundly interested in history, not the history of Mecca, to be sure, or even of Arabia; not in politics or the tribal skirmishes, the "days of the Arabs" so celebrated by Muhammad's contemporaries. The Quran's view of the past is a version of sacred history, how the divine dispensation, which began at Creation, has unfolded from Adam down to the present. The story of the prophets is rehearsed at length in the Quran, never quite consecutively in the manner of a history, but rather to make a moral point, to wit, when humankind has refused to heed the bearers of God's message, the consequences have been terrible. The lesson is clear: those who reject Muhammad will pay a fearsome price at God's hands.

Most of this sacred history is, like the Quran's eschatology, fundamentally biblical. There are some examples of Arab prophets unknown to the Bible, but most of the prophets and their stories have their biblical counterparts: Adam, Enoch, Noah, Abraham, Moses, Aaron, David, Solomon, Jonah, and others all appear there—though none of Bible's major prophets like Jeremiah, Isaiah, or Ezekiel. The familiar names all proceed easily from Muhammad's mouth and, we must assume, since there are no explanations offered as to who "Musa," "Dawud," and "Sulayman" are or where they came from, they passed just as easily into the understanding of the seventh-century Meccans who were the Quran's first audience.

The Bible and the Quran

As already noted, the presence of so much biblical matter in the Quran has prompted suspicion among non-Muslims that from the outset Muhammad was in contact with Jews who served, wittingly or unwittingly, as his inform-ants. We have no evidence that there was a permanent Jewish colony at Mecca, as there certainly was at Medina. Given the considerable presence of Jews in the Yemen to the south and in the oases to the north of Mecca, Jews likely passed through the town and their beliefs and practices were probably familiar, to some degree, to Muhammad and his contemporaries—more fa-miliar indeed than they are to us since we have little idea of the shape and heft of seventh-century Arabian Judaism. The issue of whether Muhammad "bor-rowed" anything from that quarter for his own message may come down to the degree of originality one is willing to grant prophets, or, more pertinently, other people's prophets. Islam was, and is, not simply a warmed-over version of Judaism, or of Christianity, for that matter, although some earlier Chris-tians thought so. It was a unique vision—whether from God or Muhammad's own head is precisely what separates the Muslim from the non-Muslim—preached with great conviction, and in the end with great success, over the course of twenty-two years.

Christianity confidently announced that it was the successor to Judaism: and the Quran, far from concealing its connection to the other, earlier forms of monotheism, proudly proclaims that it is a successor to both. More than once it counsels doubters to go ask the Jews and Christians whether Muhammad is speaking the truth. But the claim is, like Christianity's, supersessionist. Islam has come to replace the other two, though not, as we shall see, to abolish them.

The Quran's view of sacred history is intricately interesting, though not nearly as intricate as that of the later Muslim tradition, which supplied enormous detail, provided doubtless by its growing number of Jewish and Christian converts to Islam. According to the Quran, God is, as attested by all his visi-ble signs (*ayat*), the creator and the providential sustainer of the world—this is one of the Book's most insistent themes. God has intervened in history through his prophets, a line of spiritually gifted individuals stretching from Adam to Jesus—where the Arabian prophets fit into the chronology is unclear—who have carried God's message to his creation. In some instances this intervention was more formal in that the messenger received a sacred book—Abraham, for example, and David—but for two others there was both a Book and a mandate to establish a community (*umma*). Moses (Musa) received the Torah (Tawrat) and established the faith-community of the Israelites or Jews. Jesus (Isa ibn Miryam) received the Gospel (Injil) and established the people called Christians (Nasara).

Note: Just as the Christians used "Israelites" and "Hebrews" to denominate the Chosen People of the Bible and "Jews" (see I/1) when speaking of Jesus' contemporaries and their descendants, so the Quran prefers Banu Israil, "Israelites," for the biblical folk and Yahud, "Jews," for Muhammad's own, far less acceptable contemporaries.

The Opposition

Thus Muhammad established his own pedigree in the essentially biblical line of the prophets (as a successor in particular of Moses and Jesus), and his Book, this "convincing Arabic Quran" as it calls itself (36:69), took its place as an equal beside the sacred books of the Jews and Christians. Later, when Islam exploded into the populous habitats of those other communities, that claim to parity would take on meaning, but for Muhammad's original audience in Mecca, the references to other prophets were chiefly intended as a warning to reform, not as a prediction that a third great branch of monotheism had arisen out of the other two.

The Quraysh were not moved by either the man or his message. They accused Muhammad of being jinn-possessed, a charge usually leveled at poets (52:29–31; 69:38–43). The tone if not the content of Muhammad's "recitations" reminded his audience of the local poets and seers, though no pre-Islamic poet we know of concerned himself with preaching monotheism, much less social reform. As for the message itself—and here the reference seems to be to the Quran's biblical-type stories—some thought Muhammad had simply lifted it from the "tales of yore" that someone had perhaps told him in private and he repeated in public (16:103; 83:13). Muhammad was fierce in his denial, as steadfast as he was in his refusal to validate his message, as the very prophets he cited had, by producing a miracle. Did they doubt the divine origin of his revelations? Let them produce even a single similar piece. The Quran was its own miracle.

The accusation of Muhammad's having lifted his teachings from other sources, notably the Bible, did not end with the success of Islam, and the Muslim commentators constructed their own line of defense by parsing the Arabic adjective *ummi*, which is applied to Muhammad in Quran 7:157, 158, to mean "illiterate." If he were illiterate, the thinking went, he could hardly have stolen the material from those other Books. The point is specious, of course. It is not entirely clear what *ummi* meant. "Gentile" or "pagan" seems probable, that is, someone who was neither a Jew nor a Christian. The word apart, it is highly improbable that someone engaged in trade would be entirely illiterate, and it is even more improbable that anyone at Mecca was reading either the Bible or the Gospels in Muhammad's lifetime since neither was translated into Arabic until two centuries later. Yet in that oral culture it was hardly necessary to be able to read to know what was in those other Books.

We know more about the Quraysh's reaction to Muhammad than we do about their reaction to Islam. The only clue we are given to the latter is that they found ludicrous the doctrine of the bodily resurrection of the dead (Quran 13:5; 19:66; 27:67; 32:10–11). That teaching might indeed have seemed bizarre to the hard-headed Meccans, but it does not itself explain the fierceness of their eventual response. More likely they feared for their polytheism, or perhaps the business of polytheism to which they were attached. Muhammad's message certainly threatened Mecca's eclectic shrines and the commerce that the annual pilgrimages generated. But it is too simple to dismiss the degree of personal devotion to the deities of polytheism, whose practices seem altogether too magical and mechanical to those reared in a monotheistic and highly spiritualized tradition. But we do possess one elusive clue—albeit a highly suggestive one—that it was the loss of their gods that disturbed the Quraysh.

The "Satanic Verses"

The account that follows is absent from the Quran as we now possess it; the story comes rather from quranic commentary, notably that of the authoritative al-Tabari (d. 923). It is so unlikely to have been invented by Muslim piety, however, that Muslims and non-Muslims alike have been strongly inclined to accept at face value the tale of the so-called satanic verses.

It begins with something that *is* in the Quran, the quite explicit statement in Sura 22:52–53 that God has on occasion, with all the prophets and not merely Muhammad, allowed Satan to cast verses into the Revelation in order to test the believers, although God subsequently removed them, to be sure. There follow the commentators' attempts at sketching the particular occasion of revelation of those two quite extraordinary verses. Muhammad, the story went, was rapidly sliding into despair at the Quraysh's invincible resistance to his preaching; he was hoping, we are told, for a revelation that would somehow reconcile the Quraysh to Islam. And he apparently received it. Verses 19–20 of sura 53 were "sent down," as the process of revelation is usually described: "Have you considered al-Lat, al-Uzza, and Manat, the third, the other?" This was followed immediately by "They are the exalted cranes, and their intercession is to be hoped for." The cultic expression "exalted cranes" is difficult for us, but its main point was not lost on the Quraysh: if the divinity of the so-called daughters of Allah was not explicitly confirmed, they were certainly intermediaries, powerful intercessors with God. On hearing this revelation, the Quraysh straight away prostrated themselves and worshiped at Muhammad's side.

This happy solution disappeared as abruptly as it had surfaced. Muhammad, the story continues, immediately began to doubt the provenance of the apparent revelation, and God responded with a new and authentic one to replace the old. After "the third, the other," the Quran now says, "Do you have male (children) and He female? That indeed would be unfair. They [the goddesses in question] are but names that you have named, you and your fathers, for which God has revealed no warrant" (53:21–23). This was not the end of this curious business. The Quran felt some need to explain, hence Quran 22:52–53 about God's practice of permitting such a thing as a test of faith.

Muhammad's Night Journey and Ascension

If the "satanic verses," as that famous interpolation came to be called, have left no trace in the present Quran, the tantalizing obscurity of another verse has set in train an enormous body of tradition, some of it supposedly based on the recollection of contemporaries, but it is perhaps as much or even more the product of legendary imagination. This is the so-called night journey (*isra*) of Muhammad, to which was attached another, equally miraculous event, the "ascension" (*miraj*) of the Prophet.

On the Quran's own testimony, Muhammad stoutly refused to perform—or have God perform—miracles on his behalf, despite the fact that the Quraysh demanded such as verification of the truth of his message. At one point Muhammad did relent, and in the face of charges of being misguided or misled, he did refer, very obliquely and enigmatically, to supernatural visions he had experienced (53:1–18). There is another verse, however—Quran 17:1—that suggested to later Muslims that some other, more circumstantial supernatural experience had been given the Prophet. The verse had him carried "by night"—the Muslim biographical tradition specified he had been sleeping near the Kaaba—to "the distant shrine." The event was eventually identified as a reference to a miraculous journey from Mecca to the temple mount in Jerusalem. Later this same journey was connected with the belief that after his stay in Jerusalem, Muhammad had been briefly taken up into heaven—although this is explicitly denied in the Quran (17:95). According to the fully developed tradition, Muhammad was carried up, past his various prophetic predecessors, to the seventh heaven, which was guarded by no less than Abraham himself. Finally, he returned to Mecca that same evening. Muhammad's association with the city through the Night Journey explains in part the Muslim attachment to Jerusalem, whereas his Ascension may very well mark the occasion when the totality of the Quran's contents were revealed to Muhammad, though in "real time" they were sent down to him piecemeal and as the occasion dictated (25:32).

> **Note:** The Night Journey–Ascension complex had a long history among Muslims. It became a deeply imaginative theme for both writers and artists, and it provided in particular a canvas on which details of the Afterlife could be filled into the quranic accounts (see II/10).

Boycott

It is hard to imagine that the success of Muhammad's movement—if that is not too generous a term—troubled the Quraysh. The new prophet won a few followers, but they were younger men by and large—his cousin Ali was little more than a child at the time—and they were, neither wealthy nor powerful. Yet they were not so few as to be invisible, and everything we know about Mecca of that era speaks of shifting alliances constantly being made and re-made. In coalition politics a little counts for a lot, and so this new faction of "Muslims," whose allegiance was not tribal and whose self-interest could not be appealed to, may have counted for far more than its numbers suggest.

The rulers among the Quraysh were alarmed at any rate. Ill treatment of the Muslims yielded to more concerted and more serious action against the Prophet. No one had attacked Muhammad directly since he was under the protection of Abu Talib, the head of the Banu Hashim and the uncle who had raised him (and was also the father of the much younger Ali). Since Abu Talib would not withdraw his protection of his nephew, the two leading clans of the Quraysh, the Makhzum and the Abd Shams, declared a public boycott against their old commercial rivals of the Banu Hashim. Muhammad may have anticipated more serious troubles ahead. He arranged for some of his followers to migrate to the kingdom of Abyssinia across the Red Sea. The choice is interesting. Christian Abyssinia had long had commercial relations with Mecca, and Muhammad must surely have thought that his Muslims would receive a sympathetic hearing there, as apparently they did. Many stayed on in Africa but others rejoined Muhammad after he had resettled in Medina.

We cannot say how the boycott, which did not seem terribly effective, would have played out since events intervened, notably the death in 619 of Muhammad's wife Khadija, who was, by all accounts, one of his chief psychological supports. The same year also marked the death of Abu Talib, the uncle whose steadfast resolve in the face of the boycott was essential to his nephew's safety. The only one in fact to break ranks was another uncle, Abu Lahab, who received his recompense in sura 111 of the Quran: he and his wife shall burn in hell, the Quran assured the believers. Muhammad's days in Mecca were obviously numbered, as he himself recognized, since there was now little to restrain the Quraysh from violence. The Prophet began to search for another, safer venue for his preaching. The nearby town of Taif was one possibility, but the Quraysh were powerful there as well. He next turned to the Bedouin tribes who annually converged on Mecca and its environs. They came under the cover of a sacred truce to worship at the shrines and do the kind of business that their endless blood feuds made impossible at other times and in other places. They declined; the Bedouin had little interest in prophets.

The Hegira

Eventually Muhammad's call for help fell on responsive ears. Pilgrims from Yathrib, an oasis 275 miles to the north of Mecca, heard Muhammad preaching at one of the market fairs connected with the annual pilgrimages in and around Mecca. He interested them and they him, because, we are told, they were allied to the Jews at Yathrib. Whatever the reason for the interest, Muhammad explained submission to them and recited parts of the Quran; they were sufficiently impressed to return the following year and seek him out again. On this occasion twelve of the Yathribis concluded a kind of agreement in principle to cease their polytheism, not to steal or commit fornication, not to kill their (female?) offspring, not to plunder their neighbors, and, most important at this particular juncture, not to disobey Muhammad. There is no mention yet of formal prayer or almsgiving, probably because these had not yet been laid down as obligations in the hostile climate of Mecca where any public display of the new faith would likely have been dangerous.

The following year the Yathribis came back again, seventy-three this time—the numbers should not be taken too seriously in these accounts, particularly when they approach the numbers of Jesus' Apostles (twelve) and disciples (seventy two)—though not all were believers. They offered Muhammad a safe-conduct in Yathrib—getting there was his responsibility—but what they required in return, indeed, their motive in inviting him in the first place becomes clear only in the sequel. Muhammad began to send his followers quietly and secretly in small groups to Yathrib. He himself followed in September 622. This "migration," or *hijra*, as it was called in Arabic—Anglicized, from the Latin, as "hegira"—though unmentioned in the Quran, was regarded by Muslims as a turning point in the fortunes of the Prophet and his movement.

> **Note:** According to report, it was the caliph Umar (r. 634–644) who chose the year 622 to mark the formal beginning of the Muslim era, and documents began to be dated from it, counting, of course, by lunar years of 354 days. The first year of the Muslim era—often denoted in English as A.H. (*anno Hegirae*) on the analogy with A.D., *anno Domini*—was moreover dated back from 24 September, when Muhammad actually migrated, to the first day of that lunar year, 16 July 622.

Medina

Mecca was a parched and shadowless settlement collected around a single well—the Zamzam of Muslim lore—and a shrine. Yathrib, or, as the Muslims soon started calling it, Madinat al-Nabi, the "City of the Prophet," and now in English simply Medina, was a quite different place. It was an oasis whose underground water supply supported plantations of date palms and a comfortable population of agriculturalists. Those agriculturalists were, for a couple of generations before Muhammad's arrival, Arabs, chiefly the tribe called Khazraj, who had first approached Muhammad at Mecca, and another, the Aws. But there were other people in Medina as well, various tribes of Jews who had once controlled the oasis and were in 622 in a dependent alliance with either the Aws or the Khazraj. We do not know when or how the Jews arrived in that remote outpost of the Diaspora, but a Jewish presence is attested in many of the oases that stretched northward from Medina toward what is now the Jordanian frontier, and there was a large and powerful Jewish population in the southwestern tip of Arabia, in the Yemen. Yet we do not know in what precisely the religious beliefs and practices of those Medina Jews consisted.

Life was easier in Medina than in Mecca, or it should have been, given its natural advantages. But while the Quraysh held their fragile settlement in a shifting but nonetheless tight political grip, the Arabs of Medina had fallen to contesting ownership of the limited plantation land, and by the second decade of the seventh century social strife was beginning to pit the Aws and their Jewish clients against the Khazraj and theirs. The clans lived locked within their fortified farmsteads and awaited the inevitable showdown. These were the circumstances that brought Muhammad to the place that would one day bear his name. His audience at Mecca had said that he sounded like a possessed poet or, alternatively, a "seer" (*kahin*), both of which identifications he vehemently denied, but it was surely as some kind of *vates* or holy man that he was brought to Medina. Where today parties in conflict might bring in an impartial arbitrator with stipulated binding powers, the Medinese imported a charismatic holy man whose wisdom was not stipulated but God-given.

The Medina Accords

Several important events took place at Medina between Muhammad's arrival in September 622 and the defining military action at Badr Wells in 624. One of the first, begun while he was still at Mecca, was Muhammad's arrangement of fictive "brotherhoods" whereby his fellow "Migrants" (*muhajirun*)—whose name was a badge of honor and who soon became a somewhat privileged class—were attached, family by family, to counterparts in the still small group of Medina Muslims called "Helpers" (*ansar*) to ensure some degree of economic and social support for the penniless and resourceless Meccan Muslims. Muhammad himself lodged with Medinese supporters until a house was built for him. Its courtyard soon became the first Muslim prayer-house or mosque (see II/6).

The biographical sources on the Prophet have preserved what may be the agreement drawn up between Muhammad and the folk of Medina. The so-called Medina Accords constitute a complex document with numerous later additions, but at its heart we can discern that the Medinese agreed to accept Muhammad as their leader in the sense that they would refer all disputes to him and accept his judgment. Though he is called the "Prophet of God" in the document as it is preserved, the terms themselves demonstrate that the Medinese by no means pledged to all become Muslims. Migrants, Helpers, Medina polytheists, and Jews formed the original, strictly political umma, while the first two simultaneously began to coalesce into a religious community. There is no indication that Muhammad was intended to "run" the oasis in any sense. The arrangement simply made him the sole and final arbitrator in all disputes, and it seems likely that the settlement operated much as it had before, through a series of agreements among the various tribes and clans. What Muhammad's authority did was suspend sine die—it is difficult to believe that anyone there actually forgot or forgave—the annually compounded costs of blood feuds within the tight confines of an oasis settlement.

There is one revealing clue as to the basis of Muhammad's authority and how he chose to wield it. One clause of the Medina Accords declared that "Yathrib shall be a haram for the people of the document." Medina, in short, was going to possess the same sanctuary status as Mecca. Mecca had a physically delimited sacred space at its center and the Kaaba stood in the midst of it. But its larger territory, marked as well, as it continued to be in Islamic times, was also a taboo zone, which is the meaning of *haram*. Mecca's taboo quality was likely the result of the presence of a holy place within it, but Medina's was

humanmade, or better, human-and-God-made. The settled presence of holy
men generated such taboo zones in Arabia both before and after Islam, and
that seems to have been what was occurring in this case, save that Muhammad
insisted on rendering it explicit.

Note: The chronology of Muhammad's life at Medina is far firmer than
for the events at Mecca. Here we can trace the sequence of events and
we have some indication of the time that elapsed between them, so it
may be useful to set down a tentative chronology as a guide to the rapidly sketched events that follow.

Emigration to Medina	*September 622*
Change of qibla	December 623
Battle of Badr Wells	February 624
Expulsion of Jewish Qaynuqa	March 624
Meccan raid on Medina	April 624
Battle of Uhud	March 625
Expulsion of Jewish Nadir	September 625
Battle of the Ditch and Slaughter of Jewish Qurayza	March 627
Expedition against Mustaliq and Aisha's "slander"	December 627
Armistice of Hudaybiyya	April 628
Expedition against Khaibar	May 628
Attempt at Umra at Mecca	April 629
Expedition to Muta (Jordan)	September 629
Conquest of Mecca	January 630
Battle of Hunayn	January 630
Celebration of umra at Mecca	March 630
Expedition to Tabuk	October 630
The Great Proclamation at the hajj	February 631
Muhammad's Farewell Pilgrimage	March 632
Muhammad's death at Medina	June 632

Muhammad and the Jews

Before his arrival at Medina Muhammad had often spoken of the Banu Israil,
as the Quran names the biblical Jews. He had used, as we have seen, the
eschatological images and language current in the Jewish tradition in his
attempt to convince the Quraysh of the seriousness of their predicament and

had invoked the example of the biblical prophets both to explain his own mission and to illustrate what happened to those who resisted God's commands. The Bible was a religious terrain Muhammad shared with the Jews and the Christians. He had sent his followers to Christian Abyssinia—in belief and practice the most "Jewish" of the area's Christian cultures—with some expectation that they would be favorably received, as they apparently were. Newly arrived in Medina, he may have anticipated that his own prophetic claims would be acknowledged by the Banu Israil whose God he too worshiped.

If this is what Muhammad in fact expected, he was sorely disappointed. The parts of the Quran revealed at Medina show a notable hardening of attitudes toward contemporary Jews, now referred to as Yahud. We know too that certain religious practices Muhammad had once observed—rituals that apparently derived from Jewish ones—were altered soon after his arrival in Medina. He no longer prayed facing Jerusalem, as the Jews did and as he had previously done; his *qibla*, or prayer direction, was now the Meccan Kaaba, the old Quraysh cult center in Mecca. Nor did he any longer fast the Ashura, the tenth day of the Jews' month of Tishri or Yom Kippur. It was the day, Muhammad discovered, on which the Torah had been sent down to Moses. We cannot be certain of the chronology, but at some point after this he no longer required his followers to fast on Yom Kippur but decreed instead the fast of Ramadan, the month during which the Quran, which Muhammad explicitly compared to the Torah (Quran 11:7, etc.), was sent down to the new Moses (2:185; 97:1–5).

On the evidence we can only conclude that something went wrong between Muhammad and the Jews of Medina. It seems fairly certain that they rejected his claims to prophethood—which many Jews in Arabia and elsewhere later accepted—but there may have been a great deal more. There is no indication that the Jews there had anything to do with the civil strife that brought Muhammad to Medina in 622, but we may at least suspect that their fall from proprietors of the oasis to clients within it left some scars on the local politics, and the political overtones of Muhammad's subsequent treatment of them suggest the same. The biographical tradition is more explicit: the "Jewish rabbis"—whatever that might mean in that time and place—"showed hostility to the Messenger in envy, hatred, and malice because God had chosen the Messenger from among the Arabs." Some version of that judgment we may well have surmised on our own, but the Jews of Medina were also allegedly joining forces with Aws and Khazraj who had obstinately clung to their heathen practices and beliefs. The Jews, then, according to this and similar accounts, took religious exception to Muhammad—how loudly or publicly we cannot tell—and then made a political alliance with those Medina Arabs who, for whatever reason, were beginning to oppose the new ruler from Mecca.

The Religion of Abraham

For the moment there was no political response from Muhammad; it is unlikely that he, newly arrived in Medina and on uncertain terrain, had the
means or inclination to provide one. But he did begin to fashion a religious
retort, one that grew sharper, firmer, and more confident in its details over
Muhammad's ten years in Medina. Muhammad was the successor of the other
prophets, to be sure, and notably of Moses and Jesus. But he was not simply
adding to Judaism or Christianity—why didn't he just become a Christian or
a Jew, some were asking; rather he was chosen for something far more radical.
Islam was a renewal of the pristine—and pre-Jewish—religion of Abraham
(Quran 2:135). Abraham, the Quran pronounced triumphantly, came before
both the Torah and the Gospel (3:55–58). Abraham was, in fact, the first
muslim, the first submitter to God in absolute monotheism (2:127–134).

According to the standard *Life*, the first hundred verses of the second chapter of the Quran were sent down on the occasion of Muhammad's break with
the Jews during his first years in Medina. We cannot say if that was really the
case, but that sura is the Quran's most extended meditation on the Jewish past
and the newly revealed Muslim present in God's plan of salvation—the Muslim scriptural parallel, though with very different rhetorical techniques, to
Paul's Letter to the Romans. Among its more startling declarations is that
Abraham and Ishmael built the Kaaba (2:125–127; 22:26) and instituted the
rituals of the hajj in Mecca and its environs (Quran 22:27–30) (see II/6).

If it is true that Muhammad changed his qibla from Jerusalem to Mecca
during his first months in Medina, linking Abraham with the shrine and rituals of his hometown reflects an even more radical theological reorientation
toward Mecca. From the beginning Muhammad had identified the God he
worshiped with the "Lord of the Kaaba" (106:3), but behind the pronouncements of sura 2 lies the largely unarticulated assumption that Mecca had once,
in Abraham's and Ishmael's day, been a settlement of monotheists whose rituals were directed toward worshiping the One True God, and that in the intervening centuries it had lapsed into the polytheism that Muslims learned to
called *al-jahiliyya*, or "the era of ignorance." We do not know the extent to
which these assumptions were shared by the audience of the Quran, which
never averts or explains them, but a later generation of Muslim historians and
storytellers put robust flesh on the bare bones of Abraham's stay in Mecca and
the subsequent lapse of Muhammad's town into the heathenism into which
the Prophet himself was born.

Muhammad's career at Medina exhibits two main phases. The first, as we
have just seen, covered the two years immediately following the Hegira, when
Islam underwent a new shaping, first and chiefly by reason of Muhammad's
contact with the Jews of the oasis. Previously his preaching had taken the

form of a simple antagonistic antiphony: the monotheist trying to convert the polytheists, whose refusals, denials, and accusations fly out from between the lines of the Meccan suras. At Medina a third voice is heard, that of the Jews. It was a voice Muhammad had likely expected to harmonize with his own but it proved to be a grating discord. He did not change his tune; he simply refined and enriched it. The earliest definition of Islam was figured against the totally "other" of the polytheists: "Say," God commands Muhammad in an early sura, "you disbelievers, I do not worship what you worship and you do not worship what I worship. . . . You have your religion and I have mine" (109). At Medina it assumed a more complex identity as Muhammad, somewhat like the early Christians, had to define his faith and practice against a "parent" group, which in both instances rejected its putative offspring.

This process of religious identification continued throughout Muhammad's stay in Medina, but early in his second year there he began a course of action that would eventually make him the true master of a Muslim Medina. In 624, he embarked on a more expansive thrust that made him, before his death in 632, the lord of Arabia.

The Master of Medina (624–628)

If Muhammad's mandate was to bring peace and stability to Medina, he went about it in a curious but, as it turned out, extremely effective fashion. He had problems at Medina: there was trouble with the Jews, and some Medinese resistance to the religious preaching of this self-styled "Messenger of God" with a disturbing set of attitudes. The Medinese opposition to Muhammad is not shown in very high profile, but it glimmers forth nonetheless from the Quran. There were also economic difficulties. Muhammad had already begun to address these with his creation of brotherhood arrangements between the Meccan Migrants and the Medinese Helpers. But the landless refugees from Mecca, who could neither sow nor reap nor do any other kind of productive work in that closed oasis society—whose normal hospitality expired after three days—must have continued to be a burden to the Medinese Muslims and a source of concern to Muhammad.

It may have been anger that initially prompted Muhammad and his followers to engage in skirmishes with the Quraysh in the wastelands between Mecca and Medina, or it may have been the hope of stealing some sustenance from their enemies—and their relatives. One of the most remarkable elements Islam introduced into the hostilities of Arabia was internecine strife within families. In Arabia tribe battled against tribe, but kin fought alongside kin. Islam's claims were supertribal; they transcended blood and family, much as Jesus' own, who said he had come "not to bring peace but a sword, to set a man against his father" (Matt. 10:34–35). But Jesus' followers had never had to resort to the sword, whereas Muhammad's had it thrust into their hands. While still at Mecca, if we have the chronology right, during Muhammad's last days there, a revelation had come to him for the first time permitting Muslims to resort to force, or rather, to meet Quraysh violence with violence (Quran 22:39–41).

Nothing came of these early episodes as far as we know, but at Medina Muhammad grew more aggressive. He seems to have led attacks on isolated Quraysh bands without any apparent provocation. Economics suggests itself as a motive: when Muhammad heard of a rich Meccan caravan returning home from the north in 624, he ordered his followers to attack it, since "perhaps God will give it to us as prey." Not all the Muslims were keen on the project, which seemed imprudent—probably even more so when the Quraysh got wind of the plan and sent reinforcements to escort the caravan home. There was a major confrontation between the two forces to the west of Medina at Badr Wells. It was an astonishing success for the outnumbered Muslims, so astonishing that the Quran later cited it as an example of divine intervention on behalf of Islam (3:13). The spoils were rich enough for the Muslims to quarrel over their disposition, and a good part of sura 8, "The Spoils," is given over to the topic. The non-Muslims at Medina must have taken note of both the military success of the venture and the newfound wealth of the Muslims among them.

The battle at Badr Wells was a *casus belli* not between the Quraysh and the Muslims but between Mecca and Medina. Most of what we know about violence in pre-Islamic times has to do with Bedouin trials of honor, whereas the celebrated "battle days of the Arabs" were mostly about tribal fracases over watering holes and pasturage grounds. We know nothing of one town making war on another as was the case here. The Quraysh made two attacks on the unwalled oasis of Medina. The first, in March 625, is enshrined in Muslim mythology as the Battle of Uhud—there is a small hill of that name north of the town—when three thousand Meccans marched on the town. By all rights it should have been a Quraysh victory. The casualty figures were the reverse of what happened at Badr. Many Muslims were killed, but not Muhammad. He was wounded—struck by a thrown stone—but survived unrepentant and undeterred. Quran 3:120–199 apparently offers a lengthy explanation of what happened and why, including the assurance that God had once again sent his angels into battle, three thousand of them, with many more in reserve if necessary (3:124–125).

The Quraysh lay relatively quiet for two years; enthusiasm for an anti-Muslim crusade must have been waning at Mecca. Then in March 627 they made one final attempt on Medina. According to our sources, the attack was prompted by the Medina Jews, who were suffering growing ills at Muslim hands. Whatever the case, this was no pitched battle like Uhud, where the Muslims came out of the oasis and fought, but rather a siege. The Muslims stayed within their Medina oasis forts and apparently covered some of the open ways into the town by digging a trench or ditch. Not all were keen for the project, if Quran 24:62 refers to it, but the effort was successful. What later came to be called the Battle of the Ditch was in fact no battle at all: the Quraysh could not enter the town and the Muslims did not come out to confront them. Predictably—with our hindsight—the besiegers soon lost interest in a war of attrition far from home and began to drift off. This was pure fiasco. It was also the last serious attempt by the Quraysh to rid themselves of their homegrown prophet or, as it turned out, even seriously to oppose him.

These engagements brought most of the Medinese to the Prophet's side. They had little choice perhaps. They had offered Muhammad protection. But his aggressive actions toward the Quraysh moved the hostilities of one tribe against some of its own troublesome clansmen into a war between two settlements with no prior history of enmity between them. We hear of no mass conversions among the Medinese; there is merely the gradual disappearance of polytheism. Muhammad had indeed settled the civil unrest in the oasis but only by creating a common enemy for all parties, his own, the Quraysh. If Islam now began to seem inevitable to the Medinese, shortly it would appear profitable as well.

The Practice of Islam

The chronology of the Quran's Meccan suras can be laid out with some reasonable degree of certainty, though there are notable soft spots as to which are early, middle, or late within that twelve-year span. There is no such conviction about the long suras that date from Medina. Pieces of suras here and there can be connected with specific events like the battles at Badr or Uhud or later Hunayn, but no one has succeeded in arranging in sequence the whole or even a considerable part of them over Muhammad's ten years at Medina. We do not know, for example, when some of the primary ritual obligations of Islam began to be practiced. Ritual prayer (*salat*) would probably have been impossible in the hostile climate of Mecca; we can guess, however, that it began to be practiced soon after the Prophet arrived in Medina. Obligatory tithing (*zakat*) would likewise make sense in Medina, where early on there were Muslims of some substance, the Helpers, and others with little, the Migrants. The mention of tithing in Quran 2:177 in connection with the change in the qibla makes it seem an early act at Medina, but the Muslim tradition also connects its imposition with 9:11–12, which seems to reflect the tribes' capitulations of the year before Muhammad's death, and where it has the flavor of a tribute tax. The fast of Ramadan was likewise a Medina phenomenon (2:184–185); its specification as a religious obligation was almost certainly an outgrowth of the Prophet's early disputes with the Jews of the oasis between

622 and 624. Finally, we can be certain that no Muslim made the ritual pilgrimage until the very end of the Prophet's life: the sole hajj he himself performed was in March 632, three months before he died.

Muhammad and the Jews (continued)

Not merely modern political sensibilities make the Jews of Medina loom large in Muhammad's later career. The issue sprawls across the oldest biographies of the Prophet and runs, sometimes explicitly, sometimes implicitly, throughout the Medina suras. References to the Jews grow darker and more truculent as the Quran progresses, and the judgments are indeed more in anger than in sorrow. The Arab historians and biographers profess to explain why. Their explanations are not all of a piece, however. Some treat the theme theologically: the punishment of the Medina Jews, who were invited to convert and refused, perfectly exemplify the Quran's tales of what happened to those who rejected the prophets of old. Other early historians prefer a more political explanation, to which we now turn.

There were three principle Jewish tribes in Medina: the Qaynuqa, the Nadir, and the Qurayza. The first overt action against them took place in the wake of the military success at Badr. Muhammad, possibly emboldened by his unexpected triumph, decided to push his advantage. The Qaynuqa were invited to convert or face the dire consequences. "Don't be deceived," they answered. "The Quraysh knew nothing about war. *We* will fight!" So they fought. It was that simple. The Jews' Arab patrons, who had solemn obligations to the Qaynuqa, attempted to support them, though not apparently with unanimity or enthusiasm. The Qaynuqa locked themselves in their plantation fortresses, but to no avail. Whoever among the Qaynuqa managed to survive were driven from the oasis and the Muslims took over their properties.

A similar fate overtook the Nadir after Uhud. Here the accusation had to do with a plot to assassinate Muhammad. The Nadir took to their forts and Muhammad flushed them out. Once again the tribe was deported, men, women, and children, with whatever property they could carry. Their lands, we are told, became the Prophet's to dispose of as he would. He divided them among the Migrants, to the exclusion of the Helpers, presumably because the latter already had land of their own. Following the failed Quraysh raid on Medina in 627, it was the turn on the Qurayza, the last of Medina's major Jewish tribes. According to the *Life*, the Qurayza had urged the Meccan Quraysh to attack the oasis and then failed to help when they did. This restraint, or prudence, did not save them from the Prophet's wrath. Indeed, Muhammad received a special revelation—it is not recorded in the Quran, only as a story in the *Life*—commanding him to attack the Qurayza. He did, and after nearly a month of determined resistance, they saw the end was near. The *Life* tells another oddly heroic story about the Jews—already it had portrayed the Nadir marching off into exile with flags flying and heads held high. In this instance, the Qurayza rejected the suggestion that they convert to save themselves and likewise refused to attack the Muslims because it was the Sabbath. Finally, they appealed to their Arab patrons of the Aws. Once again, the response was unenthusiastic: no one was willing to cross Muhammad at this stage. Muhammad was conciliatory only to the extent that he allowed one of the Aws to determine the Qurayza's sentence. The latter's judgment was that the males of the Qurayza deserved death and that the women and children should be sold into slavery. It was done: between six hundred and eight hundred males of the Qurayza were publicly beheaded in the main market of Medina, and, if we are to credit the *Life*, Muhammad himself was the chief executioner. The tribe's real property was again divided among the Muslims.

That was the end of the Jews of Medina, a not inconsiderable part of the population, we can guess, though they had recently been reduced to clientage to the paramount Arab tribes of Aws and Khazraj. There is some evidence that they were the most literate Medinese and in many cases the craftsmen of the settlement. Muslim newcomers appropriated the Jews' property—their lands and inventories—but not their skills. Yet they had little need for the latter; an even more profitable windfall had come upon them.

The Lord of Arabia (628–632)

In 628, with Medina apparently in his control, Muhammad conceived the notion of participating in the *umra*, the Meccans' annual springtime religious festival. (The hajj was more "international" in character and took place in the autumn outside Mecca. See II/6.) He took with him the Migrants and Helpers, and in an effort to swell their ranks, whatever nearby Bedouin might be persuaded to go to Mecca. Though his intentions were said to be peaceful and he brought livestock to sacrifice at the Kaaba (a practice discontinued in Islamic times), we cannot know Muhammad's actual intent in this rather curious move. He already had secret allies in Mecca. The Quraysh were not, in any event, inclined to allow their implacable enemy and his followers into the town. He got as far as a place called Hudaybiyya, where he was forced to halt. Envoys were exchanged with the Quraysh, and after a homely exchange of insults on both sides and a false rumor that his close follower Uthman had been killed by the Quraysh, an odd sort of agreement was worked out. Muhammad had to agree to withdraw so that "none of the Arabs [that is, the Bedouin tribes thereabouts] could say that he had made a forceful entry," and to postpone his umra until the following year. Whatever loss of face occurred was more than made up for by the main clause: hostilities between the two sides were suspended for ten years during which people were free to join Muhammad or the Quraysh as they pleased. To discount what many may have suspected was a compromising show of weakness on Muhammad's part, a revelation was sent down declaring the Hudaybiyya agreement a "signal victory" (Quran 48:1).

The armistice, far from caving in to the Quraysh, may in fact have been a brilliant piece of strategy by Muhammad. Freed from any fear of attack from Mecca, Muhammad embarked on a series of increasingly daring raids at ever greater distances from his Medina base, all directed against the oases to the north and northeast of Medina. We do not know how the Bedouin had read the events at Hudaybiyya, but they were surely impressed by the new successes of the Muslim troops—townspeople turned raiders might be a more accurate description; these date growers and town dwellers were not born to the saddle—who, under the command of the man who called himself the Messenger of God, were imposing their will, and exacting tribute, from the richest settlements in western Arabia. Perhaps more to the point, these successful military ventures conducted in the name of religion brought a new and unexpected prosperity to the Muslims of Medina, and to whoever else they permitted to join the enterprise. The latter included the Bedouin who, ever the opportunists, began to join the colors of the Prophet in growing numbers.

Muhammad and the Jews (concluded)

Out of these successful raids a policy began to emerge. The settlements under attack were offered terms by the Prophet. If they acquiesced and surrendered, they agreed to pay an annual tax-tribute to Muhammad and the Muslim community. They retained the use of their property, but only on the understanding that it belonged to the now sovereign Muslims, who might claim it whenever they chose, which they rarely if ever did. Those who refused the terms and resisted, forfeited all prospects if they were defeated, as they invariably were. The lesson was not lost on the next settlement up the trail.

These arrangements were part of Muhammad's political and military strategy and their consequences eventually disappeared within the larger political reality of the rapidly expanding "Abode of Islam" (see I/8). What persisted far longer—indeed, down to the present day since they became part of an unchanging religious law—were the religious demands and concessions made of and to the inhabitants of these same conquered oases. Khaibar, the first of them, was largely inhabited by Jews, whose numbers were swollen by Nadir refugees from Medina. But the Jews of these oases settlements were no longer treasonous members of the Medina umma. Politically, they were surrendered foes, and their submission won them concessions; religiously, they were People of the Book, Scripturaries like the Muslims, and that theological status won them tolerance (see I/8).

The tolerance granted the Jews of Khaibar was formalized in the *dhimma*, the contract between the Muslim community and their subjects from among the People of the Book. This concordat guaranteed the latter the privilege—it is not a question of rights here; the victors are dictating terms to the vanquished—to continue to practice their religious rituals, a privilege not granted to the polytheists among the conquered peoples. They had to submit or face death, convert or perish. "Fight against those who do not believe in God or in the Last Day," the Quran forthrightly says (9:29). But the dhimma also imposed certain obligations on the vanquished Scriptuaries. The full list of privileges and restrictions later appears in a document called the Covenant of Umar. It contained the terms supposedly granted by the second caliph, Umar ibn al-Khattab, to the Christian inhabitants of Jerusalem on the occasion of the city's surrender in 635. Although the document itself is a later forgery and often brandished by Eastern Christians in their disputes with their Muslim sovereigns—in that sense it is the Muslim counterpart of the forged Donation of Constantine (see I/7)—the Covenant of Umar does embody some of the basic conditions that bind the *dhimmi*s from that day to the present (see I/8).

We can be certain that not all the later specifications were present in the dhimma dictated by the Prophet to the Jews of Khaibar—there were far more complicated, sophisticated, and aggressive People of the Book ahead for the Muslims—but it sets down the principles and conditions of all that follow. The Banu Israil of the Quran were monotheistic paradigms from a remote, unthreatening, but still educational past; the Yahud of Medina were treacherous allies who defaulted on a political contract. A third cohort was now added, the Jews who would come tumbling under the sovereignty of Islam, along with countless Christians. Many of them converted to Islam, as did many, many Christians, but others lived for more than a millennium under the universal and perpetual dhimma.

In the midst of this military activity, Muhammad in 629 did what he failed to do the previous year. He led a delegation of Muslims to Mecca to perform the umra there. It was his first visit to his birthplace since his dangerous escape seven years earlier, but he received a cold reception. After three days he was told his time was up and that he should leave. It must have been an unpleasant episode, though Muhammad's influential Qurayshi uncle Abbas appears to have embraced Islam on this occasion.

The Wives and Children of the Prophet

While briefly in Mecca for the umra, Muhammad married Maymuna, the widowed sister-in-law of Abbas. She was, by one count, his eleventh wife, and possibly his last, though early in 627 he received as a gift-concubine the Egyptian Christian Miryam. As might be imagined, Christian polemicists, who shared the assumption that prophets should be ascetic, if not celibate, had merry sport with the many wives of the Prophet, and modern Muslim biographers of Muhammad have had to address the issue at every turn. His marriages did, however, cause some problems for his contemporaries as well, not because they suggested unbridled sexuality, which could be comfortably parsed as manly prowess, but for other reasons. Arabian society was, no less than the biblical to which it was cousin, polygamous. The Quran addressed this custom and, for reasons unclear to us, though the context is one of equitable treatment of orphans, it limited the number of wives a Muslim might have to four (4:3). This is not a commandment, at any rate; it is a permission, and the very next line warns that unless a husband can be equitable toward his wives, then it is better to be monogamous. But Muhammad had more than four wives, and we can sense something in the wonder this may have caused in Quran 33:50, which explicitly states that Muhammad—"and only you, and not the Believers"—may have as many as he and the women in question may wish. The other issue that perplexed Muslims—and provided additional ammunition for the later Christian enemies of Islam—was the fact that he married Zaynab, the wife of Zayd ibn Haritha, the Prophet's own former freedman and much favored adopted son. Adoption created consanguinity among the Arabs, and custom frowned on such near-kin marriages: there may also have been talk about the unseemliness of the divorce. It is clear from Quran 33:37–38 that Muhammad feared public opinion about this marriage, and not until he received an exculpatory revelation did he dare go through with it.

Muhammad was first married to the twice widowed Khadija and to her alone for perhaps fourteen years, and she bore him all his children save one. These were the boy Qasim, who died in infancy, and the girls Zaynab (whose husband never converted to Islam), Ruqayya (who was married to the third caliph, Uthman—she accompanied him to Abyssinia with that early group of émigrés—until her death in Medina in 624), Umm Kulthum (first married to a son of Abu Lahab, Muhammad's archenemy at Mecca—Quran 111 deals with him—and then, after Ruqayya's death, to Uthman), and Fatima (who married Muhammad's cousin, and the fourth caliph, Ali). Khadija died in 619 and soon afterward, while still in Mecca, Muhammad married Sawda, the widow of one of his fellow Muslims. Also at Mecca, he became betrothed to Aisha, the then six-year-old daughter of his close associate Abu Bakr. The marriage was not consummated, however, until after the Hegira, presumably when Aisha reached puberty.

> **Note:** Aisha, by all reports Muhammad's favorite wife, had an interesting history. She is the eyewitness reporter who stands, despite her gender and age—she was only about eighteen when Muhammad died—behind many of the reports of the sayings and deeds (hadith) (see II/3) that form the core not only of the Prophet's biography but of the very substance of Islamic

(*continued*)

law. Her life with Muhammad is embroidered with a great deal of fancy, but there is a strong consensus that Quran 24:11–20, which reprimands the Muslims for believing in a scandalous libel, was about her and an incident that was thought—falsely, as the Quran itself makes clear—to have compromised her reputation. Among those alleged to have thought her guilty was Ali, Muhammad's cousin and confidant. If true, it would go far toward explaining Aisha's later antipathy toward Ali—she actually accompanied troops into battle against him—in the great political skirmishes for the leadership of the umma between 656 and 661.

It is difficult to make generalizations about Muhammad's eleven-odd wives and perhaps two concubines. Many of the relationships seem to have been political, some compassionate, some, perhaps Aisha and Zaynab, affairs of the heart. At Medina, after Aisha, Muhammad married Hafsa (his companion Umar's widowed daughter); Zaynab bint Khuzayma (already twice a widow); Umm Salama (another Muslim widow); Zaynab (his adopted son Zayd's divorced wife); Juwayriyya (daughter of a defeated Bedouin chieftain; perhaps a hostage or a spoil of war, or both); Umm Habiba (widow of an Abyssinian émigré and daughter of the powerful Quraysh leader Abu Sufyan); Safiyya (widow of the Jewish ruler of Khaibar, killed by the Muslims in 628; she converted to Islam); and Maymuna. In addition, we know of two concubines: the Jewess Rayhana of the Qurayza, who became Muhammad's property when the tribe surrendered in 627, and Miryam, the Coptic "gift" who bore him a son, Ibrahim, who died in infancy.

The Opening of Mecca

The Quraysh, who had treated Muhammad coldly, even shabbily, on the occasion of his umra to Mecca in 629, received their harsh comeuppance soon enough. The ten-year armistice of Hudaybiyya was of course still in effect, but there were, almost inevitably in those fluidly moving tribal zones, violations of the truce between the Bedouin allies of the Quraysh and those of Muhammad. They were not likely fatal since the dispirited Quraysh appeared willing to negotiate, but Muhammad would have none of it. The moment was at hand, he decided, to deal with the Quraysh once and for all.

An expedition was prepared. That fact could not be concealed, but its destination was, at least till the raiders were already on their way, this time, unusually, toward the south, toward Mecca. Luck was with them. Abu Sufyan, the leader of the Quraysh, was surprised and captured outside Mecca and was persuaded to save himself by embracing Islam.

> **Note:** Two late Meccan converts, Abu Sufyan and Abbas, turned out to
> be the progenitors of the two great Arab houses to rule Islam as an em-
> pire: Abu Sufyan of the Umayyads (661–750 in Damascus) and Abbas of
> the Abbasids (750–1258 in Baghdad). We have no preserved Umayyad
> historians so the figure of Abu Sufyan lies largely unredeemed in the de-
> bris of early Islamic history, but the many historians who wrote under
> the Abbasids did their best to rehabilitate the memory of Abbas. As we
> have seen, Muslim tradition has Muhammad marrying Umm Habiba,
> Abu Sufyan's daughter, in 628, and Maymuna, Abbas's sister-in-law the
> following year.

The Muslim troops entered the city with orders to act with restraint. Little
was necessary since resistance seems to have been negligible. There followed
a scene of quiet triumph. Muhammad entered the haram and proclaimed,
"The truth has come and falsehood has passed away." He ordered the numerous idols burned or smashed to pieces. Pictures were removed from inside the
Kaaba, all save one of Jesus and Mary that the Prophet allowed to remain.

> **Note:** The Kaaba had been rebuilt during Muhammad's youth—he had
> assisted in the project—out of timbers from a recent shipwreck on the
> Red Sea coast. The project was under the direction of one of the sur-
> vivors named Baqum (Pachomius), since the Meccans, whose dwellings
> were of mud brick, had little idea how to construct a timber roof. The
> pictures may have come from the wreck, or perhaps they were the work
> of that same shipwrecked Christian. Whatever the case, they disap-
> peared in later reconstructions of the building.

The Quraysh were treated with what appears to be remarkable leniency.
"Go," Muhammad said, "You are freed." And he left the town. Muhammad
had little to fear. Mecca had fallen to the Prophet long before he actually
entered it.

The Bedouin, the camel and sheep steppe nomads among the Arabs, were
opportunists, but they were not blind to oasis politics. Some among the tribes
scented danger in the rise of the master of Medina. We cannot follow all the
workings of what followed—the internal history of the Bedouin is written in
sand—but there was enough fear of where Muhammad was heading to gener-
ate a coalition of tribes that made one final attempt at taking him down. The
Bedouin collected their forces at a place called Hunayn, and Muhammad led
his Muslims out of Medina to meet them. The Muslims were superior in
numbers, but the circumstances of this kind of "display" battle may have been
new to them, and initially there was some panic in the Muslim ranks. They
rallied, however, and in the end it was the Bedouin who broke and ran. Once

again the Quran makes one of its few contemporary allusions. "On the day of Hunayn," it instructed the Muslims, "God sent hosts you could not see and punished those who did not believe" (9:25–26). As on the fields of Badr (8:9) and Uhud (3:121–125), God had intervened through his angels on behalf of his Prophet.

Problems before and after Tabuk

The Muslims' raiding continued. Earlier in 629, between his umra of that year and his conquest of Mecca, Muhammad had launched his most ambitious and perhaps most ill conceived expedition deep into distant Roman-Byzantine Syria. The alleged reason was the murder of one of the Prophet's emissaries to someone said to be the Arab governor of Bostra (today Busra). The truth of that does not concern us here, but the raid, which was met by government troops at a village called Muta east of what is now the city of Kerak in Jordan, is well attested—indeed, it is the first event of Muslim history mentioned by a non-Muslim source, in this case the Byzantine historian Theophanes (d. 818)—as is the fact that it was a disastrous defeat for the Muslims. Muhammad did not accompany the raiders, but he was there to console them on their return. In his weekly sermon he assured his fellow Muslims that he had had a vision of the "martyrs of Muta" at their ease in paradise.

In March 630, after his triumph at Hunayn, Muhammad made the umra to Mecca, though not the hajj, which according to the standard *Life*, "The people made . . . that year in the way the (pagan) Arabs used to do." Then he planned yet another raid far into the north, not as foolhardy as the expedition to Muta perhaps, but dangerous enough for some Muslims to balk at it. The situation was sufficiently critical that a revelation addressed it, lashing out at those who preferred to "sit at home" and "preferred to be with the women who remain behind" (Quran 9:81–86). God's advice is strong and straightforward:

> It was not fitting for the people of Medina and for the Bedouin in the vicinity to refuse to follow God's Apostle, nor to prefer their own lives to his, because everything that they would suffer or do would be accounted to their credit as a deed of righteousness—whether they suffered thirst or fatigue or hunger in the cause of God or trod paths to anger the unbelievers or received any injury. (9:120)

We are not well informed on either the motives for this expedition or the motives of the disinclined. The Helpers may have been disappointed at the almost total absence of booty from the conquest of Mecca, or the obvious leniency Muhammad showed his fellow Meccans in its sequel. The need for funds may have been growing and the obvious expedient was another raid, this time not into Roman territory as such—the Byzantines had recently driven their enemies the Persians from Syria and were reestablishing their authority—but only as far as the northernmost limits of what was now emerging as the "Medina Empire." The Prophet may have been probing. Or he may have been fishing.

On the available evidence, the Medina malingerers had little to fear. This particular raid, which was led by the Prophet in person, halted at the town of Tabuk close to the present Jordan-Saudi border and seems to have been marked by little or no fighting. As soon as the Muslims showed the flag, a number of settlements sent their delegates to Muhammad at his camp at Tabuk to signal their capitulation. Notable among them was the "ruler" of Ayla, later Aqaba/Elath, at the head of the Aelanatic Gulf. He seems in fact to have been the bishop of the city, an example of how thoroughly Roman civil authority had already deserted its own provincial towns. This was also, significantly, the first Christian community to submit to Islam and be accorded the dhimma.

When he returned to Medina, Muhammad discovered that what had been malingering at the beginning of the campaign had turned into something far more serious. The Quran tells us:

> And those who have taken a mosque in opposition and unbelief, and to divide the believers, and as a place of ambush for those who fought God and His Messenger aforetime—they will swear "We desired nothing but good"; and God testifies they are truly liars. (9:107)

This is really quite mysterious, and the Muslim historians and commentators on the Quran have no single explanation of the events lying behind it. They all agree that the Prophet himself had approved the building of this mosque before leaving for Tabuk and that when the revelation just cited was sent down, he ordered the mosque destroyed. A strong suspicion points to certain Medina Helpers as the builders, perhaps the same people who are referred to from Uhud onward by a word commonly translated as "hypocrites" (*munafiqun*), which is also the title of sura 63. What they actually were is more complex; perhaps "disaffected nominal Muslims in Medina" comes closest to describing them. But here they begin to take on the aspect of a schismatic community, a group of believers who wished to worship on their own (without the Prophet's supervision?) in a place of their own. Whatever their motives, they were judged by God himself to be in "opposition and unbelief" and the mosque was destroyed at Muhammad's own command.

The Last Years (631–632)

In the ninth year of the new Muslim era, Muhammad made his final break with the polytheism into which he had been born and against which he had been preaching for more than two decades. The move is announced in the opening verses of sura 9, called "The Immunity":

> An immunity from God and His Messenger to those of the polytheists
> with whom you have made alliances: travel through the land for four
> months, but know that you cannot frustrate God but that God will cover
> with shame the unbelievers. An announcement from God and His Mes-
> senger to the people assembled on the day of the great hajj that God and
> His Messenger dissolve treaty obligations with the polytheists . . . (9:1–3)

The biographical sources attempt to fill in the details. This "proclamation"
was not delivered by the Prophet himself but by Abu Bakr or Ali—there
was, as often, later disagreement on these points—on the occasion of the hajj
of 631. It was the last pilgrimage in which the pagans would be allowed to
participate, which may explain Muhammad's absence. All treaty obligations
contracted with them would be unilaterally dissolved. It was the formal end
of the original Medina umma, the one initiated by the agreement signed by
Muhammad and the Medinese, Muslims, pagans, and Jews, shortly after his
arrival in the oasis, and the beginning of a new umma, this one composed of
Muslims alone, a theocracy that would be at the same time a church and
a state.

The pagans were granted a four-month grace period during which all the
treaty obligations would be scrupulously observed (9:4). But once that time
was over, the consequences would be terrible:

> But when the sanctuary months are over, fight and slay the polytheists
> wherever you find them, and seize them and confine them and lie in wait
> for them in every kind of ambush. But if they repent and establish
> prayers and give the tithe, then open the way for them. Indeed, God is
> forgiving, merciful. (9:5)

Thus in the beginning of 632 Muhammad made his first hajj as a Muslim,
and, as it turned out, his last. It was also in a sense the first Muslim hajj. Previously, at least in 631, Muslims and polytheists had side by side participated
in the ritual as it had always existed, without any obvious modifications either
in the liturgy itself or in the Muslims' participation in it. In 632 only Muslims
were present, according to the proclamation at the previous pilgrimage, and
they were led by Muhammad himself, who seems to have carefully picked his
way through the elaborate ritual, changing it here and there as he went along.
The umra and the hajj were, after a fashion, combined; intercalation was forbidden (see II/6). All this occurred in connection with this famous Farewell
Pilgrimage and it became a template for all that were to follow: the Prophet's
acts and instructions on this historic occasion were recollected at length in the
biographical sources.

Muhammad returned from the hajj in March 632; three months later
he was dead. Yet his death was not sudden, though it was unexpected. To all

appearances he was still a vigorous man, hardly the sixty-two-year-old of the traditional dating, which at that time and place would have made him an old man. Indeed, he had led a dangerous military operation over a long distance less than two years earlier. We are not told precisely what his ailment was. He simply grew ill and died. He had time to make certain dispositions—he appointed Abu Bakr to lead the prayer during his illness—but not the most crucial of all: he appointed no successor. Muhammad died in bed, at his own residence, in June 632, the tenth year of the new Muslim era, as it would soon be called, surrounded by his wives and family. He lies buried in a rich tomb within the now extraordinarily grandiose Mosque of the Prophet at Medina. Nearby a place is prepared to receive the body of Jesus.

Muhammad and Jesus: Some Points of Comparison

Muhammad and Jesus are both recognized as in some sense the founders of the two religious communities that claim more adherents than any others. Both men are deeply revered among their followers and have served as role models for countless believers. But beyond that, they have little in common. At the outset, it has already been remarked that it was Jesus' life, particularly his death and resurrection, that founded Christianity, whereas it was Muhammad's message that founded Islam. Muhammad reported a revelation from God; Jesus *was* God's revelation. As his contemporaries remarked with amazement, Jesus spoke on his own authority.

Placed side by side, the two lives show remarkable differences. Jesus was born into a sophisticated religious and social milieu that already had nearly two millennia of development behind it. He read Hebrew and spoke Aramaic and likely some Greek. Though not a bookman in what was already becoming a bookish society, he had something of a local reputation as a scholar. Jesus is to us and was to his Jewish contemporaries a rather familiar figure in a very familiar landscape. Muhammad was not born and raised in a vacuum, of course, but as far as our knowledge is concerned, he might just as well have been. We know pitifully little of seventh-century Arabia, even less about the Hejaz, the region that nurtured him and where his life unfolded, and almost nothing about Mecca, his native town, save what is almost accidentally uncovered in the Quran. Muhammad was barely literate, we guess—a minor merchant we never see buying or selling. Jesus, whom we never see doing carpentry either, functioned nonetheless in front of what is for us a rich tapestry of context; Muhammad, against an almost blank screen.

In his ministry Jesus was speaking and acting before an audience of fellow Jews whom he was trying to convince that a new era, "the Kingdom," had dawned—or was about to explode in their day, an apocalyptic or eschatological notion with which they were all to some extent acquainted. Muhammad had more radically to convince polytheists to monotheism, without benefit of sign or miracle, which Jesus had in abundance. Their lifestyles differed. Jesus was an itinerant preacher, a celibate, from all the evidence. Muhammad had a home, whether in Mecca or Medina, a wife—indeed, many wives—and a large family that grew even more extended through marriage. Jesus had a specially selected and carefully trained inner circle, the Twelve. Muhammad had followers, some of them close, but he did not select apostles, nor did he even have disciples in the ordinary sense of the word. Jesus' active career lasted one year at the minimum, three at the maximum; Muhammad's, for twenty-two, during which he had the opportunity, which he manifestly took, to edit and emend the body of revelations he received. The suras of the Quran show many signs of having been rearranged and added to, and by the Prophet himself. Although he was the subject of the Gospels, Jesus obviously had no say as to what went into them, which of his sayings were reported and which not, or how accurately.

At the end of his brief career Jesus was publicly executed as a criminal, deserted by most of his followers. Muhammad was close to suffering the same fate. After twelve years of preaching at Mecca he had made relatively few converts and was himself in danger of being assassinated by enemies from among his own people. The apparent failure of Jesus' mission at Passover in 30 C.E. was "redeemed" by his resurrection, which gave his followers a new vision and a new hope. Muhammad was saved from a similar failure by his migration to Medina, where, in a new setting and under new circumstances, he began to make converts in such increasing numbers that by his death in 632 there were Muslims throughout western Arabia and the prospect of others beyond.

At Medina Muhammad became the head of a functioning community, at first an apparently civil one, but soon, with the conversion of the Medinese and the expulsion of first the Jews and then, at the end, of all non-Muslims from the umma, a community that was at once, and inextricably, religious and political. Muhammad was, in short, both prophet and statesman, pope and emperor, during the last ten years of his life. Jesus, in contrast, showed no interest in politics—"My Kingdom is not of this world." For someone to show no interest in politics in first-century Palestine was no simple matter, and the Gospels seem to go out of their way to show how Jesus avoided the political traps that his hostile questioners often set for him. Yet, for all that, Jesus was executed by a political authority on what appear to be political charges. "Kingdom," it is clear, was a term that could cut many ways in Roman Palestine, some of them dangerous.

If we cannot always come to terms with Jesus' political views, it is clear he wielded no political power. Although he was undoubtedly regarded as a leader by his disciples, it is difficult to recognize in that band of itinerants a society, or even a movement, in any ordinary sense. In any event, it was effectively ended by Jesus' death and had to be reconstituted by his followers afterward. Jesus had no personal role in the shaping of his ekklesia. This was the work of his heirs, including some, like Paul, who had never even known him in the flesh.

The Career of Mecca

Even after the capitulation of his native Mecca in 630, Muhammad preferred to remain in Medina. His first four successors, the "rightly guided" (*rashidun*) caliphs, chose to do likewise and Medina remained the capital of the rapidly expanding Muslim community until 661, when a new dynasty moved the seat of power to Damascus, then others again to Baghdad and elsewhere. Though Mecca remained Islam's premier holy city by reason of its Abrahamic associations and the hajj (see II/6), it was for most of its history a political and commercial backwater sustained by pious endowments and the income from its only business, the care and feeding of the thousands of Muslims—eventually many hundreds of thousands—who came there as hajjis on the fixed days of the pilgrimage month or as pious visitors the year round.

Whichever remote caliph or sultan claimed sovereignty, Mecca and Medina were under the immediate control of local Arab aristocrats, the sharifs. These notables claimed direct descent from the Prophet, and their location was sufficiently remote from competing authority that Mecca's sharif—the title *sharif* refers to the nobility of his descent from Muhammad; *sayyid* is also used elsewhere to denote the same honor—invariably took the princely share of the holy city's dues from pilgrims and merchants. In the first years of the twentieth century, Turkish reformers attempted to rein Mecca into their newly centralized government structure. The sharif Husayn (d. 1931) resisted and thus was born a tension that the British exploited as soon as Turkey entered the Great War on Germany's side. Husayn, whose religious credentials as ruler and guardian of "the Twin Harams" made him an attractive candidate for leading the Arabs in a revolt against their Ottoman sovereigns, negotiated with the British for a leadership role in a broad, postwar independent Arab domain. Neither the leadership nor the domain materialized, but in June 1916 an Arab insurrection against Ottoman sovereignty was proclaimed in Mecca and the Arab Revolt was under way.

From the eighteenth century Mecca had a politically and religiously aggressive neighbor in the Wahhabi-allied House of Saud in central Arabia. In 1806 the Wahhabis occupied Mecca and Medina, only to be driven out within a few years by an Egyptian expeditionary force. The Wahhabis withdrew but they did not disappear. They regrouped under Abdul Aziz ibn Saud (d. 1953), and by the outbreak of World War I the Saudis too were British clients. After the war Husayn ruled from Mecca an impoverished and marginalized kingdom of the Hejaz whose dissolution was, increasingly and obviously, the Saudi objective. British conciliation held the Saudis temporarily at bay, but by 1926 the British neither could nor would prevent the inevitable, and the Saudis once again occupied Mecca and Medina. The sharifate was abolished, and both Husayn and his son and successor, Ali, ended their days far from Mecca. The Saudis purified the holy cities religiously as well as politically, and Mecca would likely have remained an overextended and underfinanced pilgrimage town except for the flow of enormous sums of oil money into the Saudi economy. A prodigious enlargement of the Meccan sanctuary and the improvement of pilgrimage facilities from housing to sanitation were undertaken and completed in 1955. The even greater enlargement of the Prophet's mosque in Medina was finished in 1996.

Note: With the prestige of guardianship of the Twin Harams of Mecca and Medina came the inevitable responsibility for maintaining both the security and the freedom of the annual pilgrimage. The Saudis had their enemies in Islam; the hajj was an inviting time to provoke the House of Saud and, since the hajj was now televised in its entirety, to flaunt opposition to the regime before the entire Muslim world. In November 1979 the kingdom's own Fundamentalist dissidents seized the Haram and were dislodged only with force and the scandal of spilled Muslim blood in Islam's holiest place. That same year the Ayatollah Khomeini led an Islamic revolution in Iran and thereafter the new Shiite Islamic Republic used Mecca and its hajj as a world stage for demonstrating, through placards and slogans, its disdain for the House of Saud. Once again, in July 1987, there was violence in the Haram. The Iranians called for an international Muslim trusteeship over the Holy Places; the Saudis further tightened security and severely limited the number of pilgrims permitted entry from Iran. The tension persists.

4

A Kingdom of Priests

IT IS SOMETIMES pointed out that there is no such thing as "Judaism," or "Christianity," or "Islam" save what we construct as such in our own minds: there are, in truth, only Jews, Christians, and Muslims. To put it somewhat more accurately, however, those names are what the believers constructed in their own minds. The three group designators were devised not by modern social scientists but by members of the groups themselves, early on. The conceptualized "Judaism" first appears, in Greek, in 2 Maccabees 2:21; in 14:38 the phrase "practicing Judaism" is used. It is echoed by Paul (Gal. 1:13–14). "Christian" is used quite self-consciously as a very new membership marker in Acts 11:26, and "Christianity" (Gk. *Christianismos*; Lat. *Christianitas*) appears, now as a fully domesticated term, in Ignatius and Polycarp at the end of the first and beginning of the second Christian century. "Islam" has the most exalted pedigree of all. It was God's own designation of the "religion" to which he had summoned the believers. As often in the Quran, God himself is speaking: "If anyone desires a religion (*din*) other than Islam (*al-islam*), never will it be accepted of him, and in the Hereafter he will be in the ranks of the losers" (3:85).

The believers thus saw themselves as members of an identifiable group, and they organized themselves as such, even at times in a form close to something we might call a state (see I/6–8). The three faith communities are in fact metasocieties whose special quality derives from their being founded by divine decree and as part of a divine plan. The famous Covenant concluded by God with Abraham is the founding charter of that sense of community, and all subsequent claims of filiation go back to it. Although this Covenant was initiated and in a sense dictated by God, its adherents must, like Abraham himself, assent to it.

Each of the communities of Jews, Christians, and Muslims has, then, an absolute quality that sets it off from merely human societies. Its claims derive from God and so are absolute; they trump any merely human demands of loyalty toward the state or even family. Unlike civil society, which looks primarily toward the rights of its members, religious communities look chiefly to the responsibilities of the believers who constitute them. But for all their transcendent qualities, the monotheist religious communities are still made up of mortal men and women who have had to work out, with only partial help from God, their community boundaries and the identity markers of their members or, to put it more bluntly, who was in, who was out, and, always more difficult to explain, how and why.

Identity Markers

Who or what is a Jew is a legitimate, self-posed question for Jews, as is its counterpart for the other two bodies of monotheists. Each community has struggled to define and so separate itself from the various "others" who surrounded and challenged it. By defining themselves, at least in part, as Children of Abraham, the Jews laid down the initial issue of identification for both the Christians and the Muslims, who likewise claimed that title. Thus the Christians had from the outset not merely to identify themselves as the authentic Abrahamic heirs, but to deny such a claim to the Jews, to dismantle at least part of the Jews' self-identification, and the Muslims to do likewise with both the Jews and the Christians.

This is the overarching religious context of the monotheist communities' self-identification. But from the beginning, each community had also to define itself against its immediate neighbors and rivals. As we read into the Bible, it becomes clear that the first element in Jewish self-identification was that they were people of the special covenant offered them by their God, accepted by them and sealed with the sign of circumcision. Yet that is not how they referred to themselves. They were not Benei Brith, "Covenanters" but Benei Israel, "descendants" or "the tribe" of Israel. Where we might have expected Benei Abraham, they claimed instead to be the linear descendants of Abraham's grandson, Israel. That tribal identity was not enough, however. After we are told about Israel and his twelve offspring who will eventually constitute the people "Israel," we are introduced in the rest of the Pentateuch to another, more elaborate set of distinctive marks that have nothing to do with lineage and everything to do with cultural and social separation of the Israelites from their neighbors.

The Christians' problems were from the outset more complex since they had initially to lay claim to the special spiritual identity possessed since the patriarchal age by their parent community, the Benei Israel, and at the same time to maintain themselves, like the Israelites, as separate from the pagan world around them. Muhammad's first concern was, like that of the early Israelites, to define his community by its monotheism, in contrast to the prevalent idolatry and polytheism of Mecca and Arabia generally: we are "believers" (*muminun*) and "submitters" (*muslimun*); you are "unbelievers" (*kafirun*) and "associators" (*mushrikun*), the Quran asserts. As the Muslim community took shape around that basic marker, other identity issues arose, initially by the presence in Medina a Jewish community that could, and apparently did, deny Muhammad's implicit inclusion of his submitters in some supposed community of monotheists—what later came to be called, with a somewhat different marker, the People of the Book (see II/1). In its Medina suras the Quran thus takes up the task of distinguishing the Muslims from both the Jews and the Christians by recourse to the notion of a religion of Abraham, a faith community that antedated both Judaism and Christianity and of which the Muslims were the most authentic representatives (see I/3).

In and Out

The boundaries of community, once marked, had also to be wardened: the members had to decide who was to be allowed in, and how, the process that may be generally defined as conversion. Entry into the community is usually marked with a formal ritual performed either on behalf of a newborn inductee (infant circumcision in Judaism and Islam, infant baptism in Christianity) or as an adult initiation rite (pubescent circumcision in Islam and adult baptism in Christianity; bar mitzvah in Judaism, confirmation in Christianity). The community has, moreover, also to discern who is to be excluded from it, and why. Whereas apostasy is effectively self-exclusion—an individual's formal adjuration of his or her faith—banning, the Hebrew *herem*, or, as the Christians called it, excommunication, occurs when the community, acting through some competent authority, cancels the individual's membership and imposes some form of exclusion.

Judaism and Islam have very diffuse religious authority structures and so it is not entirely clear who is competent to render such a decision or how far such a writ runs. The rabbis seem to have invoked herem chiefly against those who spoke ill of rabbis, and then not very often or very effectively (see I/5). Pre-Reform Christianity, in contrast, did possess a defined and competent authority and the combination of a monarchical episcopate (see I/6) and the Church's guardianship of the merits of Jesus' redemptive death made excommunication a frequently invoked and powerfully effective instrument of theological orthodoxy and ecclesiastical policy (see II/5). With the sixteenth-century disintegration of the Church into confessional churches, however, and the redefinition of the latter's authority, jurisdictions narrowed, as did the force of excommunication.

Kinship and Covenant

The Jews were a kinship community from the beginning. The Covenant was granted to Abraham and his heirs, and the dramatic tension of the Genesis narrative is generated by the fact that Abraham had no issue. Indeed, Abraham's very first words to God in Genesis are "Lord God, what can You give me, seeing I am childless?" (15:2). Once there was an heir—the precise heir, as we have seen, was a matter of some dispute in the generations of Isaac and Jacob—the inheritance was settled permanently on the Benei Israel, the twelve tribes descended from Jacob/Israel's twelve sons. This self-appellation leaves no doubt that it is kinship identity that is at stake in the Covenant. The ethnic cleansing that occurred in Palestine after the return of the exiles (Ezra 9–10)—Israelites who had married "foreign" wives had to rid themselves of both those brides and the offspring of such unions—underlines the point forcefully, as does the later halakic or religio-legal definition of a Jew as someone born of a Jewish mother.

> **Note:** The foundation of the State of Israel as a Jewish state and the 1950 adoption of the Law of Return stating that "every Jew has the right to em-igrate to the State of Israel," and be granted citizenship therein, raised the identity issue in a new form. The Zionist founding fathers seemed willing to accept a broad self-identification—"a Jew is anyone who says he is a Jew"—as a basis for granting citizenship, but their view did not prevail. In 1959 the halakic definition of a Jew, someone born of a Jewish mother, was made the basis of Israeli naturalized citizenship. But that was by no means the end of the matter. In 1962 a Jewish convert to Catholicism in-voked the Law of Return and was denied citizenship, though he fulfilled the strict halakic definition; in 1970 the Law of Return was amended to exclude those "ethnic Jews" who had professed other religions.

"Be You Holy As I Am Holy"

But an Abrahamic birthright was never enough. There was from the beginning a form of spiritual identification among the Israelites, first defined perhaps as faithfulness to God, expressed through worship of him alone, famously signaled in Genesis by the formula "Abraham put his faith in the Lord, who reckoned it to him as righteousness" (15:6) and sealed by the external sign of circumcision (17:10–14). Another early form of spiritual self-definition had to do with holiness: Israel was to be, in the Bible's remarkable phrase, "a kingdom of priests, My holy nation" (Exod. 19:6). Holiness (*qedushah*), it was later ex-plained, is an attribute of God, and since the Israelites are God's people, that reality creates a moral obligation in them to be holy as well. "Be you holy as I am holy" is the way God puts it (Lev. 11:44–45; 19:2; 20:7–8).

The Israelites were left in no doubt about what that command involved. The imitation of God's own holiness was translated into an elaborate set of taboos, ritual and dietary, that are set out in Exodus, Leviticus, Numbers, and Deuteronomy. The same conditions and prohibitions surrounded the Is-raelites' manner and places of worship (see II/6), where taboo zones around the Jerusalem Holy of Holies, for example, protected Yahweh's dwelling from attacks of impurity. Finally, these restrictions guided the Israelites in their social relations among themselves and with their neighbors. The ethnic separation from the Gentiles (< Lat. *gentes*; Gk. *ethne*, "nations") continued to be maintained by restrictions on exogamy, while the dietary and similar laws set down markers to separate the Jews socially and ritually from their pagan neighbors.

Separation was, then, an unmistakable characteristic of Israelite holiness. Although in the Bible the thrust toward separation is envisioned as something to set the Israelites apart from the other folk who inhabited that land and who were "vomited out of it" for their unholy practices (Lev. 18:24–30), a later generation of Jews diagnosed the problem somewhat differently. We are not certain what the term "Pharisees" means—it occurs only in Greek texts—but it is temptingly close to *perushim*, "The Separate," or "The Separated," who appear in rabbinic writings after 200 C.E. The Torah had made a clear separation between Israel and the heathens (Lev. 20:26), a theme the rabbis often take up and elaborate, much as the Pharisees had in the centuries surrounding the turn into the Christian era. But the Pharisees were less concerned with the heathens than with their fellow Jews. For them a "nation of priests" meant strict observance not only of the Torah but also of the "tradition of the fathers" they invoked in their interpretation of the Law (see II/3).

The holiness program emerged in a newly tightened version from Pharisaic circles in the first century C.E., and in that form it eventually prevailed in what came to be known as rabbinic Judaism. Though their strict views on tithing, fasting, and Sabbath observance were noted by their contemporaries, their food regulations most obviously and effectively defined the Pharisees vis-à-vis the rest of the Jewish community, setting them off from the *am ha-aretz*, the "people of the land" who constituted the majority of the day's "ordinary" Jews. The Pharisees insisted that all meals be taken in a state of ritual purity as strict as that of the priests serving in the temple, a daunting requirement that restructured and delimited a basic form of social intercourse. Holiness as separation could go no further, short of withdrawal from the community, which the Essenes had already done, but the Pharisees steadfastly refused to follow them into the wilderness. They found their isolation in the dining room.

What Is a Jew?

The prophets who opposed secularizing Jewish monarchs of an earlier era were rather isolated figures whose position as revivalists and reformers rested on charismatic foundations. Opposition to the post-Exilic Hasmonaeans, in contrast, took the form of parties whose programs created neither revival nor reform, but rather schismatic fissures in the Jewish community (see I/1 and

I/5). The Sadducees, Pharisees, Essenes, and followers of Jesus held sharply differing views about past history, future prospects, and what constituted a Jewish life. What they perhaps shared was the notion that the Covenant once concluded with the entire Benei Israel had now become a special covenant observed only by a faithful remnant, namely, themselves.

There is an unmistakable air of exclusivity to the Second Temple sectarians, from Pharisees to Essenes to the followers of John the Baptist or Jesus of Nazareth. The political question of a Jewish state had been rendered moot by the Roman absorption of Judaea in 6 C.E., and although some were still willing to die for its restoration—as they did in the great Jewish insurrections of 66–70 and 135 C.E.—most of the spiritual energies of the Jewish community in Palestine were devoted to constructing new legal, ascetic, and eschatological canons to answer the question "What is a Jew?" But this was no mere speculative issue. Many of these groups attempted to live out their definition either in public life or apart from it, and to try to convince others of the righteousness of their own cause.

It was the Pharisaic answer to the question that prevailed: a Jew was someone who observed the Law, both the written Torah given to Moses and the unwritten Law, the tradition of the fathers, that went back to the same time and had the same sanction (see II/3), and whose authoritative interpreters were the rabbis who after the second devastation of Palestinian Jewry in 135 were the sole voice of Judaism. Temple and Qumran were gone, along with their guardians and devotees, and the sectarian followers of Jesus of Nazareth had chosen or been forced to separate themselves from rabbinic Judaism. More, the Romans accepted the Pharisaic disassociation from the insurrection, and in the sequel chose to deal with the Pharisaic leadership as representatives of the Jewish Covenant, not merely in a religious but also in a political sense. For their part, the Romans regarded the Jews as both an ethnic group (*natio*) and a religious community (*religio*) at whose head now stood, at their sufferance, a single official, the *nasi*, or "prince" (see I/6).

Conversion and Clientage

One acknowledgment that Judaism was, as the Romans expressed it, a *religio* as well as an ethnic category is the fact that it was possible to join the community without having been born into it, in short, to convert oneself into a Jew. The act, if not the process, appears without comment in Ruth 1:16, where the Moabite Ruth simply announces to her Israelite mother-in-law, "Your people will be my people and your God will be my God." This is an act of loyalty and perhaps a post-Exilic effort to counteract the harsh regulations requiring the dismissal of foreign wives and their offspring on the Jews' return to Judaea. But even here Ruth's child by Boaz is accepted as an Israelite—he will actually be David's grandfather—only because he is passed off as the child of Ruth's Jewish mother-in-law, Naomi. Here too the convert's family ties, his or her actual kinship links, are obliterated and a new fictive affiliation is assigned: "son (or daughter) of Abraham."

We do not know how these early conversions—see also Esther 8:14, where a great number of Persians are said to have embraced Judaism out of fear of the recently empowered Jews—were effected. There may have been no fixed process for becoming a Jew before the beginning of the rabbinic era. To be a Jew one had to live like a Jew, and that probably involved, at least for the males, circumcision. This seems more like a simple act than a ritual since it could be performed by anyone, even a non-Jew, and it apparently served to do the job even without intent, and perhaps even resistance, on the subject's part. If we may trust Josephus, the Hasmonaean kings forcibly circumcised the Idumeans (Edomites) of the Negev and the Itureans of the Galilee and so rendered both people "Jewish" (*Antiquities* 13.9.1; 13.11.3). There is no record of the conversion of females.

Evidence suggests that becoming a Jew in the Second Temple era was relatively simple, a private affair without benefit of court, credential, or ritual. Jews were apparently eager to make converts after the return to Judaea, and Gentiles were equally eager to associate themselves, in one degree or another, with Jewish practices. Some Jews may even have permitted some form of conversion without benefit of circumcision, as Paul was doing with his Gentile converts to "Jesus messianism."

Becoming a Christian

Whether as a reaction to the minimalist view of who was a Jew or as a supplement to it, immersion begins to appear in something approaching a conversion context among the Jews in the first and second centuries. In the first century both the Essenes and the Baptists of John, including Jesus and his followers (John 3:22), practiced an immersion ritual in a purely symbolic way, that is, it does not appear to be connected with the purification from any specific ritual impurity. Later in Judaism, baptism regularly supplemented circumcision, as the Mishnah makes explicit, and among the Christians baptism replaced circumcision, at least among Paul's converts (1 Cor. 1:17; 12:13; Acts 8:12–13, etc.). In addition, Jewish circumcision had now to be performed with intent, on the part of both the circumciser and the subject. The intent to convert rather quickly implicated, one imagines, the notion of instruction of the convert. That latter soon becomes standard in both Judaism and Christianity, though it is done rather more formally in Christianity since there, as in Islam, it is the *only* way of joining the community.

Among Christians the initiatory baptism was originally administered by the bishop who headed the congregation the convert intended to join. As the formal guardian of the faith and morals of that congregation, the bishop was responsible for instructing the catechumens, "those under instruction (*katechesis*)." The term *proselyte*, or "newcomer," was preferred among Jews, though this latter term was eventually used in both communities to describe the convert-to-be. In the early Church prospective converts had to pass moral scrutiny—certain professions, like acting, were regarded with grave suspicion— as well as receive formal instruction, usually throughout the Lenten season, after which they were baptized and admitted to communion on the Saturday immediately preceding Easter Sunday.

Many of these safeguards grew out of a need to mark off, and so define, Christianity from the pagan religions that surrounded it. But as time passed and as a rapidly expiring paganism no longer posed a threat to an increasingly Christian world, the niceties of instruction were often disregarded even with adult converts. It was thought sufficient to baptize them first and, if possible, to instruct them later. Sacramental baptism, after all, made them Christians, not an understanding of their new faith.

"Jew and Greek"

Christianity differed from Judaism rather precisely on the matter of kinship affiliation. "God can raise up children of Abraham from these stones," John the Baptist shouted at his Jewish contemporaries (Matt. 3:9), and although Jesus did not exactly agree with his mentor on this point, his follower Paul assuredly did. Paul was prepared to grant the Gentiles membership among the Children of Abraham without benefit of circumcision, which had been demanded even of Abraham, or Torah observance, which had been required in some degree of every Israelite since Moses had come down from Sinai. Paul's program for the inclusion of the Gentiles was not the stringent rabbinic conversion rubric as preparation for what might appear to be a kind of second-class citizenship in a kinship society, but a declaration in effect of open borders inviting mass immigration into the ranks of the Chosen People.

Paul was proposing nothing less than equal citizenship for all. "There is no such thing as Jew or Greek, slave or free, man or woman; for you are all one in Christ Jesus. So if you belong to Christ, you are all the offspring of Abraham and heirs by virtue of the promise," he wrote (Gal. 3:28). In other words, no one was born a Christian; one became a Christian by an act of faith, signaled, as the physical act of circumcision had membership among the kin of Abraham, Isaac, and Israel, by a rite called baptism. But the simple act of pouring water and reciting a brief formula was more than Christianity's initiation ritual. Unlike circumcision, a passive rite whereby the community notched its identity marker on the male body of one of its own by birth, in baptism the initiatory act was necessarily preceded by a profession of faith. The initiate must say, in effect, "I have read and agree to the terms of the contract; I wish to become a member." Only then does a representative of the community respond by pouring the water and saying, "You are a member."

Religious Tolerance: The Romans on Jews and Christians

Understood as the willingness to abide the other, whether the "otherness" is physical, cultural, ethnic, or religious, tolerance is probably best thought of as essentially a personal and individual trait. But tolerance, or its absence, also manifests itself in social acts of forbearance or persecution. These forms of human behavior are the subject of a substantial body of law, both customary and positive, both human and divine. In the present context, we are chiefly concerned with the juridical side of toleration and with an otherness that is at base theological—that is, the religious differences that Jews, Christians, and Muslims, all worshipers of the same Creator God, discern in each other. Like many of the differences that disturb, these carry with them a strong sense of "sameness" or identity with that other.

The practice of tolerance, or in this case, intolerance, goes back to the very origins of monotheism. Among the first commandments Yahweh gave his Chosen People was the warning that he is a jealous God and that they should worship no other but him. The great body of Torah law that followed this programmatic statement had in fact as one of its primary ends the separation of his holy people from the unclean masses who surrounded them and whom Yahweh had "vomited" out of the promised land. The Torah set up a protective wall of purity around both the people and their God in his temple, a wall that later generations of Jews strove to make higher, sturdier, and more impermeable.

Building a political wall around Eretz Israel was a different matter, however, and here the Israelites showed a kind of pragmatic intolerance of the people who lived around them, sometimes in and sometimes just outside the land the Lord had promised them. Where the Israelites were strong enough to impose their will, they did; where they could not, as was increasingly the case after the Exile, they lived, with difficulty, and let live. Jewish sovereignty, and so the ability to dictate political, social, or religious terms to others, ends incrementally between 6 C.E. and 135 C.E. Thereafter, the Jews in Eretz Israel and the Mediterranean diaspora lived under Roman sovereignty and, more tellingly, Roman law.

To understand religious tolerance among the Greeks and Romans, it is first necessary to grasp the role of religion in their societies. Although it sometimes led to such, religious practice was not regarded in the ancient Mediterranean world as directed toward either personal piety or higher moral standards. Religion was an affect of society: its practice was a civic ritual and its officials, the priests, were civil magistrates. Religion was regarded chiefly as being useful in establishing and maintaining civic order. The Roman state, for example, cared little—it was a matter of indifference rather than toleration, perhaps—which other tribal, national, or household gods were worshiped so long as the imperial deities were given their ritual due as a matter of civic—we might say "patriotic"— duty and as long as those other rites did not disturb the public order.

Roman indifference may indeed have yielded to tolerance with the Jews. Most of their citizens and subjects were more than willing to worship a deified Roman emperor—polytheists are not fastidious in such matters and, furthermore, participating in those rites meant sharing afterward in the sacrificial meats, a not inconsiderable protein boost to the standard Mediterranean diet. The Jews, however, would not. The Romans did not much admire the Jews or their religious practices—*superstitio* was the term most often applied to them. But, like the Greeks before them, the Romans nonetheless permitted the Jews to abstain from rites precisely on the grounds that these were contrary to their religious convictions, and provided that the Jews prayed to their own God for the well-being of the emperor and the empire, which they generally did. The Jews, in short, were a religiously tolerated minority first in the empires of Alexander's successors and then in the imperium romanum. Because they could not fully participate in civic life, which entailed religious duties, they were barred from many civil privileges and protections.

As we have seen, the Romans identified the Jews as both a *natio* and a *religio*, an ethnic community like the Syrians and a religious community like the Druids. Initially the Christians, as a barely distinguishable Jewish sect, were protected by the same tolerant exemptions as the Jews as a whole. But soon the Romans too recognized that the Christians were not Jews. The exemptions disappeared and the Christians' refusal to join in emperor worship was henceforward regarded by the Romans as an act of civil disobedience and disloyalty. The Christians, like the Jews they once were, looked on religion as an autonomous obligation, not as an adjunct or extension of the state.

Their exemption removed, the Christians were increasingly subjected to state persecution—as opposed to private or public prejudice—in the third century: to be a Christian was in effect to commit a crime, even though no specific criminal act had been committed. Christians were regarded as doubly dangerous. They refused to worship the emperor, a primary act of Roman political identification, and, unlike the Jews, whose God and rituals could easily be construed as an ethnic aberration, the Christians were preaching a universal "City of God," as Augustine later called it. Their own vision of the world, and their loyalties, apparently had, no place for the imperium romanum. Some Christians—not nearly so many perhaps as legend depicts—were executed on that charge, and so became "witnesses" (*martyres*) to their faith (see II/6), or, from the Romans' perspective, paid for their disloyalty to the state with their lives.

The World Turns Christian

Counting in the premodern era was an inexact science, and the results often move from chance to fantasy if the ancient authorities are allowed to do the counting. According to Acts 1:15, shortly after the crucifixion of Jesus there were precisely 120 Christians, all of them in Jerusalem. But no more than thirty years later, "many thousands" of Jews in Jerusalem accepted Jesus as the Messiah, this in a city with a total population at that time no higher than 20,000 and as low as 10,000. Such growth is incredible; what was more likely being said, with the rhetorical numerical flourish favored by the times, was that God was favoring the new enterprise in a highly visible way.

If we leap over the intervening three centuries and come to the emperor Constantine's critical conversion to Christianity, a new question presents itself. Was that conversion political opportunism? Was Christianity the already discernible wave of the future? Here the estimate game must be played with larger and yet more concrete figures. Gibbon may have been the first to hazard a guess as to the numbers, that Christians were perhaps—it is always of course "perhaps"—5 percent of the total population of the Roman Empire when its ruler declared the new faith. Later historians have scaled the figure upward to 10 percent, and since present estimates put the empire's total population at 60 million, there would have been 5 to 7 million Christians among them. That amounts to a 40 percent growth rate per decade from Jesus' death until about 350 C.E. After that, the rate must have notably leveled off with the progressive shrinking of the pool of prospective converts.

At first conversions to the Christian faith would likely have spread along existing networks, principally families and friends, as they did among the earliest Muslims and still do in similar cases. The next group most likely to switch allegiances would seem to be those with weak religious affiliations of their own and, predictably, the alienated and discontented; again we must think of Muhammad's Meccan converts. There are no clear-cut signs of who these first wave of Christian converts might be—earlier proposals that they were chiefly slaves have been abandoned owing to lack of evidence—but it seems highly plausible that the Jesus movement made deep inroads in the Jewish communities of the Diaspora. Those Jews would be the most assimilated to the Greco-Roman "civil religion" of their environment. In the face of the disastrous destruction of the Jewish cult and political base in Palestine and the consequent Roman mistrust of Jews everywhere, they would also likely be the most drawn to what has been described as a form of "accommodated Judaism." Later European Jews in somewhat the same circumstances made their own "accommodation" with Reform Judaism, but here an alternative—a familiar yet new and different take on Judaism—readily presented itself in those Diaspora synagogues. Rabbinic Judaism, with its stiffened boundaries, may have been as much a product of nascent Christianity's attraction to assimilated Jews in the Diaspora like Philo—Paul himself was one such—as it was of internal dynamics within the Christian community.

> **Note:** Another group from which converts were drawn to Christianity is signaled by the early churches' apparent success in attracting women, particularly upper-class women, who then provided network access to the male members of their communities. Some reasons for this are fairly obvious. The new faith condemned not only infanticide but also divorce and male adultery, thereby providing Christian women in the ancient world far greater marriage security than their pagan counterparts. Christian women also married considerably later than pagans: according to recent estimates, nearly half of the latter had wed by age fourteen, many of them even before puberty, compared to only 20 percent of Christian women. Unlike in contemporary Jewish circles and the popular cult of Mithra, Christianity's chief pagan rival, Christian women held positions of honor and responsibility in early Christian congregations.

Religious Tolerance: Christians on Pagans and Jews

With Constantine's conversion, Christianity passed rapidly from being tolerated, to favored, and then finally in 381 C.E., to the official religion of the Roman Empire. The movement brought Christianity into a long-standing and often uneasy relationship with the political and legal institutions of a powerful, venerable, and highly conservative state (see I/7). It also carried the Christians into a new relationship with their religious rivals: Judaism on one hand, and the whole spectrum of pagan cults on the other. The Church had, obviously, a well-defined set of beliefs and the energy and conviction to attempt to convince others of the truth of those beliefs. It did just that, with considerable success among the *pagani*, those last lingering Gentiles in the outback, though with rapidly declining success among the Jews and almost none later among the Muslims. The Church had few means to coerce either belief or conformity save by calling on the state. In the case of the pagans, there was little hesitation to do so: imperial legislation was enacted—in the later Roman Empire only the emperor made law—making illegal the worship of any but the Christians' God. In 453 an imperial constitution declared pagans enemies of the state, and those convicted of such should have their goods confiscated and suffer execution. Pagan temples were destroyed, as often by mobs as by the state, and in 529 the emperor Justinian closed down not only the last tolerated pagan temple in the empire—it was at Aswan, where Nubians came across the frontier to trade and, formerly, to pray—but also the last bastion of intellectual paganism, Plato's Academy at Athens, still in operation after nearly a millennium. The faculty reputedly found asylum in Iran.

The Jews were protected by Roman statute, and though it was in its power to do so, the Church refrained from an outright prohibition, as it had done with the pagans. The Jews should be permitted to exist, Christian authorities like Augustine argued, to bear witness to the "Old Testament," which was Christianity's messianic charter, so to speak. As one medieval churchman put it, "Life is granted to the Jews—they are after all our slaves—because they bear the Mosaic Law and the Prophets which attest our faith. Not only in their books but in their appearance we see the Passion of Christ." The Jews were, in short, fossils preserved by time to attest to the antiquity of faith and bear witness to a lower and now petrified form of life that had been superseded and surpassed by Messianic Christianity. They served other ends as well. They testified to the severity of God's justice—the reference to their "appearance" in the text just cited points to their social degradation—and to the eschatological climax of the drama of redemption, when an unmistakable sign of the End Time will be the conversion of the Jews.

But if the Church officially refrained from doing violence to the Jews, a great many individual Christians did not. Christianity's increasing dominance in numbers and power, excited and inflamed by an emerging theology that cast the Jews as the murderers of Christ—the charge appears formally as early as the third-century *Homily on Passover* of Melito of Sardis—led to violence against Jewish persons and property, and the (now Christian) Roman state intervened by forbidding such acts. Paganism might be a crime, but being a Jew was not. Throughout their long and tortured relationship, Jews continued to be an officially tolerated religious minority as long as there was a Christian state.

The Need of Baptism, and of the Church

Baptism was central to membership in the Christian community, in the contrast, for instance, carefully made between the baptism of John and that of Jesus (Mark 1:8). The exact nature of the act came into sharp relief, however, in the increasingly fierce persecutions directed against Christians in the third century. It is not certain what Jesus' typically aphoristic remark in Matthew 12:30, "He who is not with me is against me," meant to signify in its original context, but to a bishop of Carthage named Cyprian (d. 256), those words were a clear statement that heretics and schismatics—those who had once been members of the Church but who had wandered from its teaching or its authority—could not expect to be saved. In the North Africa of Cyprian's day wholesale defections from the Church recurred in time of persecution—Cyprian himself lived through a major Roman persecution in the mid–third century. The question for bishops like Cyprian was thus whether Christians who had received baptism from the defectors had been truly baptized. No, announced Cyprian, there is no valid baptism outside the Church's baptism and indeed, "there is no salvation outside the Church."

Though his views on baptism had soon to be rethought, Cyprian's teaching on the necessity of membership in the one catholic (that is, universal) Church—"You cannot have God as your Father unless you have the Church as your mother" was another of his pronouncements—was often reaffirmed in the centuries that followed, notably in the influential Fourth Lateran Council of 1215. In their decree concerning the Albigensian heresy, the assembled bishops proclaimed that "There is one catholic Church of the faithful and outside it no one is saved." The most notorious echo of Cyprian, however, occurred about a century later. In 1302, in an effort to assert the Church's—and the papacy's—authority before the king of France, Boniface VIII issued his bull titled *Unam sanctam*, which in its opening words unequivocally declared: "There is one, holy, catholic Church, outside of which there is no salvation." None. For anyone.

Boniface had every right to be so thunderously confident in his doctrine of *nulla salus extra ecclesiam*, "no salvation outside the Church," since the same teaching had been commonplace in the Church from the beginning and persisted, quite unchanged, till the middle of the twentieth century. Indeed, it was broadened. The Council of Florence (1431–1443), in the wake of the East-West schism (see I/6), explicitly extended the doctrine beyond "deviants" to "infidels"—those like pagans, Jews, and Muslims, who had never believed in the first place: "No one outside the Church, not just pagans but Jews, heretics, and schismatics, can share in eternal life," it declared.

Augustine and the Donatists

Cyprian had had to address the rebaptism of returned heretics in the mid–third century: the issue became even more troublesome in the early fourth, provoked by the last great imperial attempt at obliterating the Christian movement. In 303 C.E. the emperor Diocletian decreed that the Christians' churches were to be destroyed, and that the clergy had to hand over the congregation's sacred books. These measures became even more severe the following year when all Christians were required, under pain of death, to sacrifice to the gods of the empire. The enforcement seems to have been particularly vigorous in the North African provinces, and there the reactions were varied and equally vigorous. Some Christians handed over—*traditor* or "hander-over," in context, a collaborator, soon became a slogan word—both the Scriptures and their brethren to avoid prosecution, while others held on to both the books and the faith to the bitter end.

When the persecutions were relaxed in 305 and again in 311, the Christian survivors emerged from their hiding places and a vengeful reaction soon set in. The records of the living and the dead, collaborators and resistance heroes, were all scrutinized. Old wounds were opened, old debts paid. In 311 what may have been local arguments rose to a higher level of discord. A cleric named Caecilian was elected—popular episcopal elections were still the order of the day—bishop of Carthage and, by virtue of that fact, chief bishop of Christian North Africa. Caecilian was associated with a moderate and conciliatory faction among the clergy and he was, moreover, consecrated by a another bishop some accused of being a traditor. This provoked outrage by the hard-liners who thought the blood of the persecution's martyrs was being betrayed. They were also convinced that Caecilian's consecration was invalid since it had been performed by a traditor who had in effect left the Church. They elected and consecrated their own candidate, Majorinus, who soon died and was succeeded by a certain Donatus who gave his name to the entire movement, Donatism, that emerged from the affair.

At that juncture the converted Christian Constantine became emperor. He authorized an investigation into the matter that was spiraling out of control, but he referred the final decision to the bishop of Rome, Pope Miltiades (r. 311–314). He and his consulting bishops reviewed the evidence and found for Caecilian. Donatus and his fellow bishops—a dual hierarchy had rapidly developed in North Africa—were to surrender the churches that had come into their hands. Constantine was not pleased—the Donatists as the self-proclaimed Church of the Martyrs had popular support in the North African provinces—and he summoned a council of all the Western bishops to assemble at Arles in 314 and adjudicate the matter. They did—the new pope, Sylvester (r. 314–335) declined to attend on grounds of propriety and set a long-range precedent—and once again decided for Caecilian and against Donatus. They also laid down some doctrinal points. Christians were forbidden, contrary to what Cyprian had taught, to rebaptize returned traditores: baptism was baptism, and an indelible sign, no matter how evil the priest administering it.

Constantine was still not content. He summoned Caecilian and Donatus to the imperial court in Milan and heard the case in person. In the end, he agreed with the Arles bishops. Caecilian was the true bishop of Carthage; the Donatists must vacate their churches immediately. With imperial support on their side, the Catholics, for so the Council of Arles had judged them, began to carry the day. Some of the Donatist bishops were bought into submission (from the imperial treasury), some beaten into it by church and state alike, and some simply gave up. But with the accession to the throne in 361 of the convinced anti-Christian Julian, the picture altered once again. Determined to create as many problems as possible for the Church, Julian restored to the Donatists their churches and properties across North Africa. It was a time of extraordinary violence in the North African churches. The emperor's acts were matched, however, by the ordination in 395 of Augustine as bishop of Hippo, a place where there was, as in most North African cities, a Donatist bishop as well.

Augustine argued the illegitimacy of the movement on historical grounds, on the Donatists' highly inconsistent application of their own principles, and, finally, on his development of the doctrine of the nature of baptism. With Augustine as their spokesman, the Catholics now felt they had an unassailable historical and doctrinal position, and they persuaded the emperor Honorius to convene a public inquest in the form of a debate between the two sides. The disputation was held at Carthage in 411 before the imperial legate. Augustine and the Catholics obviously prevailed, and the emperor's legate gave them the judgment. In 412 Honorius issued a law once again bidding the Donatists surrender their ecclesiastical properties to the Catholics and fining those who refused. Though there were occasional battles down to the Muslims' arrival in the 630s and 640s, the war against the Donatists was effectively over.

Consensual and Coerced Conversion

Membership in the Christian community, was thought to be, as we have seen, consensual: Christians were made, not born. The making of Christians turned out to be a troublesome matter, however. Baptism has already been described as an act that required a prior profession of faith in God, Christ, and the Church. So it did early on and still does in the case of adult baptism, but the increasingly widespread practice of infant baptism, with its presumption that others might speak for the child, turned baptism into an act whose initiatory effect took place by its performance alone or *ex opere operato*, as the medieval Latin shorthand had it. It seemed like an easy way of making the reluctant into Christians: stand (or tie) the prospect in place, pour the water, and recite the formula, not just for the sheer pleasure of it, of course, but to save souls for Christ, particularly intransigent, unyielding souls who would never be reasonably converted.

"Intransigent, unyielding souls" is a passably accurate Christian description of Jews and Muslims, and Christians faced with such resistance have often wrestled with the question of forced conversion. Some jurists would permit it, but the more general sentiment was not very different from the Muslims' own. Muslims and Jews might be fought if they resisted—an argument that had more force with respect to armed and politically aggressive Muslims—but once they submitted, they ought to be neither killed nor forced to convert. But behind this conviction there was the always formidable figure of Augustine, whose exposure to the stubborn Donatists had convinced him that some coercive persuasion was legitimate. Others disagreed. Sisebut, the Visigothic king of Spain (r. 612–620), ordered the conversion of all the Jews in his domains, but a council of Spanish bishops held in Toledo in 633 presided over by Isidore of Seville rebuked the king and for the first time laid down that baptism must be voluntary and without coercion, citing Paul: "Therefore He has mercy on whom He will have mercy and whom He wills He hardens" (Rom. 9:18). But, the council's decree continued, the Jews who had already been converted were obliged to remain in the Church "to avoid blasphemy and cheapening of the Faith."

This was the Church's common teaching down to the end of the Middle Ages. It received its canonical form in the *Summa theologiae* (2–2.10.8) of Thomas Aquinas (d. 1274), who drew an initial distinction between those who have never received the faith, in which case they cannot be baptized or converted against their will, and those who were once among the faithful, whom Thomas concluded could be forcibly returned to the faith. But an important proviso provoked considerable discussion in the sixteenth century. The infidels, if they could not be converted by force, could be forcibly restrained from hindering Christian missionaries and from insulting Christ and the Christians.

An additional consideration arose out of the very nature of Christian baptism. As a sacramental act, baptism indelibly marked the soul of the baptized. Hence, it was argued, although coerced baptism might be illegal in the eyes of canon law, it was valid—that is, the baptized had, willy-nilly, become a Christian. Eventually, a lawyer's compromise emerged, and in 1210 Pope Innocent III decreed that if the infidel was, despite persistent refusal, literally forced to be baptized—bound, gagged, and baptized, so to speak—the baptism was invalid: it did not take. But if the same infidel was threatened, by terror or torture, for example, and then acceded to baptism to escape the consequences of further refusal, such a baptism was valid: the baptized was a Christian and also, somewhat more ominously, subject to Church law.

Forced conversion only works, of course, where the converter has the power to coerce, in fourteenth- and fifteenth-century Spain, for example, where the Christian Reconquista swept appreciable numbers of Jews and Muslims under Christian sovereignty. The Church, as we have just seen, had decided that the conversions of its new infidel subjects elicited by threats was acceptable practice, with the comforting pragmatic consideration that even if one could not trust the faith of the "New Christian" converts, their children at least would be genuine Catholics. Such bankrupt policies have their own penalties, and in the end the Spanish Church could not live with the hypocrisy and perjury it had itself engendered by forcing the so-called Marranos and Moriscos into the bosom of Mother Church. It expelled them all.

The Jews of Western Christendom

To the Roman guarantee of acceptance of Jewish beliefs (which were never really an issue) and practices (which often were), the Church of Latin Christendom added the guarantee of protection. It was desperately needed. Christian theology, particularly its rhetorical echo in public preaching, painted a grim and provocatively hostile portrait of the Jews. The Jews emerged not merely as stiff-necked deniers of Jesus' redemptive mission but even as deicides, the veritable murderers of the God-man Jesus. These sentiments were pronounced continuously in sermon and liturgy, often enhanced by hard political, social, or economic circumstances for which the Jews might, reasonably or unreasonably, be held responsible, and often excited local populations to resort to violent acts against their Jewish neighbors.

The Church's earliest statements of toleration and protection of the Jews were resumed and codified in Gratian's authoritative twelfth-century collection of Church canons, the *Decretum* (see II/4), which refers back to and validates the decrees of earlier sixth- and seventh-century Spanish synods. The papal and synodal decrees on the same subject are reaffirmed and updated in a later collection of canon law, the *Decretals* (1234) edited by the Dominican Raymond of Peñaforte. Raymond was, in fact, one of the most aggressive and relentless prosecutors of his century's program to convert the Jews and Muslims.

In these documents, the Jews' right to be publicly and forthrightly Jewish is affirmed, as is the secure possession of their lives, their properties, and their places of worship. But limitations were set as well, many of them reminiscent of the limitations Muslims placed on the People of the Book living under their sovereignty (see I/8). Jews might not hold public office or own Christian slaves; they should not appear in public on Good Friday. Christians were forbidden to fraternize with Jews (or Muslims), socially or sexually, and to make this segregation easier to observe and enforce, Jews—and Muslims—living in Christian lands were required to wear distinctive garb. Finally, Jews were not to be forced into conversion—as the Quran put it, "There is no coercion in religion" (2:256) —but if one of them should be forcibly baptized, this latter sacrament was to be recognized as valid and the subject regarded as a Christian. In consequence, baptized Jewish children were to be removed from their parents and sent to monasteries or orphanages for rearing in the faith.

> **Note:** The practice of separating and rearing baptized children apart
> from their parents did not end in the Middle Ages. In Bologna in 1853 an
> illiterate Catholic servant girl secretly baptized Edgardo Mortara, the
> year-old son of the Italian Jewish couple, for whom she worked, because,
> as she later said, he was ill and appeared to be in danger of dying. Five
> years later, when she revealed what she had done, the police had no
> choice but to come to the Mortara home and take the six-year-old
> Edgardo from his parents. Church law decreed that Catholic children, of
> whom Edgardo was now one, not be raised by Jews. Since Bologna was
> part of the Papal States, the areas of Italy where the pope still exercised
> political sovereignty, Church law was also the law of the land (see I/7).
>
> The canonical kidnapping of Edgardo Mortara created an interna-
> tional storm with many voices, Jewish and Christian, demanding the re-
> turn of the boy to his parents. To no avail: the then pope, the deeply
> conservative Pius IX (r. 1846–1878), took a personal interest in Edgardo
> and supervised his education. At thirteen, the young man entered a sem-
> inary and was eventually ordained under the name of his mentor. Father
> Pio, once Edgardo Mortara, died in 1940, by all accounts a pious
> Catholic and a model priest to the end.

Some of the reasons for this degree of toleration of a people regarded as
"perfidious" have already been scouted. The very existence of the Jews confirmed the fact of divine revelation: they too affirmed the Word of God and
lived in accordance with it. In a negative and perhaps more psychologically
appealing sense, the generally miserable condition of the "outcast" Jews,
Europe's gypsies before the letter, graphically and publicly illustrated the
transfer of the Covenant from them to the powerful and dazzlingly prosperous Christian Church.

The degrees of toleration (and restriction) afforded to the Jews by medieval
legislation were not always executed or enforced uniformly. Popular feeling,
fanned as often as not by the Church's own preaching, frequently overmastered Church teaching. Moreover, the Church was not the state, and in many
cases secular sovereigns, for whom the Jews might be commercially or finan-
cially useful, were generally more reliable protectors of Jewish lives and property than the Church. Then too, in the twelfth century, the theologians of
Europe's new universities, who also laid claim to the magisterium—the power
to speak for the Church—began to shift emphasis away from Scripture, where
Jews had their only legitimacy in Christian eyes, to more rational bases where
Jews had no standing at all. Finally, Christians were made increasingly
aware by Jewish apostate converts to Christianity of the contents of the
Talmud and other postbiblical Jewish writings with a discernible anti-
Christian bias. By the beginning of the thirteenth century, Jews had become

an institutionalized degraded minority, perhaps best symbolized by the Fourth Lateran Council's 1215 decree that Jews must wear distinctive clothing. The Church brought enough pressure on their monarchs to cause the Jews to be expelled in 1290 from England, in 1306 from France, and in 1492 from Spain.

The Talmud on Trial

As we have seen, the Church was long thought to have had no direct jurisdiction over Jews and Muslims as such, save to designate them as legitimate objects of evangelization or in cases where a Jew or Muslim living in Christendom might commit some offense against a Christian belief, ritual, or person. That understanding was dramatically altered by two popes in the thirteenth century, Gregory IX (r. 1227–1241) and Innocent IV (r. 1243–1254), both canon lawyers before their elevation to the papacy. In 1239 Gregory sent a letter to the archbishops of England, France, León, and Castile ordering them to confiscate all the Jewish books in their sees and hand them over to the Franciscans and Dominicans for scrutiny. His specific target was the Talmud, "the Teaching, as it is called" and "the principal cause of the Jews' obstinate perfidy," as he noted in his letter.

The immediate provocation of this act was an uproar in France brought about by Nicholas Donin, an apostate from Judaism and a convert to Christianity, who publicly attacked the Talmud as the repository of Jewish heresy and blasphemous hostility toward Christianity. His charges were loud and long enough to bring about a public disputation in 1240 in Paris before Louis IX. Donin played the prosecutor and a number of French rabbis served as lawyers for the defense at what was almost literally a trial of the Talmud. Not surprisingly, the Talmud was convicted. Gregory's earlier letter was implemented and, in 1244, twelve or twenty-four cartloads of books confiscated from the Jews of Paris were publicly burned.

The alleged crux of the matter was, as Gregory had said, the Talmud, the collection of legal exegesis and commentary at the heart of rabbinic Judaism (see II/3). The Talmud was more than an ideological and legal guide for Jews; it was also inaccessible. The Bible may have been expropriated by the Christians as their "Old Testament," but this testament to the oral Torah remained an entirely Jewish possession. According to one rabbinic story, when Moses received the oral Torah on Sinai, he asked the Lord to write it down and God replied: "I did indeed wish to give it all to them in writing, but it was revealed that the Gentiles would in the future have dominion over them, and will claim the Torah as theirs; then would my children be like the Gentiles. Therefore, give them the Scriptures in writing, and the Mishnah, Haggadah, and Talmud orally, for it is they that separate Israel and the Gentiles."

The Parisian setting of this auto-da-fé was not entirely fortuitous. The city was also the home of Europe's fledgling and most prestigious university. In 1231 Gregory had warned the theologians there to avoid the recent trend toward study of Hebrew texts. Students at Paris had been dipping their toes in the vast ocean of Jewish exegesis and the more traditional theologians were becoming disturbed. Gregory intended to curb the practice by removing the most dangerous, and offensive, of those texts from the Christian scholars' hands.

In 1244 Innocent IV, immediately after his accession, issued a bull, *Impia Iudaeorum*, which extended the Church's jurisdiction over the Jews in a new and notable way. The bull is full of vitriol: the Jews, with whom Christians were prepared to live in peace, repaid the Church's tolerance with patent infidelity, not toward Christian teachings, which they refused to accept, but to their own revelation, the Bible, which they and the Christians shared. The Jews were no longer faithful to Scripture. Innocent, the professional canon lawyer, argued, here and elsewhere, that the pope, as the vicar of Christ, who has dominion over all, possessed both the right and the responsibility of seeing that the Jews lived according to both the natural and the biblical law since their own leaders did not do so.

This was the background against which Innocent made his canonical ruling against the Talmud "which is a great book for them [the Jews] and which goes far beyond the Bible and which blasphemes against God and His Christ and the Blessed Virgin, and which they use to teach and nourish their children and render them distant and alien to the Law and the Prophets." It was by no means the end of the Talmud or of Christian attempts to suppress it and its influence. In Spain there were two more notorious show trials of the Talmud. The first took place in Barcelona in 1263 when another Jew-turned-Christian, the Dominican Pablo Christiá, made the accusations and one of the greatest Jewish scholars of the Middle Ages, Moses ben Nahman, or Nahmanides (d. 1270), was the defendant (see below). Later, in 1413, a two-year trial began in Tortosa, prosecuted by another converted Jew and the Dominican firebrand Vincente Ferrer.

Christians, Muslims, and Jews in Spain

Spain, the Arabs' al-Andalus, had a quite different religio-cultural tradition from most of Europe; only Sicily and the Balkans present parallels. In Iberia large numbers of Christians and Muslims lived for many centuries in principalities that made war on and alliances with one another irrespective of religion. Christians (called Mozarabs, or "would-be Arabs," because of their high degree of assimilation) lived under Muslim princes, and Muslims (Mudejars, or "permitted," because they were allowed to continue to practice their religion) lived under Christian ones. Amid both groups lived a substantial number of Jews. The three communities by no means loved one another, but there was a degree of respect and, more obviously, an effective degree of *convivencia*, or coexistence. It was, perhaps, forbearance rather than genuine toleration. Convivencia was most apparent on the local level, but in more ideological quarters forces of disequilibrium were constantly at work. One destabilizing force were fundamentalist Muslim Berber groups from North Africa like the Almoravids (Ar. *al-murabitun*). These were Muslim "military monks"—the *ribat* was a kind of fortified monastery—who overthrew the reigning Muslim princes and annexed al-Andalus to their North African empire. Christians and Jews in those newly conquered lands were immediately subjected to persecution, as were the Spanish Muslims whose faith or works did not measure up to severe Almoravid standards.

The process was repeated in the twelfth century. This time the Berber invaders were called Almohads (Ar. *al-muwahhidun*, or "Unitarians"). Between 1145 and 1150 they were masters of southern Spain and once again launched persecutions against Jews and Christians and purges of their fellow Muslims, among them the philosopher Ibn Rushd (see II/7). Twice, then, the generally tolerant and gracious-living Muslims of al-Andalus were reformed from within by their more fundamentalist Berber coreligionists from the Saharan margins of Islamic society.

While all this was occurring, in northern Iberia the notion of a Christian Reconquista of Muslim Spain was laying hold of both the chivalrous nobility and the Church's hierarchy. But if it was a reconquest, it was not yet a crusade. In its earliest stages the war against the Muslim states in Spain was desultory and somewhat inconclusive, though by hindsight it is clear that Christian arms were becoming superior to the Muslim capability to resist them. The Christians took Toledo in 1085, Saragossa in 1118, and in 1212 a combined Christian army met the Almohads at Las Navas de Tolosa, east of Cordoba, and broke them. Cordoba itself fell to Christian forces in 1236, Valencia in 1238, and Seville in 1248. The final stage merely waited on the unification of Christian Spain, which was effectively accomplished in 1469 by the marriage of Ferdinand of Aragon to Isabella of Castile. Granada finally capitulated in January 1492. The Reconquista was complete.

The Christian conquest of al-Andalus had tragic consequences for Jewish and Muslim Spaniards. Hardening Christian attitudes toward the Jews had little to do with Spain or the reconquest, as has already been noted; this was a European phenomenon. The Reconquista did, however, transfer ever increasing numbers of Spanish Jews from the more tolerant Muslim sovereignty to an increasingly severe and suspicious Christian one. It did the same with the Muslims. After the fall of Granada in 1492, all of Spain's remaining Muslims lived under Christian rule. In the early stages of the conquest the old convivencia prevailed and the change of sovereignty was explicitly understood, in the "Capitulations" signed at Granada, for example, to entail no change in religion. But the Muslims were too numerous, perhaps, and the Church too fearful, to abide by that agreement. Forced baptism, as understood in Church law, seemed the only solution. First it was imposed on the Jews, who as *conversos* were only partially successful in convincing the "Old Christians" that they had truly embraced the Christian faith. Christian suspicion manifested itself in the judicial instrument that lay ready to hand, the Inquisition (see I/5).

The Christian War on Islam: Peter the Venerable and Ramon Lull

The Reconquista was merely the political side of a war the Church was waging against Islam. Islam raised military threats to Christendom's well-being that Judaism never had or would, but Muslims, if more politically dangerous and more exotic to Western Christians, bore none of the heavy historical baggage that the Jews did in Christian eyes. That, perhaps, inspired some to think Islam might be conquered by means other than the sword.

While visiting Spain, Peter the Venerable (d. 1156), abbot of the Cistercian monastery of Cluny in France (see II/8), conceived of a project to assist in converting Muslims. It required a dossier that was to contain, among other pieces, a translation of the Quran, in Latin, of course. Peter persuaded the Englishman Robert of Ketton (d. 1157), a distinguished translator who had come to Spain to work on Arabic treatises in mathematics and astronomy, to put aside his scientific work and undertake the task—for a quite handsome sum, it must be added. It took Robert somewhat more than a year to complete the translation—he possibly had help; there was a Muslim on Peter's team, "to guarantee the fidelity" of the translation, and he may have worked with Robert—but when finished in 1143, this work, known early on as *The Religion of Mahumet, the False Prophet, which in Arabic is called Alchoran, that is, The Collection of Teachings*, became an international best-seller. It was included in Peter the Venerable's anthology of works on Islam, together with Robert's translation of a collection of Arab historical traditions generously titled "The Lying and Laughable Chronicles of the Saracens."

Robert of Ketton's Latin translation of the Quran is a large, sprawling work—but it is more properly a paraphrase since the translator incorporated extensive material from the elaborate apparatus of Muslim commentary available in Arabic on this holiest of books. (A second, more literal Latin translation was done at the request of the archbishop of Toledo in Spain in 1210–1211, by Mark of Toledo, a Mozarab Christian and another professional translator of Arabic science, but it never enjoyed the popularity of Robert's.) Robert of Ketton had turned, somewhat surprisingly, given the polemic nature of the collection and his own admission in his preface of hostility toward Islam, to the

Muslims themselves for an explanation of their Scripture. This first and widely read Latin Quran was, then, if not a perfectly accurate referent to what the Quran actually said, a reliable index to what Muslims understood it to say.

One of the Middle Ages' more interesting and prodigiously productive personalities, Ramon Lull (d. 1316), was known on occasion as the "crazy man" or the "Arabic Christian." He was a Catalan—"the founder of Catalan prose" is another of his claims to fame—born in 1232 on cosmopolitan Majorca into a Mediterranean world where the political tide was turning against Islam. Between 1226 and 1248 Muslim holdings in Iberia were reduced from one-third of the peninsula to the tiny amirate of Granada squeezed into the southeastern corner (where it would survive, in this reduced and impotent state, for another two and a half centuries). Castile and Aragon became enlarged in both land and population by these early thirteenth-century conquests. Castile gained an additional 10 percent in its population, but Aragon grew by a striking 30 percent, and a large number of the new subjects to the Crown were Muslims. These latter were the Mudejares, the Muslims now living in Christendom, and their presence proved both a threat and a challenge, not so much to the sovereign, who found them useful, but to the Church.

The Church's reaction to both challenge and threat was sparked by the Dominicans, a Catholic order of friars (< *fratres*, "brethren") founded by the Spaniard Dominic de Guzman with papal approval in 1216 (see II/8). Their primary mission was to preach, in the first instance against Cathar heretics in the south of France (see I/5), but their mandate was quickly broadened and they became the principal agents of the Spanish Inquisition. They were in the forefront of the missionary effort directed at the Muslims with new enthusiasm in the thirteenth century. In the wake of Christendom's stunning reversal of political fortune in Spain, there were newly buoyed hopes that Christianity's religious war against Islam would likewise reap new successes. For some years there had been a Church-run Arabic studies program on Majorca, and in 1250, (St.) Raymond of Peñaforte (d. 1275), the eminent Catalan canon lawyer and former master general of the Dominicans, sent eight Dominican friars to study Arabic there in preparation for a proselytizing mission among the Muslims.

Among the newly trained Arabists was Ramon Martí, who in the next twenty-five years spearheaded Spanish Christian polemic against the Jews and Muslims. Besides writing several works attacking both faiths, Martí was present, along with Raymond of Peñaforte, at the already noted public debate in Barcelona between Nahmanides and Pablo Christiá that was held before James I in 1263. In 1268–1269 Martí was in Tunis attempting, unsuccessfully, to convert its Muslim ruler to Christianity. It was he who carried Raymond's request to Thomas Aquinas, his old schoolmate and the reigning Christian theologian at the university of Paris, to write a summa against the infidels (*Contra Gentiles*, 1270–1272), wherein purely rational arguments were laid out to convince a Muslim of the truths of Christianity.

In this climate Lull resolved, rather impetuously, to write a book, "the best in the world against the errors of the unbelievers." Even before that, he thought, he would go to the pope and the Christian princes "to get them to institute, in whatever kingdoms or provinces might be appropriate, monasteries in which selected monks and others fit for the task would be brought together to learn the language of the Saracens and other unbelievers." This would provide the personnel "to preach and demonstrate to the Saracens and other unbelievers the holy truth of the Catholic faith."

With little encouragement from his Church but under the impulse of repeated "illuminations," Lull undertook his own campaign against Islam. He learned Arabic well enough to compose works in that language and he devoted his prodigious literary energies to fashioning and perfecting "The Art," a form of interfaith discourse that (1) did not rely on Scripture and so transcended the belief systems of the Jews, Christians, and Muslims, and (2) was constructed on the most fundamental principles he could divine, what he called the "Absolute Principles." Lull was trying to reach back, or up, to a level of abstraction where all three sets of believers could agree. He pushed even further in his quest for the deep structure of truth: the Absolutes themselves he reduced to letters of the alphabet to better manipulate them in his "combinatory art." His own writings, this aggressive and confident layman argued to the pope, would be far more effective in convincing the infidel Jews and Muslims than Scripture itself.

In 1275 Lull finally persuaded the king to open the first European school on Near Eastern Studies (including Arabic) in the Franciscan monastery of Miramar on Majorca. The institute was confirmed by papal bull in 1276 and survived until sometime after 1292. Lull subsequently attempted to persuade a succession of popes—and a Church council—to open other schools of Arabic like that at Miramar and, ever the tireless publicist, arranged for himself to give a lecture on the Universal Art at the university of Paris. It created no stir, but the lack of academic enthusiasm did not prevent him from returning to Paris again and again to castigate the faculty for relying on Aristotle and Averroes (see II/7) and for neglecting the ever growing number of works of Ramon Lull.

Lull made it to Islamic territory three times to put the Art to work first hand. The initial occasion was in Tunis, where he arrived in 1293 and immediately "engaged the men most versed in the Mohammadan religion," as his autobiography puts it. On the pretext that he might be interested in converting to Islam, Lull invited arguments on its behalf, which he then refuted with arguments of his own. The game was soon up, however, and after a spell in prison, he was deported on the orders of the local sultan. Not long afterward Lull was distracted by news of the Mongols' breaking into Syria and threatening to take Jerusalem. These events prompted the Syrian jurist Ibn Taymiyya (d. 1328) to issue his fatwas declaring the Mongols, who were professedly Muslims, to be unbelievers and so the objects of Muslim jihad (see

I/5), but for Lull and many others in Europe, the Mongols seemed like prospective converts who might rid Christendom of Islam for good. Lull went to the Latin kingdom of Cyprus and begged the Lusignan king there to send him to either the Mongol khan or the sultan of Egypt so that he might persuade one or the other or both to convert. The king declined.

In 1307, rebuffed in all his projects and expectations, Lull sailed for Bougie in what is today eastern Algeria for one last attempt—he was then seventy-four years old—at convincing reasonable Muslims of the truth of Christianity. He stood up in the public square and announced loudly in Arabic: "The Christian religion is true and the Saracen religion is false and filled with errors and this I am prepared to prove." The attendant crowd was prepared to dispatch him on the spot, but he was saved by the city's chief justice, the qadi or mufti, who also fancied himself a philosopher. They argued as reasonable men will, but the qadi soon unreasonably concluded that the visitor might be more quickly convinced of the truth of Islam in jail. Lull remained there for six months writing up his side of the argument until the local ruler had had enough and ordered the troublesome Catalan deported.

Lull returned in time to appear at the Council of Vienne (1311–1312) and argue once again for the establishment of Eastern-language schools. The bishops agreed, and Canon 11 of the council decreed the teaching of Arabic, Hebrew, and "Chaldean" (Syriac) at the universities of Paris, Bologna, Salamanca, and at the Papal Court to prepare students for missionary work. Then a startling development occurred at Tunis. The throne there was seized by a usurper who, in order to get a Christian alliance to defend him against local Muslim enemies, professed interest in converting to Christianity. So in 1314 Lull was again, after twenty-one years, back in Tunis. He got his chance to argue his case once more, orally and in writing, but after December 1315 we hear no more of him. Lull died sometime in early 1316 either in Tunis on the way back or in Majorca, where he is buried. He was eighty-four years old and had written altogether 265 books. Many of them were short pamphlets, but ten of them were between 150,000 and 250,000 words, one of 400,000 words, and one a staggering tome of nearly a million.

What of the Infidels?

Canon law has to do with regulating the behavior of Christians, not merely the true and faithful members of the Church but even those heretics and schismatics who had left or been thrust out of the Church yet were nonetheless still subject—baptism was, after all, an indelible sign—to the Church's jurisdiction. And what of the infidels, the Jews and Muslims, Buddhists and Hindus who were never part of the Church? For a very long time not much mind was paid to the distant Buddhists, Hindus, or other "heathen" residents far beyond the pale. But Jews and Muslims—Saracens, they were generally called—lived, the former throughout Europe, the latter in Spain, Sicily, and the crusader states in the Middle East, under Christian political sovereignty. The Muslims beyond the borders of Christendom constituted, furthermore, an enormous political threat to Christian Europe from the seventh to the seventeenth century. Eventually they too attracted the attention of the canon lawyers.

In Gratian's *Decretum* of 1140, only passing attention is paid to the Jews and even less to the "infidels," in both cases as the Christians' subjects. Debates with Jews and infidels were encouraged to hasten conversion to Christianity, whereas marriage with either group was discouraged because it was feared just the opposite would occur. By the time Gregory IX's *Decretals* were published in 1234, both the political landscape and the lawyers' concerns had shifted. Jews and Muslims were now regarded separately. The Jews were still treated in the context of being Christians' subjects, but the political threat of Islam was now recognized—in the ban on dealing with Muslims in arms or war materials, for example. The Crusades themselves are not taken up, however, as matter for legal consideration.

Christian-infidel relations received their first substantial treatment at the hands of Innocent IV (r. 1243–1254), himself a canon lawyer, who cast his remarks in the form of a commentary on a decretal of his predecessor, Innocent III (r. 1198–1216). *Quid super his* became the foundation of much of what followed. Is it licit, he asked, to invade the infidels' lands and, if so, why? The answer was "yes"; the Muslims were in illegal possession of lands that belonged by right to Christians, from whom they had seized them, particularly the Holy Land, "which was rightfully Christian because Christ's life and death there had consecrated the land." In the famous Donation of Constantine that emperor had specifically ceded Judaea to Pope Sylvester I (r. 314–335) and his successors (see I/7). More recently in 1229, the Holy Roman emperor Frederick II (r. 1215–1250) had by negotiation with its Muslim ruler come into legal possession of Jerusalem, a city no longer in his or any other Christian sovereign's possession.

Innocent held that the infidels, which in this context meant principally the Muslims, could choose their own forms of government, but that the pope, as the vicar of Christ, had charge of the care of their souls, a right he possessed de jure if not de facto. Although the Muslims were free to govern themselves, the pope still had the right to intervene politically in their affairs when, for example, the Muslim ruler violated, or allowed his Muslim subjects to violate, with impunity the natural law, that law immanent in all creation and to which all humankind was subject. Just as God had intervened against the perversions of Sodom and Gomorrah, which were bound not by the Torah but by natural law, so the pope could summon the princes of Christendom to invade Muslim lands, though his agents could not impose baptism there, as we have seen, since this was a voluntary act.

Innocent's argument went a step further. Given Jesus' command to the Apostles to "go to all nations and make them my disciples" (Matt. 28:19), the pope had an obligation to send missionaries to the Muslim and other infidel lands; if the infidels prevented them from entering or persecuted them for preaching or, indeed, persecuted any of their own Christian subjects, the pope was justified in dispatching Christian forces to invade those lands and even depose their ruler. Christian princes did not possess this right of themselves. Only the pope could send them into the infidel lands.

Although Innocent IV was willing to grant the infidels political control over their own lands—provided they had not been illegally seized from Christians—not everyone agreed. The canon lawyer Henry of Susa (d. 1271), better known as Hostiensis—he was bishop of Ostia, hence the sobriquet—wrote his own commentary on *Quod super his* in which he put forward the opinion that with the coming of Christ "every office and all government authority and sovereignty and jurisdiction was taken from every infidel lawfully . . . and granted to the faithful through Him who has the supreme power and who cannot err." Infidels ought then to be subjected to Christian sovereignty, and if they were, according to Hostiensis, they should be permitted to keep their property, possessions, and offices. Hostiensis was not advocating immediate invasion of the infidels' lands; a number of Crusades had already illustrated the folly of that. The dispatch of missionaries was a more practical step.

In the fourteenth and fifteenth centuries, the canonists turned their attention to the infidel Muslims in a somewhat different landscape. In Spain the Christian reconquest of the Muslim domains came to its triumphant conclusion with the surrender of Granada in 1492. The act was perfectly legal, according to the canonists, since the Christians were merely taking back from the infidels a land that had once, seven centuries earlier, belonged to them. They were further justified by the barbarous condition of the infidels. The Muslims were not, in the new view, part of Christ's flock, as Innocent IV had argued, but undomesticated wild beasts, the "wild ass" descendants of Ishmael referred to in Genesis (16:12). But once conquered and pacified, property rights again asserted their ascendancy: the Muslims were to be permitted to keep their goods and properties.

Muslims, Christians . . . and Other Christians in the Balkans

If the Arab and Berber movement into Spain in the eighth century created Muslim settlement on Europe's southwestern frontier, the Ottoman Turkish conquest of the Balkan states in the fourteenth and fifteenth centuries produced an equally notable Muslim presence on its southeastern frontier. When the Turks arrived in the mid–fourteenth century, the Balkans were already a mixture of peoples: in the north and center, mostly Slavs, who had begun to arrive in the sixth and seventh centuries; in the south, Greeks, with some indigenous Illyrian peoples squeezed up against the Adriatic coast on the west. There were budding national aspirations among the Balkan peoples, and already some of them, the Serbs and Bulgars, for example, were in the process of freeing themselves from the sovereignty of Byzantium—the Christian Greek-speaking Roman Empire of the East, with its capital at Constantinople—if not from the Byzantine political and cultural tradition.

One tradition the peoples of the Balkans had received from the Christian Roman Empire was Christianity itself. The brothers Cyril and Methodius, later venerated as saints, carried the Gospels to the Slavs in the mid–ninth century, but by the mid–thirteenth the Christianized Slavs were already divided along the same Latin Catholic/Greek Orthodox fault-line that had become formalized in the great East-West schism of 1054 (see I/6). The Croats and Slovenes in the northwest (as later the Czechs, Slovaks, and Poles) were, and remain, Latin Catholic, and attached to Rome; the Bulgars and Serbs to the east and south were Orthodox, though not tied quite so firmly to Constantinople.

By the middle of the fourteenth century the Muslim Turks were on hand in the Balkans, and from then until roughly 1700, when the tide had turned against them, the Ottomans exercised sovereignty over most of the Balkans up to the gates of Vienna in the west and well into Russian lands on the east. From the beginning the Turks did not simply occupy the land; they absorbed it into their empire, which stretched eastward to Iraq and south along the Mediterranean from Egypt to Algeria. Local Ottoman governors were appointed in the new Balkan provinces, and the Ottoman bureaucracy administered them. These functionaries were few in number, however, and to strengthen their hold the Ottomans colonized the conquered lands with Turkic (and Muslim) people brought in from Anatolia and elsewhere. The newcomers fanned out northward from Constantinople (which the Ottomans took in 1453 and made their capital) into the European hinterland in Thrace and Thessaly, and then northward through the eastern Balkans. They chiefly settled around fortified points and in the river valleys that were the peninsula's chief and most strategic trade routes. The Christian population withdrew northward into the more mountainous areas beyond Turkish control and interest.

The Turkish Muslim colonists helped stabilize the Ottoman presence yet had little effect on the Balkans in the long run. Many of them remigrated to Constantinople and Anatolia during the Balkan political upheavals of the late nineteenth and early twentieth centuries. Of considerably greater consequence were those Balkan peoples who converted to Islam, most of them voluntarily, in the sixteenth and seventeenth centuries. These were the Albanians, an Illyrian remnant northwest of Greece, and, even earlier, among the peoples who in 1376 had proclaimed the autonomous kingdom of Bosnia. The latter was in effect a frontier zone between the Catholic and Orthodox churches, and its pre-Ottoman population was made up of both groups, Croats on one side, Serbs on the other, and between them a somewhat shadowy "church" of heterodox Christians who belonged to neither the Latin nor the Eastern confession.

The first clear indication we have of the extent of Slavic conversion to Islam occurs in the Ottoman census of 1520–1530. It is not a head but a household count—in part to estimate who should be paying the Muslim tithe (*zakat*) and who the tributary poll-tax (*jizya*)—and it reveals that in the European provinces of the Ottoman Empire, Muslims constituted 18.8 percent of the total population, Christians 80.7 percent, and Jews .5 percent. The Jews, mostly migrants from Spain, whence they had been expelled in 1492, though relatively few in number, were of some consequence to the empire's economic and cultural life and remained concentrated in coastal cities like Salonika. Most of the Muslims were found immediately to the north of Constantinople, thenceforward the Turks' Istanbul, in what is today European Turkey and southern Bulgaria, and were likely Turkish migrants. But there were also sizable Muslim settlements in Macedonia and Bosnia, and these were converts, who would swell in number in the following century and later be joined by substantial numbers of converts in Albania. Moreover, the Muslims were heavily concentrated in the cities—Sarajevo, a city founded by the Ottomans in Bosnia, was by 1530 100 percent Muslim, Skopje in Macedonia nearly 75 percent Muslim, and Sofia in Bulgaria 66 percent. The Christian Serbs and Bulgars, it is clear, were mostly farmers and herders.

It is always difficult for the historian to assess motivations for conversion, particularly spiritual ones. In this instance, however, the more secular impulses are somewhat clearer. At the outset, it should be remarked that little suggests that conversion to Islam was coerced in any formal or administrative way. There were, however, in the Balkans, as always and everywhere in the Abode of Islam, notable social, economic, and financial advantages to trading in one's dhimmi status and joining the Muslim umma, but among the Slavic Christians other factors were at work. The Church in many areas, and this seems particularly true of Bosnia, as compared to Croatia or Serbia, was underfinanced and undermanned, with little or no spiritual or intellectual infrastructure: clergy, hierarchy, and churches were all lacking. Moreover, the form of Islam that the Ottomans spread in the Balkans was of the Sufi rather than the lawyerly variety, and the most active of the Sufi "orders" (*tariqa*) in the Balkans was that known as the Bektashiyya (see II/8). Bektashi Sufism had come of age in Anatolia as a heterogeneous mix of religious elements, some Muslim, some Christian, and some of very local Anatolian origin. As it spread into the Balkans it proved equally accommodating to the Slavic Christians, many of whom were themselves on the margins of Christian orthodoxy. To convert from Christianity to Islam in the Ottoman Balkans in the sixteenth and seventeenth centuries does not seem, at any rate, to have involved surrendering a great many Christian rituals, customs, or beliefs.

Naming the Others

The Quran has a good deal to say about the competitors and rivals of Islam: the Jews—both as Israelites (Banu Israil) and Jews (Yahud)—Christians (Nasara), Zoroastrians (Majus), Sabians, a group clearly conceived in the Quran but not easily identified by Muslim historians, and finally, the assorted pagans lumped together under the term "associators" (*mushrikun*), that is, those who worshiped other gods alongside the One True God. The first four groups were arguably included in the theological category of People of the Book, recipients of a genuine revelation that carried the considerable political advantage of being eligible for the special protective "covenant" (*dhimma*) granted to such (see I/8). The last group, the associators, received no such assurances: they were unbelievers (*kafir*; pl. *kuffar*) purely and simply and so had either to convert to Islam or to die.

For juridical purposes, Muslim lawyers tended to regard all three categories—Muslims, (non-Muslim) Scripturaries, and unbelievers—as simple units, with no distinctions within them. "All unbelief is one religion," the great Shafii noted, and so too all the dhimmis, despite the fact that they might differ among themselves in their beliefs. Hence, whether a Jew married a Christian or a Christian became a Zoroastrian was for most Muslim jurists a matter of supreme indifference. Others were not so certain: if the Quran distinguished between them, should not the law do likewise? What clearly did matter regarding the People of the Book was where they lived, whether under the protection of the dhimma within the Abode of Islam or outside it, in the Abode of War, where they were objects of jihad.

From another perspective, however, all those religious categories could be collapsed into two fundamental ones. After the revelation of the Quran, there were only true monotheist believers, that is, the Muslims. All others are associators, or polytheists. The thought is not far from the Quran's own, which itself convicts the Jews and Christians of polytheism, the first for their worship of "Uzayr" (Ezra?), the latter for believing the Prophet Jesus to be the son of God (Quran 9:30–31). Moreover, when Umar II (r. 717–720) forbade Jews and Christians from entering mosques—an interdict later relaxed by most Muslim law schools—he allegedly cited Quran 9:28, which prohibits the polytheists from approaching the Meccan Haram. Consensus never developed on this matter, however. Quran 2:221 forbids Muslim men from marrying "polytheist" women unless they first converted, but few lawyers thought this applied to Christian and Jewish women. The Sunni consensus permitted Muslims to marry Jews and Christians; only the Shiites thought it was forbidden.

The Making of a Muslim

Muslims use circumcision as an initiation ritual, probably in imitation of the Jews, just as Christians, with a little help from John the Baptist, took over baptism from a Jewish conversion ritual. But Islam, like Christianity, is a community of believers: Muslims too are made, not born. The Quran could easily echo Paul's sentiments that "there is no such thing as Jew nor Greek slave or free, man or woman" (Gal. 3:28), but the social realities of seventh-century Mecca differed from those of first-century Jewish Palestine. Muhammad lived, whether in Mecca or Medina, in a combatively tribal society, and in the Prophet's preaching a good deal of space and energy is devoted to taking down that tribal mind-set. The Muslim umma, as the community was called, was intentionally designed to replace a kinship society with a faith-based one. The program was successful, at least during Muhammad's lifetime. The Muslim umma was in fact an egalitarian society open to all believers.

At God's command, then, Muhammad founded a community that took as its identity marker a submission to total monotheism, an acceptance of Muhammad as God's envoy, and, consequently, of the Quran as God's words. Though the Quran frequently referred to the members of that community as "submitters" (*muslimun* > Eng. Muslims), an even more frequent designation for them was "those who have faith" (*iman*), thus, the "faithful" or *muminun*. Later some drew on this distinction between *islam* and *iman* to further distinguish the true and marginal members of the community. But as a matter of actual fact, becoming a Muslim depended directly and exclusively on making the profession of faith (*shahada*)—"There is no god but The God and Muhammad is his envoy"—sharing in community prayer, and contributing the alms-tithe, although in the beginning failing to pay the zakat seems to have had more serious consequences than neglecting prayer, presumably because it was more willful.

Adults who renounced paganism at Mecca and Medina had presumably to do nothing more than pronounce the shahada as an affirmation of monotheism, of a belief in Muhammad's divine mission, and, by implication, in the Quran's divine origin. There were baleful social consequences of such a profession in hostile Mecca—the Quran clearly reflects them—but notably less so in Medina, where the community moved inexorably to a Muslim majority. We begin to understand the long-term problem in conversion, however, in the instance of a Medinese Jew choosing, as some did, to become a Muslim and leaving his highly marked Jewish community for the equally distinct society of Muslims. Until Muslims became the majority over the entire Abode of Islam, leaving one's original community and joining the umma carried with it painful social dislocation wherever it occurred.

After Mecca's decisive submission to Muhammad in 630, the tribes of Arabia read the omens and decided that their future lay with the rising new prophet in Medina. There was no longer any need to pursue or to proselytize. Delegations came on their own accord to the Prophet and announced their submission. Most were Bedouin, though there were also representatives of some of the Christian settlements in the Yemen. Religion sat lightly on the Bedouin, as the Quran itself remarks (9:97), and for some or perhaps most of them acceptance of Islam may have meant little more than recognizing Medina's sovereignty and paying what is set down in Islamic law as a religious tithe but surely appeared to the camel nomads as a tax or tribute (Quran 9:98). This seems reasonably inferred from the fact that immediately after the Prophet's death many of the Arab tribes abruptly stopped paying the zakat and Muhammad's successor had to dispatch armed troops to enforce its collection. Muslim officials could not guarantee that everyone would say his prayers, but they surely knew whether the zakat arrived in Medina.

Conversion to Islam was readily done but difficult to realize. The *Life* is filled with accounts of the Prophet's instructing delegates of this or that tribe on the new beliefs and practices to be followed, but the process of substituting the practice (*sunna*) of the Prophet for the venerated sunna of the ancestors was not accomplished quickly or easily. Surely the best that could be hoped for in those early days was that the tribes should stop sacrificing to and otherwise venerating their idols and learn some verses of the Quran, which they could then use as prayer. But Islam quickly spread beyond the Bedouin into the sown lands of Syria, Egypt, and Iraq, where their faith did not sit lightly on Jews and Christians who for centuries had been attacking each others' faith—and variant versions of their own. We have little clue as to how the conversion process proceeded here. It must have been slow, but some of its results can be observed fairly soon in Islam's career. The accounts of early Muslim writers, chiefly historians and quranic commentators, are filled with biblical and postbiblical tales filling out the Quran's sketches; they most often seem to come from very early Christian, particularly Jewish, converts to Islam. These were later lumped together as "Israelite tales" with the label "Do Not Use." The warning came too late in most cases. The Israelite tales from the People of the Book were an influential contribution to the formulation of Islam in the first obscure century of its existence.

An Arab, and Arabic, Islam

In its earliest manifestation, Islam was the faith of Arabs revealed by an Arab prophet whose message was, it boasted, "in a manifest Arabic." In the first conversions Arabs passed from tribe to umma, losing their tribal identity (though only briefly), but not, as it turned out, any of the cultural markers of language, dress, food, and so on. Islam was at first measured by prayer, which could not be monitored always and everywhere, and by payment of the alms-tithe, which could. But when the call to Islam passed among other peoples—the Greek- and Aramaic-speaking people of Syria-Palestine, the Greek- and Coptic-speaking peoples of Egypt, the Greek- Aramaic- and Pahlevi-speaking peoples of Iraq and Iran—it sounded theologically familiar, but culturally it remained Arab. It continued to be such for a very long time—the anchor of the Arabic Quran secured it—so that Muslim converts had to assimilate to a new culture as well as assert a new faith.

The converts' cultural assimilation to Arabism was astonishingly rapid; within thirty or forty years the language of the Bedouin was being used as the language of state. Assimilation also occurred so thoroughly that it transformed the entire North African–Near Eastern land mass into an Arab cultural *oikoumene*. There were survivors—Persian culture held its breath long enough under the Arab flood that it was revived again after a century or so, though with strong Arab overtones—but the transformation was sufficiently complete that those Christians, Jews, and others who declined to embrace Islam were in the end content to speak its language.

The new converts' assimilation to Arab tribal society was considerably more difficult. The differences between peoples had always existed, of course, save in that pre-Babel world when all humankind was one (Quran 2:213; 10:19), but conversion had a particular significance in an essentially tribal society where identity and its consequent social and political protections were claimed on the basis of birth. There are ways of associating with tribal societies even if one is not born into them, but one of the most common, fictive adoption and its resultant patron-client relationship, provides the *cliens* with status of a decidedly inferior quality. What the cliens was to vestigial Roman tribalism, the *mawla* was to pre-Islamic Arab tribal societies: a freed slave, protected but dependent. It was a kind of juridical adoption whereby the newcomer became a client of the tribe, with limited membership privileges and a considerable menu of obligations.

The Arabs too were organized tribally before the coming of Islam, and though the Quran attempted to create a new type of umma where spiritual merit replaced the old blood ties—"the noblest among you in God's sight is he who is most righteous," Quran 49:13 announces in a bold reversal of tribal values—the Muslim society that emerged after the Prophet's death continued to display much of the same tribal organization and many of the status markers that had prevailed in pre-Islamic days. Thus new Arab converts could be assimilated into the rapidly expanding umma without difficulty, but non-Arabs who submitted were accessioned only through the pre-Islamic institution of clientage known as *wala*. Thus the new Persian Muslim, for example, was attached to some Arab tribal lineage as a *mawla*, or client, who depended on his patron (*wali*) for protection and, in some larger sense, from whom he took his identification as a Muslim (see I/8). This condition of clientage, a tribal hangover in a religious society that in theory recognized no tribal distinctions, though it created serious social problems in the eighth and ninth centuries, and even later in Spain, eventually passed out of Islam.

Whether to Christianity or to Islam, we do not and cannot know for certain why conversion takes place, save perhaps where a sheikh or sovereign moves and his people perforce must follow him into a new faith, as seems to have occurred in the passage of the Slavic people of the Balkans into Christianity, or that of the Arabian Bedouin and the North African Berbers into Islam. Though we can broadly calculate and weigh some of the social and economic incentives to conversion, we can take no measure of the spiritual ones, except in the rare individual cases where someone undertakes to explain. We do know that Muslims were at first a very small minority in the lands they so rapidly conquered and that eventually, after two or three centuries perhaps, they were the majority. We know too that the people who became Muslims from Spain to Iraq were originally Christians and some Jews, and farther east, Zoroastrians. Muslims were the rulers of those people, their sovereigns in power and wealth, if not in sophistication and learning. Surely it was the possibility of sharing in the Muslims' power or wealth (or at least in not suffering the liability of being excluded from the perquisites of the new order) that prompted those other Peoples of the Book to leave their home communities and join the triumphalist Muslim umma, even given the disabilities and derogation that mawla carried with it early on.

> **Note:** The conversion of entire ethnic or tribal communities to a new faith, what has been called "social conversion," sometimes leads to deviant versions of that faith as an identity marker. The later Slavic flirtation with Bogomilism, a form of the widespread Cathar heresy (see I/5), seems to fall into that category, but the Berber case is even more striking since there are multiple examples. The Berbers had originally undergone a social conversion to Christianity and then in the fourth century embraced a particular North African form called Donatism, against which the Latin and Catholic Augustine had to struggle most of his adult life. After another social conversion to Islam, the Berbers were found at the forefront first of North African Kharijism (see I/5 and I/8) and then at the center of two puritan reform groups. As Almoravids and, even more strikingly, as Almohads, they imposed their own rigorous version of Islam on the rather too easy-living but thoroughly traditional Muslims of Spain.

Islam and the Associators: The Hindu Case

After the Quraysh of Mecca, the earliest and best-organized community of associators encountered by Islam was undoubtedly the Hindus, named from their homeland of Hind in northern India. In 976 the Ghaznavids, a Persianized

Turkish dynasty established in Kabul, began their passage through the mountain passes of the Hindu Kush down into the upper reaches of the Indus Valley. According to an eyewitness, the Muslim sultan "demolished the idol-temples [of the Hindus] and established Islam in them." His more famous successor, Mahmud of Ghazna (r. 998–1030), acquired a considerable reputation in pious Muslim circles as the scourge of Hinduism. But though the Ghaznavid expeditions were advertised as jihad, they were nakedly predatory raids. The Ghaznavids had not gone to Hind to stay, as their Arab counterparts in the Middle East and North Africa had done. Their chief, and perhaps only, objective in India was to plunder, not to extend the umma or convert the Hindus. The temples they sacked were quite simply the repositories of the wealth of the Hindu kingdoms of northern India, which the Muslims took when and where they could.

The Ghaznavids were replaced in their Afghan strongholds by the Ghurids in 1186, and the armies of this new military dynasty behaved more like the original wave of Arabs who swept across North Africa in the seventh century. The Ghurids' Turkish generals led their forces across northern India from Peshawar all the way to Bengal, and the state that emerged in their wake, the Delhi sultanate (1206–1526), was the first Muslim polity in India. Nearly submerged in a vast Hindu sea, the sultans attempted to maintain their Islamic identity by swearing continued fealty to the distant Abbasid caliph in Baghdad. They had help. In the thirteenth century, the work of conversion was actively pursued, and the chief agents in the Islamicization of the lands of the Delhi sultans and their successors were the highly adaptable Sufis of the Chishtiyya tariqa (see II/8).

The assault on the Hindu temples continued, although now the intent was more distinctly political than merely looting their treasures. The Hindu temple and its image were the heart of the local raja's legitimacy, a place where the king and the god were signaled as integrated and interdependent. They became, then, a principal battlefield for the incoming Muslim rulers and the Hindu rajas they were attempting to unseat: looting or destroying a temple, or rededicating it as a mosque, was understood as a political gesture by both sides. That this and not *odium theologicum* was the primary motive for destruction of the Hindus' temples is attested to by the fact that the destroyers were invariably military men—and not religious leaders, sultans, governors, or generals—who seized the defeated king's tutelary image and, instead of destroying it as an idol, carried it back to their capital as a war trophy.

Under the Mughuls (1526–1858), another Persianized Turkish dynasty from Central Asia that ruled northern and central India from Kabul to Bengal until the arrival of the British, something approaching toleration of Hinduism emerged. Previous Muslim rulers in India seemed largely indifferent to the religious beliefs of their subjects, perhaps a wise course in many places where the Muslims remained an inconsiderable minority. Indeed, in some instances, they even granted some form of dhimmi status to Hindus, who were on the face of it textbook instances of polytheists but who clearly were, and remained, far too numerous to be coerced very effectively.

The Mughuls showed no such indifference. The greatest of them, Akbar (r. 1556–1605)—whose reign spanned the turn of the first Muslim millennium, which had its own vibrant apocalyptic associations—was profoundly interested in all things religious, particularly when they could be turned to his own political advantage. He had a quite modern fondness for interfaith conferences, in which Hindus, Jains, Zoroastrians, and even Catholic priests participated. Whether from tolerance or pragmatism, he abolished the jizya incumbent on Hindus, who were by this time generally treated as dhimmis.

If this was calculated to gain the support of his non-Muslim subjects, Akbar was not averse to taking on his own Muslim authorities. Despite the strong Sufi orientation of Indian Islam, and its fondness for integrating popular Hindu rites, festivals, and social practices into everyday Islam, the traditional *ulama* (legal scholars) were also powerful there, and Akbar challenged their authority in the name of the state. His instrument was an extraordinary decree that the leading court ulama were constrained to sign in 1579. It certified that Akbar was a "just ruler" in the technical sense of that term and, as such, was warranted to choose any quranic interpretation that he regarded in the state's best interest, even if the *mujtahid*s, the Islamic law experts, disagreed.

Akbar's strong-arm politics was accompanied by a softer and more blurred melding of Hindu pantheism and Muslim mysticism. The blend pleased few save the cognoscenti, and under Akbar's son Jahangir (r. 1605–1627), the ulama reasserted themselves. In the end, even the most eclectic Sufis deserted this flirtation with Hinduism and returned to more orthodox Muslim ways.

5

Orthodoxy and Heresy

In Search of Jewish Orthodoxy

The word "Judaism" (Gk. *ioudaismos*) first appears as a religious characterization in the Greek literature by and about Jews of the post-Exilic era. It is not defined there, but its use indicates there was something everyone, Jews and non-Jews, could identify and describe by that term. It is not "orthodoxy" in the strictest sense of the word in that it was not normative or prescriptive, as later rabbinic Judaism would come to be; rather, it is a phenomenological description. "Judaism" was constituted of what all, or better, most Jews of the period held and acted on. Most attempts at describing this "consensual Judaism" usually include God and the Torah as well as the notions of Benei Israel and Eretz Israel.

God From the beginning to the present, a Jewish core belief is that God, the Creator of the universe, is one and unique. No one but he is to be worshiped; all forms of religious syncretism are disavowed (cf. Jth. 8:18).

Torah The Bible (which was still under construction during this era; see II/1) is the Word of God. It both expresses God's will through the Law and the Prophets and describes his dealing with his people in the historical thread that runs through much of the Bible. From another angle, this principle can also be identified as "Covenantal Nomism," where emphasis is placed on the Bible as an expression of God's Law given through God's Covenant. The Law, together with its monotheism, became the distinctive mark of Israel, most notably expressed in the practice of circumcision and the observance of the Sabbath and dietary laws.

Benei Israel The Jews were a divinely elected people. God's choice had been sealed by the Covenant he had made with Abraham (Isa. 41:8–10), and it was still in force. It was renewed by the Israelites on their return from Exile (Neh. 8:1–8), and Ezra's actions in that same era, notably sending away the Israelites' foreign wives and their offspring

(Ezra 10:10–11), were directed at ensuring that the Jews would remain a people apart from all contamination by the Gentiles.

Eretz Israel   The "Land for Israel" was given by God to his people. It was and remained a holy land (see I/1).

This complex of notions and acts does not constitute "orthodoxy" in the ordinary sense of the word, which has been mostly determined by later Christian usage. It was not professed as a creed nor "defined" as dogma since there was, quite transparently, no body in Judaism empowered to decree such. It is simply observed belief and behavior, and it may be better simply to call these items the Pillars of Second Temple Judaism on the model of the Pillars of Islam (see II/4). In any event, all the themes listed above appear across the considerable literature of Second Temple Judaism, and they are visible wherever we can discern and measure Jewish religious behavior. The practice of circumcision seems universal, for example, and both the Sabbath and the Torah dietary laws were widely observed, if not always as punctiliously as some like the Pharisees might have wished. These Pillars of Second Temple Judaism are manifested very publicly in the Eighteen Benedictions (Shemoneh Esreh) of the synagogue liturgy coming into use in the latter part of this period (see II/6).

Exclusion and Banishment

Excommunication or banishment is a corollary of the very notion of community. Members may depart of their own volition, either by drifting off and away by the kind of silent attrition that affects all communities, or through a formal renunciation, the act that is now, in this religious context, called apostasy and that often carried the most severe penalties. Neither is the issue here, however; the present concern is with those members of the faith community whom the rest judge unfit or unworthy for continued association and so ban or excommunicate, cutting them off from community membership and from sharing in whatever considerable benefits may flow from that affiliation. Though it was put into these precise words only by the Catholic Church (see I/4), the belief that "there is no salvation outside the community" was a long and profoundly held conviction among Jews, Christians, and Muslims alike. To thrust someone outside the Church of the Saints, to declare that this believer or this class of believers "has no share in the Afterlife," is to pronounce a grim sentence indeed.

The Bible has two notions that appear to prescribe the act of separating an individual from the community. The first is *karet*, "cutting off," which appears to be close to excommunication. In some cases it does in fact signify ostracism, but more commonly, when the Bible uses *karet*, it means cutting off from life and is describing the death penalty for sin (see II/5). The notion of banning or banishment and its execution is more properly expressed in the Bible by the word *herem* and its derivatives. The word has the same basic meaning as its Arabic cognate *haram*, namely, that of something proscribed, removed from common usage, or, since it occurs in a religious context, something taboo. *Herem* first appears in the context of a Jewish jihad (see I/8). The booty of such biblical holy wars belonged to God alone and so must be "utterly destroyed," literally, "heremized" (Deut. 7:2, etc.). One side of this base concept of herem broadened out to include everything dedicated in whatever fashion to God's use (Lev. 27:21), like the "haramized" Muslim pilgrims about to begin the hajj (see II/6), and was thus removed from ordinary use or circulation, a point over which Jesus argued with the Pharisees (Mark 7:11). But the notion could also be applied to persons, even Israelites, who, because they worshiped false gods, are pronounced herem in Exodus 22:19, a sentence that there unmistakably means they should be executed. But *herem* at some point ceased to mean execution, whereby the perpetrator was proscribed "with extreme prejudice," and it became the more social punishment of exclusion from the community.

There emerged from the destruction of the priestly judicial system that had prevailed in Second Temple and earlier times a new rabbinically shaped and manned system of justice in the third and fourth centuries C.E. It too was centralized, though not now around temple and Sanhedrin, as in earlier days, but around a legal official and expert, the "prince," or *nasi* (see I/6). His expertise came from Torah study—he was part of the line connecting the earlier scribes and Pharisees with the rabbis then emerging—but his validation came from the Romans. Thereafter, once the norms of Pharisaic Judaism became, at least ideally, the norms of all Jews, the theory of community banning comes into somewhat sharper focus.

The earliest evidence of the practice is the addition, about 90 C.E., of three clauses to the twelfth of the Eighteen Benedictions of the synagogue liturgy. These are the "blessing over the heretics" (*birket ha-minim*), which call down not a blessing but a destruction on the Christians (*notzrim*) and "sectarians" (*minim*). There has been considerable debate over whether the minim are in fact the Jewish Christians who had accepted Jesus' messiahship but continued to frequent the synagogue, or whether they were an entirely distinct group, a sect of Jewish Gnostics, for example. But it is clear that to cast this imprecation in the form of a regular and mandatory synagogue prayer made the curse against the offenders its own effective fulfillment without trial or further process.

Under the rabbis there were other, more formal ways of distancing the offender. They ranged from reprimand to temporary ban (*nidduy*) to full expulsion (*herem*) from the community. Many of the grounds are presented as disrespect for the rabbis, but this was probably interpreted in a formal rather than a personal sense, and included failure to observe the rabbis' legal enactments. The nasi and the courts could impose such bans, of course, but it is interesting to observe that any Jew could do the same if he or she observed a gross infraction of the Law.

The Separation of the Christians

One group banned from the Jewish community may have been the Christians, the Jewish followers of Jesus of Nazareth. Jesus himself is often portrayed in the Gospels as arguing with the Pharisees, and not terribly surprisingly, his eating habits—he dined with "publicans and sinners"—was one critical issue (Luke 5:30, etc.). He and his followers constituted, like the Pharisees, a variant, of the multiple "Judaisms" of the people who called themselves Jews in the first century. They were one movement in a swirl of such eddies, a sect in a community that had, as we have seen, no apparent center or parent community that might be termed "orthodoxy"; indeed, Jesus' group was a sect on or from another sect, if his connection with John's Baptist movement is correct (see I/2). In those first days the identity of the movement's members rested on their discipleship with Jesus, and at their master's death and disappearance— his ascension into heaven, as they believed—they came eventually to be known as "Messianists" (*Christianoi*).

> **Note**: Just as "Christ" means nothing more than "anointed one," and hence "Messiah," *Christianoi* is a Greek expression probably best translated, at least in its earliest usages (see Acts 11:26), as "Messianists." To make it simply "Christians" suggests that at the outset they constituted a separate religious community, which the "Messianists" eventually became. Just as *Christos* came to be almost a name for Jesus—already Paul had dropped the article: "Jesus the Christ" had become simply "Jesus Christ"—so too *Christianoi* soon stopped referring to a messiah and meant for Christians only *the* Messiah, that is, Jesus of Nazareth.

The Christians were, then, in the beginning, a fellowship of Jews linked by their common conviction first, that Jesus of Nazareth was the promised Messiah, and second, that the messianic era had just begun, or soon would (see II/10). Neither of these beliefs, however, which were embraced by many Jews both before and after, would have led their contemporaries to regard these circumcised and observant sectarians as any other than members of the community of Jews.

Eventually, however, the followers of Jesus did constitute a religious community separate from the Jews, with lingering hesitations about the divorce on the part of the Christians and none, as far as we know, on the part of the Jews. Paul's letters and the Gospels show the process of separation in its earliest stages, where the Messianists were being harassed out of synagogues and congregations and pursued and prosecuted by the new Pharisaic leaders of the post-70 Jewish community. Why? Perhaps it was because of the increasingly "high" Christology of Jesus' followers (see I/2), who had taken to calling Jesus not merely Son of Man, the title borrowed from Daniel, but also Son of God. This latter sounds as if it *should* be offensive to Jews, as indeed it now is, but only when read through the prism of Christian Trinitarian theology of the late second and third centuries; and only if we overlook or underestimate, in the light of that theology, Jewish familiarity with such notions. Not only Philo but the post-Exilic Jewish writings generally provide various ways in which expressions like "Son of God" might still, in the first century, be understood in a manner not only acceptable but agreeable to Jewish beliefs and sensibilities.

Far more likely what thrust the Messianists out of the synagogue and turned them into Christians was the issue of the reception of the Gentiles. Every Jewish apocalyptic scenario somehow included the Gentiles, sometimes by their acknowledging the truth of Israel or even by their being gathered into it as worshipers of the One True God. Like the Orthodox Jews who saw in the creation of the State of Israel a somewhat unexpected sign of the approaching End Time (see II/10), the early Christians addressed the interest in Jesus by the Gentiles, who were already a part of synagogue audiences in the Diaspora, in eschatological terms. In that spirit, after some hesitation, they undertook to receive them formally into their congregations, without benefit of circumcision and with only the barest minimum of observance (Acts 15:19–30). We can only guess that it was the formality of that acceptance of Gentiles into the Covenant that began to trouble the other Jews. The approach of the End might excuse or explain the inclusion of the Gentiles, but for many Jews—indeed, for most Jews—the End Time was not yet, and so the Messianists' embrace of the Gentiles in increasing numbers finally brought about a rupture between the parent community and what had turned out to be a dangerously radical sect.

We cannot trace the steps from uneasiness with the Messianists to their expulsion—which it does seem more than a withdrawal. Paul and the Gospels already signal, as has been remarked, its beginnings. By the turn into the second century, we can see perhaps a further stage, as has been said, in the separation in the maledictions that had recently been introduced into the synagogue service, when the congregation prayed that the "Nazarenes . . . perish as in a moment; let them be blotted out of the book of the living." We can deduce something similar from the *Dialogue* between Justin, a Gentile convert, and the Rabbi Trypho, in which Justin says he is willing, somewhat reluctantly, to accept a Jewish Christian who insists on living like a Jew, but by no means a Jewish Christian who insists that he, Justin, a Gentile Christian, do likewise. By the opening decades of the second century, then, the Jews had disowned their Messianist brethren as false Jews, while these latter, now increasingly Gentiles who embraced Jesus as their Savior, began to reexamine, and then to question their theological and even their scriptural ties to the Jewish past.

Easter

Although we do not know the year, on the testimony of the synoptic Gospels Jesus was crucified on the feast of Passover, the fourteenth of the lunar month of Nisan in the Jewish calendar, and rose from the dead two days later, on what is called the "first day of the week" (Mark 16:2), our present Sunday. For Christians, the celebration of Jesus' resurrection is the holiest day of the entire liturgical year (see II/6), and though it is in English called Easter, after the name of the Anglo-Saxon goddess of spring, its Greek and Latin name, *Pascha*, preserves its original Jewish association. Originally the resurrection seems to have been celebrated on Friday, Saturday, or Sunday, but in 325 C.E., the ecumenical Council of Nicaea (see II/7) decreed that henceforward it was to be celebrated on "the first Sunday after the first full moon on or after the vernal equinox," that is, after 21 March. Thus, unlike Christmas, which has a fixed date, 25 December, on the solar calendar, the Christian Pascha is calculated, like the Jewish Passover, on the basis of a lunar fix ("first Sunday after the full moon"), though it is specifically tied to the solar season ("on or after the vernal equinox"), an effect the Jewish calendar brings about through intercalation (see introduction and II/6).

This was not merely a calendrical matter; in religious communities disputes about the calendar are *always* about something other than counting. At stake here was the relationship of Christian congregations to their Jewish antecedents. Many Gentile converts to the new faith may have felt freed from the requirements of Jewish law and the practices of Jewish life, but as is apparent from Paul's own letters, other Christians, and not merely those born Jewish, continued to maintain Jewish observances. Passover was one of them, which they observed, in the manner of the Jews, from sunset on the fourteenth of Nisan; hence they were later called Quartodecimans, or Fourteeners. They did not celebrate the way Jews celebrated Passover, however. Pascha, as they still called it, was understood to derive from the Greek verb *paschein*, "to suffer." In the same spirit, the Passover Exodus haggadah, the edifying retelling of the Israelites' escape from Egypt, was now read by those Christians as a story of release from the bondage to sin. There was no Passover seder since Jesus, the Lamb of God, had already been slaughtered; rather, they fasted through the day and night until past sunrise on the following morning, when Jesus' resurrection was celebrated with an agape or fellowship meal.

The Christian celebration of Passover, albeit in an altered form, must be very old, but it yielded to something slightly different around 135 when, after a second Jewish insurrection, the emperor Hadrian banned the practice of Judaism and forbade Jews to live in Judaea. It was then, according to Eusebius, that Gentile Christian bishops replaced the line of "Hebrew" bishops who had previously headed the Jerusalem church, and, we are told by another source, the now Gentile Christians moved their resurrection celebration to Sunday precisely to distinguish themselves from the banned Jews. There were thus, in effect, two distinct Easters, a Passover version and a Sunday version. Some of the Christian congregations of the East continued with their practice of a "Passover Easter," or some variant of it, until the last decades of the third century when Victor, the bishop of Rome (r. 189–199), attempted to impose the celebration of the resurrection on the Sunday after Passover on the Easterners. When they refused, citing the antiquity of their own tradition, the pope excommunicated them.

This was an extraordinarily impractical solution to a deep-seated difference on the bearing of the Jewish past on the Christian present. The parties continued to debate the Easter issue, but what turned the tide was the growing animus against the Jews by a now overwhelmingly Gentile Church with a very imperfect sense of the Jewish past and the first Christian emperor's desire to impose a Pax Christiana on the Great Church he now headed. The Council of Nicaea was instrumental in bringing uniformity, or at least conformity, on Christian belief and practice, and its decree that Easter should be celebrated on Sunday was the result.

Defining the Truth

Unlike the Jews, who regarded themselves as an ethnic as well as a religious community united by ritual and behavior, Christians were solely a religious community who ended up defining themselves more by their beliefs (orthodoxy) than by their behavior (orthopraxy).

Note:

Orthodoxy: (straight belief) is normative teaching (or doctrine) regarding a belief system. Orthodoxy is usually expressed as a "creed," as for example, Maimonides' Thirteen Principles, the Christians' Nicene Creed, or the Muslims' shahada. Deviation from orthodoxy is *heresy*.

Orthopraxy: (straight action) is normative teaching (or doctrine) regarding a behavioral system, a pattern of prescribed actions, usually expressed as a holy law. The Ten Commandments and the Torah as a whole are examples, as are the Christians' canon law and the Muslims' sharia. Although they refer to themselves as Orthodox, traditional Jews who follow the rabbinic teachings on Torah are, in effect, Orthopractic.

The normative teaching or doctrine of the faith community can take numerous forms. First, it is the body of teaching explicitly set forth in Scripture and on which there is an agreed interpretation. But this handing down of doctrine occurs in other less formal terms, as we shall see, whether through the Jews' Sinai-based oral tradition, the Christians' conviction that their bishops were enunciating a true apostolic tradition, or the Muslims' acceptance of the prophetic traditions as a veritable second revelation. Finally, doctrine may rest on a consensus, when the community has unanimously agreed, or so it seems, on some point without scriptural warrant, for example, the canon of Hebrew Scripture (see II/1), the divinity of Jesus, or that there should be a leader (caliph, Imam) after Muhammad (see I/8).

Doctrine (teaching) becomes dogma (what *must* be believed under pain of spiritual damnation and/or exclusion from the religious community) when it is defined as absolutely binding by a competent body. Generally in Christianity this is by an ecumenical or general council of bishops, where it is expressed in the form of a creed. For Roman Catholics, it is through formal pronouncement by the pope, the bishop of Rome.

In Christian circles, the custom of stating the basic tenets of Christianity as a formulary probably originated early on in the practice of (adult) baptism. The candidate signaled his or her assent to the initiation by reciting a brief statement of belief: "I believe in . . ." (Lat. *Credo in* . . .). The formula differed from church to church, but as in all else, uniformity soon set in and there emerged in the Eastern and Western Churches two main forms of the Christian creed. The Easterners took the doctrinal statement by which the bishops assembled at Nicaea in 325 expressed their understanding of Christian orthodoxy (the Nicene Creed), whereas the Latin West subscribed to a kind of agglomerate that may have had its origins in the church in Rome in the second century and eventually evolved into the version known as the Apostles' Creed.

Note: Like other venerable documents that are neither as old nor as venerable as they profess to be, an accompanying story guaranteed the authenticity of the Apostles' Creed. By this account, the Twelve, who had gathered one last time before departing to spread the Gospel to the ends of the earth, each stated what he believed about the new faith. Peter started with "I believe in God, the Father Almighty," and each contributed a clause down to Matthias, who capped it all with "and life everlasting."

The two creeds are quite similar though by no means identical. The Nicene Creed, which is longer, includes statements reflecting the theological controversy regarding the Father and the Son that brought the bishops to Nicaea in the first place (see II/7). The Apostles' Creed has two clauses not included in the Eastern creed. The first asserts that Jesus descended into hell before ascending into heaven, and the second affirms belief in the Communion of Saints (see II/10).

Reaching for Orthodoxy: The Fundamental Principles of Jewish and Muslim Belief

Among the Jews and Muslims were officials who might respond on matters of correct behavior (see II/5), but none could pronounce with the same authority as the Christian bishop, singly or in council, and none enjoyed the authority of the bishop of Rome. Yet both communities were concerned with matters of belief, what a Jew or Muslim must believe or may not believe. One of the earliest concerns expressed in those terms appears to be a Mishnah text addressed quite specifically to the Sadducees, since their opinions include them in "those who do not have a portion in the world to come," namely, "the one who says there is no resurrection of the dead, the one who says that the Torah is not from heaven, and the *Apiqoros* [that is, the "Epicurean," someone who denies divine providence]" (Mishnah Sanhedrin 10:1).

This statement, which responded to a specific and immediate need, does not, obviously, constitute a comprehensive declaration of Jewish beliefs. There had been such creedlike statements early in Christianity, prompted by profound differences within the community. But when Judaism too eventually began to produce such statements, the point of departure was not as much a need to define the community and so preserve its integrity as it was an attempt at understanding the reality that lay behind what continued to be the preeminent good of Judaism, namely, the Law. For some, that reality lay in the truths of philosophy—which were of course the truths of God himself, the philosophers would quickly add. Those truths could be pursued for their own sake, a course taken by very few of the Children of Abraham, or they could be converted to, or reconciled with, the Law, a more properly Jewish undertaking. This is what Philo undertook in Greek Alexandria in the first century, what Saadya attempted in Muslim Baghdad, and Maimonides in Muslim Spain, Morocco, and Egypt.

With Maimonides (d. 1204), the attempt to reduce the truths of Scripture to dialectical or propositional form produced not merely reflections or commentary but something that might be regarded as a Jewish creed, a systematic statement of the propositions whose acceptance is fundamental to Jewish belief. Unlike the Christian creeds, however, which were formally promulgated, and at times administered, by the authority of the bishop or of the Great Church as tests for orthodoxy at baptism or elsewhere, Maimonides' list of Thirteen Principles—which appear in his classic commentary on the Mishnah—was personal and doctrinal. Despite his own conviction that they might serve as such, his principles were never used as either a yardstick or a test for membership in the Jewish community.

The first five of Maimonides' principles have to do with God's existence, attributes, and uniqueness; they echo the kind of theological consensus that had emerged among Jewish, Muslim, and Christian intellectuals of the Middle Ages. The sixth affirms a belief in the general principle of prophecy. Only with the seventh principle, that Moses was the chief of the prophets, does a uniquely Jewish character begin to emerge. The eighth affirms that the Torah came from God, through Moses, "who acted like a secretary taking dictation," which may owe something to the long-standing Muslim view of how Muhammad received the Quran. The ninth principle affirms the absolute authenticity of the Torahs (written and oral), "precisely transcribed from God and no one else." The Muslims, it will be recalled, accused the Jews of tampering with Scripture. The tenth principle asserts God's providence; the eleventh, God's rewards and punishments: "The greatest reward is the world to come; the worst punishment is extinction." The twelfth principle asserts the necessity of believing in the coming of a Davidic messiah, though without conjecturing when. The last fundamental of Jewish belief is in the resurrection of the dead: "A person who does not believe in this principle has no real religion, certainly not Judaism."

Maimonides concludes on the significance of these principles. A Jew may sin, even grievously. He or she will be punished, but will still possess "a share in the world to come." If, however, someone cannot affirm each and every one of these principles, "he has removed himself from the Jewish community. He is an atheist, a heretic, an unbeliever. . . . We are commanded to hate him and destroy him. Of him it is said: 'Shall I not hate those who hate You, O Lord?' (Ps. 139:21)."

In the end Maimonides' Thirteen Principles had little effect on Judaism. There is no sign that any Jew was rooted out of the Jewish community or regarded as a non-Jew for violating what surely must be considered fundamental beliefs, whether thirteen, more, or less. On one level, reverence for every word and syllable of the Torah, carried all before it; on another level, a tribal community where birth and blood were the essential characteristics of membership found no commodious or convincing way of dissolving the bond of blood on the basis of either belief or behavior, no matter how unlikely or outlandish.

It is by now almost an article of Jewish faith—a dogma, no less—that there are no dogmas in Judaism. The father of this particular sentiment, Moses Mendelssohn (d. 1786), one of the earliest and most influential proponents of the Jewish "Enlightenment" (*haskalah*) is well known. For Mendelssohn, Judaism was a religion of pure reason, much as John Locke envisioned such. It possessed, for example, none of Christianity's irrational beliefs, like the Virgin Birth and the Resurrection. Jews believed only what reason suggested to them as true; personal salvation did not, in any event, depend on a Jew's beliefs but only on his or her behavior. Revelation entered the picture only with respect to conduct: the Torah was not a creed but a law code, much like that possessed by all civilized societies.

It is interesting to compare Maimonides' attempt at creating a creed with that of a Muslim thinker, another Spaniard with much the same rationalist perspective. Ibn Khaldun's (d. 1406) list of the articles of the Muslim faith are offered in his *Prolegomenon to History* as an illustration of the science of dialectical theology, the primary purpose of which was to expand and defend such Scripture-derived articles through rational arguments (see II/7). He begins, however, with Muhammad's own far more modest list of the fundamentals of Muslim belief, citing a "sound" or authoritative report wherein Muhammad declares that every Muslim must "affirm in his heart, believe in his soul, and acknowledge with his tongue" the following truths: "Belief in God, His angels, His Scriptures, His Messengers, the Last Day, and the belief in predestination, whether it be good or bad."

Ibn Khaldun's own articles derive chiefly from theology and resemble the early ones on Maimonides' list: God is one, perfect, and unique; He is all-knowing, all-powerful. He has volition. Moreover, "He determines the fate of each created thing." As in Maimonides, resurrection of the dead is an important ingredient of belief: "He causes our resurrection after death. This constitutes the final touch to His concern with the first creation. If created things were destined to disappear completely, their creation would have been frivolous. They are destined for eternal existence after death."

Prophecy occupies a far less important, and strikingly less unique, place in this Muslim theological scheme of things. "Further articles of faith are: God sent His Messengers in order to save us from trouble on the Day of Resurrection, because that Day may mean either trouble or happiness, and we would not know that. He wanted to complete His kindness toward us by informing us about this situation and explaining to us the two possibilities and that Paradise means bliss and Hell means punishment." The prophets, then, and so revelation itself, are merely supplemental to what theology can adduce about God and his work. Remarkably, there is nothing here about Muhammad or indeed of Islam.

Ibn Khaldun's essay in orthodoxy had even less effect than Maimonides' since he never enjoyed the Jewish scholar's reputation in his own religious circles. Both were in effect academic exercises by rather rarefied thinkers. The least bishop in Christendom could pronounce more loudly and consequentially on the faith than either this Jewish rabbi or this Muslim historian.

Heresy in the Early Churches

The Jewish approach to doctrinal deviance and deviants appears at times tentative and inchoate, chiefly because there was no defined standard against which to measure it nor any body competent to define it. The Church's view of its own deviants was at the same time more definite and more complex. Since it defined itself more properly through orthodoxy than orthopraxy, Christianity tended to be far more tolerant of divergencies in practice than in belief. These latter departures from the catholic or universal norm, sometimes known as the "rule of faith" and defined in increasing detail by local synods and ecumenical councils of bishops, constituted heresy. They were early and generally pursued with vigor, either through excommunication, an exclusion from the sacramental life of the Church and thus from the source of saving grace, or by formal intervention of the state.

There were doctrinal problems early in the Christian communities. So much is apparent in the Gospels (Matt. 18:15) and in Paul's first letter to the Christian assembly at Corinth. The congregation there had taken sides, some claiming the authority of Peter, others of Paul or Apollos his successor, while others said simply, and somewhat mysteriously, that they were "of Christ" (1 Cor. 1:12–13). Another harbinger of things to come was a group of Christians at Corinth known as "spirituals" (*pneumatikoi*), who were claiming a kind of preeminence over other Christians by reason of their charismatic gifts. Paul responds to the latter at length (1 Cor. 12–14), to the effect that such powers are only one of many God grants believers and, they should all recall, "the God who inspires them is not a God of disorder but a God of peace."

Paul seems not only disturbed but puzzled by such quarrels within the congregation and he tries to make some sense of them. They may be attributable, he thinks, to humans' general inclination to sin. The explanation first appears in Galatians (5:20), where "divisions" and "sectarianism" are embedded in a litany of the sins that the flesh and the spirit are heir to. In Corinthians, in contrast, Paul suggests that such factions (*schismata*) may exist "to show which of your members are sound" (11:19). Later, perhaps when such schisms seemed less useful than dangerous, he or one of his followers writes that "a heretic [*heiretikos*, the only use of that word in the New Testament] should be warned once, twice, and then the congregation should have done with him, recognizing that he has a distorted mind and stands self-condemned in his sin" (Titus 3:10–11).

> **Note:** Paul seems to be using as synonyms two terms that had no particular religious associations up to that point. *Schisma* to the Greeks meant any sort of a division, while *hairesis*, literally "choice," was used of different philosophical positions. But from Paul on they become Christian terms of art, though not interchangeable ones. "Schism" continued to mean a separation, often over the question of ecclesiastical authority, whereas "heresy" came to mean a difference over a crucial item of doctrine or belief.

This same note of distress runs throughout the Pauline writings and reaches its climax in the Letters to Timothy. Novel teachings need always have their attractions, in particular to those who are "morbidly fascinated" (1 Tim. 6:4) or "enjoy having their ears tickled" (2 Tim. 4:3). But the churches' leaders— both Titus and Timothy were such—should remain firm and resolute against them.

Paul had good reason to be concerned. The Christian assemblies were just emerging from their matrices of paganism for some and Judaism for others, and the Christians' ability to carefully distinguish their beliefs and practices from either of those others' must have been limited at the outset. Not only was there no clear paradigm of what precisely a Christian life was supposed to be; there was no agreement on what it all meant. Not until the Council of Nicaea in 325 did the Church as a whole, provoked by a great crisis in doctrine, give thought to its universal teaching (see II/7). It took another half century or more before there was universal agreement on what constituted the New Testament.

There rise up from the pages of Eusebius's *Church History*, written early in the fourth century, plentiful signs that the track between Paul and Constantine's pioneering ecumenical council at Nicaea was littered with the remains, some still breathing, of groups that had read Scripture otherwise, and wrongly in the eyes of the rest, or else (or in consequence) rejected the authority of the bishops then emerging as the Church's regnant authorities (see I/6). Some of these dissident movements were the residue of the painful process of separating what was now understood to be "Christianity" from its own Jewish past. Christian congregations and the Church as a whole (still acting by a not always or easily discernible consensus) had rather often to decide "this" but not "that" Jewish practice or conviction could be admitted. Each decision must have meant that some who could not accept the outcome first began to be marginalized and eventually ended up in those catalogs of "heresies" that early Christian authors were fond of assembling for instruction of the faithful.

Gnosticism

One the most dangerous early points of division might be either Jewish or pagan in origin. No one is quite sure where the phenomena we collect under the rubric of Gnosticism began, whether among fatally disappointed Jews, world-denying pagans, dualist Iranians, or some combination of all three, but its earliest known version appears in a Christian context. Until 1945, when the papyrus remains of a fourth-century Gnostic library were found at Nag Hammadi in Egypt, most of the texts earlier identified as Gnostic were explicitly cited as heretical aberrations by the Christian authors who quoted them. There were, however, provocatively Gnostic-type notions circulating in the very earliest versions of Christianity as well. Certain passages in the Gospels and Paul, for example, and even more explicitly in Clement's and Origen's understanding of what the Christian "tradition" was and how it was transmitted, suggest that there was a "hidden wisdom" in the Church and that it was not imparted to all. But there is no great conviction that Gnosticism was in fact a Christian phenomenon, despite the total lack of evidence for its existence in the pre-Christian era. Apocalyptic Judaism, Iranian religion, and later Greek philosophy have all been regarded as equally likely points of departure for the Gnostic worldview.

The Christian version of Gnosticism, simply, was a complex of myth and conviction. In the Gnostic view, there are two gods: a good one and an evil one. From the evil god, the God of the Old Testament, as the Christian Gnostics maintained, proceeded our material world, the *kenoma* or Emptiness, and all the evils, material and moral, contained in it. From the good god, the one worshiped by true Christians, proceeded the pairs of spiritual beings who make up the *pleroma*, the Completeness or Plenitude, most of them Platonic-type abstractions, but here personified in the mythic style.

The engagement of the two worlds begins with an event in the pleroma. One of the beings of the Plenitude, Sophia or Wisdom, sins and consequently lapses into the Emptiness and shatters into multiple points of light that then lie buried and concealed in the Here Below, most notably in the souls of humankind. Another being of the Plenitude, Christ, volunteers to assume a mortal likeness ("Jesus") and descend into the Emptiness to save Sophia. This is accomplished by bringing the Good News, the *gnosis* or saving knowledge. This he does in his mortal existence and then returns to the Plenitude after his seeming death.

The Gnostics were, then, Christians who had received the saving knowledge. This was not the Gospels as they were normally read—the literal or material meaning of Scripture was, like all things material, repudiated by the Gnostics—but subjected to a "spiritual" reading that penetrated deep beneath the surface. Gnosticism had the allure of a cosmic myth, of an intellectual explanation of spiritual reality—the emanation of multiple spiritual pleroma from the originating One is highly Neoplatonic in its conception and expression—and a satisfying explanation of the existence of evil. It also had the enduring attraction of an elitist system. The Gnostic was an adept, one of the few spirituals (*pneumatikoi*) who truly understood but who guarded that secret knowledge from the "material" (*hylikoi*) Christians.

The Gnostics thus constituted a church within a church, Christians with a privileged understanding of Scripture and a strong bias against the material world; against Yahweh, the God who created it; against the Jews who worshiped him and the Old Testament that chronicled his work. One of their most famous and influential leaders was Marcion (d. ca. 160 C.E.). The son of a bishop in what is today Turkey, Marcion eventually came to Rome and began to preach there. He was excommunicated in 144 but continued preaching and propagating his brand of Gnosticism, which directly addressed the Christians' relationship to their Jewish past. For Marcion there was an absolute antithesis between the cruel and despotic God of the Old Testament and Jesus' God of love. The true Christian should have nothing to do with the Jews' Bible and should read only Paul, who understood the difference, and an edited version of Luke. The other Gospels Marcion condemned on the grounds that they were still infected with Judaism and its worldview. This selective insistence on

Marcion's part may in fact have prompted the Church to declare the "canonicity" of all four of the Gospels (see II/1).

The Rule of Faith

How manifestly Jesus intended that there should be one body of believers, and how difficult that intention was to achieve in the face of discordant opinions like Marcion's on the most fundamental questions of faith is a commonplace theme in early Christian writing. Almost all the early Church Fathers touched on this matter of unity and schism, and by the late second century numerous solutions had been put forward. Both Irenaeus (d. ca. 200) and Tertullian (d. after 220) proposed as a touchstone of orthodoxy what they called the "rule of faith," a summary statement of the essential teaching of the Church received from Jesus Christ himself through the Apostles. This would suffice for salvation since, as Tertullian put it, "there is no need of curiosity after Christ, nor of inquiry after the Gospels." According to Irenaeus, in his work *On Heresies*, the rule of faith consists in what "the Church, though dispersed throughout the whole world, even to the ends of the earth, has received from the Apostles and their disciples."

Irenaeus sums up the rule of faith and so what constitutes the core of Christian orthodoxy in the late second century: "faith in one God, the Father Almighty, who made the heaven and the earth and the seas and all the things that are in them; and in one Christ Jesus, the Son of God, who took flesh for our salvation; and in the Holy Spirit, who proclaimed through the prophets the dispensations and the comings, and the birth from a virgin, and the suffering, and the resurrection from the dead, and the fleshly ascension of the beloved Christ Jesus, our Lord, and his future manifestations from heaven in the glory of the Father, 'to sum up all things' (Ephesians 1:10), and to rise up anew all flesh of the human race." Behind Irenaeus's confidence that he has it right is his strong conviction in the unity of the Church, which, though scattered throughout the world, had preserved this tradition intact. Cyprian too, the bishop of Carthage, trying to steer his charges through the carnage of persecution and defection in the mid–third century (see I/4), saw the essential continuity of Jesus' teachings in the Church's officers, particularly its bishops. The episcopate was an office founded by Jesus himself in declaring Peter "the rock upon which I will build my Church" (Matt. 16:18). And, Cyprian continues, "Age has followed age and bishop has followed bishop in succession, and the office of the episcopate and the system of the Church has been handed down, so that the Church is founded on the bishops, and every act of the Church is directed by these same presiding officers" (*Letter* 33).

The Roman emperor's conversion to Christianity and then his summoning the bishops of the entire Church to assemble at Nicaea in 325 made convincingly visible the notion of a single universal or catholic Church. It also gave new and persuasive force to the argument that Christian orthodoxy consisted, according to the French monk Vincent of Lerins (d. ca. 450), in adhering to "what has been believed always, everywhere, and by all" (*quod semper, quod ubique, quod ab omnibus creditum est*, in the famous words of the Latin original), with the assumption that that is a single truth. But even Vincent acknowledges that matters are not so simple, and that there have been conflicting opinions in every age. He offers what appears to be a pragmatic solution. If the contagion of heresy should infect the whole Church, then the Christian concerned with orthodoxy will consult what was held in the early Church. And if there were differences in the early Church, he will consult the more universal views of the ecumenical councils and prefer those to local divergences. But what if the councils of the past are silent on this new and suspicious opinion? "Then he will take pains to consult and interrogate the opinions of his predecessors, comparing them only as regards the opinions of those who . . . remained in the communion and faith of the One Catholic Church, and who therefore have become reliable authorities. And . . . he must also believe without hesitation not only whatever one or two but all equally and with one consent, openly, frequently, and persistently have held, written and taught" (*Commonitory* 3).

> **Note**: The term "catholic," from the Greek *katholike*, "universal," emerged as part descriptive epithet, part slogan, in the wake of the Arian crisis of the early fourth century. Arianism (see II/7) was the first "catholic" or Church-wide heresy to confront Christianity, and it was fought with precisely the same notion, that the Church itself was universal, and hence "catholic". The "Catholic Church" described what might also be called the "Imperial Church," the one that extended "everywhere," which meant in effect the Roman Empire and its environs. The Western or Latin half of that Imperial Church was early on dominated by the bishop of Rome (see I/6), and the deliberate attachment of "Roman" to the Latin Church was the work of the Protestant Reformers who wanted to point precisely to the particularity of the papal Church. The papal Church continued to maintain its claim to universality, however, and to characterize the Reformers as dissidents. "Roman" and "Catholic" thus became entwined, and it is ironic that in common usage the ecumenical "Catholic" is now as often used to describe the Reformers' putative "Roman" Church as "Roman," which was the Protestant epithet of choice.

Heresy, Witchcraft, and Reform

The prototype Christian struggle against dissidence was waged in the opening years of the fourth century. The foe was Arianism (see II/7) and the prize was often the souls of the Germanic "barbarians" newly entering the empire across its eastern European frontiers. The Church Catholic fought Arianism for more than a century in the West with councils, creeds, and abundant help and occasional interference from the now Christian Roman state. The empire's Middle Eastern provinces, however, where Arianism had in fact begun—Arius was a cleric in the church of Alexandria—proved more resistant to this particular theological challenge. At the same time, it had a more marked predilection for theology in the now prevailing Hellenic style than the more legal-minded "Romans" of the Latin West, where Greek had all but disappeared. In the fourth and fifth centuries the Christian East was riven by theological disputes that were as fundamental in their issues, the nature and person of the God-man Jesus Christ, as they were esoteric in their expression and elaboration. Monophysitism on one side and Nestorianism on the other succeeded in detaching most of Egypt and Syria, and all of Ethiopia and Armenia in the bargain, from allegiance to the Catholic Church or, as it was more commonly calle ' in the East, the Melkite or "Imperial" Church (see II/7).

The Latin Church of the West remained both papal and imperial throughout those trying times, and after the eradication of Arianism there appear to have been few doctrinal controversies to trouble Latin Christendom. The Church's enemies were more often paganism and superstition in those centuries of declining culture in both the Church and society at large. Well into the eleventh and twelfth centuries there is far more in the Church chronicles of magic, possession, and contagion than of doctrine, and the cause was frequently diagnosed as diabolical and the condition as witchcraft. Witchcraft and its attendant acts were as real as the fear of contagion, and the same remedy was applied as to the plague: carriers were eradicated by burning. The first recorded European burnings for heresy took place in Orleans and Toulouse in 1022.

Rooting out this diabolical form of the plague by burning may have been an instinctive popular response, but the pyre as a cure for heresy had a history in Christianity. If early medieval churchmen needed guidance in identifying deviant beliefs and behavior, as surely they did, they had little to turn to other than Augustine (d. 430), the Christian West's towering theological authority from his own day down to the seventeenth century. Augustine had fought both Donatists and Manichaeans, and although the Donatists, as we have seen (II/4), convinced Augustine that there was some virtue to "teaching by the rod" (*per molestias eruditio*), the Manichaeans supplied Augustine's readers with the archetype of the heretic as well as the remedies that should be applied to them. Manichaeans were burned in Augustine's day.

The dissidents of the eleventh century were about more than witchcraft or the Manichaeism Augustine's readers saw lurking everywhere. The era's laity were restless with the Church and its clergy. Ordinary Church members were growing more ascetic in inverse proportion to what was perceived as the decline in clerical ethics, where the selling of spiritual offices and benefits—the

Note: Manichaeism is the name given to the complex of religious ideas and beliefs shared by the community founded by the prophet Mani (see II/5). Mani was born in Parthian Iraq in 216 C.E. of members of one of the marginalized Jewish-Christian sects of that era. He received several personal revelations that convinced him he was chosen to complete the revelations of the Indian Buddha, the Iranian Zoroaster, and Jesus of Nazareth, whose apostle he claimed to be. He preached his message eastward as far as India, composed his revelations in numerous works regarded by his followers as Scripture, but was executed in 277 by the Sasanian shah, probably owing to pressure from the traditional Magian priesthood of Iran. His followers expected no successor: Mani was, as later Muhammad was said to be, "the seal of the prophets."

Manichaeism, like Gnosticism, to which it is obviously related, is made up of a founding myth and a series of behavioral commandments that flow from it. Its ideology was dualistic, positing an ultimate good and evil principle—the latter, following Marcion, was the God of the Jews—from which two competing worlds proceeded, a spiritual realm of light and an evil realm of darkness. For Mani these were engaged in an aboriginal warfare: the Evil One had attacked the Good, and some particles of the realm of light were, in effect, imprisoned in the material world. As in Christian Gnosticism, it is Jesus who descends and saves those fragments of light from the material darkness. This metaphysical battle is echoed in the moral sphere. Those who understand their origins and aspire to return to the realm of the Good God must free themselves from matter in any form, from consuming it to propagating it, an ethic that appears full-blown in the Cathar heresy of twelfth-century Western Christendom.

Mani's Church was made up of the Elect, who were called to and capable of full observance of this rigorous ascetic, and the Hearers, who aspired or attempted to be such. It was organized, like its Christian counterpart (see I/6), into a hierarchical episcopal structure. It was spread by energetic and skillful missionaries eastward as far as China and westward into the Roman Empire, where Augustine was first a devotee and later a fierce opponent. Eventually Manichaeism was overtaken by its rival universalist religions, by Christianity in the West and Islam in the East, and by the 800s it was in clear decline.

sin known as simony—and clerical marriage and concubinage were widespread. Eleventh-century dissidence was often an anguished attempt at reform from below, but it was noted on high as well, as witnessed by the clerical reforms enacted by the popes between Leo IX (d. 1054) and Gregory VII (d. 1085). What appeared as heresy in the towns and cities of Europe seemed like cries for help in Rome.

The Church of the Saints: The Cathars

What popular protests against clerical abuses had lit in the brush in the eleventh century took fire in the woods in the twelfth. By 1140 preachers in the Rhineland had detected a well-defined and well-organized religious movement that was quickly identified, in the best Augustinian fashion, as a strain of Manichaeism, and a group of their leaders were tried and burned at Cologne in 1143. These were the Cathars, the "Pure Ones," a group of Christians who had distanced them-selves from the mainstream Church, which they called the "Church of Satan," and lived a life of fierce asceticism in their own self-contained communities. They conferred their own baptism, called "the Consolating" (Consolamentum)—the only real sacrament they recognized—whereby proven neophytes were initiated into the ranks of "the Perfect," the spiritual elite at the heart of the movement.

The Cathars soon spread far more widely. Cathars were discovered in Lombardy and elsewhere in Italy, and they seem to have made particularly strong inroads in Languedoc, the area of southern France from Toulouse to Carcassonne. Here they began also to be called Albigensians, from the village of Albi, which was one of their centers. The Albigensians were no mere re-formers but separatists who reconstructed themselves into a more authentic Church. Like the Manichaeans, the Cathars were both metaphysical and eth-ical dualists who believed in two originating principles of good and evil and attempted to identify themselves with the former by severely distinguishing between matter and spirit in their moral choices. Catharism may indeed have come from the East, carried by eleventh-century Christian pilgrims passing, via Constantinople, between Europe and the Middle East. Thus, what was Manichaeism in Iraq became Paulicianism in Constantinople, Bogomilism in the Balkans, and, eventually, Catharism in Western Europe.

The Cathars were a two-tier community constituted by the ordinary believers and a much smaller group of the Elect who could embrace the full rigors of this dualist-inspired asceticism with its radical rejection of the world and matter: the Elect neither married nor propagated, and avoided, particularly in their diets, "all things born of coition." Put in a summary of Cathar doctrines and practices written in 1250 for the benefit of the Inquisition by Rainier Sacchoni, a former Italian Cathar turned Catholic and Dominican: "All Cathars believe that the devil made the world and everything in it, and that all the sacraments of the Church . . . do not help us to salvation. . . . All Cathars believe that conjugal relations are always mortal sin. . . . Again, all Cathars deny the resurrection of the flesh. They hold that it is a mortal sin to eat meat, eggs, or cheese, even in cases of urgent necessity, because they are the fruits of coition. . . . Secular powers sin mortally if they punish heretics or evil-doers. . . . They all deny purgatory."

In a sense, the Cathars had seized the moral high ground, a terrain more ex-posed than defended by the Gregorian reforms of the preceding century. The

Cathar Elect were their monastic clergy, thoroughly, even morbidly, ascetic in their lives, and unshakable in their convictions. Their communities lived blameless "evangelical" lives in accordance with what they claimed was a pristine Christian tradition that ran back to the age of the Apostles. And they were organized. In 1167 there was a council of Cathar leaders of France and Italy in a town near Toulouse to elect bishops and work out the jurisdictional boundaries of the Cathar "sees" in southern France.

The Church reacted in piecemeal fashion; there were local trials, convictions, and executions of dualist heretics throughout the twelfth century. In 1119 Pope Calixtus II held a council in Toulouse condemning groups sounding like Cathars—they denied the validity of the Church's sacraments, notably baptism and marriage, and rejected the Church's priesthood and hierarchy. In 1147 Pope Eugenius III, who had come to southern France to preach another Crusade against Islam, was alarmed by the number and strength of the heretics in Languedoc, where they were abetted by the local nobility (as they were not in Italy), who were jealous of the Church's vast wealth and estates there. He asked his mentor and the most eminent Christian preacher of the day, Bernard of Clairvaux (d. 1153)—who had already officially inaugurated the Second Crusade at Vezelay in 1134—to confront the Cathars of Albi and elsewhere in Languedoc. His mission accomplished little permanent good; rather, the Cathar heresy spread, with other dissident movements, northward across France into Flanders.

> **Note:** The Waldensians flourished in many of these same places and at the same time as the Cathars—Valdès preached in Lyons between 1160 and 1180 (see II/3). Although both movements had deep anticlerical roots and professed a return to Apostolic Christianity, the Waldensians were neither ethical nor metaphysical dualists in the Cathar style. Their asceticism was evangelical, in the manner of Francis of Assisi, rather than dualist, in the manner of Mani or the Gnostics.

The Albigensian Crusade

The combination of popular support and political protection by the local nobles, whether or not they actually converted, strengthened the Cathars of Languedoc, and the Church's problems with Islam and with Europe's troublesome and jealous monarchs provided the movement with breathing space in the late twelfth century. The popes sent repeated missions into Languedoc, but all were unavailing. Innocent III (r. 1198–1216), however, was more energetic and more resourceful than his predecessors. He tightened the diplomatic screws on the Languedoc nobles, and in 1205 he dispatched a French Cistercian mission to the area. They were accompanied by two Spaniards, the bishop of Osma and his canon, Dominic de Guzman. Dominic devised the strategy that finally began to make some inroads among the Cathars. The preachers sent to confront the Cathars had to be as evangelical and ascetic as their opponents and preach to the heretics where the heretics lived: in the streets. Catharism was at its heart a popular movement; only a popular appeal and popular instruction would prevail against it.

Some headway was made by the new "friar preachers" (see II/8), but it was slow going as long as the nobles protected the dissidents. In 1208, however, the papal legate to Languedoc, the medieval equivalent of an ambassador plenipotentiary, was murdered by a Cathar and Innocent III had his casus belli. For years the pope had been attempting to persuade the king of France to send his northern vassals against those in the south for harboring heretics. According to a papal mandate of 1184 titled *Ad abolendam*, the state was permitted—indeed, was required—to do just that, and Innocent had issued other similar directives in 1199 and 1207 empowering state intervention against heretics. The northern princes had been tempted—there were rich lands to be won at the expense of the obdurate southerners—and the 1208 murder dissolved whatever qualms they may have had about taking up arms against their fellow vassals of the king of France. That same year a veritable crusade was mounted against the Albigensian Cathars, and those who took up arms, and the cross, were granted the same papally sanctioned indulgences as those who fought against the infidel Muslims in the Holy Land.

The Albigensian Crusade, as it came to be known, staggered on for twenty years, interrupted by temporary submissions, followed by reneging and then renewed hostilities. The war proper ended in 1227 with a final submission of the nobles of Toulouse and the other Languedoc lands. Dominic de Guzman's increasingly active and organized "brethren"—they had been recognized by the pope as a new religious order in 1216, the Order of Preachers, more popularly known as "Dominic's Men," or the Dominicans—moved in and set up inquisitorial tribunals at Toulouse, Albi, and Norbonne. The dukes and counts had been defeated; the Church now attempted to stamp out dissidence itself. The Cathars' final and near impregnable fortress atop a formidable rocky crag in Languedoc, Montségur or "Mountain of Safety," fell in 1243 after a ten-month siege; 205 of the Elect chose to throw themselves on the pyre rather than recant.

The Holy War against Heresy

The state's involvement with the Church's treatment of its own dissidents came about through the criminalization of heresy. Just as Christianity itself had once been criminalized, and paganism newly so with the emperor's conversion, deviations from defined Christian doctrine became, in the fourth-century imperial legislation, crimes as well as sins. As a result, Roman judicial procedure came into play against heresy, most notably the one called *inquisitio*, or magistrate's investigation. In the later Roman Empire the emperor had become the sole judicial as well as legislative authority, and thus the magistrates who were his delegates were both prosecutors and judges. They could institute criminal proceedings on their own initiative or on information from an informer, search out evidence (even by torture), and render a judgment. These wide-ranging investigative and judicial powers of the Roman magistrate had nothing to do with Christianity, but from the fourth century onward they were available to the Church for the investigation and prosecution of deviant opinions.

The secular legislation against heresy was, in fact, more severe than the Church's own canon law sanctions, which stressed the reconciliation of heretics through preaching and persuasion. But the Church eventually found it necessary, or useful, to call on the state's judicial powers. One turning point came in the twelfth century, when the Cathars and the Waldensians began to gain support in southern France. The Roman Church, by now the dominant authority in Western Christendom, was sufficiently alarmed to resort to severe measures for their eradication. These were not simply divergent opinions offered in theological schools, for which there was a wide degree of tolerance, but movements—rival churches, in effect—that threatened the Church's unity and authority. The opening salvo in this holy war against heresy, a war in which church and state were partners, was fired in the 1184 *Ad abolendam*, issued jointly with the Holy Roman emperor Frederick, whereby the heretic was left to the discretion of the secular power for appropriate punishment. Furthermore, the bishop or his delegate was to make the rounds of his see at least once at year to conduct inquiry into reports of heresy and, if necessary, to prosecute the accused. The episcopal Inquisition was thus under way.

This new severity culminated in Pope Innocent III's decretal of 1199, which brought the Church's attitude in line with the imperial legislation: heresy was as treasonous a sin against the Church as it was a crime against the state. In 1207 Innocent issued a further decretal that when a heretic was found, he or she should be turned over to a secular court for punishment; in 1215 the Fourth Lateran Council defined most exactly what constituted Christian orthodoxy and institutionalized the trial and punishment of Christian heretics in accordance with Roman judicial norms. Further, it promised that "Catholics who have girded themselves with the cross for the extermination of heretics will enjoy the same indulgences and privileges granted to those who go in defense of the Holy Land."

The Secular Tribunal

The Inquisition as an ecclesiastical institution arose out of the Church's increased concern about the danger of heresy and a drawing together of church and state in the persecution and prosecution of heretics. Other factors contributed as well: the increasingly professionalized study of theology in Europe's new universities, and the creation of Church-wide fraternities of trained preacher-theologians, like the Dominicans, to bring theology to clergy and laity alike. The heresy canon of Lateran IV, for example, had said nothing about the death penalty, but the rationale for applying it was laid out by a theologian at the university of Paris—and the Church's most famous Dominican—Thomas Aquinas (d. 1274) in his *Summa theologiae*. The question under discussion there was "Whether Heretics Are to Be Tolerated?" and Thomas approached it in his usual careful manner. Heretics sinned gravely and so deserved to be separated from the Church by excommunication, he noted. They were, further, to be severed from life by execution. If lesser crimes like counterfeiting were punished by execution, how much more those who corrupted not the currency but the faith. The Church, however, always anticipated the possibility of conversion, Thomas continued, and so the convicted heretic had to be admonished, and more than once. That failing, the Church had then to look to the salvation of others: the heretic was to be excommunicated and then "delivered to the secular tribunal to be exterminated thereby from the world to death" (2–2.11.3).

Thus heretics were to be sought out or denounced, their teachings and practices investigated, and a judgment rendered. If convicted, they were summoned to recant, as Thomas noted. If they did recant, they were given a penance, some of them quite rigorous, like fasting, scourging, pilgrimage, or even imprisonment. If they refused, or if they relapsed, they were handed over to the state, the "secular tribunal," which more and more prescribed the death sentence, usually by burning.

> **Note:** John Calvin advocated, in both his writings and his governance of the Christian commonwealth he helped establish in Geneva (see I/8), the close cooperation of church and state. According to Calvin, the civil magistrates had the obligation to maintain purity of doctrine in the church; how seriously they took that obligation in Geneva is illustrated by the 1553 civil execution there of Michael Servetus, convicted of heresy against the Trinity. Calvin, no less than the pope, the emperor, and the officers of the Catholic Inquisition, believed that heresy was as much a crime against the state as an offense against God, that the state and its officials had the power and obligation to prosecute it, and if the defendant was found guilty and did not recant, to carry out the prescribed punishment, execution.

Sleeping with the Enemy

In the Middle Ages the practices of inquisitorial tribunals in Spain appear little different in objectives and means from those elsewhere in Western Christendom. Indeed, the coexistence of three distinct and powerful religious communities, Christian, Muslim, and Jewish, made Spain the most religiously and culturally diverse, and tolerant, of Europe's lands throughout medieval times. But by the end of the fourteenth century a new spirit had emerged in one important corner of the Iberian Peninsula. In Castile, a new exclusively, and exclusive, Christian identity was forged in the face of what had been a notoriously multicultural society where identities were blurred almost as a matter of course.

The blurring of distinctions in Spain often led to new efforts to define the Christian community against the other and to attempt to stand guard on those community boundaries—to keep the believers in, so to speak, and to keep the others out. The problem was as old as the Bible, whose own pages reveal, somewhat indirectly, just how attractive the other could be to the Israelites, whether in Egypt or later in Canaan. Even after Canaan had become part of Eretz Israel, the allure of the Gentiles' gods and cuisine did not diminish, nor did the inclination to marry the goyim or to commit what later came to be called, somewhat disingenuously, "simple fornication." The Bible pronounces early and often against sexual acts committed with the Gentiles. "You must not intermarry with them," God strongly warns, even though there are numerous biblical examples of acceptable miscegenation across religious lines, of which perhaps Ruth is the best known.

Among the Jews, attitudes toward mixed marriages eventually hardened, together with the increased emphasis on ritual purity characteristic of Pharisaic and rabbinic Judaism. Maimonides thought God's two chief instruments for keeping his people separate and holy were the dietary laws and the statutes against intermarriage. The rabbis went so far as to declare that every Gentile woman, for whom ritual purity was normally considered irrelevant, was, in the matter of sexual contact, to be regarded as being in a state of menstrual impurity, whether she was menstruating or not.

Christians from the outset shared Jewish anxiety about exogamy (1 Cor. 7:12–16), even though they had disavowed any tribal identity. One of the earliest councils of bishops, that held at Elvira in Spain sometime after 300, issued a prohibition of marriage between Christian women and Jewish men. Constantine introduced a similar prohibition, though somewhat ambiguously, into Roman law in 339. By 388 it was made clear and precise in the Theodosian Code: there was to be no marriage between Christians and Jews, males or females. Its violation would be regarded as tantamount to adultery, and the public at large was given the right to bring accusations. The prohibition remained in force, was reiterated—an almost certain sign that the forbidden practice had by no means disappeared—in subsequent Roman legal codes, and flowed from them into many of medieval Europe's civil statutes. Church councils reiterated the ban, but around 1000 the emphasis in ecclesiastical legislation began to shift. No longer was mixed marriage the Church's target; rather, it was extramarital sex and adultery with nonbelievers.

In Spain, of course, Muslims had also become part of the social mix, and while Christians, Jews, and Muslims living side by side might seem to represent a kind of smiling ecumenicism to some modern observers, it seemed more like a threat to Christian integrity to both contemporary churchmen and civil authorities. "If Jewish or Muslim males are found lying with a Christian woman," one Spanish municipal statute thundered, "the Jew or Muslim should be drawn and quartered and the Christian woman burned to death." With the increasing assimilation in language, dress, and customs in early medieval Spain, such misalliances must have been difficult to detect, and it was doubtless to protect itself against such interfaith sexual promiscuity that the Fourth Lateran Council decreed in 1215 that henceforward Jews and Muslims living in Christian lands should be constrained to wear distinctive clothing or other visible marks of differentiation.

The Muslim view of intermarriage was at first somewhat more relaxed than either its Jewish or Christian counterpart. According to the sharia, Muslim men might marry Jewish or Christian women, but the same right was denied Muslim women since it was understood that the child's religion would be that of the father, presumably by a kind of preemptive right, in contrast to the Jewish "linear" descent of religio-tribal affiliation through the mother. In Spain that Muslim male privilege was in direct contradiction to Christian teaching about intermarriage and, as we have seen, the Mudejares, or Muslims living under Christian sovereignty, were strictly forbidden to marry outside their faith community.

The Spanish Inquisition

The Inquisition came late to Spain. Its European beginnings are dated to about 1232, almost the very year that King Ferdinand III of Castile was proudly calling himself "king of the three religions." The Spanish Inquisition properly so-called was instituted at the request of Ferdinand and Isabella, by a papal bull issued in 1478 that licensed priests to investigate heretics but principally lapsed Jewish converts or conversos. Three Dominicans were appointed to the task and set to work in 1481. A year later the first public executions—an auto-de-fé, or "act of faith"—took place. The Inquisition grew in size and strength over time, and its task was rendered more complex by the growing religious and ethnic anti-Semitism that regarded any taint of Judaism suspect and reprehensible. Jews did not normally belong to the Church's inquisitorial jurisdiction, which had only to do with Christian deviants, but there were very broad exceptions: allegations of Jewish blasphemy, usury, or magic, proselytizing among Christians, or aiding or encouraging lapsed Jewish converts to Christianity all brought Jews into the purview of a Christian inquisitorial tribunal.

Finally, in 1492, the same year that Granada fell to their armies and their intrepid captain Columbus set foot in the Americas, Ferdinand and Isabella decreed the expulsion of all Jews, conversos or not, from Spain. The Jews who left scattered all across the Mediterranean basin. The safest refuge was in the

Abode of Islam, in North Africa just across the straits and in the more distant Ottoman lands in the Balkans and the Middle East, where, as self-styled "Spaniards," Sephardim, their rituals and practices took root in the local Jewish communities (see I/6).

Note: Reports on the number of Jews expelled in 1492 have varied widely, but one recent estimate puts Spain's Jewish population just before the expulsion at no more than 80,000. Of these, some became Christians and stayed—conversion was always an unspoken option to exile—rather than lose their property, and some even returned and accepted baptism after a short stay in the Muslim Maghrib. Hence, perhaps forty thousand Jews were permanently expelled from Spain in 1492.

The Christians called the Spanish Muslims "Moors" (*moros*) a word derived from the Romans' name for the inhabitants (*Mauri*) of their short-lived North African province of Mauretania, presently Morocco. But after 1526, when compulsory baptism began to be imposed on them as it had on the Jews, they began to be called by the not entirely affectionate diminutive Moriscos, or "Little Moors." The Moriscos presented a very different problem for the Christian rulers of Spain, lay and ecclesiastical, than had the Jewish conversos. To begin with, there were a great many more of them than Jews, and they were important for the prosperity of the Christian seignorial class. Their faith seems at the outset to have presented less of a direct threat to Catholic Christianity than either Judaism or Protestantism, those other Inquisition targets, and the thought that the forced Muslim converts might actually be turned into true Christians lingered far longer than in the case of the Jews. The Christians might have discovered how unlikely this prospect was had they known about the fatwa issued by a mufti in Oran around 1504 giving leave to Muslims to practice taqiyya, or dissembling true belief in the face of persecution (see II/4).

Their separateness and their cultural solidarity—they continued to speak Arabic and cling to other cultural markers like food and dress—made the Moriscos an obviously alien presence among the Christians of Spain. Nor were the Moriscos terribly careful about concealing their disdain for Christian beliefs like the Trinity or practices like the Eucharist. Finally, the Muslims, whether as straightforward Moors or converted Moriscos, represented a far graver political threat than the Jews. Islam was at war with Christendom on several fronts—a great naval battle was fought between the Christian and Ottoman fleets at Lepanto in the Mediterranean in 1571—and the large Muslim, now Morisco, population of Christian Spain had all the apparent makings of a fifth column.

In 1526, the same year baptism was required of all Muslims living in Spanish lands, the center of the Inquisition was relocated to Granada, the heart of al-Andalus. Decrees were issued prohibiting distinctive dress and the use of

Arabic—outside Granada all Moriscos by then spoke some form of Castilian—and Spanish books written in Arabic characters (Aljamiado)—called "Qurans" whatever their contents—were collected and burned. The Moriscos held the Inquisition temporarily at bay by paying a large annual indemnity, but in the 1560s, 1570s, and 1580s, Morisco revolts in Granada and uncovered plots of Morisco connivance with French Protestants and North African Muslim princes ended any attempts at reconciliation. The Inquisition turned on the Moriscos with a vengeance. In Aragon and Valencia Moriscos were by far the largest number of defendants before the tribunal, and in Granada Moriscos represented 82 percent of the prosecuted between 1560 and 1571. Finally in April 1609, the Crown decreed that expulsion was the only solution, and eventually three hundred thousand Moriscos were expelled from their homeland, with only twenty thousand left of what had once been a large population of Spanish Muslims.

Who Possesses the Truth?

The primacy of the See of Rome, a claim that stretches far back into the history of the Christian Church (see I/7), was only rarely understood, or acted on, in the manner it has been since the nineteenth century. In the early Church the Roman See regarded itself as the final judicial authority, while synods and councils of bishops generally formulated the norms of Christian belief and behavior. In the Middle Ages the pope had to share even his juridical authority with national princes who were as eager as the bishop of Rome to control such a rich and powerful institution in their realms. The Church had also to compete for power with the emperor, the Frankish or German lord who claimed at least the western half—there was a profoundly legitimate, albeit Greek-speaking, Roman emperor resident in Constantinople until 1453—of the now divided mantle of Constantine and, in consequence, a jurisdiction as universal as that of Peter's heir in Rome. But papal power did not diminish; in the sequel it merely flowed into new channels.

With the reforms of Gregory VII (r. 1073–1085), the papacy began the long and difficult process of freeing itself from outside political interference. At the same time, Gregory proclaimed his own jurisdiction over all Christians, clergy and laity alike. To administer this enlarged jurisdiction, the papal diwan, the Roman curia, grew into an effective instrument of policy, and, as a counterweight to the theologians, canon lawyers began their rise into the Church's hierarchy of power and prestige (see I/6). One index of the change in papal perspective is the frequency with which we hear invoked the title *vicarius Christi*, the deputy of Christ—now no longer merely of St. Peter—and so the trustee of all the powers bequeathed to the Church. Once those papal powers were moral; increasingly, from Gregory onward, they were also juridical. And the canon lawyers were not far behind in their statements of papal powers and prerogatives.

The pope, like all bishops, possessed both priestly and jurisdictional powers, but at issue here was the magisterium, the teaching authority in the Church as it applied to matters of faith and morals. Early on, the canonist Gratian (see II/4) had remarked that Christ had given Peter "the keys of the kingdom" or, more precisely, the key of knowledge and the key of power, the first now in the hands of the "doctors"—the experts from Augustine and Jerome onward—and the second in the apostolic succession of bishops, and most notably Peter's own successor, the bishop of Rome. But there were other claimants to the keys. From the early thirteenth century, another set of voices in the Western Church provided authoritative guidance on the moral order. These were the professionally trained and certified *magistri*, or masters, on the theological faculties of Europe's newly minted universities. These faculties were corporate, collegial bodies of highly trained clerics who offered instruction on Scripture—not through clerical pastoral preaching or episcopal pronouncement, the two earlier channels of moral instruction in the Church—but through teaching or, to put it more instrumentally, by lecture, the "reading" of the sacred page, or by public disputation. Understanding the Word of God had become increasingly complex, as had its display as reasoned discourse or theology; the rise of a professional class of exegetes and theologians both met and shaped the need for universal understanding of the faith. Theology became a science in the thirteenth century (see II/7) as did the study and teaching of Christianity.

The Church, then, had two orders of teachers: the bishops who pronounced authoritatively by reason of their episcopal office and the theologians who taught with increasing authority by reason of their professional training. This is, rather precisely, the difference between the Shiite Imams and the Sunni ulama, the utterers of the Word and its bonded unpackers. In the thirteenth and fourteenth centuries there were occasional conflicts. A bishop of Paris, Stephen of Bourret, put the matter in perspective in 1325: the magistri taught but the Church decreed, "the Holy Roman Church, mother and teacher (*mater et magistra*) of all the faithful, to whom belongs . . . the universal norm of orthodox truth, the approval or disapproval of teaching, . . . the determination of which opinions should be held and the condemnation of errors."

Stephen Tempier, another bishop of Paris, where, Christendom's most prestigious and outspoken magistri theologiae resided, raised the same issue for an earlier generation of bishops and theologians. In the case of theological truth or, more tellingly, error—that is, heresy—whose opinion should be preferred, the bishop's or the theologian's? Few in that Latin Christian universe would deny that either the pope or a council of the universal Church's bishops could define dogma or condemn heresy. But what of an individual bishop, like Stephen Tempier, who issued his own "syllabus of errors" in the face of the theology faculty of the university of Paris? Tempier's condemnation was revoked in 1325 by Stephen of Bourret, but the question remained: was the original condemnation valid and justified and, if so, did its revocation make Tempier himself a heretic?

Papal Heresy

Pope John XXII was an early lightning rod for a discussion of papal infallibility. Between 1322 and 1324 he issued a series of decrees first questioning and then denouncing what had become the standard Franciscan teaching on poverty, striking down the notion, previously affirmed by a bull of Nicholas III (see II/8), that neither Francis of Assisi and his followers, nor in fact Jesus and the Apostles before them, could absolutely renounce their dominion over material goods since their use of them, in eating and drinking, for example, showed that they were exercising some degree of right over them. John went even further and ruled that property was not a result of the fall of Adam: it existed by divine decree from the beginning and Adam himself had possessed antelapsarian property in Eden.

The pope's rulings were unacceptable even to moderate Franciscans like Michael of Cesena, the minister general of the Friars Minor, or William of Ockham, one of the fourteenth century's most considerable theologians. Both men had just argued their case at the papal court at Avignon, but they took their hasty leave when the pope's decision on Franciscan poverty came down. They found protection at the Munich court of King Louis IV of Bavaria, who had his own problems with the pope. John excommunicated both Cesena and Ockham when they refused to submit, and in 1324, he excommunicated Louis for assuming the title and prerogatives of emperor without papal approval. Somewhat after these events, John moved on to other, more ethereal matters. In a public sermon, the pope announced that the saints, though doubtless in heaven, would not enjoy the vision of God until the general resurrection of the body at the End Time. This teaching was reversed by John's successor, Benedict XII (he did not, however, rescind John's ruling on Franciscan poverty), thus rendering John, according to some, a papal heretic.

For the next twenty years, until his death in 1349, the Franciscan Ockham attempted to convince all who could read that both John and Benedict were doctrinally in error in their ruling on poverty. In his writings, Ockham argued that although the Church as whole had a scripturally guaranteed infallibility—Jesus had said to his disciples, "I will be with you all days until the end of time" (Matt. 28:20)—nothing protected any *part* of the Church, whether bishop, pope, or council, from falling into error. Ockham's understanding of infallibility was, in fact, as restrictive as possible. God would not permit all Christians to be in error at any given time; there would always be someone to keep the faith and oppose the errors of the majority. Orthodoxy, then, was what was received without opposition, a retrospectively discerned consensus of the faithful. What all Christians have believed is undoubtedly true, and this Christian consensus may be parsed as de facto infallibility.

According to Ockham, what made a heretic was not merely the assertion of an error but pertinacious perseverance in it despite correction. In his eyes, pertinacity was not always transparent, but one type was easy to discern. When someone maintains that a teaching must be held, he or she is either correct or pertinaciously in error: irrevocable assertion constitutes pertinacity. Although apparently arguing generally, Ockham had in mind both John XXII and Benedict XII and their dogmatic assertions about Franciscan and evangelical poverty. Ockham did not deny the pope jurisdictional authority: he was, after all, the Church's chief executive officer. But the bishop of Rome did not create the Church's truth; he merely settled controversies among the true experts (*periti*), the Church's theologians. When these latter differed on questions of doctrine, the pope, by careful investigation, had to make a determination as to which position was true. John XXII did more than adjudicate, however. He reversed papal decrees, that of Nicholas III on poverty and that of Innocent III on the Beatific Vision—decrees not only founded on Scripture but accepted by the whole Church. The pope, it followed, was a heretic.

This did not follow for all, however, or perhaps even for many Christians. But the dispute undoubtedly weakened papal power, or better, the papacy's moral authority, which had already suffered from the move to Avignon and the Christian experience of not two but three popes contesting the throne of St. Peter (see I/6). When the next great attack on the papacy occurred, it would not be an accusation leveled against a pope but against the papacy itself. The Reformers aimed to reduce the pope from the claimed head of all Christendom to the more modest status of bishop of Rome, with a jurisdiction limited to the (benighted) souls there.

The Umma Divided:
Sects and Sectarianism in Early Islam

The Quran's division of the world into true believers (*muslimun* or *muminun*), qualified believers (the People of the Book; see II/1), and unbelievers proved not quite adequate for the realities of the world it had itself created. Already in the Quran there was talk of "hypocrites" (*munafiqun*), those apparently who had accepted Islam at Medina but whose actions belied the strength of their new faith. This disparity between faith and act continued to trouble the nascent community. How observant did the believer have to be, the Kharijites asked, to be considered a believer? Did failed or faulty observance make one, ipso non facto, an apostate? The Kharijites thought so, but most Muslims did not. Failed observance was simply that; faith dwelled in the heart.

The issue of the genuine Muslim and so of membership in the community arose early in Islam. The Medina suras of the Quran speak often of munafiqun, and though the allusion, like much else in the Quran, is not entirely clear, it seems reasonably certain that the reference was to Medinese Arabs who had at least nominally professed Islam but were not Muslims in their heart. Some hearts were easier to read. At the Prophet's death in 632, many of the opportunistic Bedouin tribes of Arabia thought of leaving Islam, at least to the extent of not paying into the Muslim treasury the alms-tithe that was a sign of their submission. Muhammad's successor as head of the umma had to make an immediate decision: was it possible to secede from the Islamic community? The answer was a decisive "no." The "secession" (*ridda*) was put down when armies were sent against the tribes to coerce their adherence to Islam.

Entry into the community of Muslims was regarded, then—as it was among Christians—as only partially reversible. A Muslim may be banished from the community but may not willfully withdraw from it. That latter act is called apostasy and is viewed exceedingly gravely in all three faiths. In most cases apostasy requires a formal act of disavowal on the part of the believer, but the question was raised in Islam, as it was among the radical Reform Christians we lump together as Anabaptists, as to whether nonobservance was, in fact, a kind of apostasy. The Kharijites certainly thought so, and were willing to visit the fatal consequences of apostasy on those who did not pray daily or fast during Ramadan.

In the classic form cited above, the shahada is purely a verbal formulation and leaves open the questions of interior intention and the relative importance to be placed on interior faith and external good works. The Kharijites, who supported Ali until shortly before his death and then broke with him, had greatly emphasized the latter: whoever did not act like a Muslim was in fact not a Muslim, and should be treated accordingly. "Accordingly" in this context meant as an apostate, the penalty for which was "termination with extreme prejudice." In the few places where Kharijites actually gained political control of the community, they were, as one might suspect, most circumspect about killing off all the other Muslims who did not share their view of Islam.

Heresiography and Comparative Religion

One of the richest genres of Islamic religious literature is that given over to cataloging and describing the various "sects" (*farq*; pl. *firaq*) that arose within the community of believers. Although the narrative context is invariably theological, as are the issues over which these groups were thought to have separated themselves from the umma, social and economic conflict lurks barely concealed beneath the bland and rigid categories that in Christendom might be called heresies.

The Muslims were every bit as fastidious as the Christians in identifying and cataloging dissident opinions that occurred among Muslims. One of the first to have done so was the theologian al-Ashari (d. 935), whose *Opinions of the Muslims* attempted to sort out what was already a troubling variety of Muslim sects. Later works, which were often called "Book of Religious Communities and Sects," added, under the first of those rubrics, a discussion of non-Muslim religious communities.

Christianity's recognition of a comparative religious perspective was satisfied by the inclusion of the Jews' Old Testament in their own body of Scripture and theological reflection on the passage of the Abrahamic promise from the Jews to themselves. The Muslims had a far broader horizon. The invitation to comparative thinking is already explicitly present in the Quran's acknowledgment of a religious category called People of the Book. That established a fruitful way of thinking about religious communities related, across Scripture, to Islam, but the Muslims' conquests and the only partial absorption of Zoroastrians, Manichaeans, Buddhists, and Hindus into the umma broadened the Muslims' view of the others in ways that never occurred to Christians until much later. The two most widely read medieval Muslim texts on religious communities and sects, those by the Spaniard Ibn Hazm (d. 1064) and the Iranian al-Shahrastani (d. 1153), are in fact filled with comparative, if not always sympathetic, perspectives on humankind's other religions.

Innovation and Heresy

In a muslim society that possessed no institution or office capable of defining "orthodoxy" in the familiar Christian sense, one norm against which a Muslim's actions or, somewhat less certainly, opinions could be judged as to rectitude was the "custom of the Prophet" (*sunnat al-nabi*). The notion that the sunna might serve as an Islamic yardstick gained widespread currency in legal circles only in the early ninth century, but neither it, nor deviations from it— *bida*, "innovation"—serve as a very useful guide for understanding what was actually happening within the Islamic community in the first century and a half of its existence, nor even, perhaps, thereafter.

On a closer inspection of the notion of bida, with its attractive heuristic possibilities as an Islamic equivalent of "heresy," it soon emerges that the term covers both more and less than is historically useful. The Quran presents itself as both a permanent and a closed revelation, and the Muslim believer, no less than his Jewish and Christian counterparts, is invited to accept the notion that God had here laid out, definitively, immutably, and exhaustively, his will for humankind. To add, subtract, or otherwise change God's Word was, therefore, an "innovation," whose Arabic expression stands suggestively close to the etymon for "creation," a power reserved exclusively to God.

God, as it turned out, had not said his Last Word, even in the believers' eyes, and what followed in Islam was an attempt to interpret, to flesh out, and, somewhat less ingenuously, to modify the divine message. The hadith's function is clearly to gloss and explain the revelation, and there is considerable innovation vis-à-vis the Quran's pronouncements within the extraordinarily flexible limits of the custom of the Prophet. Some of this had in the end to be accepted as permissible innovation in grudging acknowledgment of at least some evolutionary energy at work within the community. At the other end of the belief spectrum, however, stood *ghuluw*, "extremism," a type of innovative practice or belief that violated even the elastic limits of the lawyers' patience. Beyond that lay only *kufr*, total and irreconcilable unbelief.

Taking the shape and measure of bida exercised the legal ingenuity of the Islamic lawyers, but the *ghulat*, the "extremists," have attracted the attention of the historians since in their ranks can be traced the deep and powerful opposition to what was developing into an Islamic consensus, an opposition that in many cases was drawing its ideology from other religious traditions in the Middle East. Most of the ghulat causes were lost, but in at least one instance their voice continued to be heard discordantly in the increasingly harmonious chorus of Sunni Islam: Shiism eventually embraced and held firm to many of the ghulat premises, such as the transmigration of souls and the divinization of the caliph Ali and his successor Imams (see II/9).

Taking the Measure of Early Islamic Sectarians

To recite the often bewildering sequences of the various firaq in the same terms as the original authors of the Islamic heresiographies is simply to produce another catalog. Before the material there becomes comprehensible, the premises of the heresiographers themselves have to be examined, and their methods understood. But this process alone, difficult as it is, does not yet convert the appearance and disappearance of those multiple "sects" into episodes in the community's history; they must be somehow related to the Muslim historians' accounts of those times and places. This way it is possible to understand many of the earliest sects in terms of political opposition to the dynastic ambitions of the Umayyads. That much is relatively straightforward, since the historians were essentially writing political history. The going gets rough in attempting to integrate social and economic factors, which the historians did not much reckon, into the growth of Islamic sectarianism.

Both Kharijism and the early movements associated with Ali and his descendants illustrate the complexities of the problem. The Kharijites, or "Seceders," who appear as a sect in all the heresiographies, played an active political role in the events between the Battle of Siffin in 657, when Ali accepted arbitration in his dispute with Muawiya, and the fall of the Umayyads in 750. The Kharijites had withdrawn their support from Ali after Siffin, been attacked by him in turn, and mounted insurrections against him, while continuing to resist the claims of Ali's family, but not until sometime past the mid–eighth century did they begin to put together the rudiments of a theology. The Kharijites' original "secession" from Ali's cause has been read in both religious and economic terms. In like manner, some have interpreted the movement's later manifestations in terms of the self-interest of the tribes that made up the bulk of the Kharijites, whereas others have preferred to see in Kharijism a kind of tribal solidarity and egalitarianism that in the end viewed the umma as a quasi-communistic "charismatic" community. From this perspective, Kharijism represented an Islamic and quranic transformation of the pre-Islamic tribe, particularly on the North Arabian model, which was thrust into revolt by tensions between their own traditions and the emerging bureaucratic and centralized structure of the Umayyad caliphate.

The Kharijite position, as it finally emerged, was that the umma was a community based entirely on the Quran and that its members consisted only of those who held to true Islamic beliefs. This might seem rather self-evident and not terribly consequential, but the Kharijites proposed to measure those beliefs by behavior. Where most Muslims were willing to accept the profession of faith at face value, or, as the more theologically minded put it, to "suspend judgment" on the quality of that faith, the Kharijites wished to measure faith by deeds. Thus, the sinner—someone who violated what was understood by the Kharijites, appealing to common norms, as Islamic behavior—was not merely a nonobservant Muslim but in fact an unbeliever (*kafir*). In Christianity such a judgment might lead to a kind of sacramental execution, a cutting off from the grace of salvation, but for the Kharijites, sin amounted to apostasy, and the punishment for apostasy was death. The Kharijites gravely proposed not to excommunicate sinners but to execute them.

Kharijism's subsequent history shows some of the political and social contexts in which a sectarian form of dissent might be useful. A moderate version of Kharijism identified as Ibadi spread to the Persian Gulf ports and thence to North Africa, where there were frequent revolts against Abbasid sovereignty and eventually independent Kharijite "states" appeared. Kharijism put down wide, though perhaps not very deep, roots among the local Berber population. And although North African Kharijism as such was dead by the mid–tenth century, it was at the outset the most acceptable form of Islam to the Berbers. Once embraced, it permitted the spread of the new faith away from the coastal plain, where it had been planted by the original Arab conquerors, into the interior mountains and steppes that were the Berber domains. What made Kharijism attractive to the montagnard and nomadic Berbers was surely its conviction of the equality of all believers, a notion that nonetheless coexisted comfortably with a legitimist veneration for Ali's family, which permitted the rise all across North Africa of various dynasties called "Sharifian" (a *sharif*, or "noble," was understood to be a direct descendant of Muhammad, in this instance through Fatima and Ali).

Defining the Umma: The Sunni View of Islam

Before the sunnat al-nabi or custom of the Prophet became a criterion for orthodoxy, there was another, older idea to which many Muslims could rally and
which, by its choice of issue, effectively set political limits against "sectaries."
This was the principle of a united community, jamaa, and it survived in the common centrist conjunction of "people of custom and the united community" (*ahl
al-sunna wa al-jamaa*). The connection between the two notions may date back
to Ali (r. 656–661), when that caliph refused to accept the extension of the sunna
concept, the notion of normative behavior, beyond the Prophet to his immediate successors. The partisans of jamaa, in contrast, regarded the community and
its sunna as a continuous process and so were willing to accept the sunna of the
first three caliphs as authoritative and normative as that of the Prophet himself.

The jamaa partisans or "political Unitarians" supported the Umayyads
in the name of community solidarity, while the ruling regime suppressed its
Shiite and Kharijite dissidents. The jamaa position found powerful support in
the influential lawyer Hasan al-Basri (d. 728), but there remained the problem
of Ali versus Uthman or, as some Shiites saw it, Ali versus the authority of
all three of his predecessors in the caliphate. Another lawyer, Ahmad ibn
Hanbal (d. 856), was chiefly instrumental in refusing that dilemma in the
name of the political centrists. All four of the first caliphs were "rightly guided"
(*rashidun*); Ali was no longer an enemy of the community, as some had regarded him in the events of 660–661, and his sunna was accepted along with
that of the others. The basic Sunni position of the Islamic umma as a single,
undivided whole was thus essentially in place, and those who had sought to
rend it, the supporters of civil strife (*fitna*) and sectarianism, could be readily
disavowed.

But *sunna*, as it turns out, means something more than the "custom of the
Prophet," Muhammad's customary way of applying the Quran to the world. It
also meant the "custom of the community," which, according to one Prophetic
tradition, would "not agree in error." The Muslims' frequent, if often unac-
knowledged, acceptance of community consensus as a normative guide for
human acts had its origins in the absence of authoritative directives—the silence
of the Quran, for example—whence it led to majority acceptance of the familiar
but unquranic practice of male circumcision and the equally unquranic but probably improvised institution of the caliphate. When such directives did eventually surface in the guise of Prophetic traditions, the problem appeared to be
solved. But only very briefly: the superabundance of problem-solving traditions quickly undermined their own authority (see II/3) and what emerged
was a consensually agreed-on base—that A is applicable in this case and B is
not—while all counterevidence could be cancelled or simply ignored (see II/4
and II/5).

Important in the Sunni view was, then, staying close to "catholic" Islam as defined by consensus. This was true in a political sense, by following the commander of the faithful or leader of the community: praying with him, paying the alms-tithe into his hands, following him into holy war if he so decreed, abiding by his application of the punishments prescribed by the Quran. "Whoever secedes from the Imam of the Muslims," said Ahmad ibn Hanbal in his *Creed*, "when the people have agreed upon him and acknowledged his caliphate . . . , that rebel has broken the unity of the Muslims and opposed the tradition coming from God's Messenger." But there is an even more profound sense in which consensus defines the community. The Prophet is reported to have blessed Muslims who "kept close to the community," a phrase that for Shafii, Islam's most influential jurist, meant there should be no deviation "from what the community of Muslims maintains. . . . Error arises in separation. In the community there can be no total error concerning the meaning of the Book, of the Prophetic tradition." And taking a large step outside the cover of revelation, he added, "or of analogical reasoning, please God."

Sunnis and Shiites

If the Kharijites were willing to exclude the grave sinner as well as the unbeliever from their midst, others such as the early jurist Abu Hanifa (d. 767) regarded faith (*iman*) as separate from the moral activity of the individual Muslim. Neither view entirely prevailed in the end. Abu Hanifa's definition of faith as "confessing with the tongue, believing with the mind, and knowing with the heart" was generally accepted by Sunnis as applicable to membership in the community of believers whose profession rendered them subject to the Islamic law. All agreed, moreover, that the one unforgivable sin of polytheism (*shirk*; "association," that is, of other gods with *the* God) excluded one from that community. As regards other grave sins such as murder and fornication, eternal punishment in the Afterlife was probable but not inevitable. The sinner could only put his hope in God's goodness and the Prophet's intercession; for their part, the other Muslims here below must suspend judgment.

The Shiites (see I/8) would not have it entirely so. In Shiite eyes, the Sunnis are assuredly Muslims (muslimun) in that they have professed the essential monotheism of the shahada; but only the Shiat Ali were muminun, true believers. Shiites have not hesitated to enforce this conviction on Sunnis when they have had the power to do so—in Safavid Iran, for example—but more often the power shoe was on the Sunni foot. To avoid having Sunni practices forced on them under threat, Shiites, despite their deep veneration for the martyr, have resorted to the practice of dissembling (*taqiyya*) their true beliefs (see II/4). Neither Sunnis nor Shiites, however, despite their often antagonistic feelings toward one another—often most openly and violently manifested on the hajj or annual pilgrimage, when they are in close quarters and religious emotions run high (see II/6)—have read the other out of the umma.

The Sunnis often distinguished among the Shiite dissenters. Those who contented themselves with praising Ali and his successors in the Imamate as the best Muslims were thought merely to have "wandered" from the truth and abandoned "tradition and the community" or "the consensus." Those Shiites who attributed prophethood or even divinity to Ali, however, like the Alawis (see II/9), were more severely judged: they were guilty of (kufr) and so vacated any claim to be a Muslim.

Obvious deviance apart, the Sunnis' tolerant attitude of suspending judgment on the moral conduct of one's neighbor had some extremely disagreeable political implications that were, in fact, the chief point in the discussion. Postponement of judgment effectively removed the religious and moral issue from the political life of the Islamic empire, and the acceptance of this principle marked another stage in the secularization of the caliphate, whose tenants could no longer be challenged on the grounds of their personal morality. The predestination argument led in the same direction—*de facto* was in fact *de Deo*. The predestination versus free will argument drifted off into quite another direction, into the metaphysical thicket of atoms, accidents, and "acquisition," but the postponement thesis held because it represented some kind of ill-shaped Muslim consensus that custom and the community were more important than tossing dead sinners into hell and live ones out of office or out of the community.

Note: Two of the most recent deviations from catholic Islam are the movements called the Bahais and the Ahmadis. The former, the product of a number of earlier peelings off from Imami Shiism, are the followers of Baha Allah (d. 1892), who proclaimed himself the "promised one," promised, that is, by an earlier Shiite charismatic, Mirza Ali Muhammad. Baha Allah's prophetic teachings, and their understanding by his followers, have moved progressively farther from Islam. In many places Bahais are regarded as members of a distinct religion. In Iran, however, they are still considered Muslim apostates and treated severely as such. The Ahmadis are the followers of Mirza Ghulam Ahmad (d. 1908), a Punjabi who began by denouncing Western colonialism as the Antichrist and ended by declaring himself not only the Mahdi (see II/10) but also the Second Coming of Jesus and the last avatar of the Hindu god Vishnu. The followers of Ahmad, whose center is now in Pakistan, are divided on the nature of his prophetic status, but those who grant him a prophethood on par with Muhammad's have been explicitly rejected by the main body of Muslims. Both Bahais and Ahmadis are energetic proselytizers and have enjoyed notable success in the more tolerant atmosphere outside the Abode of Islam.

The Zindiq Inquisition

One form of "innovation" that the medieval Muslims found particularly disturbing was what they called *zandaqa* and whose somewhat shadowy practitioners were termed *zindiq*s. As best can be discerned, the zindiq was originally a dualist of the Manichaean type; indeed, the Zoroastrians may have used the term for the Manichaeans who departed from Zoroastrian orthodoxy by putting their own "interpretation" (*zand*) on the Avesta. What made the Manichaeans particularly dangerous for the Muslim was their apparent embrace of Islam—as they earlier seemed to embrace Christianity—without renouncing their deep-seated belief in two gods, one of good and the other of evil. Hence the zindiq was a crypto-Manichaean, and in the eighth century was regarded as a danger to the state. It was that aspect of zandaqa that prompted the famous "inquisition"—famous chiefly for its uniqueness—instituted by the caliph al-Mahdi in 780 with specific directions that all zindiqs were to be apprehended and brought before the caliph himself. There was even an official inquisitor appointed to direct the search for the heretics. As in its later Christian counterpart, this Muslim inquisition stipulated that individuals could be taken into custody under either suspicion or denunciation and questioned by either the caliph or a competent official. If found guilty of zandaqa, they would be invited to recant; failing to do so, they were executed, either by decapitation or some form of crucifixion.

Zindiq must have been a popular (or frightening) term since the appellation was soon extended to mean any kind of freethinker, skeptic, or suspected atheist and, in the end, anyone whose behavior seemed either erratic or insincere.

The Enemy Within: Ibn Taymiyya

Holy war *jihad* is, as we shall see (in I/8), a religious obligation for Muslims, a duty, whether for the community or the individual, forcefully to resist the enemies of Islam. The division of the world into the Abode of Islam—the territories under Muslim political sovereignty—and the Abode of War—the lands beyond that pale—draws a rather precise line between the community and its enemies. But the early Muslim jurists who laid down those boundaries were aware that the political and religious reality they sought to define was far more complex. The very first problem faced by Abu Bakr (r. 632–634), Muhammad's immediate successor as the head of the umma, was whether to use force, in effect, whether to invoke jihad against those Arabian tribes who, at Muhammad's death, refused to pay the alms-tithe required of all Muslims. This was judged apostasy (*irtidad*), and so the use of force to coerce the defiant tribes was legitimate. The decision to do so redrew the boundaries of jihad: holy war, the *only* war permissible to Muslims, might also be waged against God's enemies within the umma.

The attack on the faith to which jihad is a legitimate and necessary response most often came from external enemies, from that area designated by classical jurisprudence as the Abode of War, because its inhabitants either were in fact hostile to Islam or were constantly in a state of war among themselves. But as soon became apparent, Islam had its enemies within, those who also threatened the faith, either as apostates (*murtaddun*), like those who had refused the pay the zakat, or dissenters like the Kharijites. Jihad was waged against both groups.

By the thirteenth century the problem of internal enemies had changed not as much in kind as in scale. Central Asian newcomers called Mongols had entered the Abode of Islam and threatened to destroy the very fabric of the umma. In 1258 Baghdad, the heart and seat of the caliphate, was taken, sacked, and so thoroughly destroyed that the city never quite recovered. But the Mongols, who were inexorably pushing westward toward the Syrian and Egyptian heartlands, were by then themselves Muslims and so not enemies but members of the umma; indeed, its de facto rulers. Might they be fought?

The question was posed to the most eminent, and notorious, jurist of the day, the Syrian Ibn Taymiyya (d. 1328). In his tension-filled lifetime, he had fought against both state and church and paid for it with spells in prison; he died a prisoner in the Damascus citadel. The issue now was the Mongols, whether a jihad might be fought against these new, powerful, and destructive Muslim warlords. In two fatwas, or judicial responses (see II/4), and then more systematically in his treatise *Public Policy in Islamic Jurisprudence*, Ibn Taymiyya rendered a judgment that still resonates today among Fundamentalist Muslims. Profession of Islam was not enough. Though by the criterion of the shahada they were Muslims, the Mongols violated the broader requirements of Islam. They still lived according to their own pagan law, which rendered them, in effect, unbelievers. Jihad against them was not only licit but required. The duties of Islam are both explicit, like those detailed in the Pillars of Islam, and implicit, Ibn Taymiyya argued in his *Public Policy*. The true Muslim must not marry his sister, eat impure foods, or, significantly, "attack the lives and wealth of the Muslims." "Any such trespasser of the Law should be fought," he concluded, "provided he had a knowledge of the mission of the Prophet. It is this knowledge that makes him responsible for obeying the orders, the prohibitions, and the permits (of the sharia). If he disobeys these, he should be fought."

Despite his own problems with some of the rulers in Islam, Ibn Taymiyya was a firm believer in the two swords of temporal and spiritual power and responsibility, distinct but firmly linked in Islam. The state, whose function is described in the popular phrase "to command the good and prohibit evil," possessed, and was obliged to use, its coercive might (*shawka*) to protect the integrity of the faith and observance of the law, while it was the function of sharia and its guardians to maintain justice in the community.

Fundamentalists as the Faithful Remnant

Ibn Taymiyya has been a powerful ideological model for the theoreticians of the modern movement called Islamic Fundamentalism, or, as some prefer, Revivalism. Whatever the appropriate name, this is the Muslim version of what is in fact a much broader phenomenon called fundamentalism, a term that was originally applied to evangelical Christian sects in the 1920s. Fundamentalism, whether Muslim or any other variety, is generally (though not invariably) characterized by a series of positions that are at the same time theological (Scripture is infallible); philosophical (Scripture is not subject to so-called critical analysis); historical (it envisions a return to origins); political (it advocates revolution in the name of religion); and, of chief interest in the present context, sociological (the movement is a "Church" within the "Church").

Muslim political power, or better, the political power of Muslim states, has been on the wane for many centuries. One reading of this progressive waning sees it as the result of an ideological attack from secularism, which is represented in modern times by Western states. The effects of the onslaught are everywhere apparent: the era of colonialism, the West-abetted foundation of the State of Israel and continued Western dominance of the political economy, the erosion of Islamic political, judicial, and educational institutions. Two basic and contrasting solutions have been offered (with many compromises in between). One is to adopt Western ways, in short, to modernize Islam—the position is called Modernism—and bring it into conformity to the needs and demands of the modern era. The other is to return to Islam, either to struggle for the preservation of the best of the past, what is called Traditionalism, or to seek, as the Fundamentalists, or Islamists, as they are now often called, do, a renewal or revival (*tajdid*) of the past.

Fundamentalism has arisen in the Islamic world from this latter perspective. It has issued its "call" for a moral and social movement to establish the Islamic order, realized in the Jamaat-i Islami in Pakistan and the Muslim Brotherhood in Egypt. It is firm in its denial of nationalism and its repudiation of the nation-state in the name of a single umma. Islamic Fundamentalism struggles—not always successfully; consider Saudi Arabia and the Islamic Republic of Iran (see I/8)—to be nonsectarian. It seeks the reconciliation of Shiite and Sunni differences. And if it is willing and eager to embrace the technology of modernity, it is resolute in its denial of the ideology of secular and pluralistic modernism. It points, with great effect, to the failure of two modern Muslim experiments in modernism and Westernization, republican Turkey and prerevolutionary Iran.

> **Note:** In the case of Islam, a distinction must be drawn between a Muslim state, one in which the majority of the population is professedly Muslim, and an Islamic state or society, whose laws are based to a greater or lesser extent on the sharia. Syria, Egypt, Iraq, and Turkey would be examples of the first, whereas Iran, Saudi Arabia, Taliban Afghanistan, perhaps the Sudan and Pakistan, and fitfully Libya might all be argued—and disputed, chiefly by each other—as Islamic states.
>
> "Jewish" and "Christian" do not allow the same distinction. It is of no matter in the first case since there is only one state or society that qualifies in either sense of the word as "Jewish"—the State of Israel—even though it has no constitution and many Jews cannot or prefer not to imagine it as Jewish in the religious sense. There are, however, still many states where the majority of the population professes Christianity, but only one surviving state, the Holy See or State of the Vatican City, population 870, is governed by a version of Church law.

What distinguishes Fundamentalism from Traditionalism is its flexibility, its willingness to practice ijtihad (as Ibn Taymiyya did) and to adapt sharia to the modern world. It is a critique not only of the West but of the Muslim status quo. Islamic Fundamentalism understands Islam as a totalizing experience and so rejects the separation of Islam from politics or any other aspect of modern life. The Islamists, like all other such groups, see themselves as a faithful remnant, the true Muslims, who stand in sharp contrast to others who profess Islam but who follow the values of the derogatory *jahiliyya*, the "era of ignorance" used to characterized pre-Islamic days. Hence they are also willing to follow Ibn Taymiyya's lead with respect to the Mongols and to condemn other Muslims as unbelievers, most notably the rulers of other "Muslim" countries, a conviction that led directly to the assassination of Anwar Sadat, president of Egypt, in 1981.

Catholic Judaism

"Catholic" or "Sunni" Judaism made its appearance considerably later in that community than in Islam. Jewish reliance on consensus, though probably latently present throughout the rabbinic period, became doctrine in certain Jewish circles in the nineteenth century. It was, in fact, the centerpiece of the movement called Conservative Judaism. Its most eminent champion was Solomon Schechter (d. 1915), who left his academic post at Cambridge in 1902 to take up the presidency of the New York's newly founded Jewish Theological Seminary, the academic flagship of Conservative Judaism in America (see II/3). For Schechter, the consensus of Jews was "the collective conscience of catholic Israel as embodied in the universal synagogue." Schechter's emphasis on "catholic

Israel" (*kelal Israel*), like that on its institutional counterpart, the "universal syn-agogue," was the intended antidote to the sectarian "Israels" emerging from the rabbis' conflict with the "pietists" in Eastern Europe and from rabbinic en-counter with modernity's promise of "enlightenment" and "emancipation." The sunna of Conservative Judaism was preserved in the Bible's historical record of the Jewish experience and shown forth in the beliefs and practices of Jews.

As already noted, Vincent of Lerins attempted to sum up Christian ortho-doxy in the phrase "what has been believed always, everywhere, and by all." Schechter might have agreed if the phrase "and practiced" were added to "be-lieved." The core beliefs and practices of Jews across the centuries was Judaism's grounding authority. Traditional Judaism had validated itself by reference to the oral Torah, the "second revelation" bestowed on Moses at Sinai and transmit-ted—and interpreted—by the rabbis who stretched in an unbroken chain from second temple times to Schechter's own. But he and the Conservatives would not have it so. The Jewish people themselves, and the tradition they carried, in a historically verifiable manner, over the generations were their own validation.

Shades of Black: Orthodox Judaism

Despite its traditional trappings, what is commonly called Orthodox Judaism is a relatively modern phenomenon. The broad outlines of Jewish belief and practice throughout the "long" Middle Ages from the closure of the Talmud in 600 C.E. down to the appearance of Reform Judaism in the nineteenth cen-tury may be generally characterized as "rabbinic"—that is, they were shaped by the academic lawyers who constituted the primary Jewish elite during those centuries. Those beliefs and practices were by no means uniform since Jews lived under quite different political and cultural regimes—Muslim in Spain, North Africa, and the Middle East, Christian principalities and then, more recently, secular nation-states in Europe. That basic difference led to a distinction between Ashkenazi and Sephardic Judaisms (see I/6), a difference more of style than of substance. Nor was the rabbis' stewardship untroubled: it was challenged, by a denial of its very premises, the oral Torah, by the Karaites (see II/3) and then by the messianic claims of Sabbatai Zvi in the Middle East and their various aftershocks in Eastern Jewry (see I/1).

A broad and rich strain of mysticism developed within this cultural synthesis, but the Kabbalah, as it was called (see II/9), was so esoteric that its effects were for long felt almost entirely within learned circles of rabbinic adepts. In the eighteenth century that began to change. The movement of popular devotion called Hasidism carried a more accessible form of Kabbalah into the Jewish communities of Eastern Europe (see II/8). The Hasidim with their charismatic *rebbes* and their preference for experiential faith over punctilious observance represented a direct challenge to the centuries-old rabbinic synthesis. Their "opponents" (*mitnaggedim*), particularly those in the Lithuanian yeshivas, the most learned in Eastern Europe, stiffened their own practices, and a serious fault line appeared between a populist, devotional Judaism and a learned, observant Judaism at the far eastern edge of Europe, which in the eighteenth and nineteenth centuries had developed a substantial Jewish population.

What aborted the schism and drove the Hasidim and Mitnaggedim into each other's arms, and so, in effect, created Orthodox Judaism, was the appearance of what both sides perceived as an even greater threat to Judaism's integrity. The very notion of the European nation-state required that it grant freedom and civil equality to all its citizens. Hence the movement toward "emancipation" freed European Jews of the centuries-old civil disabilities under which they had lived before. But if the Jews were invited into the civil state in the nineteenth century, they had necessarily to leave some of their baggage behind. That same political philosophy dictated that the modern secular state could no longer tolerate the existence of autonomous bodies within it. For the Jewish community, the *kehillah*, this meant the loss of whatever immunities it possessed or whatever autonomous civil powers it exercised. Finally, the modern nation-state aspired to cultural uniformity, and to that end it established a system of secular state-run schools where citizens would be uniformly instructed in the nation's history and the state's ideals. For the Jews, as for the Christians, this meant surrendering education, which was usually a schooling in the elements of Scripture and the Law, to a secular authority.

In the nineteenth century, the walls of the ghettos were coming down all across Europe, tunneled under, clambered over, or simply walked through by increasing numbers of Jews who now belonged to Europe's new bourgeoisie. In France and Germany, the European Enlightenment was creating a Jewish Enlightenment (*haskalah*) with many of the same characteristics as its determinedly secular counterpart. Jews began to move out of their own communities and to share in the cultural and civil life of Europe. Some Jews simply disappeared into the new secular world open to them; some attempted to "reform" their traditional beliefs to bring them into line with what now appeared to be enlightened thinking about religion. Still others tried to work out an accommodation between the society in which they lived and the venerable religious tradition to which they yet adhered.

Today Orthodox Jews fall into three large and often diverse groups: the fairly well-defined and organized Modern or Neo-Orthodox: the heterogeneous segments that constitute the Ultra-Orthodox or Haredim; and between them, a third group, perhaps simply the Orthodox, who are chiefly characterized by their denial of the fundamental premises of the other two. The Modern Orthodoxy movement traces its origins back to Samson Raphael Hirsch (d. 1880), a German rabbi who early on adopted elements of the "Reform" style—discarding the rabbinic "habit," shaving the beard, conducting services in German—that was sweeping Germany, with the encouragement of the

German government. As the Reform movement showed itself ever more radical in jettisoning the past, Hirsch began to move back toward the traditional ways, though always with the hope that they were compatible with the secular culture amid of which most German Jews now lived. *Torah im Derech Eretz* was his slogan for that desired accommodation: the Torah was compatible with the "ways of the country." The latter were mostly a question of style, Hirsch argued, and living *im Derech Eretz* required no major changes in either Torah beliefs or talmudic practice. Hirsch was, and thought others could be as well, a good German and a good Jew. Modern Orthodoxy has continued in that same tradition of actively adapting to the modern world—sober not somber, a conservative gray rather than an assertive black—without, sacrificing what it regards as the essentials of traditional rabbinic Judaism.

The Haredim, in contrast, literally "those who quake" with concern for God's word (Isa. 66:5), thought no accommodation could or should be made with modernism. These were the "black monks" of Judaism, the traditionalists who emerged from the nineteenth-century battles between the pious devotees of Hasidism and the yeshiva-learned Mitnaggedim, two schools that discovered they had more in common with each other than with any brand of Reform (see II/8). Far from compromising with modernism, even in the mild form taken up by the so-called Modern Orthodox, the Haredim fled from it. Hasidism on one side and Lithuanian yeshiva traditionalism on the other closed ranks against "the world" of the nineteenth century and, even more resoundingly, the twentieth. European shtetl Judaism created new, invisible community walls as rapidly as the physical ones disappeared. When that European prototype community of traditionalist Jews was all but annihilated in the World War II, it was lovingly reconstituted in Brooklyn and Tel Aviv, where the Ultra-Orthodox Haredim, both Hasidic and non-Hasidic, cling to the old ways inside tightly knit and tightly guarded communities.

Between the mildly accommodating Modern Orthodox, who think accommodation is good, even necessary, for Jews, and the passionately unaccommodating Haredim, who think accommodation is evil, stand the "merely" Orthodox, who more quietly and pragmatically pursue the traditional rabbinic ways without either advocating accommodation as a policy or denouncing it as evil. Orthodox Judaism in this sense is the modern, evolved form of rabbinic Judaism, neither deliberately "reformed" like Modern Orthodoxy nor more or less consciously "reactionary" like the various communities grouped as Haredim.

The three types of Orthodox Jews have been sorted here across a spectrum of degrees of accommodation with the modern world in which most Jews have lived since the beginning of the nineteenth century. That accommodation displays itself in other ways that supply equally plausible methods of distinguishing among Orthodox Jews. Accommodation, and one's attitude toward it, governs observance, and some level of observance represents the "floor" that separates the Orthodox—who are really more concerned with orthopraxy than orthodoxy—from those who are nonobservant. All observance is Torah observance among the Orthodox; where they differ is in the relative weight they give matters like dietary laws, ritual purity, talmudic unpacking of the Torah (Orthodox more weight, Modern Orthodox less), and, beyond that, to customary laws' enlargements and refinements of the Talmud (Haredim more weight, Orthodox less).

Orthodox Judaism rests on "markers" precisely intended to signal its members as Jews in a Gentile world, but variations in those same markers (clothing, head coverings, facial hair, etc.) serve, sometimes quite intentionally—the skullcaps known as yarmulkes or kipahs, for example, are often worn like battle flags or old school ties among the observants—to distinguish one group from another. Modern Orthodox males shave; Orthodox and Haredim do not. Haredim wear side curls; Orthodox and Modern Orthodox do not. There are other, more substantial indices as well, although with considerable fuzziness around the edges and occasional cross-cutting in the middle. The attachment to political Zionism tends to run stronger on the left of the observants being discussed here and weaker on the right, where there are Haredi groups resolutely opposed to the State of Israel (see I/7 and II/10). Likewise, the segregation of women in synagogue services and the coverings prescribed for them in public increase sharply from left to right across the observant communities.

6

Community and Authority

IF ALL THE PROCEDURES described in the preceding chapters were directed to defining and wardening the community, the question of who was to govern the society of believers, and how, had also to be addressed. Prophetic or charismatic leadership, as given by Moses, Jesus, and Muhammad, for example, is unique and temporary, and can scarcely be replicated by later generations. God had sent the Guide; the community itself had to find or choose its leader.

A People Called Israel

The Hebrews (which appears to be a designation rather than a name) were "ruled," if that is the word, by their tribal sheikh Abraham and other members of his family, from one of whom, Israel (formerly Jacob), they took their distinctive tribal name of Benei Israel, the "Children of Israel." Despite confusion and overlapping in the biblical texts, and despite modern scholars' inability to settle on a chronology for the various pieces put together to compose the Bible, there is unanimous testimony that the creation of a people called Israel after its supposed tribal ancestor was the result of a covenant (*berit*) thought to have been concluded between their God Yahweh and a people of his choice. Yahweh had deserved well of this people: He had led them out of bondage in Egypt; they in turn must submit to his will, as subjects to a sovereign. If they do so, they will be rewarded, most notably by the possession of a land long ago promised to them, a "Land for Israel" (Eretz Israel).

Neither the provisions of God's will nor the exact boundaries of the promised land were spelled out at that point. Abraham received no law save the command to circumcise. The Torah followed centuries later in the Sinai revelation, but working out a law governing the new Israelite manner of life probably had to wait on the conquest of Canaan. Once they were only a people called Hebrews—perhaps simply "wanderers," apparently a rather mixed bag of seminomadic families—but as Israelites some of these same wanderers set up cult centers in honor of Yahweh, henceforward to be their God to the exclusion of all others, as he himself had demanded.

In what sense the Israelites first understood themselves as one people in Eretz Israel, is difficult to say. They were clearly organized along clan lines, and the fact that there were twelve clans or tribes has suggested to some that they were united in a kind of confederation around a central shrine where they would periodically resort to commemorate with ritual the covenant that gave them their identity. By all appearances the confederation was a loose one: there was no single leader and no apparent apparatus of central government. Individuals the Israelites generally called "judges" came forward when need or circumstances dictated.

A Kingdom Called Israel

Only hesitantly with Saul (1 Sam. 8:1–22), then notably with David (ca. 1000–960 B.C.E.), did one of these "occasional leaders" unite the Benei Israel into a somewhat unified whole, and only under David's son and successor Solomon (ca. 960–922 B.C.E.) did a centralized and institutionalized monarchy of a familiar Near Eastern type emerge. Cult center and liturgy were by then firmly established in Jerusalem, where Solomon's newly energized commercial enterprises financed the construction of a magnificent temple.

Thus Israel became a polity ruled by a hereditary king, but its "constitution" was still God's Covenant. The latter had become increasingly explicit over time through the growth of a positive law whose provisions reflected Israel's conversion to a sedentary agricultural society. None of this was by the king's writ, however, but according to the "law of Moses," the divinely inspired leader who had guided them from Egypt to the Land of Promise. The evolutionary character of the community's laws was concealed beneath an appeal back to the original Covenant and a Sinai revelation so that all that had occurred thereafter, whether through custom or design, was progressively incorporated into the charter of Scripture.

The Israelite monarchy proved unstable. Internal tensions between northern and southern clans shattered the kingdom's fragile unity, and, on the Bible's own testimony, foreign cults began making headway against Yahweh. Successive invasions by more powerful external enemies, and part of the population's departure into exile in Babylonia left David and Solomon's political achievement in ruins. But the united monarchy and the Mosaic Covenant were not so closely identified that the destruction of the first necessarily signaled the end of the latter. New charismatic leaders, now prophets rather than earlier warrior types, arose in Israel to preach fidelity to the Covenant and, through it, the identity of the Benei Israel.

Far more lasting than the polity called the kingdom of Israel was the notion of a Davidic kingship. According to God's own promise, David's kingship will descend to his heirs, and remain there forever: "Your family shall be established and your kingdom will stand for all time in My sight, and your throne will be established forever" (2 Sam. 7:16). David himself, the poet-king, later sang: "He has made a pact with me for all time, its terms spelled out and faithfully kept, my whole salvation, all my delight" (23:5). And they will rule not only over Israel but over all nations (22:44–51). Finally, David himself provides the appropriate descriptive term: "So, Lord, I will praise You among the nations, and sing psalms in your name, to one who gives His king great victories and in all His acts keeps faith with His anointed king" (Ps. 18:49–50). "Anointed" in Hebrew is *mashiah*, a term with enormous implications in all three Abrahamic religious communities (see I/1). The dream that the Davidic line would be reinvigorated, that one day "a shoot shall grow from the stock of Jesse" (Isa. 11:1), did not die easily among Jews.

After the Exile

The Babylonian Exile is a mysterious period in the life of the Israelite community, since there are almost no sources to assist historians. Some of the exiles did return to Judaea—how many remained behind we cannot tell, though the number must have been considerable—and restored some semblance of liturgy and some degree of self-government within the rather loose structure of the Persian Empire, of which Judaea was now part. By Persian royal decree, the Mosaic Law was publicly repromulgated by Ezra, who was, in the new order of things, neither king nor prophet but a priest (*kohen*) and a scribe (*sofer*).

Post-Exilic Judaea was first a temple-state under the general sovereignty of the Persian shah, later of the Greek Ptolemies of Egypt, and then, after 200 C.E., of the Greek Seleucids of Syria. It was ruled by a crown-appointed governor who consulted on local matters with the hereditary high priest of the temple and a council of elders, the Sanhedrin. But "Judaea" was merely an administrative arrangement, and although it had within it the cult center of the Jews and was served by an official Jewish priesthood, there were also offspring of the Covenant in the other Persian provinces into which Palestine and the Transjordan had been divided, as well as even farther abroad, dispersed in Syria, Egypt, and Babylonia (see I/1).

The Jewish Diaspora was not an exile, and those who lived outside the Judaean temple-state did so by choice, not by constraint. In a sense, they regarded themselves as one community, and the single name *Ioudaioi*, "Judaeans," was applied to all, whether living in Judaea or not. All Jews were bound to contribute a half shekel toward upkeep of the temple in Jerusalem, and many made pilgrimage there. In the larger centers of population abroad they constituted a "corporation," a Hellenistic notion that gave official sanction to a semiautonomous community of non-Greeks who had their own internal organization, guaranteed rights and privileges, and, very probably, their own formalized religious cult.

The Maccabean-Hasmonaean revolt of the 160s B.C.E. and the consequent restoration of a Jewish monarchical state in Judaea had little effect on the Jewish sense of community except to underscore a premise already implicit in the first experiment in monarchy: a Jewish state, as the ancient Near East understood the latter term, was not identical with Covenant Judaism. Much as the prophets had made that point against the Israelite kings of an earlier day, others now came forward to instruct the Hasmonaeans. But whereas earlier charismatic preaching had been the Covenanters' chief weapon against the monarchists, now the contest about an authentic Jewish life was waged in open political warfare. The Hasmonaeans appear to have envisioned a peculiar hybrid state that was demographically Jewish but culturally Hellenized; their expansionist policies included Judaizing newly occupied lands, while they themselves became progressively more Hellenized in both their mode of government and their personal lifestyles. Finally, the Hasmonaean head of state was both Hellenistic king—certainly not Davidic—and Jewish high priest, the first in Israel's history to have held such dual authority.

Israel's political career dwindled to a rather inglorious end. At this remove, the later Hasmonaeans may be reckoned ineffectual rulers, but in the second century B.C.E., the Near East was increasingly ruled, if not yet openly governed, from Rome, not from Alexandria, Antioch, and or provincial Jerusalem. It was Rome that judged the Hasmonaean monarchs useless for their purposes. They found a better client monarch in the Hasmonaean vizier Herod. From 37 to 4 B.C.E., this descendant of an Idumean converso family, a murderous scoundrel, a supple politician, and the greatest builder since the Pharaohs— among many other projects, he built the last and most grandiose version of the Jerusalem temple—was the faithful Jewish guardian of the Pax Romana. When he ended his days and his heirs proved less able than their progenitor, Rome ended the clienthood of the Jews and simply annexed Eretz Israel piecemeal—Judaea became a province in 6 C.E.—into the Roman Empire. The Jews of the Palestine provinces revolted twice, in 66–70 and in 132–135, but to no avail. If the Jews were to survive, it would not be as a state.

Zionism

Zionism in its most general terms may be defined as attachment to Eretz Israel, the Land of the Promise (see I/1). That attachment turned into nostalgia as the Diaspora grew in size and importance and Eretz Israel was torn from Jewish political control in the first century C.E. This longing for Eretz Israel, which increasingly focused on Jerusalem after its destruction by the Romans in 70 and again in 135, may be called spiritual Zionism, and it echoes like an anthem throughout most of medieval Jewish literature. Many Jews did return to visit and even settle in Jerusalem, which was under Muslim sovereignty after 635, but no one thought there was any realistic chance of regaining political control of it until late in the nineteenth century, when Theodor Herzl inaugurated modern political or secular Zionism, whose purpose was to establish a national homeland for the Jews. The vision of Herzl and his followers was based on nationalist rather than religious aspirations—these Zionist pioneers were rather markedly secular in their orientation—but with the 1948 foundation in Palestine of the State of Israel there slowly came to the fore within the Jewish community a more fundamentalist religious Zionism that held that the state should be not merely for Jews but a Jewish state in the sense that its law was the Torah (see II/4) and its boundaries those of the biblical Eretz Israel.

A New Political Order

Before and after the Exile, the high priest was Israel's chief religious authority, but he was not without some degree of competition, mainly from a non-priestly officer who served as president of the Sanhedrin (see II/4), the *nasi*. Nasi or "prince," is a title and an office that runs deeply, albeit somewhat blindly, back into the post-Exilic Jewish tradition. An official called by that name presided over the Sanhedrin from early on and possessed such important duties as fixing the calendar—tied then, as now, to visible sighting of the new moon—overseeing the process of intercalation, that is, periodically inserting days into the lunar calendar to keep it generally in step with the solar year, pronouncing bans and excommunications (see I/5), and sending forth legates (*shelahim*, "apostles") to the various Jewish communities, both in Palestine and the Diaspora, to apprise them of new legal enactments and to bring back information and alms.

All these functions of the nasi were religious offices, though clearly with political implications as well. Then came the catastrophes of 70 and 135. After those Jewish insurrections and their bloody repression by the Romans, there was no longer any question of a Jewish state or Jewish sovereignty within the empire. But the Romans nonetheless continued to regard the Jews, as they had in the past, as both a *natio* and a *religio* and continued to deal with them on a corporate basis. The Romans also acknowledged the nasi as the head of the empire's Jews. Whatever privileges they had acquired—to hold assemblies, conduct judicial proceedings, or practice their national or religious customs— had been granted to the Jews as a whole, not merely to their Palestinian political entity. Earlier, the high priests in Jerusalem or the "ethnarchs"—a kind of tribal or national sovereign acknowledged by the Romans—had a limited geographical jurisdiction. The nasis, in contrast, who now held both political authority as the recognized Jewish representative to Rome and the chief religious, judicial, and legislative power within the community, knew no such limits. They were "princes" not only of Palestinian Jewry—the nasi generally resided at Tiberias—but of the Diaspora as well.

Patriarch and Exilarch

The Romans translated nasi as "patriarch," and that was the title conferred on the scholar now recognized as the spokesman and leader of the Jews throughout the Roman Empire. The title, its powers, and its perquisites may have owed more than a little to what was occurring in Parthian Iran to the east. The rulers had granted the head of the yeshiva there the title of exilarch or "leader of the Jews of the Exile" and recognized him as the head of what once had been the Jews of "Babylonia" but who were now subjects of the Parthian rulers of Iran.

If we review the powers and functions of the Jewish patriarchs from Gamaliel II (ca. 80–117 C.E.) down to the abolition of the office in 425, we see that they not only presided over the Sanhedrin but announced the appearance of the new moon, which determined the date of Jewish liturgical festivals, among other things. He or his shelahim collected funds from Jewish communities all over the Diaspora and determined and pronounced sentences of excommunication (see I/5).

The nasi's political powers were created, in a sense, by the Roman authorities, who chose to deal with him as the official representative of the Jews of the empire, and all the evidence points to general Jewish acceptance of the nasi's acting as such. He was accorded most of the honors of a client king in the Roman Empire, and was granted dispensation from various provisions of the Law to ease his necessary dealings with Gentiles.

As already noted, at about the same time the Romans were recognizing the nasi as patriarch, a parallel institution, that of the exilarch (*resh galuta*), was emerging under the Parthian dynasty in Iraq and Iran. The office was thought to have originated among the successors of Jehoiachin, the Israelite king carried to Babylonia in 597 B.C.E. Not all the Jews had returned to Eretz Israel when Cyrus had given them leave to do so. Some of those who remained behind in Babylon may have attempted to continue the royal Davidic line through recognition of a resh galuta. That much is surmise. More certain is that sometime about 70 C.E., the Parthians, who then ruled the empire of the shahs, did formally recognize a single head for the various Jewish communities living in their Iraqi provinces; that the official in question claimed Davidic descent; and that, like his counterpart on the Roman side of the frontier, he had considerable power, including the disposition of a police force. The relationship between the resh galuta and the rabbinic community in the Iranian Empire was an uneasy one, and jurisdictional and political questions often divided them. But for all that, the patriarch and the exilarch were the two poles of Jewish authority in the Middle East, divided by the frontiers of the Roman and Iranian Empires. Each was the head of an often scattered community, responsible for the administration of justice among the Jews in religious matters and, where jurisdiction was allowed, even in civil cases.

The exilarch was essentially a secular authority—the Romans' patriarch traced his lineage back to the head of the venerable, and biblical, Sanhedrin—and in post-temple Judaism he had to share his power and prestige, just as the Israelite kings had in an earlier era to share their authority with the temple priesthoods. The Parthian exilarchs had powerful rivals in the Palestinian-trained rabbis who staffed and directed the Babylonian yeshivas, and they eventually won out. The institution that succeeded both the patriarchate and the gradually disintegrating exilarchate illustrates the triumph within Judaism of the yeshivas and their rabbis over all other competitors, social and political.

The Geonim

When the Muslims came to power in the Near East in the seventh century C.E., they adopted the same kind of system favored by their predecessors. Groups that constituted some kind of religio-social unity outside the Muslim community were treated as semiautonomous entities, which in much later Islamic times came to be called millets (see I/8), and were permitted considerable self-regulation. Christianity, with its well-established hierarchical structure, presented few problems in this regard, but when the Muslims had to choose a representative of the Jewish community to the centralized caliphate, they turned to the prestigious "eminences" (*geonim*) who headed the two great academies of Sura and Pumbeditha in Iraq. Palestine had its own *gaon*, and he too was a rabbi who stood at the head of the Galilean academies.

The rabbis attempted to preserve and strengthen the Torah-Talmud bond that united their communities. Efforts were made to standardize and simplify the text of the Bible for reading purposes. Furthermore, the rabbis had been trained in a common legal tradition, and so accepted on behalf of themselves and their communities the geonim's religious and legal authority. For their part, the geonim intervened directly in the lives of the various communities by setting the liturgical lunar calendar and resolving legal disputes that could not be settled locally. Formal bans continued to be invoked. To cite only one of the most notorious, in 1232 the rabbis of France imposed the expulsion ban (*herem*) on anyone who studied philosophy, or, more particularly, who read Maimonides' *Guide for the Perplexed* and the philosophical introduction to his

Mishneh Torah. Some Jews denounced the text as blasphemous to the Christian authorities, who were conducting their own war on philosophy (see II/7) and so obligingly burned the books in the market square of Montpellier. Maimonides' supporters reciprocated by cutting out the tongues of the informers who had denounced the texts.

Ashkenazi and Sephardic Jews

Just as Christian communities divided along a cultural line marked by the split into Greek- and Latin-speaking worlds, Jewry of the Middle Ages separated into two distinct components: the European Jews who lived under Latin Christianity and those of Spain and the Middle East who lived under Islam. Although the division between Eastern and Western Christians eventually spawned profound differences on theology and authority, the differences between Ashkenazi and Sephardic Jews were considerably less substantial.

A man named Ashkenaz is numbered among Noah's descendants in Genesis 10:3, and a place called Sepharad is mentioned in Obadiah 1:20. Whatever the original intent of these two obscure references, rabbis after 800 C.E. were identifying the first name with Germany and the second with Spain. By the tenth century Rhineland Germany was in fact the most important center of Jewish life in Christian Europe. The manner of Jewish social and religious life of these "Ashkenazim" passed thence westward into France and eastward into the rest of Germany and Bohemia. Thus, there was a kind of German tradition in exegesis and ritual that can be termed Ashkenazi, and even when this particular Jewish way of life spread ever eastward into the Slavic lands and eventually into the English-speaking world, it continued to be identified as the Ashkenazi or "German" tradition.

There was a similar development of the name Sepharad (or Sefarad). The "Sephardim" were originally the Jews of Spain, who from the eleventh to the fifteenth century developed a rich and distinctive way of life. With the expulsion of 1492, many Spanish Jews migrated to North Africa, the Balkans, and the Middle East (and eventually South America), where their traditions in the end prevailed over those of the local communities until the term "Sephardic" came to be used generally of Jews from the Muslim lands.

Ashkenazi and Sephardic have different pronunciations of Hebrew—which until modern times only the learned could use. Most of the Ashkenazim spoke German or the German-Hebrew hybrid called Yiddish, whereas the Sephardim spoke Arabic or Castilian. But the most notable differences between the two are in ritual, the wording or addition of prayers to the synagogue service, and the variety of local customs in food, dress, and so on that reflect European versus Middle Eastern styles of life. Both use the standard lawbook published by the Sephardic scholar Josef Karo (d. 1575) of Safad in Galilee, the *Shulkhan*

Aruk (see II/4), but the Ashkenazim include the "supplements" made to it by the Polish scholar Mosheh Isserles (d. 1572).

Note: In pre-Holocaust times the Jewish world was 90 percent Ashkenazi, but the destruction visited on European Jews and a higher Sephardic birthrate has reduced that majority to less than 80 percent. Israeli Jews are more evenly divided between Ashkenazim and Sephardim, and there are chief rabbis and parallel religious organizations for each group.

Judaism under medieval Islam was much what it had been under Christianity, though without many of the religious and political pressures, and in the full enjoyment of the new economic prosperity that came to the Near East in the wake of the Muslim conquest. The Jews who lived as dhimmis in this network of communities across the face of the Islamic empire, the later Sephardim, probably felt some kind of ethnic identity—culturally they were eventually Arabized, though Hebrew and Aramaic continued in use as learned and liturgical languages. But their more deeply felt bond was, as it had been for many centuries, a common observance of the Mosaic Law and its talmudic corollaries, and a longing for Zion.

The Christian Ekklesia

The earliest Christian community was not unlike a Pharisaic or Qumran conventicle. Like the former, it had a formal table-fellowship with a common meal (*agape*), although the eucharistic communion was already at a considerable symbolic and liturgical remove from a Pharisaic understanding of a community meal. And like the Qumran associations, it was a community united in eschatological expectation. The Christians held common prayer services on the model of a synagogue liturgy, and there was a familiar Jewish program of philanthropy to take care of widows and orphans (Acts 6:1–6). Jesus' immediate disciples stood at the head of the community, and at *their* head stood not precisely Peter, who seems to find preference in the Gospels (Matt. 16:17–19), nor even James and John, the sons of Zebedee who are also singled out there (Matt. 17:1; 26:37), but James, the almost unnoticed "brother of the Lord" (Acts 12:17; 15:13–21; Gal. 1:17).

As is clear from the Acts of the Apostles, James did not act alone at Jerusalem, as a later bishop might; he was a first among peers. But it is equally evident that he was in a real sense the head of the congregation (*ekklesia*) there, and that he was succeeded in that office by other of Jesus' relations, all of them practicing Jews of strict temple observance. Elsewhere other congregations came into being, often in connection with Jewish synagogue communities in the Diaspora, and there "elders" (*presbyteroi*) were appointed to govern them.

From the beginning, Jesus' followers had to face the question of their own Jewishness. Hellenized and Pharisaic Jews made poor bedfellows and worse tablemates, inside or outside the Christian community, but Jesus' own exaltation of the act of faith in himself over a strict observance of the Law raised even larger issues. Jesus, who did not observe a marked degree of ritual purity, might fit ill into a strict Christian fellowship, but Gentiles would scarcely fit at all. Some accommodation had to be worked out, at least for a time, but Paul for one refused to surrender the issue to pragmatic solutions.

Paul's attitude toward the Jewish law must be placed inside the context of his thinking about the Church. In Jesus' own words, a New Covenant had been sealed by his death and resurrection; a new Chosen People, a new Benei Israel, had been elected—a notion strongly underlined in the Letter to the Hebrews, which was included in the New Testament canon. The original Covenant had eventually been detailed by laws governing the behavior of God's people, laws regulating purity and sacrifice. The New Covenant had no need of such laws, in Paul's view. Jesus now dwelt in the body itself, transforming it from within. Each Christian was his own temple and his own priest: the new sacrifice was eucharistic.

Bishops and Priests

As we shall see (II/6), Jesus was thought by Christians to have presided over his Last Supper in the manner of a priest, which would mean, of course, in that very Jewish world of the early Christians, a *kohen*, or Jewish priest. "In the manner of" is the operative phrase since neither Jesus nor any of his early followers were of priestly descent, and the *kohenim*, moreover, performed their priestly functions within the Jerusalem temple, an institution that ceased functioning in 70 C.E., and with it, the primary role of the Jewish kohenim. In his lifetime, Jesus participated in those temple rituals—as a layman, of course— as did his followers after his death (Acts 3:1), and the chief "Christian" activity of the latter was, in those early days, preaching, which was sometimes attended by cures. As for the Eucharist, Jesus appointed no one to stand in for him, whatever form that ritual took at the beginning. His only appointment was of the Twelve to "sit on thrones and judge the twelve tribes of Israel" (Luke 22:30), to proclaim the coming of the Kingdom, and to heal and exorcise, as Jesus himself had done (Matt. 10:5–8). There is no sign that he made them priests as either he or they might have understood that word.

As Paul's letters show, the earliest Christian communities, Jews all, had various authority figures. Initially these were the Apostles and elders in Jerusalem (Acts 15:2), but as the movement spread along the arteries of the

Jewish Diaspora, other figures ("teachers," "prophets," "elders," "overseers"; see 1 Cor. 12:28) appeared, all of whom "received the gift of the Spirit," though there is no very clear indication who performed which tasks. It may be assumed that all reflected current synagogue practice in the Diaspora. Fairly soon, however, it was the holder of the office of overseer (Gk. *episkopos* > bishop) who had assumed the leadership role in each ekklesia. The bishops' power and authority grew rapidly with the emergent theory that they were the successors of Jesus' original Twelve (see II/4). Already at the end of the first century, in the letters of Ignatius, for example, an office that seems to have made James a "first among equals" was taking on special status as "overseer," who was coming to be recognized as the single "successor of the Apostles" and so the bearer and interpreter of the authentic Christian tradition (see I/8). As in the case of rabbinic ordination (*semika*) in Palestine during the same period, the Christians' "laying on of hands" or ordination of the priestly presbyters, and par excellence of the bishops, was a charismatic act. Bishops were ordained by other bishops as part of the apostolic succession; presbyters were ordained by the bishops of their own communities, whose delegates they were in the performance of liturgical functions.

The bishops, by reason of their succession to the Apostles, were thought to possess the teaching power (*magisterium*) in the Church (see II/5), and it fell to the individual bishop not only to instruct prospective converts in the Christian faith but also to judge the orthodoxy of the opinions of those already members of his flock. The evolution of the elders of those early Christian communities into a Christian priesthood seems to be a separate but parallel development. Already the New Testament Letter to the Hebrews announced Jesus as the new high priest inaugurating a new priesthood, "according to the succession of Melchizedek" (Heb. 6:20) (see I/1), but in the earliest sources it is invariably the bishop presiding at the Eucharist. Indeed, bishop and presbyter may have begun as a single office (with deacon as the second; see below) and become separated over the course of the second century as Christianity spread into more remote areas. The presbyter emerged as a distinct officer charged with performing some of the bishop's functions, like presiding over the community Eucharist.

Very early on bishops were chosen from among the ranks of the presbyters and so shared in Jesus' priesthood, though the teaching power remained the bishop's prerogative by reason of his episcopal and not his priestly office. As such, like their Jewish priestly antecedents in the temple, the priests, and so the episcopate, were solely males. In the fully developed sacramental system, the priest was the ordinary minister of the sacraments, save for Confirmation and Holy Orders, which were reserved for the bishop. The deacon (Gk. *diakonos*, "servant," "assistant") is also a very old office in the Church (see Acts 6:2, 6; Tim. 3:8–13) and had assorted churchly duties, most of them administrative. Women as well as men held this office in the early Church.

> **Note:** The Jewish priests were held to a stringent code of ritual purity (Lev. 21), which women, who were subject to systematic onsets of ritual impurity by reason of their menstrual periods, could not observe. Women were thus excluded from the priestly office and, indeed, restricted to the outer courts of the temple.

Hierarchy and Structure

With the spread of the new beliefs and the appearance of Christian communities both within and beyond the Roman Empire, the individual parts of the Great Church began to arrange themselves, as neither Judaism nor Islam was to do, in an organic and hierarchical system. The local government of the bishop had sound precedent in the early practice of the Church, and the passage of the Christian message at first created no great discrepancies in the practice of the local churches that constituted the Great Church. But the simple relationship between the bishop and his community yielded to considerably more complex arrangements once Constantine embraced the Great Church as his own.

The social, political, and economic consequences of the emperor's conversion constrained the local churches to fashion for themselves, and for the Great Church, an organizational structure congruent with their new responsibilities. In some instances, existing institutions were adapted, some of them going back to apostolic times; in others, totally new offices were created. In almost every instance the model followed by the Church was the parallel institution of the Roman Empire. The bishops within a single region began to conform to the hierarchical municipal pattern of that region: metropolises, cities, towns, and even villages had bishops at their head, but the bishop of the metropolis or provincial capital—later called an archbishop—had precedence and jurisdiction over the others.

Thus by the third or fourth century there came to be only three major spiritual offices or orders in the Christian Church: deacon, priest or presbyter, and bishop, all of which were bestowed, in ascending order, through a consecration signaled by the laying on of hands by a bishop or bishops, in what was later termed the sacrament of Holy Orders (see II/5). Everything else—patriarch, pope, cardinal, monsignor, etcetera—is merely a title of importance or honor.

Patriarchs were somewhat like metropolitan bishops. The bishops of certain prestigious sees, they were acknowledged as having wider jurisdiction than a mere province: Constantinople, Alexandria, and Antioch, to which Jerusalem was later added almost as a form of ecclesiastical courtesy. Rome too fell into that category, though its bishop preferred the honorific of pope. The patriarchate was in fact an Eastern Christian title, even though the honor was later extended to a few Latin bishops, like those of Venice and Lisbon. In more recent times the title has proliferated in the Eastern Churches.

Cardinals began their careers as "hinges" (Lat. *cardines*) between local parishes, where they served as ordinary priests, and the episcopal chancery, where they part-timed as administrators. At Rome the chancery, (*curia*) of the bishop, also known as the "pope," grew so large and complex that the "cardinals" there could no longer moonlight, even though they were still nominally attached to local parishes as priests or deacons, or even to nearby dioceses as bishops. All three types of cardinals—cardinal-bishops, cardinal-priests, and cardinal-deacons—became in effect full-time administrators in the Roman curia. They, together with the pope, formally constituted the Ecclesia Romana, the "Roman Church" (see I/7).

In the 1050s the new college or assembly of cardinals was being described as the equivalent of the ancient Roman senate and, according to a decree issued in 1059, by Pope Nicholas II, the cardinal-bishops would henceforward be charged with the duty of electing a pope. It was not stated, however, whether there had to be unanimous agreement on a candidate or how disagreements should be resolved. Just such discord arose at the death of Pope Hadrian in 1159. Two rival candidates were both named pope by their cardinal supporters, one as Victor IV, the other as Alexander III. The emperor, Frederick I Barbarossa, who strongly favored Victor, proposed to call a council to settle the matter. When his authority to do so was questioned, Frederick could cite the cases of Constantine and Charlemagne and, had he wished, even more recent practices in Church history: emperors had summoned councils to settle schismatic papacies, where there were in effect two popes, in 1046 and 1064. A council, chiefly of bishops under imperial control, met in Pavia in 1160 and duly pronounced for the emperor's man, Victor IV.

Not everyone was convinced by the process, however, and for nearly twenty years a political and propaganda war was waged between Frederick and Alexander and his supporters, until in 1177 Frederick recognized his cause as lost and acknowledged Alexander III as the legitimate pope. Two years later Alexander issued a new decree on papal elections that stipulated that agreement of a two-thirds majority of cardinals was required for a valid election and that, should anyone of the minority refuse to accept the will of the two-thirds, he should be excommunicated. The practice remains in force in the Roman Church today.

In 1586 Pope Sixtus V placed the maximum number of cardinals at seventy—emulating the seventy elders of Moses—but the limit was lifted by John XXIII in 1958. In modern times all the cardinals of the Roman curia are bishops. These are lifetime appointments made by the pope, though after the age of eighty the cardinal loses his right to participate in the papal election.

Councils of Bishops, Local and Ecumenical

The question of the bishop's powers became more complex when deviant opinions spread into other sees and other bishops' jurisdictions. The bishop's capacity to pronounce, like his power to adjudicate, was limited from the beginning. The episcopate was not an ecumenical (churchwide) office: every bishop was the bishop of some place, his bishopric or see (< Lat. *sedes*, "seat" or "residence"), and his authority is limited to that locality. Some bishops might speak for larger areas—the archbishop or metropolitan bishop for all the sees of his province, for example, and later the bishop of Rome for all the bishops of the Western or Latin Church—but bishops could formally and authoritatively give voice to the apostolic tradition only when they were assembled in an ecumenical council.

From as early as the 250s and 260s bishops had taken to meeting regionally in synods, usually under the presidency of the area's metropolitan bishop, in order to deal with larger issues of heresy and orthodoxy within a province. In the fourth century, however, the crisis of Arianism (see II/7) spread across the entire Great Church and prompted the Christian emperor Constantine—none other had the authority perhaps—to summon all the Christian bishops to an ecumenical council at Nicaea (Iznik in present-day Turkey). In 325 they condemned Arianism as a deviant way of thinking about Jesus and his Father and promulgated the Creed of Nicaea setting out the orthodox position.

At Nicaea the bishops also pronounced the Church "one, holy, catholic, and apostolic"—a single universal community, heir to Israel's claim to be "a holy people," and, finally, descended, in its authority, from Jesus' own Apostles. Thus from Nicaea onward the Church could claim a common doctrine, rooted, it was maintained, in Scripture, and ruled by an institution, the episcopate, thought to be grounded in Christ and his chosen Apostles. The notion of the Church's singular universality persisted through strain and even schism for another twelve centuries, until the emergence of "confessional churches" in the wake of the Reformation.

The Laity

The separation of Christians into clergy (Gk. *kleros*, "lot," hence, *klerikoi*, either "the chosen" or those who have "elected" the better way) and the laity (Gk. *laos*, *laikoi*, "people") is not very apparent in the earliest Church records, but it is fully attested at the end of the first century in the letters of Clement of Rome, who notes the continuity between the Jews' high priest, priests, and Levites and their Christian counterparts, the bishops, priests, and deacons. The latter all have a special function in the Church, but so too do the laikoi—Clement was writing in Greek—who were bound by "the precepts proper to the laity." About a century later the Latin Tertullian thought authority separated the two. Even in the churches the bishop and his presbyters sat in the sanctuary, while the laity were collected in the *quadratum populi*, the rectangular nave of the basilica. Augustine later attempted, not terribly successfully, to define the laity by what they were not. They are "at the junction of the world and the Church; they are neither clerics nor monks."

These distinctions of responsibility and function were rendered more juridical when Constantine began to grant statutory privileges to the *clerici*. Indeed, as time passed, the upper Christian clergy often acted as state functionaries, particularly in the wake of the progressive collapse of Roman political authority in the fifth and sixth centuries. Functionally, too, the clergy had unique control over the Christian's primary public acts, whether liturgical or juridical. The laity, for their part, found fulfillment in the sacraments (see II/5), whose benefits recognized no distinction between clergy and laity, in the cult of first the martyrs and then the saints, and in the pilgrimages that were the outgrowth of both (see II/6).

These spiritual distinctions eventually elided, at least in Western Christendom, with a social hierarchy that drew even sharper distinctions. The laity became synonymous with the lowest order of medieval society, beneath the aristocratic knights and the literate clergy as a third estate of illiterate peasants and laborers. The most elevated of the laity took spiritual refuge in monasticism (see II/8), a path to perfection that made no class distinctions, though in the end the clergy among the monks came to rule the monastic roost. There were also alternative forms of monastic life that allowed the laity to be both in the world and in the cloister, the so-called third orders pioneered by Francis of Assisi that allowed the layman or laywoman to share in monastic life without embracing all its rigors.

The laity's share in governance of the Church, which was largely nonexistent, surfaced somewhat abruptly as an issue in the fourteenth-century movement called Conciliarism. It arose with the nobility's growing importance in Church affairs, chiefly fiscal but juridical as well. The investiture controversy—who had the primary right, king or pope, to appoint holders of ecclesiastical benefices, and so control their income?—was the opening shot of an ongoing dispute between state and church, between nobility and clergy. Although the Church won the investiture battle, it lost, at least temporarily, the larger one of the layman's role, albeit the noble layman, in Church affairs. In the strifeful Church councils of the fourteenth century, not only bishops sat in judgment but kings and representatives of the emerging "nations" of Europe, the French, Germans, and English among others, in the same way medieval Europe's powerful new institution, the university, organized itself.

The Primacy of Rome

Theoretically all bishops were equal in the light of the apostolic succession, but some were clearly more equal than others in the Roman provincial organization. The Christian Church and the Roman *imperium* exerted a reciprocal influence on one another through the fourth, fifth, and sixth centuries, but the pull of the empire's hierarchical structure on the Church's episcopate, which was both multiple and in theory egalitarian, chiefly concerns us here.

The Jesus movement, soon called "Christianity," had spread from Jerusalem through large metropolitan centers such as Alexandria, Antioch, and Rome. Rome had a true claim to the apostolic succession in both Peter and Paul, who early carried the Gospel there; it was, moreover, no mere provincial capital but the head of the empire. As the churches emerged from the catacombs into their privileged position as the Great Church under the Christian emperor Constantine (see I/7), the episcopate began to conform ever more closely to the Roman administrative system. Bishops of provincial capitals became metropolitan archbishops with jurisdiction over their episcopal peers in lesser cities and towns, so that the eventual organizational chart of the Christian Church resembled that of the Roman Empire that housed it.

There were differences at the very top, however. The Roman executive rose through provincial governors, thence through diocesan prefects to a single autocrat at the apex of power. The Christian hierarchy rose no higher than its metropolitans or archbishops; above them were only the bishops of the prestigious patriarchal sees. These were an ill-sorted group that included Antioch and Alexandria, two enormous cities at the head and heart of the east's most powerful and prosperous regional jurisdictions, Syria and Egypt; Jerusalem, the venerable "mother of churches" with its sanctity, historical prestige, and considerable endowments, though no political importance; and Rome, still an important city, with the grandeur of empire clinging to it, and a place whose bishop could claim a spiritual lineage that went back to Peter himself.

Although the bishop of Rome was unmistakably accorded a kind of primacy of honor among his episcopal and archepiscopal peers, the question of absolute primacy never arose in the early Church. The presence of many venerable and flourishing centers of Christianity, each ruled by a bishop who stood in a direct and equal line of descent from the apostolic tradition, would have rendered such claims nonsense. Absolute primacy arose only when multiplicity had been reduced to polarity, when Rome and Constantinople, where Constantine had transferred the imperial capital in 330, each stood alone at the head of a separate spiritual, cultural, and political tradition. Rome did intervene in the affairs of other churches from the beginning; no one protested, and there are even examples of the Roman church being appealed to in certain cases. Only in the fourth century did Rome's bishops, who bore the unofficial title of "pope," began to insist on their de jure right of final jurisdiction based on Peter's position vis-à-vis the other Apostles.

> **Note:** "Pope" is a nickname rather than a juridical title for the prelate who was, and is, the bishop of Rome. The word derives from the Greek *papas*, "father," and was also used by the bishop or patriarch of Alexandria. The English "pontiff," as in "supreme pontiff," comes from the Latin *pontifex*, literally "bridge builder," and was a title, and a sacred trust, assumed by the head of the priestly guilds in pre-Christian Rome. Roman emperors arrogated both the office and the title, *pontifex maximus*, to themselves in their quest for dignity, and in the fifth century it was assumed by the pope in turn. In the Middle Ages the popes ruled the Papal States of central Italy as sovereign. In the nineteenth century these were absorbed, much diminished, into the newly formed nation-state of Italy. In a concordat or treaty agreed on with Italy in 1929, the Italian republic recognized Vatican City as a sovereign state and the pope as its ruler. Most of the other states followed suit.

This particular line of argumentation found its definitive expression in the sermons of Leo, bishop of Rome between 440 and 461, who claimed, on his Petrine authority, a universal jurisdiction. The Council of Chalcedon in 451, although accepting Leo's doctrinal formulation of a solution to the theological problem of Monophysitism, did not accept the Petrine argument. Its twenty-eighth canon spelled out the message in unmistakable terms: the Roman emperor and the senate were now in Constantinople, which consequently enjoyed equal privileges with the Old Rome, though it ranked second after it in protocol order. Rome, which supplied the theology of the council, did not put its name to Canon 28; the Eastern bishops did.

The so-called Petrine argument—that Peter was the head of the Apostles and that the bishop of Rome, as his episcopal successor, was the head of the Church—was deeply resisted in the Eastern Church, from beginning to end. There was no argument over the Gospel testimony that Peter was indeed the head of the Twelve and that Jesus had vested a special authority in him. But, the Easterners contended, such an enactment made Peter the first and the type of the Christian bishop and not merely the bishop of Rome. Jesus had endowed Peter with episcopal authority, which he shared with the other Apostles: every church in Christendom had a "Peter" sitting on its episcopal throne. "Peter is the teacher of the universe" is the way Nicholas Cabasilas, a fourteenth-century bishop of Salonika, expressed it; "the pope is only the bishop of Rome."

Western and Eastern Christianity and Christendom

Rome and its natural rival on the Bosporus were only beginning their poisonous struggle, which had its roots somewhat less in theology than in the administrative history of the Roman Empire. Toward the end of the third century, the Roman Empire had been divided into an eastern and a western region, with matching administrations and capitals. The move was made in part for administrative reasons: the polity was far too large to be administered from a single center in an age when long-distance travel was slow and uncertain, and when there were growing pressures on the distant frontiers. But the division was also rooted in another economic and cultural reality. When the Romans had first come to the eastern Mediterranean, they had conquered, and then attempted to absorb, a Hellenic milieu whose culture was not only different from their own, but, as the Romans themselves felt, superior. They had become masters of eastern peoples who, if politically less disciplined than the Romans, possessed compensatory energy and originality. The western provinces of Gaul, Germany, and even Spain were no match for Egypt, Syria, or the cities of Anatolia. This Greek-speaking "eastern" Roman Empire was thus privileged in the administrative reforms of the late third century, and Constantine early in the fourth gave the East a rival to old imperial Rome in his new city. Once Byzantium, the town thenceforward was to be called Constantinople, a name that even the Ottoman and Turkish "Istanbul" somewhat uncertainly echoes.

In 1054 the Eastern and Western branches of Christendom were divided along the same Latin-Greek fault line by mutual anathemas, and though there were occasional brief and opportunistic patch-up jobs, the rifts remain till this day. The causes of the East-West schism, as it came to be called, were complex, but it seems safe to say that the question of authority was a more powerful catalyst than any of the theological differences that one side cited against the other. The issue of authority and jurisdiction did not begin in the eleventh century, of course. It lay implicitly in the third-century division of the Roman Empire, and once that empire became Christian in the fourth century, it worked its way into a wide variety of theological discussions. Rome in the west and Constantinople in the east both represented imperial ambitions, first parsed in political and now more recently in ecclesiastical terms.

Among the Western Churches Rome had no rivals: the other Latin sees had suffered grievously from the incursions of the "barbarians" from the great steppes that the Byzantines had managed to fend off before the arrival of the Slavs. These Huns, Goths, and Vandals were eventually converted, but they nonetheless destroyed much of the fabric of Roman society in Gaul, Spain, and Africa. In power and plenitude the bishops there were no match for the bishop of Rome. Constantinople, in contrast, was an eastern upstart: Antioch, Alexandria, and Jerusalem all had prior and greater claims to ecclesiastical authority. But by the seventh century these once proud sees had disappeared within the Abode of Islam, and from that point on Rome and Constantinople, with a bishop in each and an empire behind, faced off as implacable rivals.

The Competition for Souls

What are generally referred to as the Eastern or Orthodox Churches are those that had grown to maturity in the eastern or Greek-speaking part of the Roman Empire, roughly the lands east of a line drawn southward from Poland, Czeska, and Croatia, continuing, on the southern side of the Mediterranean, east of Tunisia, which was the Latin-speaking province of Africa, and west of Greek-speaking Cyrenaica, the modern Libya. The two halves of the empire, distinct from the beginning in their language and culture, began to be administered separately in the late third century, when East and West had different emperors, bureaucracies, and capitals. There were attempts to reunite the two politically but they were never terribly successful. In the fifth century invasions of new peoples from the eastern steppes reduced most of the western empire to rudimentary forms of political, cultural, and commercial life. The East, which was immune to those early waves of conquerors, held on to a continuous existence down to 1453, even though many of its Middle Eastern and North African provinces fell to the Muslims in the seventh and eighth centuries.

Tensions were apparent between the empire's Eastern and Western churches almost from the outset, bred of the linguistic and cultural differences between Christianity's original Middle Eastern seedbed, which produced the Greek Gospels and then a number of brilliant churchmen to interpret and expand on them, and a West that had to read a translated Scripture and struggle to interpret the thought and expressions of Paul, Origen, and others in their own Latin idiom. This breeding ground of differences was nourished by the rise of the bishop of Rome to a position of absolute supremacy among the Western Sees, while in the East, Alexandria, Antioch, and Jerusalem guarded their ancient privileges and Constantinople asserted its new imperial ones.

Even before Europe's newly arrived tribal peoples, Germans and Slavs, found their settled place within the empire, Christian missionaries, some Latin and some Greek, moved into their midst to bring them the message of the Gospels. Greek and Latin evangelists met in the Balkans, where, in the ninth century, the two Christianities found a new issue to divide them: the conversion of the Slavs. There is reason to believe that the emperor Heraclius may have asked for papal assistance in converting Croats along the Adriatic in the first half of the seventh century—the Croats became and remained Latin Catholics in any event. But the issue became more political, and so more complex, in the mid–ninth century. In Moravia, a Slavic prince, in order to counterbalance Frankish missionaries from the west (he judged, probably correctly, that conversion to Frankish, i.e., Latin, Christianity would invite Frankish political dominance as well) asked for and received Christian missionaries from Constantinople. Two brothers, Constantine—or, as he later came to be known, Cyril—and Methodius, devised a new Greek-derived alphabet with which to transcribe the oral Slavic of the prospective converts (Old Church Slavonic) and began their work in Moravia in 863. The pope heard of the mission, summoned the brothers to Rome, and after an inquiry, gave his blessing to the enterprise. Cyril died in Rome in 869, but Methodius returned to Moravia, where he continued his work until the ruler was overthrown and his pro-Frankish successor invited in Latin priests to continue Christianizing his country. Thereafter all papal support went to the Latin missionaries and later in the ninth century papal pronouncements disavowed the Slavonic liturgy and its growing complementary literature.

Pope, Patriarch, and the Bulgarian Church

In 863, Boris, the ruler of the increasingly powerful Balkan kingdom of Bulgaria, announced his own conversion to Christianity. But just as the Moravians had sought instruction from Eastern-rite Constantinople because they feared the political consequences of the Latin-rite Franks' missionary activity, Boris preferred to approach the more distant Franks rather than nearby, and palpably more dangerous, Constantinople. His instinct may have been correct, but it came too late. The Byzantines marched against Bulgaria and Boris quickly agreed that Eastern Christianity was his preferred creed. A Greek clergy came to Bulgaria and the process of Christianization began shortly after 864.

Boris remained uneasy, however, with his ecclesiastical dependence on Constantinople, and he shortly requested of Photius, the patriarch there— and a man whose appointment had been strenuously opposed in Rome—that his kingdom be granted its own independent patriarch. Further, Boris addressed to Photius a long series of questions on some problematic Christian practices in Bulgaria. Photius denied the request for a patriarch and ignored the questions. Boris, miffed, turned quickly toward the pope and the Frankish king, both of whom responded with alacrity. Pope Nicholas was conciliatory: there would soon be a Bulgarian archbishop. Moreover, he answered Boris's questions in a way that showed he was willing to be flexible concerning local religious practices. The Franks for their part dispatched missionary clerics to serve and instruct the Bulgarians.

Photius was outraged, his anger fueled by the banished Greek clergy's reports on what the Latins were permitting in Bulgaria, including the information that the Romans had added a new clause to the Church's traditional creed, namely, that the Holy Spirit "proceeded from the Father *and from the Son*," the latter phrase, in Latin, *filioque.* The patriarch convened a local synod in

---

Note: The insertion in the creed of the phrase "and from the Son" seems to have first appeared in Christian circles in Visigothic Spain in the seventh century as an attempt to underline the symmetry of the three Persons who make up the single but triune God. This manner of examining the Trinity was Augustine's insight, and it worked its way deeply into the Western understanding of that difficult subject. For the Easterners filioque was not merely an innovation; it ran counter to their own sense that they knew nothing about the essence of the Godhead. For many of them, the essence of God was unknown and unknowable; it was revealed to us only through its attributes or "energies," a manner of putting the question that led to another violent disagreement on the immediate experience of God (see II/9).

Constantinople early in 867, condemning both the practices and the addition of the filioque clause in Bulgaria. Later that same year, at a larger assembly of bishops in the capital, the condemnation was formally extended to the whole Bulgarian Church and Pope Nicholas was declared excommunicated for condoning and abetting them. Nicholas died before he got the news; it came instead to his successor Hadrian II. There was a new emperor in Byzantium as well, Basil, who was so alarmed at what was occurring that he removed Photius and restored the former patriarch, Ignatius. Hadrian was not mollified. He convoked a council in Rome, excommunicated Photius, and declared all the bishops appointed by him invalidly consecrated. Another council met in Constantinople in 869–870 to affirm the pope's ruling, but the Eastern bishops were deeply divided on the question.

The council of 869–870, made up chiefly of Eastern bishops, did make another important decision: in response to a request from Boris, it declared the Bulgarian Church under the jurisdiction of Constantinople, not Rome, and appointed a semiautonomous archbishop for the kingdom. Boris had gotten his way, and so had the Easterners: the Greek clergy promptly returned to Bulgaria to continue Christianizing the country.

The so-called Photian schism was patched up in 877 when Photius, once again patriarch at the death of Ignatius, though he refused to apologize for his past positions, conceded that the Bulgarian Church should be under Roman jurisdiction, perhaps with the comforting knowledge that Boris would never agree to it, as he did not. Bulgaria was and remained Orthodox, though not, as it turned out, very long Greek.

Methodius, it will be recalled, was preaching in Moravia at this point and spreading the use of the Slavonic liturgy there. But there was a change in regime, and the new prince of Moravia decided he preferred the Franks after all. Methodius was arrested, and although the pope intervened to have him freed, Rome too decided it preferred the Franks and henceforward there was a notable cooling toward the use of Slavic in church services. A decade or so later, in 886, some of Methodius's liturgical disciples showed up in Bulgaria, where they began to spread the use of Church Slavonic, and indeed, to translate additional works into the new ecclesiastical script. Boris grasped its value for political purposes and threw his support behind the Slavic missionaries. From a monastic center at Ohrid in Macedonia monks trained in the new language skills penetrated deep into the countryside. Services and preaching in Slavic rather than Greek turned out to be a powerful tool not only for turning Bulgaria into a Christian country but for creating a national tongue and, in effect, a single people. Whatever the Turkic origins of the Bulgars, by Boris's era Bulgaria had become a Christian country and the Bulgarians a Slavic people.

> **Note:** Shifting ecclesiastical and cultural allegiances left another legacy in the Balkans. The dualist heresy called Bogomilism originated in Bulgaria in the tenth century at least in part as a popular reaction to the imposition of an alien Greek clergy in a bewildered peasantry not far removed from paganism. See I/5 for the Bogomils and their spiritual descendants in the south of France, the Cathars and Albigensians.

The Parting of the Ways, East and West

The Photian affair was papered over by both the Eastern and the Western Church since it was in the interest of neither to continue it, but the rift between the two Christendoms—many more in fact, but Islam had enveloped and stifled a number of them in embryo, and Moscow, the "Third Rome," was still in the wings—could not be long concealed or another open breach long averted. There were simply too many issues: two diverging cultures, one Greek and one Latin, with two equally distinct ways of worshiping God and two increasingly different theologies. The Greek was inclined toward the dramatic, the mystical, and the quietist approach to the truths of Christianity; the Latin's penchant was for a legal and rapidly Aristotelizing scholasticism and a centralizing and hierarchical authority structure. There were also the papacy's increasingly assertive claims to primacy among the bishops of the Great Church. Finally, like tinder beneath all that highly flammable fuel, there was, in the mid–twelfth century, the troublesome issue of Byzantine Sicily and southern Italy. This was the Magna Graecia of the ancients, a Greek cultural and Byzantine political enclave recently freed from its Muslim sovereigns by the Normans.

In the 1050s, Leo IX, an energetic reforming pope later canonized by his Church, made the mistake of campaigning against the Normans in southern Italy. The Normans had driven the last Muslims from Sicily and were marching northward and menacing the papal domains. The Normans made short work of the papal forces, took Leo captive, and kept him under a kind of house arrest. Though they were struggling for possession of the land, Leo and the Normans agreed that the land should be Christian, and Christian in the Latin fashion. Even as he was facing the Normans, Leo was establishing a Latin hierarchy in the once Greek Christian cities of the south, with his friend and adviser Humbert of Silva Candida as archbishop of the entire island of Sicily. The Byzantine emperor could make little political response—the Seljuq Turks were advancing well into the eastern marches of Anatolia—but his patriarch, Michael Cerularius, could and did. He closed the Latin churches of the Pisans and the Genoese in Constantinople; the Latins used unleavened bread in the Eucharist, against tradition, it was claimed. Leo responded from his confinement (he died shortly thereafter): he dispatched Humbert as his legate to Constantinople, and there in May 1054 the archbishop lay the papal decrees of excommunication on the high altar of Hagia Sophia. Two weeks later Michael Cerularius excommunicated the legate in turn.

The events of 1054, for all their drama, were more symbolic than actual. The break between the two Churches owed something at least to the two headstrong individuals who threw down the gauntlet. But while the theology that stood between Greek and Latin could be, and was, subsequently discussed, the political damage in Sicily, where the two Christendoms actually touched, was deep and damaging, and in the next century broke into an open and festering wound.

A Misbegotten Crusade

From the Christian perspective, a crusade was an engaging notion: an attempt to displace the infidel Muslims from the Holy Land that was believed to be illegally (and impiously) seized Christian soil. But Palestine, and indeed much of the Muslim Near East, was Christian in another sense perhaps not grasped or appreciated by the Latin knights summoned by Urban II in 1095 to take the cross against the Muslims. These lands were (like Sicily) former domains of the Eastern Roman Empire, and the sovereign of that empire still held sway in Constantinople and expected a political as well as a religious restoration in the wake of a Frankish success. Well before that success was accomplished—Jerusalem fell to the crusaders in 1099—the Byzantine emperor was given to understand that the Latin crusaders had no intention of turning over their conquests to his imperial hands. A Latin, not a Byzantine, kingdom was established in Palestine, ruled by a series of Latin kings and their feudal princes and counts; and a Latin clergy controlled the churches of "liberated" Palestine, under a Latin patriarch in Jerusalem who had been appointed by the pope.

The success of the First Crusade lasted less than a century. By 1187 Jerusalem and most of the Holy Land was won back by the Muslims under Salah al-Din, while the Franks clung precariously to a few Mediterranean ports on the Palestine coast. The fervor for the crusade enterprise, though doubtless abated, lived on, however. Egypt was one rich and promising target, as Tunis would later be, and in 1203 knights were assembling in Venice, where the Venetians contracted to carry them to Egypt. Alexius Angelos, the son of a deposed Byzantine emperor Isaac, made them an offer that both the crusaders and their grasping Venetian ferrymen found impossible to turn down: a large sum of money and submission to the Church of Rome if they would restore him and his father to the imperial throne in Constantinople. Thus began the Fourth Crusade, which ended with the crusaders looting the imperial city so thoroughly that Europe began to be filled with a Byzantine treasure in gold, jewels, manuscripts, and relics—Venice got the lion's share—and the Greeks never forgot or forgave the violation of their house and its possessions. There was no need for the Easterners to submit to the Roman Church. The crusaders had simply taken over Byzantium. A Latin knight, Baldwin of Flanders, was elected emperor by his fellow knights and a papally appointed Latin bishop presided in Hagia Sophia as patriarch of Constantinople.

Church Reunion

In 1261 a new Byzantine ruler, Michael VIII Palaeologos (r. 1261–1282), was finally strong enough to put an end to the Latin adventure in Constantinople, at least for the moment. There were other dangers, however: the inexorable presence of the Turks in what remained of the empire and, the new and intimidating figure of Charles of Anjou in the West. This younger brother of Louis IX of France had been invited to take the crown of Sicily by the pope as a counterweight to the German emperor, but Charles's eyes were wider than that island: Byzantium itself beckoned to him. Michael, who cared little for theology, judged the time ripe for a rapprochement with Rome and the alliance that must inevitably follow, which would save his throne and his house from both the Turks and Charles. In 1267 he made a highly conciliatory approach to Clement IV, who welcomed his interest and told him in effect that the Greeks would have to come to terms first. The terms, which Clement put in the form of a creed to be signed, were no less than total capitulation on all the points of theological and jurisdictional dispute between them. The response was not a happy one.

Clement died the following year and was succeeded, after a lapse of three years, by a very different man, Gregory X. When elected pope in 1271, he was a cleric with the crusaders in Syria, and a successful crusade, a united Christian assault on Islam, was very much on his mind. He took up Michael's offer, and when Michael signaled his continued willingness to cooperate, Gregory summoned a general council to meet in Lyons in 1274 to unify the Churches and to reinvigorate the idea of a crusade. The first session met in May 1274 with three hundred bishops and sixty abbots in attendance as well as a number of theologians (Aquinas died on his way to the council), King James of Aragon himself, and representatives of the sovereigns of France, Germany, England, and Sicily. Michael's hand-picked delegation of Eastern bishops— the patriarch Joseph, who declined to attend, was deposed and replaced by a more complaisant cleric, Germanus—finally arrived in June, proxies from five hundred metropolitan bishops in hand. In the fourth session, on 6 July 1274, the issue of reunion was dealt with quickly when Michael's delegates signed the creed originally formulated by Clement IV, requesting only that Greek practices like the use of unleavened bread in the Eucharist be allowed to continue.

The Latin and Greek Churches were thus reunited by an act of cold political calculation on the part of Michael Palaeologos but no one was deceived. When Michael died in 1282, his son and successor, Andronicus, immediately renounced the Union of Lyons, restored the patriarch Joseph, and refused to allow his father to be buried in consecrated ground.

A Papal Crisis: Celestine and Boniface

At the opening of the fourteenth century the Western Church stood on the brink of disaster, some of which might have been foreseen, but other elements—like the election of the elderly hermit monk Pietro da Morrone as Celestine V in 1294—seem entirely, and extraordinarily, circumstantial. From Celestine's election and brief five-month papacy flowed long-term political and religious consequences that emptied directly into the Reformation a little more than a century later. In the short term, they carried the papacy from Rome to Avignon.

A Neapolitan of peasant stock, Pietro da Morrone became a Benedictine at age seventeen and spent most of the rest of his life as an ascetic recluse in the mountainous Abruzzi. In July 1294, the saintly Pietro was abruptly and unexpectedly elected pope by a befuddled and hopelessly deadlocked college of cardinals. He accepted and took the name Celestine V. The eighty-year-old Celestine appears to have enjoyed being pope, at least at first. He gave everyone what he craved, including the same benefices to several different people. Twelve cardinals elected Celestine: six Romans, four Italians, and two French.

Celestine doubled the size of the college, creating seven new French and five Neapolitan cardinals, the latter out of regard for Charles II. Very soon, however, everyone, including Celestine, seemed to understand that this papacy had been a very bad idea. After five months Celestine decided to resign. Was it possible for a pope to abdicate? The chief lawyer of the college of cardinals, Gaetani, said yes, yes. Gaetani succeeded Celestine as Boniface VIII. The new pope immediately abrogated all his predecessor's decrees and then tried to arrest the old man. Pietro made it back to the Abruzzi but was eventually apprehended and kept under a kind of surveillance arrest until he died in 1296. He was canonized in 1313.

At the election of Boniface VIII (r. 1294–1303), the papacy was deeply embroiled in European power politics, in part because of Celestine's maladroit pontificate but more fundamentally and consequentially by reason of the increasing internationalization of the papacy by popes like Innocent III (r. 1198–1216) and the growing tensions between the rising European monarchies and a Church that was the largest and richest landowner in their domains. King and pope were locked in an almost inevitable struggle between national and secular aspirations and the most powerful institution in Europe. In Italy those secular aspirations had not yet risen to the level of monarchy—when they did, in the nineteenth century, the Church once again stood in the way (see I/7)—but were borne by powerful families like the Guelphs and Ghibellines, Colonnas and Orsinis.

The strong-willed and irascible Boniface had the additional burden of facing in Philip IV of France a ruler as determined and persistent as himself. Boniface had canonized Philip's grandfather, Louis IX, in 1297, but the issue was not the sanctity of the dead but the power of the living, Philip's power over the Church in France and Boniface's power over the Church universal. Boniface may be judged to have had the last word or, if not the last, at least the loudest, since the words of his famous bull *Unam sanctam* (1302) still reverberate in the ears of Catholics and non-Catholics alike. Here Boniface made his famous declaration that there was "no salvation outside the Church" (see I/4). The ringing finale spelled out the pope's message to Philip, and to everyone else: "We declare, affirm, and define as a truth necessary for salvation that every human being be subject to the Roman Pontiff." There has never been a stronger statement of papal power.

Philip's response was not prudent. A French minister of state and a member of the Colonna family, with whom Boniface was locked in a mortal feud, tracked down the pope at Anagni in 1303, struck him when he refused to resign, and then stripped him of his tiara and vestments. When his antagonists fell to quarreling whether to kill him on the spot (the Colonna position) or to take him captive to France (the more sensitive French proposal), Boniface, then in his eighties, managed to escape but died quite suddenly a few months later.

The Popes without Rome: Avignon

Boniface's successor lasted only eight months before he too died, in his case, of dysentery. The college of cardinals was now sharply divided between pro- and anti-French factions. After a contentious eleven-month debate, they chose the French bishop of Bordeaux—who was not a cardinal—and he took the name Clement V (r. 1305–1314). The election, Clement's subsequent coronation at Lyons, his almost immediate consecration of nine new French cardinals, and his willingness to support the king's patently false charges against the Knights Templar (see II/8) all loudly proclaimed the victory of Philip of France in his war against papal power.

Clement chose not to go directly to Rome, in that era a politically unstable and dangerous place. Instead, in 1309 he settled, temporarily, it was thought, in Avignon, a city in the territory of the Holy Roman Empire but just across the Rhone from the domains of the king of France. Soon Rome began to come to him. The Roman curia, the papal bureaucracy, by degrees transferred itself to Avignon and conducted its and the papacy's business from that city. The cardinals came, too, and when Clement died, they elected another Frenchman in his place.

Nine popes in all resided at Avignon, seven as the sole successors of the prince of the Apostles, from Clement V to Gregory XI, who moved back to Rome in 1376, and two more, Clement VII (r. 1378–1394) and Benedict XIII (r. 1394–1417), who contested the restored Roman papacy in what has come to be known as "the Great Western Schism." With the pope, the Roman curia, and the college of cardinals, the latter now overwhelmingly French, all present and in residence, Avignon was in every sense an imperial court. The city eventually had an outsized and quite splendid palace complex that housed the considerable papal household, while the city itself had to struggle to house the twenty-three cardinals and their thousand-odd retainers, the papal bureaucrats (chancery, tribunal, and alms-ministry), representatives of most of Italy's banking houses, and all who had something to sell to that grand company.

Avignon was not the Papal States, the pope's considerable possessions in Italy, but rather the emperor's city, albeit one that stood in the very dense shadow of the king of France. The papacy lost much of its independence at Avignon, and with it, a substantial amount of its income since many were reluctant to pay Church dues that would end up in the French king's pocket. The Avignon popes had necessarily to become efficient, which they did, and also, in the process, more grasping. Simony, the buying and selling of spiritual offices, became almost routine as did, almost as a corollary, the practice of attaching fees to the granting of spiritual benefits, the system known as indulgences (see II/5).

But the Church lived on, and sometimes with vigor. John XXII (r. 1316–1334) was an energetic and contentious pope who defied the emperor and his privileges, brought the controversy over Franciscan poverty to a thunderous conclusion, and ended his days accused of heresy (see I/5 and II/8). Innocent VI (r. 1352–1362) managed to restore some semblance of papal control and order to the Papal States in Italy, and Urban V was in Rome just long enough to receive the Byzantine emperor John V Palaeologos into the Roman Church. Finally, Gregory XI (r. 1370–1378) was filled with high hopes, of returning to Rome, for example, of uniting Eastern and Western Churches, and of rekindling the zeal for a crusade against Islam. He did in fact return to Rome in 1376—his other hopes came to naught—but the continuing political turmoil prevented him from accomplishing anything serious.

The Great Western Schism

Gregory did die in Italy, which meant that the next papal conclave met in Rome. Eleven of the sixteen voting cardinals were French and wished to return as quickly as possible to Avignon, but the Roman mob had its way: the terrified cardinals voted for an Italian, the archbishop of Bari, who took the name Urban VI. The affair was by no means finished. As soon as the French cardinals got out of Rome, they declared they had voted under duress. They reconvened and elected a new pope, a Frenchman, Clement VII, who promptly returned to Avignon. There were now two popes, Urban VI in Rome and Clement VII in Avignon. Christian Europe was split in its allegiance: France and Spain declared for Clement, while Italy, Germany, England, Hungary, and Poland continued to recognize Urban as the only legitimate bishop of Rome and heir of St. Peter.

The impasse yielded no easy solution. Neither the Italian nor the French pope, each elected by a conclave of cardinals and each with what had become, in the fourteenth century, strong national support, was willing to yield. The Empire, England, and the Papal States stood behind Urban; France, its ruler, and the prestigious theologians of the university of Paris backed Clement, along with Naples and Scotland. National churches were in the making—that of France was already far advanced—and the concessions now granted them by the two contenders in hope of support simply accelerated the process. There were even saints on both sides: Catherine of Sienna with Urban, Vincente Ferrer with Clement.

Urban died in 1388 and was promptly succeeded in the Roman line by Boniface IX (r. 1389–1404), who practically redefined simony with his sale of offices, then briefly by Innocent VII (r. 1404–1406) and Gregory XII (r. 1406–1415). Amid this undistinguished company, however, an element of sanity (or despair) appeared among the Roman cardinals. Those who elected Innocent

VII each took an oath before the election that if chosen, he would resign if his Avignon counterpart did. Once elected, Innocent VII showed no inclination to resign, even in the face of unmistakable signals from Avignon. Other solutions began to surface. In 1394 the theologians of Paris, among them the chief Christian intellectuals of the day, were losing enthusiasm for the ongoing schism and proposed that either both contenders should resign and a new pope be chosen or else a general council should decide which of the two was the genuine pope. Clement in Avignon did not take the news at all well. When he heard the proposal, he had a stroke and died. A French conclave immediately elected Benedict XIII in his place. At first Benedict seemed inclined to conciliation. In 1404 he sent a delegation to sound out Boniface's willingness to negotiate. Boniface had no interest in the proposal, nor did Innocent VII after him. By the time the eighty-year-old Gregory XII had put on the Roman tiara in 1406, neither side seemed prepared to budge.

Pisa and Constance

Dissatisfaction finally overcame the obstinacy of the papal rivals. The French king, who had early on lost his enthusiasm for his French pope, signaled that perhaps a council should intervene, and the idea was eventually taken up by a number of eminent churchmen. There were enough of them, at any rate, to encourage some cardinals and prelates to detach themselves from Avignon and others from Rome and come together at Livorno, where they issued an encyclical summoning the bishops of Christendom to a general council that would convene in Pisa in March 1409. Gregory and Benedict responded by summoning their own councils, but the assembly at Pisa had the most general and distinguished attendance. In the end there were four patriarchs, twenty-two cardinals, and eighty bishops at Pisa, with proxies for many more. Neither Gregory nor Benedict chose to appear, however, though explicitly summoned. On 5 June the assembly unanimously declared both popes schismatics and heretics "openly scandalizing the universal Church." With the schism now apparently ended, the cardinals met in conclave on 15 June 1409 and elected a new pope, an Italian Franciscan who took the name Alexander V. He never made it to Rome. He died at Bologna in May 1410. The cardinals quickly reconvened and chose another Italian from among themselves as John XXIII.

At this almost hopeless juncture the Roman emperor (and German prince) Sigismund intervened. Acting on the precedent of Constantine, he summoned a council to meet at Constance within his own domains. It was formally convened in 1414 by John XXIII—who doubtless thought it would confirm him in his office—and included numerous cardinals, bishops, heads of monasteries, theologians, and canon lawyers. The council voted to depose all three papal claimants and then elected a new pope, Martin V. This time the council had some claim to be ecumenical and so the depositions stuck. But the price to the papacy was considerable. Even before this new election the council issued a decree, *Haec sancta*, setting forth as dogma that a general council's authority was higher than that of the pope. When the election did occur, the council was organized in the manner of a university into corporate bodies of "nations," with each of the five nations present represented by six electors, who cast their votes together with the cardinals.

> **Note:** The Council of Constance posthumously condemned the teachings of the English reformer John Wycliffe (d. 1384), who had asserted the English government's right to confiscate the endowments of corrupt clergy and, in fact, to undertake, on its own authority, the reformation of the Church in England. The Bohemian reformer Jan Hus (d. 1415), chancellor of the university of Prague, who had condemned papal corruption and taught that the laity should participate in the wine as well as the bread in the Eucharist, was invited to Constance under immunity from Sigismund, but once he arrived he was arrested, tried, and, when he refused to recant, burned at the stake.

Conciliarism

The Council of Pisa did not succeed in ending the schism—in a sense it made it worse by adding a third pope, Alexander and then John—since national supporters of the Avignon and Roman papacies were not yet ready to desert their candidates, even though many churchmen had. But it had made clear to nearly everyone where the solution lay, in a general council of the Church, and it was that solution to which the Council of Constance put its hand in 1415. The discussion around and under that pragmatic way of clearing the ground of the intransigent rivals and starting afresh had forced the Church's canon lawyers and theologians to consider more profoundly, and to define more carefully, the powers of an assembly of the universal Church and how they squared with those of the office of the bishop of Rome, whom all parties to the discussion recognized as head of the Church.

The movement organized around this issue is called Conciliarism. Although the unmistakable crisis that gripped the Church gave it urgency, Conciliarism's form and shape derived in no small part from the fact that these assemblies were in truth general councils. That is, they were formally constituted not only of bishops but of abbots of monasteries, heads of the Church's new religious orders, university theologians, and secular princes. They were, in reality, what some of the later theorists called a *congregatio fidelium*, an assembly of all of

Christendom or, as some even would have it, a *representative* assembly of all Christians with powers that were only dimly conceived.

The Papacy under Attack:
Marsiglio of Padua and William of Ockham

The radical notion of a representative assembly had been championed by an outspoken critic of the papacy a century earlier. Marsiglio of Padua (d. ca. 1343) was a lawyer who was briefly rector of the university of Paris and then served as political adviser to the Ghibellines, the antipapal and proimperial party of the Italian cities. He wrote his principal work of political philosophy, *The Defender of Peace*, in support of their position. The tract was published anonymously in 1320, but when his name leaked out, Marsiglio was branded a heretic and had to flee Italy to escape ecclesiastical sanction. He took refuge at the court of King Louis IV of Bavaria, who was having his own argument with the papacy, and from that safe haven Marsiglio declared Pope John XXII a heretic and supported Louis's secular coronation as emperor in Rome in 1328 (see I/7).

The Defender of Peace is a defense of an Aristotelian-derived state as necessary for the preservation, at almost any cost, of the order of civil society. The authority of the state, and, in fact, all sovereignty, derives from the people. So too in the Church, sovereignty belongs to the "general council of all Christians," who alone have the power to make laws concerning bishops and priests, including to remove a pope, to regulate the sacraments, to excommunicate, and, in general, to exercise all the powers claimed in Marsiglio's day by the pope. For the state to properly achieve its end, he argued, the power of the Church must be strictly limited. The state possessed authority; the Church was merely an instrument, and it is the state that authorizes the Church. No bishop or priest has any coercive power over any layman.

Another influential thinker, and papal critic, was William of Ockham (d. 1349), who belonged to a somewhat different milieu but ended up on the same path as Marsiglio. An Englishman and a Franciscan, he was a theologian and moralist of subtle ingenuity (see II/5). He too taught at Paris—he arrived the year after Marsiglio departed—and later, like Marsiglio, was a condemned heretic (though for his views on poverty, not for his politics). Ockham too spent the last years of his life under the protective wing of Louis of Bavaria. Where the two men differed was in their motives. Marsiglio had grave philosophical problems with the Church, its offices and functions; Ockham had ecclesiastical problems with John XXII and that pope's views on the subject of the Franciscan life (see II/8).

Ockham's political ideas are found chiefly in his *Dialogue*, written in 1343 in the form of an imagined conversation between student and teacher. In it Ockham argues as strenuously as Marsiglio whose work he had read (and disagreed with in the matter of Marsiglio's denial of the Petrine argument for the supremacy of the bishop of Rome), for limiting the Church's authority to purely spiritual matters. Again like Marsiglio, Ockham was convinced that the state, in this case the empire, needed no validation, neither a papal coronation nor any other ritual. The emperor was made by the electors, not by the pope. The Church's authority comes from possession of the truth, which is vested not in the pope or in a bishop but in the community of the faithful. Infallibility is a mark of the Church, not of the pope. It follows, then, that a pope may lapse into error, as Ockham believed John XXII did on the matter of Christ's poverty. The pope's power is likewise limited, according to Ockham, by the freedom granted to Christians by both New Testament revelation and the natural law, and there are times when the state may be the guarantor of that freedom.

Conciliarism drew on Ockham's ideas about the limitations of papal power, but even more powerfully on Marsiglio of Padua's view of the people's sovereignty and even on the Roman law precept "what concerns all, all have a right to judge." These notions were clearly operative in Councils of Constance, Basel, and Florence in the fifteenth century, which set themselves to reform the Church in both its head and its members. All opened their decrees with the statement "As representatives of the universal Church . . ." The definition of the Church as a corporate aggregate of Christian believers was developed by the most influential figure at Constance, the canon lawyer Francesco Zarabella, who argued that "the Church is nothing else than the congregation of the faithful."

The Voice of the Council: Haec sancta *and* Frequens

By its decree *Haec sancta*, the Council of Constance asserted a council's authority over the papacy, not in general terms but only in cases where the pope was seen to be in error or leading the Church astray. The council did not embrace Marsiglio's radical views that vested spiritual sovereignty in the faithful, which was then exercised by their representatives in council. Those who expressed themselves at Constance still thought that both spiritual sovereignty and spiritual powers came from on high, but that they rested inherently in the bishops (including the bishop of Rome) and not by delegation from the pope, who was their head. Those powers could be exercised for reform apart from and even despite the pope in cases of crisis or emergency, which no one denied was the case in the opening decades of the fifteenth century.

A restored papacy eventually managed to neutralize the sense and intent of *Haec sancta*. In 1436 Pius II issued his bull *Execrabilis* prohibiting all appeals over the pope's head to a council's authority. But the notion of national churches that the Council of Constance implicitly endorsed by its organization and voting format was of more lasting consequence. Nationalism was on the rise in Europe, and the papacy with its universalist claims was in a sense its natural enemy. In the following century the independence of national sovereigns in Germany and England, for example, provided precisely the kind of political shelter required for the earliest stages of the Reformation to take root. The papacy, which had once claimed universal jurisdiction over a united Christendom, now had to deal with nations and their princes piecemeal. In this era the new instrument of the concordat, in effect a treaty between the Church and a national government, also appeared.

The conciliar movement was far from dead, however. In 1417 Constance had issued another decree, *Frequens*, that attempted to institutionalize general councils by requiring that they be held regularly to carry out the reforms mandated at Constance, the first two at intervals of five years, and then every ten years. In fulfillment of that decree, there was an abortive council at Pavia (later Siena) in 1423–1424. The few bishops who had assembled there decreed another council in 1431 in Basel, over which a new pope Eugenius IV (r. 1431–1447) presided. But pope and council soon fell out and Eugenius almost immediately dismissed the Basel conclave. Recriminations continued on both sides until Eugenius transferred the council, which simply refused to go away, to Ferrara. Some of the bishops moved to Ferrara; others hung on in Basel until 1449, when they finally gave up and went home. They took with them the notion that the council was somehow above the pope. The Council of Ferrara-Florence, which concluded the final act of reunion with the Eastern Churches, was firmly under the control of the bishop of Rome.

The Emperor and the Pope

In the mid–fourteenth century, another beleaguered Byzantine emperor, John V Palaeologos (r. 1341–1391), had attempted some personal diplomacy with the West. John was faced from within by powerful pretenders to his imperial throne and a Serbian "province" that in 1346 declared itself independent and its Church autonomous—the patriarch of Constantinople promptly excommunicated its head—and from without by the Ottoman Turks, who had now entered Europe and all but surrounded the capital city. The emperor was in fact their tributary, and a demeaning part of that tribute was the service of his son Manuel and a military force to fight *with* the Turks against the last Greek outposts in western Anatolia. John decided to go West in person and seek help.

That was in 1367, the same year Urban V thought the moment had come for the pope to leave Avignon and return to Rome. The two men, pope and emperor, met in Rome in October 1369, where, in St. Peter's basilica, John Palaeologos publicly announced his adherence to the Church of Rome. Yes, he agreed, the pope was the supreme spiritual authority of all Christendom, and yes, the Holy Spirit proceeded from the Father *and* the Son. There was no sequel, however. Urban V once more deserted Rome for the safer confines of Avignon and John attempted to return to Constantinople. He nearly didn't make it: he was arrested in Venice for unpaid debts and kept in prison until the dutiful Manuel came and ransomed his imperial father. The union of the Churches was likely dead before the emperor finally reached the capital.

"Better the Turban of the Turk..."

The final attempt to put together what theology, culture, and politics had relentlessly rent asunder was made in the second quarter of the fifteenth century when the Eastern Churches had largely disappeared into the Abode of Islam, and what had once been the Eastern Christian Roman Empire was reduced to Constantinople, its hinterland, and an inconsequential slice of the Peloponnese, a pitiful island surrounded on all sides by an Ottoman Muslim sea. The Ottoman Turks stood poised to overwhelm even this spit of land, but they had pressed deeply enough north and west into the Balkans that the Latin West too had grown alarmed at this latest aggressive thrust of a Muslim power.

Once again the Byzantine emperor, now John VIII Palaeologos (r. 1425–1445), turned to his only hope, the West, fully understanding that the price to be paid for any form of help was reunion with Rome, once again on Roman terms. This time the pope was Eugenius IV and the conciliar setting was first Ferrara and then Florence. This council had a long and troubled pedigree reaching back to the Council of Constance and the 1417 *Frequens* decree that mandated regular conciliar assemblies. But in the sessions held in Ferrara in 1438, and then in Florence in 1439, the conciliar issue that had dominated much discussion in these assemblies yielded to the pressing question of reunion of the Latin West with not only the Greek East, the reduced patriarchate of Constantinople, but all the Eastern Churches under Islam's domain.

Unlike at Lyons in 1274, there were serious theological discussions at Ferrara-Florence, chiefly because in the large Eastern delegations there were now churchmen interested in union. The emperor wished it, of course, for his own, principally political reasons, but both Joseph, the patriarch of Constantinople, and Mark, the metropolitan bishop of Ephesus, were strongly opposed. The union had two powerful Eastern champions, however: Isidore of Kiev, metropolitan of Moscow, and Bessarion, archbishop of Nicaea and a scholar already imbued with the humanistic ideals of the Italian Renaissance.

In the end, probably not so much their arguments as cold political necessity carried the day. In its session in Florence on 6 July 1439, the council issued its Decree of Union, signed by the emperor and most of the delegates. Joseph was by then dead, and Mark of Ephesus refused to put his name to the document.

The council's Decree of Union was promptly repudiated by both the clergy and people of Constantinople. "Better the turban of the Turk than the cap of a bishop," it was said. The patriarchs of Alexandria, Antioch, and Jerusalem all declared against it. Both Isidore and Bessarion, now named cardinals in the Roman Church, returned to Italy, where Bessarion in particular became an important figure in the European Renaissance—"the best Latin among the Greeks and the best Greek among the Latins," another humanist called him. But John VIII and his brother Constantine IX, the last emperor of Byzantium, who died defending the city against the final, successful assault of the Turks in 1453, both remained loyal to their pledge of faith to Rome.

Moscow, the Third Rome

Kiev had been the earliest center of Christianity among the eastern Slavs, but near-destruction at the hands of the Mongols and then absorption into the political spheres of Latin Poland and Lithuania brought the Ukraine into the orbit of the Roman Church. Only Moscow remained a Slavic bastion of Eastern Orthodoxy, and its metropolitan bishops were customarily appointed from Constantinople. But after the 1439 Decree of Union, Constantinople was and remained officially Roman, and in Moscow, where the decree was never accepted, the council of Russian bishops began to elect their own primate.

With the emperor's death and the Turks' entry into Constantinople in 1453, a new Greek patriarch felt free to repudiate the union of Florence and restore relations with Moscow. But no longer on the old terms: with the fall of the city, the last great independent see of the East passed under Islamic sovereignty, as had the patriarchates of Antioch, Alexandria, and Jerusalem and the independent Churches of the Serbs, Bulgars, Armenians, Syrians, Chaldeans, and Abyssinians. Moscow alone stood free, and in the last quarter of the fifteenth century, the grand duke of Moscow began to assume the full imperial titles of "autocrat" and "Caesar" (Russ. *tsar*). The Church was not far behind. Sometime around 1510, the monk Philotheus wrote to Czar Basil III drawing what had to be an inevitable conclusion. Rome had fallen to the barbarians because of its heresy and Constantinople to the Muslim Turks for its embrace of Rome. Just as there was one true Christian sovereign left in the world, so there was one sovereign Orthodox Church, that of Moscow: "Two Romes have fallen, but the third stands, and a fourth will not be." The metropolitan of Moscow did not have himself declared patriarch until 1589, however, and even then only as fifth in ecclesiastical rank behind Constantinople, Alexandria, Antioch, and Jerusalem.

Note: The Eastern Churches are not united under a single authority, as the Western sees were until the Reformation. Rather, they consist of nine or so autonomous (or autocephalous) Churches. Four of these are under the patriarchs of the ancient sees of Constantinople (accorded a kind of primacy of honor and the title of ecumenical patriarch), Alexandria, Antioch, and Jerusalem. Chiefly in the lands proselytized from Constantinople and as a consequence of Constantinople's disappearance into the Dar al-Islam, the patriarchates of Russia, Serbia, Romania, Bulgaria, and Georgia were later added. Eventually independent Orthodox Churches developed in Greece, Cyprus, Czechoslovakia, Poland, Albania, and, finally, the United States.

Reformation and Counter-Reformation

In 1515 or thereabout, the Augustinian monk Martin Luther (d. 1546) reached his understanding that the Christian is justified by faith alone (see II/10). This teaching flowed naturally from reading Paul and Augustine, yet it profoundly undermined the foundations on which the Christian Church—Augustine's, certainly, if perhaps not yet Paul's—had been raised. At some point, Luther believed, the development of that Church had gone terribly awry. The preaching of indulgences, which had forced Luther to go public with his accusations, was but the last false note in a centuries-long distortion of scriptural truth. Luther understood what he was about. Justification by faith was, he said, "the article by which the Church stands or falls." The Catholic Church had lost its authority in a manner that could be expressed almost syllogistically: "Where the word is, there is faith; and where faith is, there is the true church."

Luther was too good an Augustinian, and perhaps too good a Catholic, to deny absolutely the existence or validity of a Church possessed with the authority to teach and administer the "scriptural" sacraments of Baptism and the Lord's Supper, as the Eucharist was coming to be called (see II/6). He attacked the corruption and malfeasance of the Roman Church, its institutions and officers—whose authority, he maintained, was no different from those of secular officials: it arose not from status but from their work. He created no other institution in its place, perhaps because he thought, along with others, that the protestors' separation from the Catholic Church would be a temporary affair, awaiting only a radical reformation. But that was not to be so. A conference of conciliation held at Regensburg in 1541 between the Reformers and Catholic representatives foundered irretrievably. The Reformers could not and would not rejoin a Church that had no intention of reforming itself in matters they considered crucial to its validity as an instrument of God's will.

An alternative was already being worked out. In 1536 John Calvin, whose *Institutes of the Christian Religion* had already sketched a blueprint for a kind of ecclesiastical organization, was invited to Geneva to attempt to put his ideas into practice. He failed on this occasion, but after 1541 he returned and began constituting not merely a Reformed Church but a veritable Christian Republic (see II/8).

The Reformers did not wish to destroy the Church. The institution was, after all, founded by Jesus. What they desired was rather a return to the pristine Church, the Church of the Gospels and the Apostles, which, on their reckoning, survived unblemished only as far as the Council of Nicaea (325 C.E.), but could still be found, in orthodox sources, as late as the sixth century. It was this latter conviction, a form of Christian consensus, that some on both sides thought, at least at the outset, might be the basis for a reconciliation between the Church and its Reformers.

The Reformation challenged the right of the Roman Church and its hierarchy, particularly its chief authority, the bishop of Rome, to speak for the Church of Christ. It attempted to wrest the truth of Christ, if not out of the hands of the Church, where Reformers and Catholics alike agreed it somehow resided, then out of the sole control of the Church's spokesmen. At stake was the right of the Roman Church's authorities to possess the magisterium, the power to teach authoritatively on matters of faith and morals (see II/5).

The Radical Reformation: The Anabaptists

Luther and Calvin shared the same vision of the Christian Church as a body of believers united in faith and practice under the guidance of authority. But the Reform generated other, very different notions of the Church. In Switzerland, Germany, and the Netherlands the 1520s groups of believers quickly dubbed Anabaptists or "Rebaptizers" appeared. Their quarrel was with infant baptism, which they held invalid and hence insisted be administered again, to the publicly confessing adult. The movements joined, somewhat too generously, under the rubric Anabaptist had other, more radical views on the calling of the Christian. For them the Church was an entirely voluntary association (hence adult, consensual baptism) that prized not conformity but freedom of conscience and advocated pacifism in those troubled and violent times. In the words of their *Schleitheim Confession* of 1527, "There shall also fall away from us the diabolical weapons of violence—such as sword, armor, and the like, and all of their use to protect friends or against enemies—by virtue of the word of Christ: 'You shall not resist evil'."

The Anabaptists left force to the political authority, the magistrate, as an "ordering of God outside the perfection of Christ." But for those who followed Christ, and who nevertheless, "being inadvertently overtaken," lapse into sin, the "ban" is invoked: the sinner is to be admonished privately twice, publicly if there is a third occasion. If there is still no mending of his ways, the sinner is excluded and shunned.

Note: The sixteenth century was as turbulent in its economic development as in its theology. The early Anabaptists, whose descendants survived decades of fierce persecution from all across the Christian spectrum and live on as the Amish, Mennonites, and Hutterites, among others, engaged the era's emerging capitalism with an equally radical proposal. "Private property," the Hutterite Peter Walpot (d. 1578) wrote, "does not belong to the Christian Church. Private property is a thing of the world, of the heathen, of those without divine love. . . . But the true community of goods belongs among true believers. For by divine law all things should be held in common and nobody should take for himself what is God's any more than the air, rain, snow or water, the sun or other elements. . . . Owning private property is contrary to the nature and conditions of His creation." Walpot and other advocates of what they called "true yieldedness" could appeal to the practice of the early Church (Acts 4:32–35) and the preaching (but no longer the practice) of the Christian Fathers from Clement to Chrysostom and Augustine, but they failed to convert many Christians, Catholic or Reformed, to their ideal of Christian communism.

The Confessional Churches

The Reformation and the Catholic response through the Council of Trent converted an institution that still, with the exception of notable secessionists like the Lollards in England and the Hussites in Bohemia, regarded itself as a single Church into what became, in effect, four distinct Churches, or, to use a more accurate term, "confessions." Where the earlier Church had defined and preserved its unity through its conciliar creeds and attendant canons, the post-Reformation era witnessed the issuance of statements put forth by, or in the name of, a body of believers setting out their own particular beliefs (chiefly those that separated them from the Roman Church) together with at least an outline of the principal institutions by which it proposed to organize and govern itself. The earliest of these is the Anabaptists' *Schleitheim Confession*, but the best known is probably the Lutherans' *Confession of Augsburg* (1530) and *Book of Concord* (1580), followed by the Calvinists' *Helvetic Confessions* of 1536 and 1556, their *Canons of Dordrecht* (1619), and finally the Anglicans' *Book of Common Prayer* (1549) and *Thirty-Nine Articles* (1563). For what might be called "Reformed Catholicism," the decrees of the Council of Trent, particularly the *Profession of Faith* of 1564 and the various enabling bulls of the post-Tridentine popes fall into the same category.

7

Church and State:
Popes, Patriarchs, and Emperors

THE BIBLE is inexorably history-minded. After a mythic prologue and a kind of tribal prose epic of the patriarchal age, its narrative settles into the form of a continuous history focused on the kingdom of Israel. There are prayerful asides, long legal interpolations, moralizing stories, and prophetic glosses on past events and predictions of future ones, but the chief players are God, Israel's royal house—with the prophets ranged round them like a Greek chorus—and Israel's enemies, from the Canaanites and Philistines of old to the Greeks of the most recent era. The latest book of the Bible, Daniel, disguises the Hellenes in a fable-allegory (the four beasts of Daniel 7–8) and projects the future in the form of a vision of conflict, chaos, and triumph. The vision is marked with some precision. The history of Israel unfolds in terms of "weeks," that is, multiples of seven (9:24–27), which flow directly and seamlessly from historical events into the cosmic metahistory of the End Time.

That is not the way a later generation of Jews read the Bible, however. The order we find in the Septuagint translation was a different one, and at the end of the canon after the so-called Writings stood the Books of Ezra and Nehemiah and two Books of Chronicles, the latter a matter-of-fact—they are neither up-lifting nor apocalyptic—summary of the history of the Jews from Adam to the Babylonian Exile. Chronicles, like Kings and many other books of the Bible, keeps one eye on God and the other, somewhat more attentively, perhaps, on the doings in the royal palace. These were, after all, royal chronicles, the records and recollections of a people who also for a time constituted what in ancient times passed as a state.

The Jewish Experience: From State to Church

As we have seen, the Jews began their recorded history as Benei Israel, a tribal group whose primary bonds were supplied by kinship and whose leadership, where we can discern it, was now patriarchal, on the model of a Bedouin sheikh, and now charismatic. Abraham typified the first whereas Moses spoke on behalf of his people—now considerably more numerous than Abraham's extended family—before the Pharaoh. The ruler of Egypt himself became the archetype of the secular sovereign who is either oblivious or uncaring—in any event, obdurate—in the face of a monotheistic community's loyalty to a different and higher authority.

Moses' contest with the Pharaoh and his wizards on behalf of the Israelites' God is reported, in even greater affective detail, in the Quran (7:103–126, etc.). In Jewish eyes, Egypt, Israel's longtime political enemy across the wastes of the Sinai, overshadowed the Pharaoh as a symbol of pagan opposition to the people of God. But for the Muslims, who after all made Egypt politically their own land, the Pharaoh was the very embodiment of the tyrant, Muslim or not, medieval or modern.

Joshua, Judges, and Samuel tell the prolonged story of Israel's struggle up the ladder of political evolution—possession of the land was crucial here— from a loosely knit confederation of tribes eponymously identified with the twelve sons of Jacob, the literal Children of Israel, who acknowledged common lineage and worship of Yahweh in shrine centers across the new Eretz Israel. These are obscure times for us, but, as has already been noted (see I/6), the outlines of a recognizable Israelite polity emerge with the rather overargued explanation in 1 Samuel (8:1–22) of how Israel came to be, with God's reluctant approval, a kingdom.

The kingdom of Israel survived, with a major interruption between 597 and 164 B.C.E., from Saul's day before the dawn of the first millennium down to Rome's dissolution of it in 6 C.E. We know a good deal about its early kings from Kings and Chronicles, and about its restoration monarchs after 164, the Hasmonaeans and Herodians, the latter from the Jewish historian Josephus, whose political sense was somewhat more acute than that of the Hasmonaeans' own propagandists, who provided us with the books of Maccabees. Kingship was undoubtedly royal in Israel—Solomon's Jerusalem palace was even larger than his grandiose temple—and unmistakably sacred. Kings, like priests, were God's anointed (*mashiah*) in Israel, and the Psalms give us some idea of the religious ritual that accompanied a royal enthronement.

But though sacred in his office, the king of Israel, like the later caliphs of Islam, possessed no religious powers: he neither spoke for nor legislated on behalf of God. The king eventually dwelled on the western hill of Jerusalem, where the Muslim tradition imagined even David lived and where Herod's palace near the Jaffa Gate became the Romans' praetorian headquarters. Across the city, on its eastern hill, were the temple and its priests, the latter the religious authorities, if not of the state, then assuredly of the people. The kohenim controlled both the House of the Lord, where they alone conducted his prescribed rituals, and the Law of the Lord, whose sole authoritative interpreters they were. The king commanded the army and levied the taxes; the priests managed the temple Israel's major corporation and exacted their tithes in God's name.

Israel was discernibly a theocracy—the word is Josephus's own—if by that we mean that God's was the founding and principal authority and that the behavior of its members was governed by God's will as expressed in what the Jews called Torah and the Greeks "the Mosaic constitution." But the kings had their own authority as well, which was unprotected by either divine revelation or the promise of personal infallibility; indeed, the Bible's later books are filled with unvarnished accounts of both the political follies and the moral failings of the Israelite kings. Yet it was not the priesthood that corrected them. The kings were guided, not always in a kindly fashion, by the prophets, men who at times stand as a kind of spiritual adviser/consultant to the king, and on other occasions appear unbidden before the throne as God's extraordinary envoy to the monarch.

The Babylonians dissolved Israelite sovereignty in 597, not by annexation but by looting the people of their rulers and their treasure. The kings were gone— they would briefly return later as the Hasmonaeans for another quick century of Jewish sovereignty—but they left their distinctive palm prints all over Jewish consciousness. As already noted, the king was God's anointed, and every later Jewish dream of restoring either the glory or sovereignty of Israel had built into its scenario a return of a member of the House of David, who would rule Israel forever. Judaism remained steadfastly messianic, and the shadowy but powerful figure of the Messiah was explicitly and unmistakably royal. "David, king of Israel" as a prayer and a slogan has never ceased to stir Jews.

The Israelites' neighbors and rivals took over what was left of David's and Solomon's inheritance, which was by then only the former tribal land of Judah. When the exiles, though not the treasure, were restored in the late sixth century B.C.E., the Jews were still a people and a religious community, as they had been before and as they had remained during the Babylonian Exile, but they no longer possessed a state. Rather, the Judaeans, as they were now called (see I/1), were the provincial subjects of the shah of Iran and later of the Greco-Macedonian kings of Egypt and Syria, a "church," perhaps, within someone else's state. In the 170s that someone else was the Greco-Macedonian Antiochus IV Epiphanes, lord of Greater Syria and hostile to Jewish beliefs and religious practices.

It is not quite clear whether Antiochus persecuted his Jewish subjects in Judaea as a church or as fractious subjects. The Books of Maccabees argue the first; Josephus more strongly suggests the latter. It made little difference perhaps: to persecute the Jews as Jews, whether the motive was religious, political, economic, or simply allophobia, was an act with religious consequences against a community, one of whose own identity markers was the worship of a unique God. Antiochus struck at both temple and Torah, installing an altar to one of his own gods on the temple mount—the "abomination of desolation" of Daniel 9:27—and ordering copies of the Law be burnt.

The Jews were but one religious community in Greco-Roman antiquity, but they had unique privileges. From very early on, rulers were considered divinized in the Middle East, and from Alexander onward, both the Greek *basileis* and the Roman *imperatores* were acclaimed, in life or after death, as godlike. *Theios* and *divus*, "god" or "godlike," did not carry for the pre-Christian Greeks and Romans the same heavy theological freight that "God" does among the monotheists, and the population at large had few problems publicly acknowledging that their rulers were beyond human. But the Jews could recognize an altar and sacrifice when they saw them, and they could not participate, either by throwing incense on the altar or by sharing afterward in the meats of sacrifice. Nor could they, or would they, many of them, violate the Sabbath or the dietary laws to perform civic duties. The Greeks and Romans understood and, somewhat more extraordinarily, accepted this, and by reason of their national "superstition," as it was called, the Jews were exempted from performing these basic acts of ancient *patria*-ism and political solidarity.

This yielding of state to church was not in the end enough, at least for some Jews. There were three major Jewish insurrections against the Roman imperium, in 66–70, 117–118, and 132—135 C.E., none of them on unmistakably or chiefly religious grounds—although the messianic figure of Bar Kokhba emerged in the 132 uprising—and all falling in what is generally considered the most enlightened era of that empire's history. At the end of the last of them, the Jews found themselves cast into another exile, banned by statute from living evermore in the Roman province of Judaea—they did not return until the Muslims brought an end to Roman rule there in the 630s—and dispersed into the midst of their fellow Jews of the Diaspora (see I/1). Thenceforward the Jews lived as subjects in the empires of others, from the fourth century onward in a Christian Roman Empire, where they had to deal with both church and state, and then after the seventh, many of them in the Abode of Islam, where the church was in effect the state, and where their status was the subject not of secular but of religious law (see I/8).

"Render to Caesar..."

The life of Jesus of Nazareth unfolded against a darkening political background in Palestine although the Gospels themselves only occasionally look skyward and take note of the changing weather. For the modern critical reader, the Gospels are filled with plentiful clues to the dangerous political storm building between Jews and Romans behind, and often directly over, Jesus' life. It is difficult to overlook the fact, for instance, that he was tried by a high-ranking agent of the Roman Empire, Pontius Pilate, for what was palpably a political crime, in one of the empire's most incendiary provinces, in a city attacked, besieged, and battered down by the Romans no more than forty years after Jesus' own execution. If those facts are not concealed in the Gospels, the political overtones certainly are, and both Jesus and his followers are presented in a manner that almost completely disassociates them from any involvement or interest in the political causes or currents coursing through Palestine in the first century C.E.

This is not to say there were no attempts at drawing Jesus into those currents. The Roman tax was an issue in Judaea as it was elsewhere, and the Gospels depict provocateurs attempting to get Jesus to pronounce on the inflammatory subject of whether or not a Jew should pay that tax. When he asked to be shown the appropriate coin—many coinages circulated in Palestine—he was handed a Roman coin with the effigy of Tiberius. Although the deified emperor's depiction was already a sore point with some strongly aniconic Jews, Jesus answered in his customary parabolic way: "Render to Caesar the things that are Caesar's and to God the things that are God's" (Matt. 22:21 and parallels). It was a successful retort—his questioners left discomforted—but later Christians, who did not read these words simply as a clever response but as words falling from the mouth of the Son of God, and had, moreover, very different political concerns, understood them as benchmarks for dealing with all secular authority.

Paul had his own troubles with the Roman authorities—he seemed particularly adept at inciting riot—and when we last hear of him in the Acts of the Apostles he is in Rome waiting to stand trial before the emperor. The tradition adds that he was executed there, along with Peter, not for the crime that had brought him there, but rather because the emperor Nero had, it seems, decided to make Jesus' followers in Rome scapegoats for some of his own imperial mischief. But for all his problems with the state, Paul does not seem to have been very concerned with, or even much interested in, politics. He advocated abiding by the political status quo (Rom. 13:1–6; 1 Tim. 2:2; Titus 3:1), perhaps as a nonrevolutionary Jew who, like many others, had come to terms with empire, the Romans' and others'; or perhaps as a good Roman who saw imperial authority as part of a divine order (so Rom. 13:1–2); or, most probably, as a Christian who had his heart and mind's eye turned toward the rapidly approaching End Time. The New Age was rushing in for Paul, and that fact rendered political and even personal questions, like marriage, somewhat beside the point.

The Pauline words of political restraint were most probably addressed to fellow Christians who increasingly needed them. The Roman Empire was suspicious of anything that threatened order, and the Christians with their talk of "the Kingdom" and their private meetings and rituals—private particularly when Jesus' followers were no longer welcome in the synagogues—were attracting official Roman notice. But if Paul could urge and practice a kind of nonchalant restraint with respect to civil authority, that posture was not so easy for a somewhat later generation of Christians. The quite extraordinary buffing-up of Pilate's image in the Gospels—and the darker light thrown thereby on the Jews—shows that in the 70s, 80s, and 90s, when there was still no sign of the End but many signs of Roman intervention in the lives of Jesus' followers, the Christians had every reason to be, at the very least, wary of Roman authority and power.

The Christians and the Empire

If the Jewish reader of the second or third century closed his Bible on Chronicles, the Christian found something else in his Old Testament. Daniel's apocalyptic visions were concluded with the twelve "minor" prophets' assurances that the days of hope would indeed come to pass. The Gospels with which the New Testament begins fit comfortably into that same apocalyptic paradigm. Though the Gospels themselves invite one to read them as history—Luke in particular, but the other evangelists also provide comforting historical touchstones in their narratives—the core of their message is undeniably apocalyptic: "The Kingdom of God is at hand" (Mark 1:15).

The New Testament ends with its own Daniel, the book called Revelation, which assured the Christian that Jesus' Second Coming would initiate a triumphalist cosmic era that would supersede all previous earthly history. But that understanding was defeated, in a sense, by the very history it sought to terminate. The Parousia did not occur, and soon the Christians turned from expecting the eschaton to counting the days, or rather the years, till its arrival (on millennialism, see II/10). That was one alternative, an occasional one, as it turned out. Another was to internalize the Kingdom, to render it a spiritual state shared by all Christians at baptism. What chiefly concerns us here are somewhat more literal approaches to parsing Jesus' promise of a Kingdom. The first was overtly political and took wing with the unlikely wedding of the Christian ekklesia and the Roman imperium: the Kingdom simply awaited its king, a Christian sovereign who would establish Christ's rule over the earth.

The Persecutions

The first signs of trouble between the followers of Jesus of Nazareth and their Roman sovereigns remain mysterious. In 64 C.E. Nero (r. 54–68) publicly executed some Christians at Rome—Church tradition insists that both Peter and Paul were among them—on the grounds that they were responsible for a destructive fire in the city. This may have been scapegoating, purely and simply, for the emperor's own crime, as Tacitus later thought. But when that Roman historian reported the event a half century after the fact, he could nonetheless characterize the Christians as a despised and antisocial lot and moral reprobates. Accusations of moral reprobation were not fatal at Rome; far more dangerous was the likely widespread Roman conviction that what the Christians themselves thought of as otherworldliness and group solidarity was in fact antisocial behavior. Two things militated against the new movement. First, Christians were perceived, as has just been said, as a group apart, mysterious and even clandestine in their rituals and practices; and whatever they did not know, the Romans, like many others, feared and maligned. Second, it became increasingly clear to the Romans, as it was to the two parties concerned, that the Christians were not Jews. Jews were assuredly not beloved by the Romans but, for all their peculiarities, they enjoyed exemptions and protections under Roman law. The Christians, cast or fled from the synagogue, did not.

The first to press the matter was the emperor Domitian (r. 81–96), who embarked on a broad persecution of the Christians, not so much for their beliefs—as a modern sensibility might suspect, since beliefs were not much of a concern to the Romans—as for their refusal to accord him divine honors by sacrifice, an act the ordinary Roman would regard, correctly, as an act of political loyalty and a Christian, equally correctly, as an act of worship. There were some imprisonments and some executions—we cannot be sure how many—and then the storm passed. Other subsequent storms occurred across the vast empire: property was confiscated, clerics were arrested, Christians were killed—their fellow Christians proudly kept records of the trials and executions of these "witnesses (Gk. *martyres*) to the faith"—but the circumstances were often different, as were the point of the attacks and the victims targeted. The persecutions had little effect; the numbers of Christians slowly grew, in high places, even the very highest, as well as low.

In 250 C.E., when the empire was beginning its unmistakable descent into economic and social depression, what has been called an "age of anxiety," the emperor Decius (r. 249–251) launched a systematic persecution of Christians throughout the empire. Each citizen was required to bear a certificate attesting to the fact that he or she had sacrificed to the imperial deities as witnessed by and in the presence of special officials. Many believers deserted the faith; others dissimulated by buying themselves certificates (see I/4). Shortly after, Valerian (r. 253–260) more precisely targeted bishops and the senior clergy for arrest and execution. Finally, in 303, the emperor Diocletian, whose administrative and fiscal reforms rescued the empire from dissolution, inaugurated the last and greatest series of persecutions of Christians and the Church. He decreed that all churches should be destroyed and all Christians forced to sacrifice under pain of death.

Diocletian and his coemperor resigned in 305, planned as an orderly step in the imperial succession, and two designated successors acceded to the purple, Constantine in the West and Galerius in the East. There were already Christian influences at work in Constantine's household and so Diocletian's measures were quietly abandoned in the Western provinces. In the East, however, Galerius pursued the Christians in fierce earnest until his death in 311.

In 312, at the Milvian Bridge in Italy, Constantine had called on the Christians' God for aid in a struggle against one of his rivals. As the Christians later told the story, he was given a heavenly vision of a cross—"In this sign you will conquer"—and victory came to him after he had the cross emblazoned on his soldiers' shields. Thus in 313, when Constantine met in Milan with his then coemperor Licinius—whom Constantine would later remove to rule alone—it is not surprising that the final communiqué of this imperial summit included a proclamation of religious toleration for all religions of the empire and the restoration of all confiscated property.

Constantine

Constantine made no formal declaration of his own Christianity. Although he was not baptized until shortly before his death in 337, which was not entirely unusual at the time, from 313 onward the emperor seems to have regarded himself a Christian, albeit still in rather easy conjunction with the current and official imperial cult of the Invincible Sun. These were new times and new circumstances, and Constantine, like many another, was undoubtedly feeling his way.

Constantine's conversion, whenever or however it occurred, brought the emperor, the sole source of political authority in the late Roman Empire, into direct contact with the Church's own increasingly influential leaders (see I/6). Whereas the emperor claimed universal jurisdiction, however, the bishops were local or regional authorities. Every bishop was a bishop of some place, where his writ prevailed; the emperor, in contrast, ruled everywhere. And this particular emperor ruled from a new place. Under Diocletian the empire had multiple capitals, east and west, as it had multiple *augusti* and caesars. But Constantine chose to rule alone, and from his own city, Constantinople, the site of the former town of Byzantium.

Rome's replacement by Constantinople as imperial capital was consequential not yet to the relationship of church and state, which was a later, theoretical question, but to how the Christian bishops viewed their sovereign and how he dealt with his Christian subjects and their—and presumably his own—spiritual leaders. At Constantinople Constantine was free to create his own imperial tradition, borrowing from the Roman past when it suited his purposes, but without the aristocratic Roman guardians' of that past looking over his shoulder. His city on the Bosporus was also remote from Christianity's most populous Middle Eastern centers—Antioch, Alexandria, and the revered Jerusalem—and even more remote from its emerging Roman claimant to episcopal autocracy (see I/6).

Like the later caliphs of Islam (see I/8), Constantine had no precedents in dealing with his fellow Christians as their sovereign. But unlike an Abu Bakr, the Christian Roman emperor possessed fully developed instruments of rule, the power to legislate—by the fourth century the emperor was the sole source of law in the empire—and to execute, to carry out the imperial will-become-law.

Constantine and his successors legislated for the Church, not directly, to be sure, but to the extent that Church's officials and properties were privileged by law, while the Church's enemies, paganism without and heresy within (see I/5), were prosecuted and persecuted. Constantine also undertook, at imperial expense, the identification and enshrinement of his new faith's holy places in Palestine—Jesus' birthplace in Bethlehem and his tomb in Jerusalem, for example—and both Jerusalem's bishop and Palestine's governor were bidden to put their shoulders to the task (see II/6).

The emperor clearly could order what and whom he would, and in 325 he summoned to Nicaea near his capital all the bishops of what would be, by the time they left, the Great Church. The occasion was the appearance of what was seen to be a pernicious teaching in Christian circles. It is doubtful that Constantine on his own could have recognized pertinacity of doctrine, but the danger of what came to be called Arianism (see II/7) was that it threatened the fabric of the entire Church, which concerned the emperor. Hence, the bishops in council at Nicaea, with Constantine at their head as mover and guide of this novel Christian enterprise (see I/6), created the first formal statement of Christian Church–wide orthodoxy, enshrined in the doctrinal communiqué known as the Nicene Creed, and the first formal Church-wide heresy, Arianism, was condemned without appeal in the creed's appended anathemas. By summoning the Church's leaders and then confirming their decrees, and through his undoubted and undisputed power to do so, Constantine had effectively created a Church united in doctrine and quite as universal—the preferred term was "catholic" (see I/4)—as the imperium romanum united under a single ruler. The notion of a single Church persisted until the Reformation (see I/6) and that of a single imperium even longer, though perhaps not so continuously.

The Contest Begins: Ambrose and the Emperor

Constantine had no political rivals in Constantinople and no episcopal ones at Nicaea; his power and authority were unquestioned. It remained to be explored, however, how far that power and authority extended into Church affairs, and indeed, what the Church's affairs were. The investigation was conducted chiefly in the West, with its own Roman imperial tradition and, in the fourth and fifth centuries, a diminished ecclesiastical regard for that tradition. Viewed from Italy or Latin Africa, the empire was in crisis in late antiquity, perhaps fatal crisis. Voice was given to Christian anxiety and its desire to seek its own identity not by the bishop of Rome, however, but by two other powerful and cultured clerics: Ambrose, bishop of Italy's premier city, Milan, and Augustine, bishop of Hippo in the prosperous Roman province of Africa, roughly modern Algeria and Tunisia.

Ambrose had become bishop of Milan in 373 but his political career did not begin until 375, with the death of the emperor Valentinian. Valentinian was succeeded in the West—Constantine's single empire had by then reverted to its earlier, Diocletianic dual form—by the sixteen-year-old Gratian, over whom Ambrose soon began to exert a marked influence. The Eastern emperor, Valens, had allowed great latitude to the Arian Christians of the Balkans, particularly when that form of Christianity seemed appealing to the Gothic tribes streaming into Rome's Balkan provinces from the east. Relations with the invaders broke down, however, and in 378 the Goths inflicted a crushing defeat on the Romans at Adrianople in which Valens himself was killed. To replace him Gratian appointed the Spaniard Theodosius emperor of the East.

Gratian was murdered in 383, aged twenty-five, and Theodosius soon gained complete control of the empire. The new autocrat was no Gratian, who had permitted Ambrose to intervene often and decisively in matters of state, and soon he and his powerful archbishop in Milan were clashing over diverse issues. The breaking point occurred when Theodosius, to punish an insurrection in Salonika, lured seven thousand inhabitants expecting to see a special performance into an amphitheater. Instead, they were slaughtered, men, women, and children. "It is the office of bishops to judge Christian emperors," Ambrose had written, "and not for emperors to judge bishops." And he did not hesitate to judge *his* emperor. The bishop of Milan excommunicated the emperor of Rome and required a public confession and penance before the ban could be lifted. Theodosius capitulated. It was the first real trial of arms between Christian Church and Roman state, and the Church, in the person of its most powerful bishop, had its way.

The City of God and the City of Man

What is called in shorthand the problem of church and state masks several different issues that elide into one another depending on circumstances of time and place. From one perspective, it is a subset of the larger clash of values inherent in the preaching of Christianity: the spiritual ones God's Kingdom is thought to exalt here on earth and the material ones that move "this world," the antithesis of God's Kingdom. The latter are the same that asceticism seeks to control and tame (see II/8). In this instance, however, the values of this world manifest themselves in political form, in the constitution of the "City of Man," founded by Cain and that stands in contrast, and often in conflict with, the "City of God," those of humankind who make up Christ's Church here on earth. Or so it seemed to Augustine.

The earliest Christian emperors in Constantinople and Rome must have seemed, from time to time, like attractive candidates for the role of lord of God's Kingdom. But when the fourth century turned into the fifth, the Roman

Empire showed signs of expiring all along its extended frontier and the Roman emperors appeared to be somewhat less than obedient sons of the Church. One Christian, at least, thought it a fit occasion to separate Christianity from its still fresh association with the Roman imperium. Augustine, student and admirer of Ambrose and later a bishop in turbulent Roman North Africa, was a theologian rather than a historian (see II/7), and so his celebrated meditation on history, the *City of God*, was prompted more by a desire to explain salvation history than to write its profane counterpart.

It is not odd, then, that Augustine's reading of the contrast and clash of the Church and the Roman state unfolds in his *City of God* on the high plains of theological metaphor and is laced with biblical examples. But there is also no doubt that for Augustine Christ's Kingdom was historically embodied in the Church (*City of God* 20.9), a position that remained firmly embedded in Christian consciousness until the Reformation and in Catholic thinking down to the mid–twentieth century. But "Kingdom" is not Augustine's preferred metaphor for the Christian dispensation; rather, it is "City of God." This is a polity (*civitas*) that is God's work, eternal, and, though "on pilgrimage" here on earth, its fulfillment and its destiny are in heaven. It stands in sharp contrast to the "City of Man," an ephemeral creation that seeks power and glory and that in the end will come to naught. Augustine regards these as two distinct systems, and though often in conflict, they are not necessarily opposed. The "City of Man," whatever its form, is a necessary political remedy for the anarchy created by Original Sin; it enables fallen humanity to live together in a species of social harmony.

In *City of God* Augustine addresses the notions and values, not the actual reality, of the two contrasted societies and so he does not concern himself with either their institutionalization or their leaders. But the Catholic Church had leaders or, as Augustine would have it, a supreme leader in the bishop of Rome, and the Roman Empire assuredly had a leader, and only one, the "Autocrat of the Romans," who resided in Constantine's city of the Bosporus, and would continue to do so for a millennium after Augustine. Thus, the conflict of church and state in late ancient and medieval Christendom often took the form of a conflict of claims of the heads—pope and emperor—of the two systems to which most Christians, including those two rulers, belonged.

Viewed in those terms, the problem may be further shorthanded to "Caesaropapism," the conflict of the overlapping and imbricated spiritual and temporal powers of pope and emperor. The issue was precisely because of the imbrication. Unlike a later age that proposed separation of church and state, the pre-Reformation controversy involved a single universal church and a single universal empire. Each conceded lawful and legitimate jurisdiction to the other. The emperor had a God-given right to rule and the pope had a God-given right to teach and judge in matters of salvation. But how far did each jurisdiction extend, and to what extent did one office have to suffer judgment or even contumely from the other?

"Two There Are..."

"Two there are, august emperor, by which the world is chiefly ruled," wrote Pope Gelasius (r. 492–496) to Emperor Anastasius in Constantinople in 494, "the sacred authority (*auctoritas*) of the priesthood and the royal power (*potestas*)." This letter became a fiercely contested document in that it set out the Western Church's teaching on the relationship between church and empire, the spiritual and temporal authority, that was to prevail for centuries. Gelasius cast his argument in the form of a comparison of the priesthood and the kingly or imperial office, but, as he made quite explicit in his letter, primacy in the first belonged to the bishop of Rome as surely as the second was embodied in Anastasius and his predecessors in Constantinople. By the fifth century the notion of Petrine and so Roman primacy was universally recognized in the Western churches and was even accorded a degree of assent among the Easterners, if only of the bishop of Rome as a *primus inter pares* or as enjoying a kind of protocol of honor.

Gelasius conceded that the emperor was the first of humankind in dignity, that the existence of the imperial office was a matter of "divine disposition" and that Christians were bound to observe the emperor's laws. But it is equally true, as Gelasius called on the emperor to acknowledge, that "no one can by purely human means raise himself to the privilege and place of him whom the voice of Christ has set before all," namely, the bishop of Rome. Ten years later Gelasius spelled out the distinction of powers still further. Christ himself had established the two functions, with the result that "Christian emperors would need priests for attaining eternal life and priests would avail themselves of imperial regulations in the conduct of temporal affairs." Thus the "soldier of God" would not be involved in worldly affairs, and "he who was involved in worldly affairs would not seem to preside over divine matters." It was a pious wish only rarely realized in the centuries that followed.

In Constantinople, meanwhile, things were seen from a slightly different but equally consequential perspective. Justinian (r. 527–565), the activist emperor who attempted, with what turned out to be only temporary success, to restore imperial dominion over the western lands—Italy, Spain, and Africa—that had once been Roman and then had fallen into barbarian hands, revisited the question of church and empire in one of his laws regulating—or as Gelasius might have put it, "presiding over"—the conduct of bishops and other clergy. "Nothing shall so preoccupy emperors as the moral well-being of priests. . . . We therefore exercise the greatest care concerning the true doctrines of God and the moral well-being of priests."

In so thinking and acting, Justinian was doing no more than following Constantinian precedent. Anastasius had provoked Gelasius's rulings by formally embracing a theology that Rome found contrary to Christian orthodoxy, and the emperor was being told not to meddle, that the two jurisdictions, spiritual and temporal, were separate. Justinian, whose reputation for orthodoxy was impeccable in Rome, could therefore follow the example of his illustrious predecessor Constantine in claiming the right to protect Christian doctrine and oversee the morals of the clergy.

Even at this early stage the complexities of resolving the emperor's right to rule and the Church's right to judge were emerging. They became infinitely more complicated in the West when the pope too came to possess the *potentia* of political power and western monarchs came to understand that they also shared in a kind of spiritual auctoritas by reason of their being God's anointed.

How the Pope Became a Prince

The foundation of papal power lay in the misfortunes that fell on the Roman Empire in the West during the fourth and following centuries. The Eastern Empire managed to hold the Gothic and then the Slavic invaders of the Balkans away from the imperial capital of Constantinople; to settle, convert, and to some extent tame them; to rule the Slavic peoples as vassals or to enter into uneasy alliances with them. Behind the shield of Constantinople, Anatolia and the East survived and prospered, and even after the Muslim armies overwhelmed the eastern provinces from the south in the seventh century, the ecclesiastical structure there remained intact, even though it was no longer in direct communication with the imperial patriarchate in Constantinople.

Not so in the West. The Latin-speaking provinces from Italy to Spain and across western and central North Africa were overrun in the fifth to the eighth centuries by successive waves of Huns, Goths, Vandals, and Germanic peoples. Roman secular authority largely perished beneath this flood, and all that was left to bring order out of the chaos that followed on what one historian called "the meeting of German primitivism and Roman decrepitude" was the Church. The Christian bishops in the end had to make peace and then political arrangements with the Gothic and Germanic kings who ruled Europe. Chief among those bishops was the bishop of Rome, already the claimant to primacy among his episcopal peers by reason of his Petrine credentials and the undoubted cachet of Rome as the symbol and bearer of all that survived of Roman order and tradition.

Romulus Augustulus, the last feeble pretender to the Roman imperial title, vacated his claim in 478, and thereafter Roman *potentia* was effectively represented only by the bishop of Rome. Pope Leo I (r. 440–461) negotiated the city's fate with the Huns in 451, and by the time of Gregory II (r. 715–731), the pope was unmistakably the ruler of the city and its territories. In 727 Rome was under attack by the Lombards, who had already taken over most of the remaining imperial holdings in the north of Italy and were then threatening to occupy Rome as well. The emperor current in Constantinople was Leo III, who was involved in a profound dispute with the Western Church over the veneration of images (see II/6). Gregory had no doubts about Leo's legitimacy, but he also had little hope that the emperor would help save the city. In 727 he warned Leo not to think of intervening in the West: the popes were quite capable of taking care of affairs in Italy.

And so they did, chiefly by finding a counterweight to both the Byzantines and the Lombards in the rising power of the Franks west of the Rhine. The king of the Merovingian line who ruled there, Childeric, was a nonentity; true power rested with the majordomo, Pepin. Pepin sent a query to Rome inquiring of the pope whether it was permissible to depose Childeric, since he was, for all his legitimacy, powerless. The pope responded affirmatively—the sovereign must be appropriate to his office—thus effectively ending the reign of Childeric, who was sent off, perhaps gratefully, to a monastery, and elevating Pepin to the kingship of the Franks. He was anointed and crowned at Soissons in 750 by Boniface, the monk who was responsible for organizing the conversion of the Germans and who was then archbishop of Mainz and the voice of Rome among the Franks. The grateful Pepin drove the Lombards out of most of their newly acquired possessions in northern and central Italy, kept some of them for himself, and in 754 handed over the remainder to the pope and confirmed the transfer in writing.

An important event had occurred at Soissons in 750. A papal legate had, with full papal approval, anointed a new king of the Franks in the manner of consecrating a bishop. The imperial autocrat in Constantinople had long been viewed in a priestly light and the imperial ceremonial was as redolent of a church ritual as it was of a courtly one. The Frankish kingship, however, had hitherto been a purely secular office and, indeed, an elected one. By this papal act, the notion of a theocratic divinely ordained king was introduced into the Western tradition of sovereignty. We shall return to that development; of interest here is Pepin's reciprocal legitimation of the pope's own temporal sovereignty. The bishop of Rome was now openly a prince, the temporal sovereign of lands that continued to exist as Papal States until their dismemberment between 1859 and 1870.

Somewhere between Pepin's coronation in 750 and that of his son Charlemagne in 800, the pope's princely power was further and substantially advanced by a document that has come to be called the Donation of Constantine. In it the first Christian emperor deeded to the then pope Sylvester I (r. 314–335) and his episcopal successors guardianship of all the empire's possessions in the West: "all provinces, palaces and districts of the city of Rome and Italy and all the regions of the West." To the pope also belonged the Holy Land (see I/4), the Lateran palace in Rome, and all the symbols of imperial sovereignty—the diadem, scepter, stole, and purple cloak. As we shall see, the bequest was given as of 30 May 330. The reported occasion was Constantine's transfer of the imperial capital to Constantinople, "since it is not right that an earthly emperor should have authority there [in Rome] where the rule of priests and the head of the Christian religion have been established by the Emperor of Heaven."

The Donation of Constantine was a forgery, and indeed it may have been created in the papal secretariat to convince Pepin of the pope's right to the lands that the Frankish king actually ceded to him. Whatever the occasion, the Donation of Constantine was widely regarded as genuine throughout the European Middle Ages—it was first unmasked as a forgery by the humanist scholar Lorenzo Valla (d. 1457)—and established in theory what was already a matter of fact: that the pope was a prince among the princes of Europe.

The College of Cardinals and the Roman Curia

The circumstantial formality of the papacy changed in accordance with this new sovereignty status. Whereas the papal government had consisted largely of a "bureaucratic oligarchy" dominated by noble Roman families, from about 1050 the popes gave a different and more effective shape to the papal state that had come into being, chiefly by reforming and restaffing two important and related institutions: the college of cardinals and the papal curia (see I/6).

In its earliest history, the collegium or corporation of cardinals—the principal (Lat. *cardines*, "hinges") bishops, priests, and deacons who served in or near Rome—had primarily a liturgical function. The seven cardinal bishops, those whose sees adjoined Rome, were called on in turn to perform the sacred services at the pope's own Lateran basilica. In the mid–eleventh century, however, their duties began to change. The cardinal bishops became the pope's chief advisers and the ministers of the emerging papal government. More, the newest cardinals were appointed from outside the narrow circle of Roman aristocrats. Men like Peter Damiani and Humbert of Silva Candida gave the institution an international flavor and an intellectual panache it had not previously possessed, one appropriate to what was increasingly felt to be an ecumenical organization.

Besides placing the cardinal bishops at the head of the various branches of the papal government, Urban II (r. 1088–1099) further created an administrative body of bureaucrats on the model of the curias of contemporary royal courts, though the papal version soon outstripped the royal curias in size, skill, and sophistication. The curia romana or papal curia had three departments: the camera or financial administration, the chancery or secretariat, and finally, the chapel, the last charged with the supervision of papal liturgy and ceremonial.

The creation of the papal curia was contemporary with the new prominence given the study of Roman law in Italian centers like Bologna, and the growth and propagation of a body of Church or canon law (see II/4). The Roman curia chiefly recruited its personnel from the ranks of these trained legal scholars, and their training and professionalism added new strength to the Church's organization.

The institution that linked the curia to the other churches of the newly imperial—and now self-consciously ecumenical—Roman Church was that of the papal legates. There was more than one type of papal deputy, but two chief forms of delegation. The papal vicar or legate plenipotentiary—in effect, the papal representative—was usually a cardinal, accountable to the pope but with full powers to pronounce, or denounce, in the pope's name, or even to convoke a provincial council, over which he presided. The papal nuncio was a legate sent on a special mission, most often, as the name implies, to deliver a message to a sovereign or a church.

How the Prince Became a Priest

As already remarked, Roman emperors were regarded as godlike from the very beginning of the imperium, as Greek kings and various Middle Eastern rulers had been before them. The *imperator*'s investment with sacred qualities accelerated in the third century C.E. through contact with the imperial traditions of Iran, whose investiture and ceremonial underlined the shahs' sacral character in unmistakable fashion. It was precisely at this religious veneration of the *divus augustus* that the early Christians, like the Jews before them, had balked and so brought grief on themselves and the Church.

When the Roman emperor became a Christian, adjustments obviously had to be made in the imperial cult, and it was perhaps the sovereign's sacerdotal rather than divine quality that began to be brought into relief. All sacrificial honors to the emperor were abandoned, and priesthoods and temples dedicated to him disappeared. But court ceremonial continued to emphasize the sacral quality of the holder of the imperium, surrounded by his sacred consistory or council and dwelling with his household in the *sacrum palatium*.

Early Christian writers made no effort to diminish or denigrate this implicit claim to imperial sacrality. Although one strand of Christian thought agreed with Augustine and regarded political sovereignty as a necessary consequence of human moral weakness, most preferred to follow Paul in recognizing temporal sovereignty and lordship as part of God's ordained order and, by extension, as a kind of divine appointment. In the emperor Justinian's words, "priesthood and emperor . . . both proceed from one and the same source and provide for human life."

Although that latter generous view continued to prevail in the Eastern Empire—and the Eastern Church—until the last *autokrator* perished in the defense of Constantinople in 1453, the West experienced the rise of a new kind of Germanic kingship in the land beyond the Alps. For the Franks and the other Germanic peoples, kingship was a fundamentally and thoroughly secular elected office. But we have already seen how papal acceptance of the deposition of the Merovingian Childeric in favor of Charles Martel's son

Pepin was followed in 750 by the anointment and coronation of that same Pepin by the papal legate Boniface—an act that changed European kingship and made it at once theocratic and tied in a still undefined relationship to the papacy.

In 800 the act was repeated for the benefit of Pepin's son, and with even greater emphasis: Charlemagne was crowned not king but emperor—a challenge and, as it was read in Constantinople, an insult to the emperor there— and not in Soissons by a papal legate but at St. Peter's in Rome by the pope himself, Leo III. Charlemagne may not have been pleased by the honor bestowed on him by the pope; he seems to have preferred the more modest and less dangerous title of king of the Franks and the Lombards. His son Louis the Pious and grandson Charles the Bald both seem to have embraced the honor, however, as well as its implication, that they were in fact Roman emperors and the anointed of the Lord.

> **Note:** Some of Charlemagne's successors were less amenable to papal approval and control, most notably Napoleon, who invited the pope to his imperial coronation on 2 December 1804 but, lest there be any misunderstanding, there in the pope's presence, he did the honor of crowning himself.

The question of empire became moot with Charles's death. His grandfather's "empire" rapidly disintegrated into a mosaic of petty princedoms, where the nobility severally ruled over large estates and controlled the military as well as the political and legal institutions of what had become a decentralized society. Part of that decentralization was bound up with the Church's lessened powers. Europe's feudal lords had most of the Church's properties under their control. They did not appropriate or secularize them, to be sure, but they distributed tenancy of these benefices, as they were called, to prelates of their own choosing, in the manner of fiefs, as a reward for services rendered or in prospect of such. With the dissolution of the royal or imperial power at the top of the system, the lords, now only nominally vassals of the king, became a law unto themselves, including, of course, the bishops and abbots who had essentially become lords of their own ecclesiastical estates.

West of the Rhine the imperial dream passed from among the Franks with the last of Charlemagne's line, but eastward the high Frankish lords, still following the Germanic tradition, chose as their new king Conrad, duke of Franconia. His grandson, Otto I (r. 936–973), resurrected the Roman imperial ideal by having himself crowned by the chief bishop of the German churches, the archbishop of Mainz, and at Charlemagne's old capital of Aachen. Otto immediately set about asserting his authority over the German churches by claiming the right to appoint all the empire's prelates to their sees or benefices, churchmen who thus became his vassals. In 955 Otto became the hero of Christendom by defeating the invading Magyars. His jubilant troops acclaimed him emperor, and in 962 he was crowned by the pope in Rome.

The triumphant Otto was succeeded by his son, Otto II (r. 973–983), who married a Byzantine princess and died fighting the Muslims in Sicily, and then by his grandson, Otto III (r. 983–1003). Otto III in particular envisioned a new union of empire and church, the first represented by himself, of course, and the latter by Gerbert of Aurillac, a Frenchman educated in Muslim Spain, whom Otto contrived to have elected pope as Sylvester II (r. 993–1003). All the evidence suggests that Otto and Sylvester had a grander plan between them. At the same time that Otto announced Rome was once again the capital of the world, he proclaimed the Roman Church the "mother of all churches." The emperor also reached out to Poland and to Hungary, the now pacified kingdom of the Magyars, to incorporate them in some fashion into his revived Roman Empire. Sylvester for his part seemed willing to allow the emperor his temporal sovereignty and to limit his own jurisdiction as Western Christendom's leader to matters of the spirit.

Rome Redivivus: The Holy Roman Empire

Otto I's coronation had united the crowns of Germany and Italy, to which the emperor Conrad in 1033 added broad domains in France. After this the rulers begin styling themselves "Roman emperors" and their realm the "Roman Empire." Eventually it became "Holy" as well, not as a reversion to the practices of the third- and fourth-century Roman *imperatores*, who, as we seen, regarded everything about their person and rule as sacred, but now in competition with the Church. Frederick I (r. 1152–1190), called Barbarossa, was a fierce advocate of the *imperium* in the face of the papacy—he convened a Church council in Pavia in 1160 to settle a disputed papal election—and he first adopted the protocol *sacrum imperium*, "sacred empire," to describe his sovereignty in 1157. "Sancta" had long been one of the Church's earmarks, and an unstated argument for its superiority to the state, and Frederick now had his own rhetoricial weapon in his ongoing contest with the papacy. The joining of the two notions into "Holy Roman Empire" did not officially appear until 1254, however.

The issue of "holy" came to a boil in the first half of the fourteenth century when Louis of Bavaria, once elected emperor in 1328, chose to be crowned in Rome, but not by the then pope, John XXII (r. 1316–1334), who had not supported his election. Louis had on his side a weighty philosopher, Marsiglio of Padua, and an even weightier theologian, William of Ockham, both of whom were under his protection. Each wrote a tract defending the notion of a secular empire independent of Church validation (see I/6), but the pope still wielded more public and political authority and Louis's grand gesture came to very little in the end.

The sovereigns who followed the Ottonians as rulers of this now considerable European territory known as the Holy Roman Empire were all elected rulers, at least from the time of Lothair, who was elected by his fellow German princes in 1125. Which imperial German princes had the right to elect the emperor was the subject of some dispute, and to settle it, the emperor Charles IV in 1356 issued a "Golden Bull," an imperial decree with a golden seal, that regulated election and coronation procedures. It restricted the elector privilege to the prince-archbishops of Mainz, Trier, and Cologne, the king of Bohemia, the count palatine of the Rhine, the duke of Saxony, and the margrave of Brandenburg. The imperial office itself became hereditary, though still subject to at least a nominal election, and in 1438 it passed to the House of Hapsburg, where it remained until Francis I renounced it in 1806.

The Two Swords: Gregory VII and Henry IV

We have already seen how Pope Gelasius in the late fifth century attempted to separate ecclesiastical and imperial powers. His letter on the subject made fairly explicit that in his judgment the pope's spiritual power was superior to and took precedence over the emperor's temporal, secular, and political power. His view served, with bumps and halts, over the intervening centuries, as a defining statement on the issue of church and state, to be parsed as either side saw fit. When Gregory VII (r. 1073–1085) assumed the papal office, the Gelasian formula of two distinct offices, the priestly and the kingly, each established by God and each disposed of its own powers and responsibilities, was still the common coin in Rome. The imperial power was wielded in Gregory's day by Henry IV, with whom Gregory expected, as perhaps did Henry, to work in close cooperation. On occasion they did, but a serious issue of contention between them unraveled whatever rapport the pope may have had with Henry—namely, the emperor's right to invest or appoint prelates to powerful and lucrative offices within his empire. With the title of bishop went control of important cities and their hinterlands. The practice was not new in the eleventh century, but it was increasingly under attack as one of the root causes—buying and selling spiritual offices constituted simony—of what was universally understood to be a progressive ecclesiastical decadence, a condition Gregory had vowed to root out.

Henry resisted Gregory's attempt to deprive him of what he regarded as the royal power of episcopal investiture, and Gregory responded by laying out more exactly the extent of papal authority. He had at hand Gelasius's pronouncements on the subject, to which he and, as it turned out, Henry, could add what came to be a popular scriptural text in the struggle between emperor and pope. According to Luke (22:36–38), Jesus, before setting out for Gethsemane after his Last Supper, remarked that if anyone possessed a sword, now was the time to have it at hand. "Lord, they said, we have two swords here.

Enough, he replied." The point in the Gospel context is obscure, but it was not to the eleventh-century disputants about church and empire: the "swords" of the text were understood allegorically to represent spiritual authority (embodied in the pope) and temporal power (embodied in the emperor), with the former holding not only a sword but most of the cards. The emperors, needless to say, saw it somewhat differently.

When Henry refused to give over his right to invest the empire's high prelates and proposed to name a bishop to the important see of Milan, Gregory threatened to exercise a right he had claimed for the papacy from the beginning of his reign: that of deposing an emperor. It seemed to some that Gregory had gone too far, that he had in fact violated the Gelasian separation of offices and functions, temporal and spiritual. So it seemed to Henry, who in 1075 summoned a council of German bishops he prevailed on to denounce Gregory as immoral and a usurper of the papal office. In February 1076 Gregory formally excommunicated Henry and declared him deposed from office. Henry attempted to defend himself. In a letter to the pope he insisted on his own divine right to rule and accused Gregory of being not a pope but rather a false monk. He also explained to the German bishops that Gregory had attempted to combine in his own person the offices of king and priest. Both sides of course displayed the two swords of the Lucan passage.

What followed was a test of the powers of the men and their offices. Each had to convince the German princes, on whom Henry's authority rested, as well as the German bishops, whom the pope needed and who were capable, at that precise juncture, of separating themselves from Rome and constituting a German Church. Gregory succeeded in the end, and in January 1077, in a famous moment at Canossa in northern Italy, the emperor stood in the snow outside the pope's residence and pleaded for forgiveness. The pope relented. The excommunication was lifted and Henry was restored to his imperial office. More followed between the two men and their successors, but the principle had been put forward with great clarity: the priestly office, more specifically the papacy, was not only distinct from the temporal; it was also superior. And for the first time a pope claimed and exercised the power not merely to excommunicate an emperor, which had been done as early as the fourth century by Ambrose to Theodosius, but to depose him from the office to which he had been duly elected by his own princes and which had been regarded in most circles as God-given as the pope's own.

The Papacy versus Frederick II

There were, then, two generally held views among canon lawyers on the relationship of temporal and spiritual authority, the two swords. One held that the sovereign's temporal power was autonomous and independent of the spiritual, held by the ruler from God by virtue of his office for the good of Christendom but without the meditation or, as some bold souls were later moved to say, the recognition of the Church. The other view was that, as Bernard of Clairvaux had argued, both swords were placed firmly in Peter's hands, and thus of his successors, who delegated temporal power to the sovereign and continued to regulate its use for the good of the Church.

The conflict between the rival and clashing claims of pope and emperor reached a violent climax under Innocent III and his successors in the see of Peter and the emperor Frederick II Hohenstaufen. Innocent III (r. 1198–1216) was the most autocratic-minded and absolutist of the medieval popes (see I/5), and he made his views on the power of the papacy known early in his reign. In the first of two decrees he published in 1202 he adduced the papacy's favorite evangelical text, the one giving Peter the power to bind and loose whatever he would on earth, with the assurance that it would also be so in heaven (Matt. 16:19). Innocent then went on to point out that the pope was not merely Peter's successor but no less than Christ's vicar. Indeed, the office had been foreshadowed in both Testaments in the reference to "a priest according to the order of Melchizedek" (Heb. 7:17, reflecting on Gen. 14:18–20). Melchizedek had been both a priest and a judge and so too, Innocent argued, were Christ and his vicar or deputy, the pope, who possessed universal judicial and sacerdotal rights. In a second decree Innocent applied that right to the matter of the imperial succession. The German princes certainly had the right to elect the emperor, especially since this right and power came to them from the Apostolic See, which had transferred the Roman imperium from the Greeks to the Germans in the person of Charlemagne. But it belonged to the pope, he concluded, to examine and judge the person elected since it is the pope who "anoints, consecrates, and crowns him."

But principle had to be translated into reality. The emperors of the house of Hohenstaufen had recently acquired the kingdom of Sicily in addition to the German federated imperium, a situation Innocent read as a threat to the papal power in central Italy, and the pope managed to steer the imperial election away from the natural Hohenstaufen heir into the hands of the more manageable Otto IV, who had no claim to Sicily. Otto turned out to be less docile than Innocent anticipated and the pope turned instead to the young Hohenstaufen heir in Sicily, Frederick II (r. 1215–1250), who dutifully promised to surrender his Sicilian throne when he became emperor. He did not, and when first Innocent III died in 1216 and then Otto IV in 1218, Frederick became emperor and the papacy was faced with its most formidable medieval rival.

Frederick, educated in Islamic-Christian Sicily and married to Isabelle of Brienne, the heiress to the crusader kingdom of Jerusalem, envisioned himself as lord of all of Italy, and in 1239 he had possessed himself of the imperial domains in the peninsula's north. The then pope, Innocent IV, as stubborn and determined as Frederick, was forced to take action. The earlier Gregory IX

(r. 1227–1241) had already excommunicated Frederick in 1227 for failing to fulfill his vow to go on crusade—Frederick actually went in 1228 and negotiated the transfer of Jerusalem from Muslim to Christian hands—and again in 1229 for invading the Lombard lands in the north. He then seized most of the papal lands, and when Gregory summoned a general council to deal with the emperor, Frederick seized the bishops on the high seas and was on the point of taking Rome when Gregory died in 1241. So it rested first with the briefly reigning Celestine IV and then particularly with Innocent IV (r. 1243–1254) to deal with the emperor known as Stupor Mundi, the "Wonder of the World."

Innocent IV's first task was to save himself. He slipped out of Rome, and in 1245 in the safer confines of Lyons he convened a council that deposed Frederick and promulgated a crusade to remove him. We will never know how successful it might have been since Frederick died in 1250 before any real action was taken. The crusade was now directed against his son Conrad, who himself died in 1254. Here the imperial Hohenstaufen line ended—it lingered on in the kingdom of Sicily until 1268—and with it the greatest imperial threat to papal power in Italy. After a spell of princely jostling in Germany, Rudolf of Hapsburg was elected emperor in 1273, and the Hapsburg rule of what was now known as the Holy Roman Empire began.

Though the aggressive Hohenstaufen threat against papal holdings and authority in Italy had passed, the issue of investiture had not. Philip the Fair, the king of France (d. 1314), for one, was particularly aggressive in asserting the emerging medieval state's rights against the papacy, its power to tax the Church, for example, and later, to remove a bishop from office. This last act elicited from Boniface VIII the most grandiose of all papal claims to authority in the bull of 1302, *Unam sanctam* (see I/4). Philip replied by arresting Boniface, who died soon afterward. Boniface's successors were made of less stern stuff and the decline in papal secular fortunes reached its nadir in1309, when Clement V was constrained by Philip to leave Rome and take up residence in Avignon (see I/6).

The Reformation as Political Event

In 1517 the Augustinian monk and theologian Martin Luther publicly attacked the teachings and practices of the Church, notably what appeared to be the papal sale of indulgences in the empire's German cities (see II/5). He continued and deepened his criticisms in a stream of publications and public statements, and Pope Leo X formally condemned and excommunicated him in 1521. What was principally an ecclesiastical affair became political as well when Luther's call for reform began to be implemented in German towns and cities, and later in 1521 Luther was summoned to appear at Worms before the Reichstag or Diet.

This was the empire's representative assembly, which was convened by the emperor, in this case by the newly elected Charles V, and attended by some two hundred of Germany's principal prelates, princes, and civic dignitaries. Luther was called on to recant. He refused and left the meeting with a limited safe-conduct to reconsider his position. As a faculty member at Wittenberg, Luther was under the jurisdiction of Frederick, the prince-elector of Saxony. In what may have been the most important political decision of the entire Reformation, Frederick, despite his friendship and support of Charles in what had been a very controversial imperial election, chose to offer his protection to this obdurate priest-monk. The emperor issued a warrant for Luther's arrest. To assist the reformer was now treason as well as abetting heresy.

For nine years, between the Reichstags of Worms in 1521 and that in Augsburg in 1530, the emperor Charles V, who was now Luther's judge and executioner, did nothing about his famous outlaw theologian. By the time he convened the Diet of Augsburg in 1530, the Reform was deeply entrenched in Germany and elsewhere, not merely by reason of acceptance of its principles, but, even more difficult to reverse, with the confiscation of Church lands and properties and their redistribution to new and different proprietors, clerical and lay. Charles had reason to delay. He had to fight not only political opposition from the papacy but a long war against his chief European rival, Francis I of France (r. 1515–1541) and at the same time defend the empire's southeastern border against the oncoming Ottomans, who in 1526 crushed a Hungarian army at Mohacs and were marching on Vienna.

Only in 1530, when both the French and the Ottomans had been chastised, at least for the moment, could Charles V turn to Luther. Luther, who was by then a cause célèbre in Europe, did not attend the Reichstag at Augsburg but his deputy Melanchthon presented, with Luther's approval, both a *Confession* and an *Apology* in defense of the Lutheran position. It was supported by some of the princes who had already declared for and enacted the Reform in their territories but rejected by the Catholic majority. The 1521 Worms condemnation of Luther was confirmed.

The empire's Protestant princes, three of them imperial electors, now formed their own defensive alliance, the Schmalkaldic League, to protect their interests should the emperor turn to force, as seemed likely. But in 1534 the empire's problems grew more complex when a revitalized Francis I concluded an alliance with the Ottoman sultan Sulayman. Thus the emperor had to take up arms not only against the allied French and Turks but even against his own princes. In 1544 Paul III announced the convocation of a general council to deal with the Reform and strongly supported Charles's decision to suppress the Reformation by force of arms. In 1547 the imperial and league armies met at Mühlberg near Dresden and the emperor was victorious.

The Reformation seemed over when the Protestant princes accepted Charles's terms. But not so. One of them, Moritz of Saxony, with the support of the French king, who was always willing to bring grief to Charles, drove the emperor and his army out of the German lands and then came to terms with Charles's brother, and his deputy for the eastern half of the empire, Ferdinand. The eventual result, in 1555, was the Peace of Augsburg wherein both emperor and princes guaranteed and certified the religious status quo in the various principalities, Catholic and Protestant—or in a formula enunciated a few years later, *cujus regio, ejus religio*, "whose the rule, his the religion," without prejudice, it was hoped, for the *religio* of the *regio* next door. The agreement meant, moreover, that the princes were the guardians of this "religious peace" and so of both the well-being of their churches and the believers' consciences.

Luther and the Princes

From the moment of his excommunication and outlawry in 1521, Luther depended for his personal safety and the survival of his movement on the support of German princes, in the first instance Frederick of Saxony and then a growing number of others. In 1520 one of his tracts, *To the Christian Nobility of the German Nation*, called on those princes to take action on a broad front, from depriving the papacy of its wealth and the reform of the religious orders, both of which were likely to be highly profitable enterprises, to revising the theology curriculum in their universities, which was likely not.

In this and his other early writings, Luther envisioned, much as Calvin did, a productive concord of aims between the spiritual and political leaders of Reformed Christendom. Luther's hopes in this regard were soon dashed, not merely by the hostility of *the* sovereign, the emperor Charles V, but by the self-interests of even those princes committed to the Reform. It was in this climate of growing pragmatic concern for the independence of the Church—Luther still thought in "catholic," not confessional, terms—that he published in 1523 *On Secular Authority* or so the title is often rendered in English, although the German for "secular," *weltlicher*, is perhaps better translated as "worldly." In it Luther argues for the total independence of the Church as a free congregation in which all members are equal, and each is "King, Priest, and Prophet." Secular and spiritual governance are two distinct realms and should be kept separate. This separation of functions was based on an at least implicit understanding that "the things that are Caesar's and . . . the things that are God's," were also separate—a position difficult to maintain in the sixteenth century when things as diverse as property (the Church's) and the media (the printing of the vernacular Bible) were hotly contested between ecclesiastical and political authorities.

In the end, Luther settled for something less than either perfect cooperation or complete independence of church and state: a piecemeal reform guaranteed by the ruler of this or that particular territory in the patchwork that was the Holy Roman Empire. From well before the Reform, the European political map had been reshaping itself into national states. England, France, and Spain (until its king was elected emperor as Charles V) were not part of the revived medieval version of the Roman Empire and so did not share in the nostalgic dream of a single universal imperium. All were developing into recognizable facsimiles of their modern selves, a polity embracing a people sharing a common history, living in defined territory, under the rule of a stable political regime. This development carried in its wake, though on a much more turbulent course, the formation of national churches.

Calvin's Two Kingdoms

John Calvin (d. 1564), the French-born Reformer who converted Geneva into a Christian commonwealth, was a firm believer in the "two kingdom" theory of authority, or as he often called it, the "two powers, civil and religious," which in his view should be complementary. In both his writings and his practice in Geneva, he promoted their combination in a single polity, so that "minister and magistrate seem to be parallel offices of a body at once ecclesiastical and religious." Indeed, the two ought to work hand in hand. The magistrates, Calvin believed, no less than Paul, were ordained by God, to cleanse the church of offenses by "punishment and physical restraint," whereas the ministers of the Word assisted the magistrates with persuasion and instruction to the end that few might sin. Far from separating church and state, he described their union in his *Institutes* in language that would be at home in Tehran in the late twentieth century as he convinced the Genevans it should be in the sixteenth, though Calvin gave civil officials far more latitude to decide church matters than the Iranian Constitution granted their secular counterparts (see I/8).

According to Calvin, civil government has as its appointed end to cherish and protect the outward worship of God, to defend sound doctrine and piety and the purity of the church, to form our behavior to civil righteousness, to reconcile us one to another, and to promote general peace and tranquillity. The magistrates must govern by laws—human laws, to be sure—that may vary from state to state, but all of which should reflect the natural law that God has made accessible to humanity from two sources: the moral teachings of Moses as summed up in the Ten Commandments—Calvin, like Aquinas and the Catholic tradition generally, did not think the judicial and ceremonial laws of the Old Testament were binding on Christians—and their natural law counterpart inscribed on the conscience of all humankind. Calvin also agree with Thomas that the natural law reflected no more than God's will, experienced explicitly in revelation and implicitly in the order found in creation. The next century a quite different, and highly influential, view of the natural law was put forward by the jurist Hugo Grotius, who wrote in his "On the Law of War and Peace" (1625) that "the legal principles so identified [as natural law] would have a degree of validation even if there was no God," a sentiment that Calvin and Aquinas alike would have found incomprehensible.

Church and State in the Counter-Reformation

Papal claims to temporal jurisdiction had become unraveled in the Reformation, and the Counter-Reformation did little to mend the damage. Indeed, the fatal blow to papal pretensions to secular jurisdiction was likely dealt by one of the Church's own preeminent intellectuals of the post-Trent era, the Jesuit theologian Robert Bellarmine (d. 1621). The papal claim was based in part on Innocent III's emphatic identification of the pope as the vicar or deputy of Christ as well as of St. Peter, and on the conviction of some that Jesus had possessed, not merely as God but as man, royal jurisdiction over all humankind. In the volume of his *Controversies* published in 1586, Bellarmine summoned up a wealth of patristic evidence to refute the latter contention. The pope, he maintained, enjoyed full sovereignty within the papal lands, which were then still considerable, but elsewhere sovereignty belonged to the ruler, whose authority, no less than the pope's, also came from God, though in this latter case it was mediated through the people. It was a clear-cut statement of the separation and equality of spiritual and temporal sovereignty—indeed, so clear-cut that the then pope Sixtus V placed that volume of the *Controversies* on the *Index of Prohibited Books*. The *Index* was already in print and awaited only final promulgation when Sixtus V died; his successor quietly and speedily removed Bellarmine's name from the *Index*.

The Papal States

Theoreticians of the bishop's powers had inevitably to address the reality that the pope *was*, in fact as well as theory, a temporal sovereign who governed defined territories and taxed, conscripted, and otherwise supervised the everyday lives of thousands of subjects in what was called the patrimony of St. Peter or, to use a more modern term and concept, the Papal States. It refers to lands, chiefly in central and eastern Italy, over which the bishops of Rome exercised varying degrees of political sovereignty for more than a millennium, from 754 to 1870.

We have already seen how the basis of that sovereignty was laid down in 754 by Pepin's "restoration" to papal control of the Italian lands that had once been part of the Byzantine Empire—and to which they still belonged, according to the Byzantines—and more recently in the hands of the Lombards. The

Byzantine claim on them was neatly rebuffed by the Donation of Constantine certifying that emperor's bequest of his Italian lands to the custody of St. Peter's successor. Two years later, in 756, the Lombard king enlarged Pepin's grant with new territories, and eventually the bishop of Rome acquired as well the area on the Adriatic from Ravenna to Ancona. Finally, in 1077 the duchy of Beneventum in the south was acquired by treaty from the Normans.

Beneath papal sovereignty the cities of central and eastern Italy were forging their own local republican traditions throughout the Middle Ages, and the trend toward municipal autonomy was both reinforced and hastened by the popes' removal to distant Avignon (1309–1377), followed by the competition of two or even three popes during the Great Western Schism that began in 1419 (see I/6). The powerful Renaissance popes, particularly the aggressive and warlike Julius II (r. 1503–1513), attempted to reassert control over the papal domains, and they succeeded at least in putting together a well-defined territory that stretched from Parma and Bologna in the north, along the Adriatic coast and through Umbria, to the Campagna south of Rome.

The clerically governed Papal States, as it now seems fair to call them, fared neither better nor worse than Italy's other petty polities in the seventeenth and eighteenth centuries, but the somnolent march toward centralization was interrupted by Napoleon's conquest of Italy in the 1790s. The Papal States were taken from the pope and first, in 1798–1799, attached to the Napoleonic republics created in Italy and then, in 1808–1809, incorporated into the kingdom of Italy that was to form part of the French Empire. The then pope Pius VII excommunicated Napoleon and the emperor in turn arrested the pope, who was held at Fontainebleau until 1814. After Napoleon's final defeat at Waterloo, the Congress of Vienna in 1815 restored the Papal States to the bishop of Rome.

But it could not turn back the tide of the French Revolution. Republican sentiment was running high in Italy, and in the 1840s and 1850s there was also growing sentiment for unification under a monarchy of all Italy's states, to which the independent Papal States were obviously a major impediment. In 1843 a clerical Italian patriot publicly proposed unifying of all the Italian states under papal leadership, that the pope be in effect Italy's monarch, with Piedmont providing the muscle and with all foreigners—France, Austria, and Spain had little appetite for a united kingdom of Italy—excluded from peninsular affairs. Others wanted to begin reform in the clerically ruled Papal States themselves by creating a republican-style bicameral legislature.

In 1846 there was a new pope, Pius IX (r. 1846–1878). At first he gave signs of sympathizing with the swelling sentiment for republican reform, and he introduced modern institutions of government into the Papal States: a council of state made up of provincial delegates, a cabinet, and a citizen militia in the papal domains. In 1848 he even proclaimed a fundamental law for the States, including a bicameral legislature to vote into effect laws drawn up by the council of state. But there were limits that showed how little Pius trusted the public will: the parliaments could not interfere in spiritual matters nor even those "mixed" matters with spiritual implications, and more fatally, the college of cardinals had the right to veto all legislation. They essentially had, much the same power possessed by the council of guardians vis-à-vis the assembly in the Islamic Republic of Iran (see I/8).

There would be no national union under the pope. Pius made it perfectly clear, in an encyclical no less, that he could never sanction a war against a Catholic power—Austria, for example, whose military intervention in Italy was one of the essential props of papal power and which was, of course, the bête noire of the Italian monarchists. In 1848 a republic was proclaimed in Rome and Pius IX was saved only by escaping in disguise to the still-friendly kingdom of Sicily. This time the French were invited to intervene: they occupied Rome and Pius was able to return—but to little effect. In 1859 Umbria, Emilia-Romagna, and the Marches voted to join the kingdom of Italy, and in 1870, when the French finally withdrew from Rome to fight the Germans at home, Italian troops moved in and occupied that last enclave of papal sovereignty.

Pius IX refused to acknowledge the legitimacy of the Italian annexation and with little other alternative remained a "prisoner in the Vatican," as he liked to call himself. There the question remained frozen until 1929, when by the Lateran Treaty of that year, the pope, Pius XI, acknowledged Italy's sovereignty over the former papal domains and, in return, the Italian government (eventually followed by many others) recognized the political autonomy of "The Holy See" or Vatican City, a "monarchical-sacerdotal state" as the U.S. fact sheet calls it, "population 870 (est.), natural resources, none."

8

The Church As the State:
The Islamic Community

THE HEBREWS were a "polity" from the outset, albeit on the modest scale of an extended family or clan that led an apparently autonomous existence among the scattered tribes on the margins of the Middle Eastern agrarian societies of the Stone Age. Eventually they grew into something more substantial—as God himself had promised—and the kingdom of Israel survived politically in its exposed Palestinian home for more than three hundred years. In the end, however, there were too few Israelites for their "state" to be politically viable in the Fertile Crescent of the seventh century B.C.E., and in Babylonia in the opening decades of the sixth century the Jews began their millennia-long experiment in maintaining their identity and some degree of integrity as a people under the political sovereignty of others. For long periods those "others" were their own monotheistic offspring, and rivals, the Christians and Muslims.

Christians were born into the same politically subordinate status as the contemporary Jews of the first century, though they soon had to deal with their Roman masters from a far more exposed position than had the Jews. But the Christians, like Jesus himself, seem to have developed no distinct policy toward the Roman Empire in particular or toward worldly political power in general. The Christian churches had, in effect, a three-century period between Jesus and Constantine before they had seriously to think about the secular state and its place in the scheme of both sacred history and their own lives. Islam's experience was profoundly different. Almost from its inception, the Muslim community, the umma, was both a religious and a political association; Muhammad was his own Constantine.

The Umma

In 622 Muhammad accepted an invitation to leave his native Mecca, where he was the charismatic leader of a small conventicle of believers, and to emigrate to Medina as the ruler of a faction-ridden community of Arabs and Jews. This was a crucial period in Muhammad's life, and the years following his migration were spent trying to forge some kind of community in accordance with his religious principles and the political realities of the situation. As described in the Medina Accords (see I/3), Muhammad's original "community" at Medina included not only his fellow Migrants from Mecca and the newly converted Helpers at Medina, but Jews and Medinese pagans as well. The Jews were soon purged from both the umma and the town, and the pagans were dragged willy-nilly into it; the umma finally became a community of believers who accepted Allah's dominion and both the prophethood and the leadership of Muhammad.

These were not artificial associations. Muhammad's role as a prophet within a community that he himself had summoned into being necessarily included the functions of legislator, executive, and military commander. God's revelations continued to spill from his lips. Now, however, they were not only threats and warnings to nonbelievers, but more often legislative enactments regulating community life, and particularly the relations of one Muslim with another. Thus was constituted an exclusively Muslim umma, and its institutionalization can be charted in the Medina suras of the Quran, which are devoted not merely to shaping the Muslim sensibilities of the believers but to laying out some of the basic ritual requirements later summed up in the Pillars of Islam (see II/4).

Holy War: The Islamic Case

The complex of concerns and conditions that have collected around the Muslim notion of holy war (jihad) reduces itself to a discussion of the circumstances under which an individual Muslim or, more commonly, the community of Muslims is faced with the obligation to use force against an enemy. Although some considerations are directed to the extent or degree of that force, the main thrust of the discussion in Muslim circles from the Prophet down to the present has been about the enemy and the hostile act that triggers the use of force. In the quranic passages on jihad, there is certainly a wider dimension to the term than the use of force. The believer must energetically strive "in the path of God" to overcome the temptations of the world and his own inclinations to sin: that ethic of striving, the jihad of the heart, is built into the Muslims' moral code. The question at hand, however, deals with the other component of jihad, the jihad of the sword, the use of force, or "killing" (*qital*) as the Quran calls it in what appears to be the earliest revelation (22:39) to address the issue: "Leave is given to those who fight because they are wronged . . . who were expelled from their dwellings without right." The date must have been soon after the Hegira and the verse obviously looks to the cause of the Migrants who had recently had to take refuge in Medina. Permission was granted to take up arms against their Meccan oppressors.

If the Meccan suras of the Quran are circumspect on the subject of violence— the few and defenseless Muslims there would almost certainly have suffered in its use—and generally appear to counsel its avoidance (15:94–95; 16:125), the mandate for force granted at Medina was eventually broadened (2:191, 217), until, it seemed, war could be waged against non-Muslims at almost any time or any place. Quran 9:5—"Slay the idolaters wherever you find them"—is as broad a permission for war against the infidels as can be imagined (but for the circumstances, see I/3). In the traditional Muslim understanding of the passage, it was thought to have "abrogated" (see II/1) all earlier limitations on the use of violence against nonbelievers.

It was the thrust of these texts, and of the body of hadith that grew up around them, that led Muslim jurists to divide the world into the Abode of Islam (Dar al-Islam), where Islamic law and sovereignty prevailed, and the Abode of War (Dar al-Harb), lands that were not yet subjected to Islam's moral and political authority. In theory, the Abode of Islam is in a permanent state of warfare with the Abode of War, as the very name suggests—at least until the latter submits—and jihad is the instrument by which that subjection will be accomplished. Hostilities between the two spheres may be suspended by armistice or truce, but they can never be concluded by peace, only by submission.

A systematically framed doctrine of jihad emerges in the work of the Muslim jurist al-Shaybani (d. 804). His *Law of Nations* became one of the foundation texts of Muslim thinking on the subject, and it was often glossed and expanded by later lawyers. It is worth noting that this formulation of a doctrine of jihad occurred during the full tide of Muslim expansion, when the Abode of Islam was growing ever larger by conquest. But it was also a period when the unity of the original umma was being replaced by local Muslim polities whose rulers found the conduct of a jihad a convenient and persuasive way of establishing their Islamic legitimacy.

Al-Shaybani and other early jurists appear, however, to have exercised a certain caution on the matter of hostilities with the unbelievers, which is the essence of holy war, and required that some degree of provocation be present. This was not so with al-Shaybani's somewhat younger contemporary Shafii (d. 820). In his view, war with the Dar al-Harb was not an occasional circumstance but a permanent and continuous state since the cause was precisely the others' unbelief (*kufr*). Jihad was, in the words of a later commentator, "a duty enjoined (on Muslims) permanently till the end of time." It was in fact this notion of obligation that much exercised the jurists. The obligation to wage jihad was, Shafii explained, a collective one (*fard kifaya*) since all that was required was that *some* Muslims—the obligation bound "adult, free men who had the means and the health"—take up arms against the infidel. If no one did, the punishment would fall on all, however.

The discussion of warfare is prolonged and detailed among the jurists, who tried to make sense of what the Quran said about such matters and what the hadith revealed about Muhammad's own counsel and practice, though obviously in quite different circumstances. The degree of harm that might be inflicted on the enemy, to his person, property, or liberty, was a major concern. The caliph had large discretion in such matters, whether to pardon, ransom, enslave, or kill prisoners of war. All agreed that adult males might be slain during hostilities but not women and children, provided they were not involved in the actual fighting. There was, however, a sharp division of opinion—the Quran and Prophetic example were unclear here—on whether it was legitimate to execute prisoners of war. At issue was the reason there was warfare in the first place: if it was, as many alleged, because of unbelief, then there should be no exceptions to the death sentence. If, however, it was all about war, then the capacity to fight was the determinant and the elderly, infirm, monks, and perhaps many others might be spared.

Finally, there is a nice discussion that finds a later juridical echo in the Christians' *Requerimiento* regarding the infidels of the New World who had to be "invited" to become Christians before they could be attacked. According to some Muslim jurists, the infidels of the Abode of War had also to be read a version of their Miranda Rights before they were assailed. The Quran has God say, "We never chastise them until We send forth a Messenger" (17:15), a statement that, when taken with the pertinent hadith, was understood to mean that hostilities with the unbelievers could not begin until they had been formally summoned to Islam and had refused. This was not a majority opinion, however. There were enough reports of Muhammad's own unannounced attacks to make most jurists conclude that in this instance, "the practice of the Prophet had abrogated his words."

In the centuries after Muhammad, the combination of juridically imposed conditions and political realities has diminished the effectiveness of jihad as a practical instrument of policy, though it remains a potent propaganda weapon both for Muslim Fundamentalists to brandish and for their Western opponents to decry. Muslim jurists have rarely agreed on the exact fulfillment of the conditions they have laid down for a genuine jihad (and Muslim public opinion even less often), while the umma on whose behalf it is to be waged has now been divided, perhaps irretrievably, into nation-states that generally subscribe to a quite different (and decidedly non-Islamic) version of international law.

There was a final important development in the medieval theory of jihad in the fourteenth century. The prominent Syrian jurist Ibn Taymiyya (d. 1328) no longer subscribed to Shafii's understanding that jihad required a permanent state of hostilities with non-Muslims. Rather, he took the more pragmatic view that jihad meant only that the Abode of Islam had to be defended against attack. This far more limited notion of jihad as defensive warfare may have been a return to an earlier view of the subject—the conservative Ibn Taymiyya relied heavily on the opinion of "the Fathers" (*al-salaf*)—but it may also have been counseled by concern over another, much closer, and more threatening enemy. The Central Asian Mongols had cut a wide and bloody path across Iran and in 1258 they sacked Baghdad and killed the caliph. In 1260, three years before

Ibn Taymiyya's birth, their advance on Egypt was checked at Goliath's Spring near Nazareth, in Galilee but the devastation they had visited on Syria, Iraq, and Iran was still everywhere visible, as were the Mongols themselves.

Under these circumstances Ibn Taymiyya issued two fatwas on the Mongols. Over the preceding half century they had become officially Muslims, but, as the question was proposed to Ibn Taymiyya, were they really Muslims? No, Ibn Taymiyya ruled with great consequence. Despite their pronouncement of the shahada, the Mongols were not Muslims because they did not live according to the sharia, and thus, according to a second ruling, the lands under their control were neither Abode of Islam nor yet the Abode of War but a new intermediate state. Ibn Taymiyya had in effect ruled what the Kharijites had much earlier held: that observance—not mere profession—made the Muslim, and that under those circumstances it was permissible to take up arms against such. Though his rulings had little immediate consequence, they were "rediscovered" by modern Muslim Fundamentalists who have used the fatwas to justify the assassination or forceful overthrow of Muslims who are not, in their opinion, truly submissive.

War and Religion: The Jewish and Christian Cases

While the classical Islamic legal tradition prohibits all war (e.g., tribal warfare, raids, blood feuds) except on religious grounds, Western ethical theories, on the contrary, have sanctioned "just wars" on certain natural law grounds but never on the basis of religious ones. This latter attitude is altogether quite modern and altogether secular since most religious communities have permitted and even encouraged war in the name of God. Yahweh was a warrior God (Exod. 5:3; Isa. 42:13), and the Bible is not unnaturally filled with conflicts that are palpably holy wars (see I/6). The Israelites, quite like the pre-Islamic Arabs, even carried their God with them into conflict on occasion (Num. 10:35–36). Deuteronomy 20–21 provides rules for war, with God as the leader, and its terms are similar to those dictated by Muhammad, except there is no agreeable dhimma status granted to the Israelites' enemies. With the progressive loss of Jewish sovereignty (and so the capacity to employ force against its enemies), war was eventually reduced to an anticipated eschatological event among the Jews, and then, with the diminution of messianic enthusiasm, a school exercise for the rabbis, who laid down the rules of war in the eternal present of the Talmud.

The Christian Church is not a state as such and so cannot formally declare or conduct a war. It has, however, on occasion permitted and even encouraged both warlike acts and formal wars in the name of religion. An example is the Crusades, the first of which was called for by Pope Urban II at Clermont in 1095. The Crusade—its formal title was *peregrinatio in armis*, "armed pilgrimage"—had as its stated objective freeing the Christian holy places in Jerusalem from the Muslims (Jerusalem fell to the crusaders in 1099, was retaken by the Muslims in 1187), and it was garlanded with the Church's spiritual rewards and indulgences (see II/5) for those who voluntarily participated in this and later attacks against Muslim lands.

Originally the Crusades had nothing to do with attempts to persuade or force the Muslims to convert—European Christian missionary activity among the Muslims was rarely attempted and notoriously unsuccessful—but the later Crusades began to adopt it as an objective, particularly as attempts at taking and holding Jerusalem and Palestine began to seem increasingly illusionary. As already noted, coerced baptism never found much favor among the Church's canon lawyers. It was just such a canon lawyer, however—Innocent IV, as he was known when he was elevated to the papacy in 1243—who defined the Church's position: though nonbelievers might not be coerced into conversion, the pope, as vicar of Christ on earth, had the authority to order even non-Christian powers to admit preachers of the Gospels into their lands, and, if they refused, to authorize Christian states to use force to effect their entry. Thomas Aquinas, in his *Summa theologiae* (1265–1271), echoes Innocent's reason and adds three other grounds that justify a state's use of force against the infidel: the latter's hindering the Christian faith by "blasphemies, evil suasions, or open persecutions."

Dhimma and Dhimmis

Muhammad's attitude toward the People of the Book, as he called those who shared the same scriptural tradition with Islam, was generally favorable. Early on, in fact, he had called on them to verify his message. But as time passed, the Quran came to look on Jews and Christians as adherents of rival rather than collegial faiths. Some of this change in attitude was dictated by events at Medina itself, where Jewish tribes made up part of the population. Not only did the Jews of Medina reject Muhammad's prophetic claims; they began secretly to connive with his enemies in Mecca to overthrow him. Muhammad's own reaction was determined and progressively more violent. As Muhammad's political strength grew, the Jewish tribes of Medina were first banished, then taken and enslaved, and finally executed on the spot. This quite extraordinary behavior is matched by nothing in the Quran, and is quite at odds with Muhammad's treatment of the Jews he encountered outside Medina. We must think then that it was essentially political, prompted by behavior he read as treasonous, not by some transgression of the law of God.

A later encounter with Jews took place in 627 in the course of a raid on Khaibar and Faydak (see I/3), oases north of Medina whose population was mostly or wholly Jewish, including some Muhammad himself had exiled from Medina. He settled terms on them, and this and other similar arrangements rather than his own conduct at Medina provided the model for the Muslim community's disposition of the non-Muslim peoples who were being rapidly swept under Muslim political sovereignty. Beginning with the capitulation of Khaibar to Muhammad himself, settlements in the path of the Muslim raiders were offered quite specific terms: either submit peacefully or be conquered by force. Those who resisted could expect little mercy for themselves or little respect for their possessions. Most, however, appear to have submitted on the Muslims' terms. The newly conquered had to pay their new political masters (as they had to their old) a tribute in the form of an annual head tax (*jizya*; Quran 9:29), in addition to the traditional land tax. If they were pagans, they had perforce to become Muslims. Jews and Christians, however, though they too had to pay the jizya, were under no compulsion to convert. As People of the Book, Jews and Christians were offered a kind of concordat or pact (*dhimma*). According to the Prophet's own terms, the vanquished recognized Islam's political sovereignty and in turn were permitted the free practice of their religion, subject to certain limitations.

> **Note:** The Zoroastrians (*Majus*), members of the state-established religion of Iran, were probably peripheral to the seventh-century world of western Arabia that received the Quran. They are mentioned only once there (22:17), as among the religious communities that will be judged on the Last Day. With the early conquest of Iraq and Iran, however, Zoroastrianism became an issue for Muslim jurists and politicians. A hadith that seemed to settle the issue of their treatment was in circulation. The Prophet was reported to have treated them "as if they were People of the Book" and advised his followers to do likewise. Despite some occasional juridical doubts, the view prevailed that the "Magians" were eligible for the dhimma. Whether they were in fact People of the Book was a different matter. There were objections, but their early acceptance as dhimmis seems to have carried in its train the conclusion that they were Scriptuaries as well, though no Muslim exegete or historian appears to have been well instructed on their "Book." How grudging was that admission is nevertheless revealed by the fact that the jurists never permitted Muslims to marry Magian women or eat meat slaughtered by them, as they did with the Jews and Christians.

The limitations waxed and waned in number and specificity in the early decades—many of the Christian versions claimed their parentage in the spurious Covenant of Umar, the terms supposedly granted to the Christians by the second caliph, Umar ibn al-Khattab (r. 634–644), when he accepted the surrender of Jerusalem in 635—but most of them are rather self-evident. The dhimmis, as they were called, were forbidden to attempt to convert the Muslims, to build new places of worship, or to make public display of their rituals.

But in other instances, depending on the circumstances of time, place, and ruler, the social and financial disabilities imposed by dhimmi status were more severe and humiliating. Jews and Christians were not persecuted within the Abode of Islam, but neither did they enjoy the full rights and privileges of the Muslims.

Muslim Dhimmis in Christian Spain

People of the Book is a theological category and describes peoples who have received a genuine revelation; dhimmi is a political category and refers to those People of the Book who have accepted and live under Muslim sovereignty. People of the Book may be found inside and outside the Dar al-Islam, dhimmis only within it. The Christians recognized no such affinity with Islam. They permitted the Muslims to live in convivencia among them (however briefly) for social and economic, not theological, reasons. One group of them, the Muslims living under Christian sovereignty in Spain, underlines the religious and theological significance of the dhimma.

As the Christian Reconquest pushed ever southward in Spain, and more and more Muslims passed from Muslim to Christian sovereignty, they fell under what was known as the *mudéjar estatuto*, a series of legal agreements whose final and most comprehensive version we can see in the terms concluded between Their Catholic Majesties Ferdinand and Isabella of Aragon and Castile and the Muslim lord of Granada at that city's capitulation in 1492. By its terms, the Muslims were guaranteed the free pursuit of their religious and social life under their traditional institutions. They became, in effect, Muslim dhimmis. But there was a crucial difference.

The dhimma concluded by the Muslims with their Christian and Jewish subjects was a religious pact, guaranteed by God and sanctioned by the practice of the Prophet himself; as such it formed part of the sharia, the canon law of Islam (see II/4). The Christian statute, in contrast, was a political agreement concluded by secular authorities as an affair of state. It could be abrogated by the dictating party, and it shortly was by Ferdinand and Isabella in 1502 with respect to the Muslims living in Castile, who were then given the inevitable choice between exile, death, or conversion. The same choice was extended in 1526 to cover the far more assimilated Muslim dhimmis living under the Christian Crown of Aragon. We do not know how many Muslims chose death in the aftermath of the abolition of the Mudejar status, but many did leave for Muslim-ruled North Africa and others converted to Christianity. Note has already been taken of the sad fate that overcame this latter group, now called Moriscos, or "Little Moors," who in 1609, as Christians, were expelled from their homeland (see I/4). The dhimma granted by the Muslim umma to the People of the Book could never be abrogated and never has been.

> **Note:** The dhimmi issue is generally moot in modernizing Middle Eastern states with Western-style constitutions, which guarantee freedom of religion and equal political rights for all citizens. Yet the dhimma remains an active—and provocative—component in many Muslims' vision of the Islamic state, whether in being, as in Iran or Saudi Arabia, or as a prospect, as in the program of the Muslims called Fundamentalists or Islamists.

Conversion by Levy: The Devshirme

Islam accepted the preexisting institution of slavery in the same manner that Judaism and Christianity did, and, like the other two, gave the slave parity with the freeborn in matters of faith, if not in matters of law. From the beginning, Muslims used slaves for various tasks, from menial domestics, through concubinage, work in the bureaucracy, service in the caliph's praetorian guard, to soldiering generally. Berbers, Turks, Kurds, and Circassians all served as Islam's soldiery as the Arabs grew disinclined to go to war. The Circassians in particular formed a remarkable military caste, the Mamluks—the word means "something possessed"—who ruled Egypt from 1250 until their overthrow by the Ottomans in 1517.

Islamic law forbade the enslavement of Muslims, and so the future Mamluks were purchased or captured as young boys outside the Abode of Islam, enslaved, then converted, and finally given a strenuous military training before entering service. In the 1390s the Ottomans added something new to the practice, the *devshirme*. In the course of their conquest of the Balkans, they began to exact as the sultan's traditional fifth share of the booty of conquest young boys from among the Christian Slavic population—very few Greeks or Armenians were taken. The boys were neither captured nor purchased but simply collected from their parents at irregular intervals, apparently as need arose. They thus became the sultan's slaves. They were converted willy-nilly to Islam—at their age and in that time and place there seems to have been little resistance—and shipped off to training camps in Anatolia. There they were subjected, like the Mamluks, to rigorous training, but not, in this case, in the martial arts alone. They were evaluated for intelligence, character, and general bearing, and the best and brightest were sent to palace schools in Istanbul, to take their place eventually in the Ottoman administrative hierarchy. The others continued their military training to emerge as the sultan's "new army" (Turk. *yeni cheri* > Janissaries), who fought, along with the traditional Turkish cavalry, the spahis, in defense of the expanding Ottoman Empire.

These two groups of the sultan's slaves, both Slavic Christians by birth, though Muslims by conversion and Turkified by training, replaced the ethnic

Turks as the administrative heart and military sinews of the Ottoman Empire during the three hundred–odd years (ca. 1390–1690) the devshirme was practiced, a period that also corresponded with the apogee of Ottoman power and wealth. Both the enslavement of the dhimmis and their forced conversion were illegal in terms of Islamic law, though there seem to have been no strenuous protests. The victims had the fairest of prospects, the road to Istanbul, opened to them, and the religious authorities' fealty to—and dependence on—the sultan was almost as profound as that of the *kapi kullari*, the "slaves of the court."

The Millet System

The dhimma defines and regulates the status of the People of the Book living under Muslim sovereignty. It makes no distinctions, however, among them: Jews, Christians, and later, Zoroastrians were all equal before the Islamic law, granted the same privileges and subject to the same restrictions. In 1453, the same year he took Constantinople from its last Eastern Christian defenders, the Ottoman sultan Mehmed II organized his "flock" (*reaya*), that is, the 90 percent of his subjects who were not part of the Ottoman ruling institution. The flock was divided horizontally according to profession and occupation, but Mehmed introduced a new vertical distinction by *millet*, or religious community. In theory, the Muslims of the flock constituted a millet along with the others, but in reality the millet organization applied only to the Jews, the Armenians, and Orthodox Christians.

Or so they were called. The Orthodox millet was headed by the newly appointed Greek Orthodox patriarch of Constantinople, George Scholarios, known as Gennadius II, a monk strongly opposed to all plans for reunion with the Roman Church (see I/6). His millet jurisdiction included not only the Greek Christians but the Churches of Bulgaria, Serbia, and Bosnia, whose liturgical language was not Greek but Slavonic. The members of these latter Churches spoke Serbo-Croatian as their vernacular, and all of them were at the time of the Ottoman conquest well on their way to becoming jurisdictionally independent (autocephalous) Christian Churches. Likewise, the Armenian patriarch in Constantinople presided over the fortunes not only of his own Church but of the bundled Monophysite Churches in the Ottoman lands, notably the Copts of Egypt and the Jacobites of Syria and Iraq (see II/7). The Jewish millet was presided over by the chief rabbi of Istanbul and included both Sephardic and the less numerous and influential Ashkenazi Jews of the empire.

The sultan dealt with his non-Muslim subjects through the heads of the millets, who naturally favored their own proper constituents. In the Balkans this led to increased estrangement between the Slavic Churches and the Greek Orthodox Church under whose jurisdiction they were now placed. For their part, the three millets became in effect Ottoman institutions, organs of administration in the sprawling bureaucracy of the empire.

The Caliphate

Muhammad no more appointed a successor than Jesus had. Christians' immediate eschatological expectations made that absence of concern seem natural, but there is little trace of such urgently imminent End Time expectations in Islam, either before or after the Prophet's death. Muhammad's illness and death in Medina in 632, if unexpected, were by no means sudden. There was ample opportunity to make provision for the succession, and though some Muslims maintain that he did, the majority agree that he did not. As the story is commonly told, at Muhammad's death the Migrants, those who had originally come with him from Mecca ten years earlier, and the Helpers, the inner cadre of the Medina converts, met separately to plan what to do next. When they learned of the other caucus, the Migrants led by Abu Bakr hurried to join the other group, presumably to head off a preemptive choice of successor by the men who had, after all, once ruled the oasis. There appears to have been a rather secular and political debate on the relative merits of the two groups. The Medinese pointed out that the Migrants were merely guests in Medina, and Abu Bakr countered with the rather astonishing (to us) claim that the Arabs would consent to be led only by a member of the Quraysh. There was a proposal for dual leadership of shared authority. Finally, and we do not know what settled the matter, though expedience suggests itself, it was agreed that the senior Migrant Abu Bakr should assume leadership of the umma. All present took an oath of allegiance, Bedouin fashion, to the new Caliph.

If we are unsure how or precisely why Abu Bakr was chosen, we are equally uncertain about how the succession was viewed. The title chosen for Abu Bakr comes from *khalifa*, used in the Quran of Adam and David as God's "deputies." But Abu Bakr, far from deputizing for God, seems not even to have acted in that capacity for the departed Muhammad, at least in any prophetic or charismatic sense. From what we can gather from his acts—he decided to send an army against the Arabian Bedouin who at Muhammad's death signaled their opportunistic withdrawal from the umma—he seems to have succeeded Muhammad merely as head of the umma. Thus Muhammad's charismatic leadership possessing both spiritual and executive powers was routinized in the form of a chief operating officer. As one of the subsequent early caliphs, Umar II (r. 717–720) put it: "There is no Prophet after ours and no Holy Book after ours. What God has ordered or forbidden through our Prophet remains so forever. I am not one who decides but only one who carries out, not an innovator but a follower."

Thus the caliph was neither above the law—in the umma's case, God's Law—nor its maker. Indeed, Abu Bakr and his successors were closer in function to another title used of the early caliphs, commander of the faithful (*amir al-muminin*). They appointed and removed political subordinates. They decided military strategy and served as commander (*amir*) of the armies of Islam. The caliph was the chief judge and chief fiscal officer of the new regime. Most of the caliph's military, judicial, and fiscal responsibilities were soon delegated to others, however; the community was actually a number of armies on the march far from the centers of power, and though decisions might be made in the name of the caliph, they were increasingly made by others.

If the caliph and his delegates could decide, they could not or did not legislate. For their guidance, they now had the closed and completed Quran, and they could not add to that text, which, like Jewish law, addressed itself in great detail to matters of personal status but was mute on the political governance of what was rapidly becoming an immense empire. The caliph and his delegates resorted instead to many other devices to shape their purpose: tribal practices, local customs, pragmatic necessities, and, to some extent, whatever precedents the Prophet's practice suggested to them. There is little suggestion that the caliph regarded himself or was regarded by others as possessing special spiritual powers. He was the head of the umma, and though the umma was based entirely on a shared acceptance of Islam, the caliph was not so much a religious leader as the leader of a religion.

The Powers of the Caliph (and Others)

The caliphate was in a sense an improvised office. Its tenants tested it as they proceeded, freed from any inhibition save the collective sensibilities of Muslims but likewise deprived of any counsel from either the Quran or the hadith. Later, some jurists spoke at length on the powers and responsibilities of the caliph, or the Imam or "leader," as he is often called in the technical literature, but only after the office had already evolved through historical circumstance—including those improvised decisions of the early caliphs—and the main outlines of the Islamic law, the sharia, had been created (see II/4). The sharia had laid out the main behavioral norms for a Muslim without a great deal of concern about the persons or institutions responsible for their oversight and enforcement. When that subject finally did arise, the jurists' eyes began to turn toward the caliphate.

In discussing the question of jurisdiction, Islamic law recognizes two large domains of action where different "claims" (*haqq*; pl. *huquq*) prevail. God's claims, all parsed as religious, needless to say, are those that the Islamic community or umma has over the individual Muslim. Individuals' claims are the responsibilities Muslims have in relation with one another. These two domains fall broadly into two different jurisdictions. Individuals' claims were the very stuff of Islamic law—family law, inheritance, civil actions, and injuries—and disputes regarding them were settled by the *qadi* in his sharia court (see II/4). The protection and enforcement of God's claims fell into the purview of the political authorities, the caliph-Imam or his delegates. What precisely those claims were was never entirely resolved by the jurists, but most understood them to include punishment of crimes (penal law, only very sketchily touched on in the Quran), collection of the alms-tithe from Muslims and the tribute-tax from the subject peoples, ensuring that public worship like the Friday prayer be carried out, and responsibility for the wealth and property that belonged to the umma as a whole.

Tensions in the Community

The caliphs, the earliest ones at any rate, had to face a problem that Muhammad himself had forestalled with great difficulty during his lifetime. There was a tension in the community from the beginning between the notion of Islam as a universal religion that claimed the allegiance of all humans, and that of the Arabs as a final version of the Chosen People. The catchphrase is Judaism's own, of course, and speaks to God's election of Israel as a fellow in his Covenant. Muhammad's own perspective was perhaps somewhat different. He knew, from his own understanding of history, that previous revelations had constituted their recipients a community, an umma. It had been true of the Jews and Christians and now, in the final act of the drama of revelation, it would be so with the Arabs.

If this revelation of a "clear Arabic Quran" through an Arab prophet to Arabs of western Arabia was calculated to create a sense of unity among those peoples, the project cannot be judged entirely a success. Muhammad had problems with tribal rivalries in his own day, between the mighty and the low in the complex hierarchy of tribes and clans that dominated not only his native Mecca but most of the peninsula's Bedouin population. Boasting and vilification were common pre-Islamic instruments for establishing and maintaining that order, and though Muhammad decreed that the only aristocracy in Islam was that constituted by piety and merit, the tribal divisions of Arab society long outlived his efforts to suppress them in the name of either a single Arab umma or a universal religion for all humankind.

With the Prophet's death, the umma rapidly began to disintegrate. Only through the strenuous military efforts of his first successor, Abu Bakr (r. 632–634), was Islam successfully reimposed on the tribes across Arabia who had read Muhammad's death as the death knell of Islam and declared their secession from the community by refusing to pay the alms-tithe. What followed was more subtle and perhaps more insidious in the long run. The enormous wealth that came to the community as booty and tribute was distributed according to a system devised by the second caliph, Umar (r. 634–644). It recognized and rewarded the merit of early conversion and a concomitant willingness to bear arms against the enemies of Islam, but in institutionalizing this system of rewards and pensions, Umar restored the distribution rights to tribal chieftains, permitted this to be done along tribal lines, and allowed it to be effected in the new Islamic garrison towns whose social organization was precisely tribal.

The consequences of these purely administrative decisions were twofold, and each was far-reaching in its social impact, as we have already seen (I/5). They preserved and perhaps reinforced the old pre-Islamic tribal rivalries, which continued to disturb the equilibrium of the Islamic body politic for at least a century afterward; and they conspired to create a distinction between Arab and non-Arab within the bosom of Islam. It is not certain that Muhammad intended an egalitarian community. What actually emerged was a society where both tribal and ethnic rivalries died a lingering death.

The caliphate, though an obvious pragmatic success, did not exhaust the possibilities of leadership in early Islam. There was among some Muslims the concept of the head of the community as a prayer leader (imam) or an eschatological chief or Mahdi literally "Guided One." The latter has been invoked from time to time in Islamic history as a challenge to the caliph or a magnet around which to energize Muslim political action (see II/10), but its successes have been short-lived, and the figure of the Mahdi receded, like that of the Messiah in rabbinic Judaism, into an indefinite future.

Ali ibn Abi Talib (601–661)

Some saw, and continued to see, the office and role of the head of the umma in a quite different light. This is the Shiat Ali, or "Party of Ali," who trace their origins back to the person and history of Ali ibn Abi Talib.

Ali ibn Abi Talib was Muhammad's much younger cousin—thirty-one years younger by the traditional chronology—and it was his father who raised Muhammad when the latter's grandfather and guardian died. Although Ali was only nine at the time, tradition has remembered him as the first after Khadija to submit and accept Islam. Ali, at twenty-one, migrated with his cousin to Medina in 622 and thereafter he began to play an increasingly important role in the life of Muhammad and the consolidation of Islam. How important depends on whether one reads the standard Sunni biographies of the Prophet, which certainly do not downgrade Ali's importance, or the Shiite hagiographies, which not only exalt him to the heavens—Ali's military prowess is equaled only by his eloquence—but in their reading of some otherwise opaque passages of the Quran (e.g., 5:55; 13:7), and in their remembrance of other events in Muhammad's life, understand the Prophet to have explicitly promised the succession to Ali and his family. On his deathbed Muhammad is said to have called for pen and ink, "So I may write for you something after which you will not be led into error." But death came before anything could be recorded. According to the Shiites, as the Shiat Ali are called in English, Muhammad intended to put into writing God's appointment of Ali as his successor. Sunnis also remember the occasion, but have different explanations of what was intended by Muhammad's cryptic remark.

The Succession

The story of how Abu Bakr came to be chosen caliph has already been told. The Shiites remember it somewhat differently. By all accounts Ali, who was then thirty-one, was not present at the meeting of the Migrants and Helpers after Muhammad's death. All further agree that once the choice of Abu Bakr was made, Umar and others went to Ali's house to ask—apparently to demand—that he too take the oath of allegiance. Ali may have resisted, though on what precise grounds we do not know. What the Shiites do recall, however, is that some who urged him to assume the leadership himself, and he declined. These included his uncle Abbas, the eponym of the later Sunni dynasty of caliphs, the Abbasids, and even Abu Sufyan, the head of the house of Umayya, another Sunni dynasty that some twenty-odd years later attempted to exterminate the house of Ali.

Where Sunni and Shiite historians totally disagree is on what followed between Abu Bakr's accession to the caliphate in 632 and Ali's own in 656. The Sunnis maintain that Ali accepted the legitimacy of his three predecessors, Abu Bakr, Umar, and Uthman; the Shiites vociferously deny it. Ali certainly had his enemies—Muhammad's favorite wife, and Abu Bakr's daughter, Aisha, prominent among them—but they seem not to have included the first three caliphs. When Abu Bakr died in 634 he secured the succession for Umar ibn al-Khattab. The latter attempted to regularize the succession process by appointing a council of six men, including Ali, to settle the caliphate at his death. When Umar was assassinated in 644, the choice once again passed over Ali for another early and devoted follower of the Prophet, Uthman, of the rich and influential house of Umayya. Uthman's caliphate (r. 644–656) is best remembered for his promoting the first standard edition of the Quran (see II/1) as well as his appointing relatives to important posts in the rapidly expanding Muslim empire. His reign was in any event a troubled one, and he was murdered by a conspiracy of pretenders to his office. Ali was not himself directly involved in Uthman's death, and in its wake he was named caliph to succeed him. Ali was then fifty-five, married to the Prophet's daughter Fatima (among others) with two sons (among others) who had been Muhammad's favorites, Hasan and Husayn.

Ali's caliphate (r. 656–661) was as plagued as his predecessor's. Important posts were still held by Uthman's appointees, who were often his own Umayyad relations, chief among them Muawiya, the governor of Syria, who orchestrated and maintained a steady drumbeat of criticism against the new caliph on the grounds that he, if not complicitous in the deed, was doing nothing to bring to justice, and may even have been sheltering, Uthman's murderers. Others, like Talha and Zubayr, abetted by Aisha, who had been slighted—perhaps even slandered—by Ali during the Prophet's lifetime, saw their own chances for the succession dashed by Ali's appointment and were resolved to unseat him.

Ali, who had been forced to move from Medina across the steppe to Iraq, disposed of Talha and Zubayr at the Battle of the Camel near Basra in 656 and Aisha was sent into permanent retirement. But Muawiya's campaign was more persistent and his power in the end more effective. He had the troops of Syria under his command and support in the other provinces as well. Ali moved his own army to oppose him and then, after an inconclusive battle at a place called Siffin in Syria in 657, he made what proved to be a fatal error: he agreed to submit his dispute with Muawiya to arbitration. Immediately he lost a considerable contingent of his followers who "seceded" from his cause—they came to be called Kharijis, "Seceders"—and turned against their leader. Ali had first to deal with these troublesome rebels, which he did at Nahrwan in Iraq. He won the battle but lost his life: while the dispute with Muawiya dragged on, the fourth caliph of Islam was struck down by a disgruntled Kharijite in January 661. Ali was buried, as the story goes, at Najaf in Iraq, which has become a major Shiite pilgrimage center.

The Umayyads (r. 661–750)

Muawiya acceded to the caliphate, moved the capital of the Abode of Islam out of the still rebellious Holy Cities to Damascus, where his own troops and power lay. He and his successors ruled not as the tribal sheikhs that the first four caliphs seem to have been, but closer to the style of kings on the Byzantine or Iranian model. The rule of Islam now belonged to a family, the Banu Umayya, or Umayyads, and the crown passed dynastically from head to head until it was seized in turn by another family, the Banu Abbas, or Abbasids, in 750.

The Umayyads were widely condemned by later generations for introducing "kingship" (*mulk*) into the Islamic community—they were in fact proud of the title of king—and of showing more concern for the secular pleasures of the world than for the spirit and practices of Islam. Their style was indeed imperial, and Muawiya upset tribal if not Islamic precedent by appointing his son as his caliphal heir. But the Umayyads did have discernible Islamic sensibilities. They made a clear-cut theological claim to the caliphate. The monument of the Dome of the Rock in Jerusalem is an Islamic building with an Islamic function, and the same Umayyad caliph who conceived that building was also the first to devise an Islamic coinage for the new regime. He too began the Arabization, and thus indirectly the Islamization, of the still nascent apparatus of Islamic government.

At Ali's death the Muslim community had already begun to display signs of serious schismatic disruption. The secession of the Kharijites from support of Ali ibn Abi Talib's uncontestably legitimate caliphate has been noted (II/5). It is clear the dissenters possessed a far different view of the umma and, consequently, of who should stand at its head. Puritan-egalitarians who thought that the grave sinner ipso facto became an unbeliever and, in effect an apostate, the Kharijites, held that any Muslim might head the umma. They did not enjoy any great success among Muslims and their point of view did not survive long. The Shiites, in contrast, were more tenacious and in the end more successful.

The Holy Family: Ahl al-Bayt

Sunnis and Shiites both speak of the "people of the house" (*ahl al-bayt*), by which they commonly mean Muhammad's family. Whereas the Shiites restrict the descent of that family to the offspring of Ali and Fatima, the wedded cousin and daughter of the Prophet, the Sunnis have a wider understanding of the expression.

"People of the house" seems to have been a commonplace pre-Islamic designation for the leading or noble members of a tribe, but its appearance in the Quran, and the political wrangles that went on over leadership and preference in the Muslim community, gave it other, highly charged resonances. "People of the house" appears three times in the Quran, where it means "family" or "household." Most Muslim commentators thought the phrase must refer to Muhammad and his family: "God wishes to take the pollution from you, O people of the house, and to purify you thoroughly" (33:33). Others argue that the context requires that the reference be to Muhammad's own wives, who are the subjects of the verses that precede and follow. That the first interpretation had a clear political intent is revealed by the gloss put on it in a famous Prophetic tradition, the so-called hadith of the robe, where Muhammad is reported to have spread his robe around his immediate family and said, "This verse [i.e., 33:33] was revealed for me and for Ali, Fatima, Hasan, and Husayn," with the occasional addition of "I am the enemy of their enemies." These traditions were accepted by Sunni authorities and so it seems likely that the extension of Muhammad's metaphoric robe to include *all* the male heirs of Ali—it was argued that women (in this case Fatima) do not confer nobility, only the males in the line—was accomplished by the Abbasids. The latter overthrew the Umayyads in 750 and, as we shall see, assumed the caliphal office on the grounds that they were Ali's legitimate descendants. That descent was more juridical than linear, however. The Abbasids claimed that their founder had been "deeded" the caliphate by Ali's grandson Abu Hashim, the son of a certain Muhammad born of one of Ali's wives known simply as the Hanafite woman. Thus the Abbasids responded to mounting Alid criticism of their legitimacy by putting into circulation this broader interpretation of Quran 33:33, whereby the "people of the house" included their own ancestor as well as the Fatimids descended from the union of Ali and Fatima.

That leadership should belong by right to a family rather than rest on the choice of the community or society has struck some as a rather non-Arab notion. But it has characterized support of Ali from the beginning. Simple loyalty to the house of Ali (Alidism) became Shiism when it began to acquire, besides a memory of Ali's importance in the earliest days of Islam, an ideology to explain the transfer of Muhammad's spiritual charisma, if not of his prophetic gift, to Ali and thence to certain members of his house. When or how that happened is not easy to explain since there are no Shiite documents earlier than the tenth century, when that ideology was already fully developed.

The historical footing grows firmer in the events of 680, when Ali's second son, Husayn—the first, Hasan, is almost invisible in these narratives—was lured from Medina by promises of support for his family's cause across the steppe toward Kufa. Husayn was intercepted by Umayyad forces at a place called Karbala, where he and most of his followers were slaughtered. It was the end, for the moment, of Alid political aspirations, but the massacre at Karbala was also, as it turned out, one of the foundation stones of religious Shiism (see II/6).

The Abbasids (r. 750–1258)

There was no single Shiite view of the Imamate or leadership of the community and no greater degree of agreement among various Shiite factions than among the Sunnis, save on the principle that rule over the umma belonged by right and by designation to the descendants of Ali ibn Abi Talib, Muhammad's cousin and son-in-law and the actual fourth caliph, and that that ruler should possess religious as well as secular powers. Which descendant and which powers were much debated questions. The Umayyads never succeeded in destroying a strong sense of loyalty to Ali, his sons (notably the martyred Husayn), and their offspring. For their part, the Alid loyalists' claims to power generally came to naught. One group, the followers of Muhammad ibn al-Hanifiyya, another son of Ali, found a zealous propagandist in a certain al-Mukhtar who proclaimed him Imam and Mahdi (see II/10). The claim was taken seriously enough by the first Abbasids, who had seized power from the Umayyads in 750 and attempted to eradicate their rivals, for them to have put out the story that the Imamate had been transferred to them, the descendants of Abbas, by the son of Muhammad ibn al-Hanifiyya.

Later, during the reign of the Abbasid caliph al-Mahdi (775–785), new grounds of legitimacy were put out by the House of Abbas: their preeminence, it was now claimed, rested on the merits of Abbas himself—an uncle of Muhammad and a notoriously late convert to Islam—and therefore the caliphate belonged by right to his family, which was, after all, the Prophet's own. The issue thus became political rather than purely theological. On one side was what has been called an absolutist or autocratic party that essentially reflected the views of early Shiite theoreticians and found its chief support among the new bureaucrats in the nascent government ministries in Baghdad and among the still active Arab tribespeople on the nearby Syrian steppe. Chief among the latter were tribes that had migrated from the Yemen who were familiar with, and perhaps preferred, a "royal" tradition among their rulers. On the other side were the "constitutionalists," those who saw the will of God vested in the collective wisdom of the umma a wisdom committed to the protection of the ulama, Islam's emerging lawyer class (see II/4). In this view, the caliph's legitimacy was manifested in his receiving the *baya*, the oath of allegiance and loyalty once sworn by the Bedouins to their sheikh and now to the caliph by the representatives of the umma.

The early Abbasids attempted to keep a foot in both camps. They extended their patronage to the bureaucrats of the *diwans*, men whose absolutist tendencies seem to have derived not so much from Alid loyalty as from a nostalgia for the gone but still potent imperial traditions of Sasanian Iran. The Abbasids' relations with Ali and Fatima's actual family were somewhat more circumspect, however, since these latter were, after all, potential rivals for the throne that was being so carefully reared in Baghdad. This cautious policy foundered during the reign of al-Mamun (813–833), when that caliph accepted both the theory of Alid absolutism and their practical claim to the office by appointing the Alid Imam presumptive Ali al-Rida as his successor. Al-Rida died soon thereafter and al-Mamun's experiment failed. The caliph's Arab armies in eastern Iran were replaced by staunchly Sunni Turkish praetorians, who effectively curbed whatever absolutist claims or dreams the Abbasids may still have had.

Though kept under tight rein by their Turkish wardens, who wielded the actual power (sultan) in Allah's Commonwealth, the Abbasids continued to rule for many centuries. Caliph succeeded caliph in Baghdad until 1258, when the city was all but destroyed by the Mongols. Soon thereafter an Abbasid "survivor" surfaced in Cairo and was enthroned as caliph by the Mamluk sultans who ruled there from 1250 until they were unseated by the Ottoman Turks in 1517. The Ottomans, no nicer than their predecessors in such matters, arranged another "transfer" of the caliphate to themselves.

From Alidism to Shiism

The movement around Muhammad ibn al-Hanifiyya was one of the earliest signs of what was later branded "extremist" (ghulat) Shiism and the initial stage of a movement from loyalty to Ali's family to the clearly defined ideology that we call simply Shiism. The other stages toward the final formulation of this latter remain obscure since, with the accession of the Abbasids, the Shiites appear to have abandoned any real claim to the caliphate and to have contented themselves with wielding considerable political, though not doctrinal, influence on the Abbasid caliphs. But there were some radical Shiite theoreticians even then, and they seem to fall into two chief groups. The Rafidites maintained that God, through Muhammad, had designated—"designation" (*nass*) was a key Shiite contention—the Prophet's cousin Ali as his successor. The critical text appointing Ali head of the umma had been removed from the Quran, they claimed, and Muhammad's companions had conspired to deprive Ali of his rightful position and to appoint the usurpers Abu Bakr, Umar, and Uthman as Imams in his stead. The Zaydis agreed on Ali's prior designation as head of the umma, but they were not ready, as the Rafidites were, to read the other *rashidun* out of the caliphate and the venerable Companions of the Prophet who had recognized them into error.

The more moderate Zaydis had some political success: they installed one of their Imams in Tabaristan in 864 and another in the Yemen in 901. The Rafidites made no visible political headway, however, save for al-Mamun's already noted flirtation with making one of their Imams his heir in the caliphate. But their doctrinal development, which probably began in earnest in the circle of Ali's great-great grandson Jafar al-Sadiq (d. 765), proceeded, in ways invisible to us, until a coherent picture of what was by then called Imami or "Twelver" Shiism begins to appear in our sources sometime early in the tenth century.

The Shiite Imamate

Although our clearest view of the formative process of Shiism comes in the earliest years of the tenth century, the roots of the movement go back, as has been said, to the circle around Jafar al-Sadiq in the eighth. By the tenth century, however, most of the basic tenets of Imami Shiism were in place: Ali was the designated Imam in succession to Muhammad, and after him had come, likewise by designation, and likewise from among Ali's descendants and heirs, consecutive Imams, all of whom had been gifted with infallible spiritual powers for guidance of the community. This line came to a temporary end with the "concealment" (*ghayba*) in 878 of the twelfth Imam. This "Hidden Imam" would return one day, but only at the end of time as the Mahdi.

> **Note:** *Imam* is a generic Arabic term for leader. Besides its technical use by Shiites, the word is also often employed, generally uncapitalized, for either the leader at mosque prayer or the head of a Muslim congregation.

Thus, in the late ninth century, the Shiite Imamate apparently vacated history and politics for the safer ground of eschatology. By trading in their political claims for spiritual vindication, the Shiites ceased posing a threat to the current, strongly Turkish-buttressed Abbasid regime, and indeed there are signs that in the late ninth and early tenth centuries the caliphs began to take a more relaxed view of Shiism and Shiites. It was in this climate that the Shiite theologians constructed their new doctrinal synthesis on the Imamate. In summary, the Imami or Twelver Shiites regarded the Imamate not as an evolutionary consequence of the religion of Islam but as one of its basic and necessary ingredients, as fundamental as belief in the One God or in the Prophet's mission. The Imamate had been established by God as part of the primordial nature of things. There was a cycle of transcendental Imams in the *pleroma*, and in their historical manifestation they are the intermediaries between that transcendental world and the universe of humanity. Each Imam is God's "proof" (*hujja*), and as such they are all impeccable and infallible. Moreover, they are the sole repositories of the understanding of the true, albeit hidden (*batin*) sense of Scripture. This divine knowledge was transmitted to Ali, the first Imam, by the Prophet himself and by Ali to his successors in each generation.

According to most Shiites, the Imamate passed from generation to generation by designation at the hands of the previous Imam. Where there are major differences of opinion is on the designated heir of the sixth Imam, Jafar al-Sadiq. The question arose whether the Imamate passed to his eldest son Ismail (d. 760), whom he had formally designated his successor but who predeceased his own father, or to his younger son, Musa al-Kazim (d. 799), whom Jafar had designated Imam after Ismail's death despite the fact that Ismail had a surviving son, Muhammad. Could the designation be taken back, in effect, or did it necessarily descend on the dead Ismail's infant son? The different answers to this question set in train the division between the so-called Ismaili Shiites who regarded Ismail's son Muhammad as the only genuine Imam, and Imami Shiites who recognized Musa al-Kazim and his descendants as Imams.

This was the distinction in the eighth century, but by the tenth the two groups had taken an additional and significant step apart: the Imamis embraced, as we have seen, the notion of the concealment of the twelfth Imam in their line. This reportedly occurred sometime about 878, and though the direction of the community rested for a spell in the hands of deputies, by the mid–tenth century the Imamites had accepted the fact that there was no longer an Imam in the flesh and that until his return as the Mahdi, they were solely a spiritual community, a concession that, for all its attractiveness for the intelligentsia, had surrendered the Imamis' claim to the highest political power in Islam.

Sunnis and Shiites

The Party of Ali thus maintained that (1) the umma was primarily a spiritual community, a "church" that runs a "state," so to speak; (2) its leader or Imam—a term they preferred to "caliph"—should likewise be a spiritual leader; if not a prophet like Muhammad, then a charismatic governing and teaching authority; and finally (3) God in the Quran—Shiites eventually dropped their accusations that the actual text had been tampered with—and Muhammad in his public pronouncement (since suppressed) had announced that Ali was rightfully that Imam and that his family would hold the office after him. They never really did so; the actual power remained in the hands of the majority Sunnis, shorthand for "partisans of custom (sunna) and the unity of the umma," who were content to accept the "facts" created by history in all its worldly imperfection.

The point at issue thus is who shall rule the umma. The Sunnis were willing to accept the verdict of history as reflected in the choices of that "whole first generation" of Muhammad's contemporaries and their immediate successors. The Shiites argued against history in asserting Ali's preeminence, but in so doing they were forced, to one degree or another, to attack the consensual wisdom of the Companions of the Prophet from whom all the Prophetic sunna ultimately derived. Disappointed by history, the Shiites turned where some Jewish groups may also have resorted, to a Gnostic wisdom, a kind of particularist and underground sunna transmitted, generation after generation, by infallible Imams of the Alid house or by their delegates. In fully developed Shiism, which found its most lasting base by connecting itself with Persian nationalism, the entire range of Gnostic ideas is on display: the exaltation of wisdom (*hikma*) over science (*ilm*); a view of historical events as a reflection of cosmic reality; and a concealed (*batin*) as opposed to an open (*zahir*) interpretation of Scripture. It was simply a matter of time before Shiite Gnosticism found its siblings within Sufism and philosophy (see II/9).

When Westerners returned to the Middle East at the beginning of modern times as travelers, traders, missionaries, and merchants, some thought they could best understand the Sunnis and Shiites as, respectively, a version of Catholics and Protestants. Or so it seemed to some Catholic adventurers who saw the Sunnis as the "orthodox" Muslims and the minority Shiites as some species of heterodoxy, an attiitude that has not entirely disappeared. Functionally speaking, the opposite seems closer to the truth. The Christian bishop and the Shiite Imam show the same charismatically transmitted powers and may speak definitively, if not infallibly, on behalf of God. The Roman Catholic view of the papal magisterium is in fact very close to that of the Shiites toward the Imam (see II/6). One difference, however, is that whereas in Islam the transmission of that magisterium is by both designation and descent from the Holy Family, the Christian episcopate is an office held by a clergy that is celibate and so, by definition, without issue: the bishop receives his teaching powers by designation alone.

The Hidden Imam

The eleventh Imam in the sequence followed by the Twelver Shiites was Hasan al-Askari, whose tenure began in 873. He died the following year, but had a son, it was reported, born in 868 or thereabouts, bearing the Prophet's own name of Abu Qasim Muhammad. There were problems: some Shiites had apparently not heard of this son and turned instead to Hasan's brother Jafar, who denied there had been any son. Most were convinced that young Muhammad was the true Imam. He was nowhere to be found, however, and thus there began to circulate the same story of a concealment or an "occultation" that had earlier been broached in extremist and Ismaili circles.

Note: The place of the Imam's final concealment was later identified as a cave near the tombs of earlier Imams at Samarra in Iraq. Within it was a well down which Muhammad was said to have disappeared. The caliph al-Nasir had the place walled off in 1209, but Shiites continue to visit and pray for the return of the Hidden Imam.

There was confusion for a spell among the Shiat Ali, some following Jafar as the twelfth Imam while others were convinced that the disappeared Muhammad was the legitimate successor to the Imamate. A certain Uthman al-Amari put himself forward as the Hidden Imam's spokesman; he had in fact held that same position under both the tenth and eleventh Imams, who had rarely appeared in public for fear of Sunni reprisals. The new phenomenon of a Hidden Imam must have seemed little different from the prevailing custom of an Imam who had little or no public presence. Thus the system continued to function through an intermediary or delegate who, one after another, appeared to speak for the concealed Muhammad. They brought him the monies paid by the Shiites as their alms-tithe and carried back answers to questions posed to the Imams.

There may have been doubts about this arrangement from the beginning, and there were problems with the four "delegates"—they called themselves "gates" or "ambassadors"—of the now long-departed Abu Qasim Muhammad. There was a rather abrupt solution. In 941 the last of these deputies produced a document from the Hidden Imam announcing that the period of the Lesser Concealment was over and that henceforward there would be no delegates or spokesmen, no direct communication. The Lord of the Ages, who was still alive, though in another, spiritual dimension, had gone into a permanent Greater Concealment, not to return until the events preceding the Day of Judgment.

The concealment of the Imam, the infallible guide and head of the community, had repercussions on the entire structure of Shiite Islam. It was first thought that at the Great Concealment in 941 the Imams' functions were in abeyance, that everything from the conduct of a holy war, to the enforcement of the sharia, to the collection of the zakat had effectively lapsed. No law-based community could survive, however, without an executive or judicial authority of some sort, and soon Shiite lawyers were exploring the possibility of the delegation of at least some of the Imam's powers. By the fifteenth century it was fairly generally established among Shiites that their ulama exercised what they called a "general representation" of the Hidden Imam and thus were empowered to collect the zakat on the Imam's behalf and even to declare a jihad in defense of the faith. In the end, their ulama, particularly in Iran, had established a wide-ranging authority among the Shiites.

The Twelver or Imami Shiites generally remained politically quiescent under the watchful eyes of the Abbasid caliphs down to the concealment of the twelfth Imam of their line. Thenceforward they remained a closed, scholarly community, with ties to some of the Sufi movements of the day (on Sufis, see II/9), preserved from extinction by their willingness to dissemble when necessary, and ruled by an indifferently trained body of clerics. The other major branch of the Shiat Ali opted for a more activist, radical, and even revolutionary course. Supporters of the Hidden Imam Muhammad ibn Ismail appeared at various points in the Abode of Islam in the ninth century as "announcers" (*dais*) of the return of that Imam as Mahdi in eastern Iran, Syria, and southern Iraq, where sometime about 875 they recruited a certain Hamdan Qarmat.

Political Ismailism: The Fatimids

Sometimes called the "Seveners," the followers of Ismail, son of Jafar al-Sadiq, and of his descendants, led an obscure existence in the Abode of Islam for most of the eighth and early ninth centuries. Then, in the second half of the ninth century, two diverse movements sprung from the same Shiite soil, the Qarmatians and the Ismailis properly so-called. Their "call" (*dawa*), as these early Ismailis called their movement, was heard in southern Iraq and Bahrain—this latter the proper locus of the Qarmatian "branch" of the larger movement—as well as northwestern Iran and North Africa. The original substance of the call was the announcement of Ismail's infant son Muhammad's concealment and the promise of his eventual return as the Mahdi. There, however, the two groups parted company. Whereas the main body of Ismailis believed that the return of the Imam had taken place in a person named Ubaydallah in Ifriqiyya (modern Tunisia), the Qarmatians continued to await the perhaps distant End Time return of their leader.

The main base for the ninth-century Ismailis was at Salamiyya in Syria, where there came into existence a line of "grand masters" who were regarded as the "guarantor" or proof (*hujja*) of the expected Imam-Mahdi. Missionaries were dispatched throughout the Abode of Islam, and particularly to the Twelver Shiite communities still in disarray after the death of the eleventh Imam and the announcement that his son and presumed successor was in concealment. The call enjoyed some success in Iraq, the Yemen, and North Africa, enough apparently for the fourth grand master to announce in 899 that he was in fact the Mahdi. The proclamation was filled with consequence. For those unwilling to accept the claim, like the Qarmatians, it meant at best separation and at worst outright hostility toward those who believed the messianic voice from Salamiyya. For those who did heed and accept, it meant the kind of overt, and obviously dangerous, political action that ensued with the onset of Islam's messianic era.

Action was taken: there were Ismaili insurrections in the name of the Mahdi-Imam in Syria and the Yemen, but the call was most successful among the Berbers of North Africa. The Mahdi himself left Syria and took up residence in what is now Morocco, where he directed military operations in Algeria and Tunisia. In 909 the Tunisian metropolis of Qairwan fell to his troops and the Imam took up residence in his newly founded capital of al-Mahdiyya, declared the existence of an Imam state, and assumed the caliphate under the title of Abdallah al-Mahdi. There were, however, none of the signs expected at the onset of the eschaton, or End Time, and Abdallah's son and designated successor, who not unexpectedly called himself by the Prophet's own name of Abu Qasim Muhammad ibn Abdallah, had to suppress the voices of dissent. The triumphant Ismailis soon conquered Egypt, where in 969 they lay down the foundations of their new city, Cairo, and then moved on to Palestine and Syria, where they reigned as spiritual and political sovereigns until they were dislodged by the Turks in 1171.

The Fatimids—as the dynasty was known, to stress its descent from both Ali and Fatima in contrast to the Abbasids, who claimed descent from Ali alone—soon vacated their eschatological claims. The End—the *qiyama*, or "resurrection," in Ismaili parlance—was not yet, and in the meantime there would be an indefinite line of caliph-Imams to rule the Abode of Islam. This meant that the traditional Islam of the "Pillars" and its traditional law (sharia) were still firmly in place. The Sunnis now under Ismaili political control were not constrained to embrace Shiism—such a course may have been far too dangerous, politically speaking—but the Fatimids did make strenuous efforts to convert them. Missionary dais were trained in the new dawa center in Cairo, al-Azhar, which eventually turned into Islam's largest, most prestigious, and influential (Sunni) school of religious studies and still dispatches Muslim missionaries all over the globe. From al-Azhar they were sent into the Fatimid provinces to instruct and persuade the Sunni majority and sent under cover into the caliph's domains to subvert the Sunni regime, which they attempted—unsuccessfully, as it turned out—with a combination of propaganda and terrorism.

The foundations of Ismaili Fatimid political power had originally been laid down among the perennially dissident Berber tribes, who had already bucked the tide in their adherence to Donatism in the fifth century and Kharijism in the seventh. The Ismaili call was not dissimilar to those earlier appeals or to the later ones that carried the Berbers into Spain as Almoravids and Almohads: a heightened sense of community, a puritanical ethic, and a call to holy war against the "false" Muslims outside the movement. Within the new community of Ismailis a warrior class was recruited from among the Berber tribes, and the Berbers provided the bulk of the fighting force that carried the Fatimids across North Africa to conquer Egypt and nearly the caliphate itself.

The Fatimid claims to the Imamate varied over the period covered by the initiation of the call in Ifriqiyya, through the critical reign of the Imam Muizz (r. 953–975), down to the last fatal schism in the movement at the time of Imam Mustansir (r. 1036–1094), but it varied, in any event, from the more straightforward call to apocalyptic revolution being broadcast by the Qarmatians. The Ismaili Fatimids had by contrast an elaborate metaphysics of the Imamate and a state that developed along lines not very different from those of the Abbasid caliphate. From the beginning the Fatimids underlined the special religious and eschatological qualities of the new Imamate. Later, under Muizz, they backed off somewhat from these claims and cast their emphases instead on a speculative theology of a cosmic Imamate and their own position as *locum tenentes*.

We know a good deal about that version of Ismaili theology and its marked Gnostic and Neoplatonic coloring from one of the chief surviving documents of esoteric (*batin*) Ismailism, the *Tracts of the Brethren of Purity*. This was a kind of encyclopedic statement of the Ismaili message for the use of their missionaries sent forth from the propaganda center in the new Fatimid capital of Cairo (see II/9).

Muizz's reforms neither intended nor succeeded in secularizing the office of the Fatimid Imam whose titles and ceremonial remained filled with echoes of Mahdism and quasi-divine powers. The "materialization" of these tendencies culminated in the divine claims of the Imam al-Hakim (d. 1021) and the creation of the Druze sect, named after one of its prominent missionaries, al-Darazi. Al-Hakim's view of himself as a divinized or divine Imam found little support among his subjects, and his successors returned to a modest posture on the Imamate as simply a more authentic alternative for the Sunni caliphate. With the return to modesty came a turning as well to another Abbasid pattern, the delegation or loss of powers to more secular and military forces, the viziers and generals of the realm.

With the decline of the Fatimid power center in Egypt, the widely scattered Ismaili diaspora—the creation of those energetic dais—was increasingly left to its own resources. There was a considerable Ismaili apparatus in Iran, which, with schism and political impotence in Cairo, was taken over by the dai Hasan ibn al-Sabbah, who sometime before 1090 installed himself in the impregnable fortress of Alamut in Daylam, south of the Caspian Sea. Hasan never claimed the Imamate for himself; he was merely the hujja, here understood as the custodian of Ismaili doctrine until the return of the Imam-Mahdi. One of his more desperate, or optimistic, successors went considerably beyond that. The Mahdi had returned; the eschatological resurrection was at hand (see II/10), and with it the abrogation of traditional Islam. It brought climax but no satisfaction. The entire movement went down under the deluge of the Mongol invasion.

Apocalyptic Ismailism: The Qarmatians

The Qarmatians, who took their name from their founder, Hamdan Qarmat, are a branch of the Ismaili Shiites who found fertile ground for the call in southern Iraq and in settlements along the western coast of the Persian Gulf. Wherever they made inroads, they prepared a kind of redoubt, a fortified place called a dar al-hijra, or "migration shelter," that would serve them as the same kind of refuge that Medina had once been for the Prophet. In 899, as we have seen, the new grand master of the Ismailis announced that the movement was no longer about the return of the Imam because he was in fact the Imam. The Qarmatians refused to believe the claim and so diverged in both ideology and politics from the parent group that was by then firmly established as the Fatimid dynasty in Egypt. The Qarmatians were just as deeply established in southern Iraq—though rather too close to the caliph's military forces, who finally tamed them—and at Bahrain and other centers on the gulf. From these they raided widely across the entire Fertile Crescent and took particular advantage of pilgrims heading to and from Mecca. In 930 the Qarmatians stormed Mecca itself and carried off the Black Stone from the Kaaba. They held it for more than twenty years until the Abbasid caliph managed to buy it back from them.

The Qarmatians never relented in their opposition to the Egyptian Ismailis and their Imams, though at one point in 931 their chief *dai* announced that a young Iranian prisoner of war was in fact the Imam-Mahdi and that the End Time had begun. That move aborted, as did all initiatives at reconciliation with the main body of the Ismailiyya. The Qarmatians survived as an organized community in some gulf settlements until the fourteenth century, when they gradually and almost imperceptibly became Twelver Shiites.

The Sultanate

At the height of their power, the Ismaili Fatimids had extended their call from their base in Egypt westward across North Africa to Morocco—the Umayyad declaration in Spain that theirs was a genuine caliphate was a reaction to the approach of the Fatimids across the straits—and eastward through Palestine and parts of Syria that they held. Their agents were spreading the revolutionary message at the very heart of the caliphate in Iraq and Iran in the eleventh century. Sunni, caliphal Islam was under a grave threat and was likely saved by the arrival on the scene of intrepid warrior bands who were as loyal to Sunnism and the caliph as they were implacable soldiers. But they also brought a new element of power into the Abode of Islam: if the Turks saved the caliphate, the caliph had thenceforth to share his throne with the newcomers.

Sultan is a quranic term meaning simply power or authority, and early in Islam it came to be applied without a great deal of technical precision to sovereign political authority, frequently as a synonym of *mulk*, "possession," hence "kingship" or "sovereignty." The Abbasids used it that way, and it is noteworthy that they spoke of conferring *sultan* on the "amir of amirs." In the latter office, that of grand amir or commander-in-chief, lay the true origins of the sultanate as a distinct and autonomous power in Islam. In 936 the caliph al-Radi formally appointed as the first tenant of that office the Turkish general Ibn al-Raiq and so vested in him the highest civil and military functions of the state, functions formerly divided between a civilian vizier or prime minister and a military amir or commander. The grand amirate passed to successive military families who filled the post and exercised its functions until the arrival in Baghdad of the Saljuq Turks.

The Saljuq captain Tughril assumed the title of sultan in 1038, and it appears that the chiefs of another Turkish dynasty in Afghanistan, the Ghaznavids, began using the same title shortly thereafter. Like the Saljuqs, the Ghaznavids were nominally delegates of the caliph with respect to their Islamic sovereignty—their purely Turkish or tribal sovereignty was quite another matter—and there were the usual negotiations between caliph and Ghaznavid sultan concerning titles, honors, and jurisdiction. But the Saljuqs eventually lodged themselves in Baghdad, as the Ghaznavids did not, and so became, like others before them, the actual custodians of their nominal sovereign.

There was no real difference between the office of the grand amir and that of sultan, the title preferred by the Saljuqs to describe the same sovereignty, power, and privileges: full financial, military, and administrative control; the mention of the sultan's name immediately after the caliph's in the Friday prayers; the right to coin money, to grant and confiscate fiefs; and, finally, the use of Islam's now considerable stock of honorific signs, badges, and titles.

Nor should the authority be regarded as essentially secular. The sultan's titles had the same religious aura about them as the caliph's own. The grand amirs of the Buyid family unashamedly promoted Shiism in their domains at the heart of the caliphate, while the Ayyubid sultan Salah al-Din restored Sunnism to Egypt, and both the Ghaznavid and Saljuq sultans relentlessly pursued Ismailis. Finally, the Saljuqs were intimately involved in the promotion of the Shafite-Asharite brand of jurisprudence to a position of well-advertised prominence in the Abode of Islam.

The coexisting caliphate and sultanate have been called "superimposed monarchies" in that both offices possessed a power that was at the same time personal and absolute. The sultan had to be invested by the caliph with his sovereignty—he was constitutionally the caliph's delegate—but once in possession of such sovereignty, the sultan's power was in fact unlimited. The sultan was, of course, bound by Islamic law. But that point was largely moot since there was no instrument to guarantee its observance in the face of such sovereignty. What most severely limited the sultanate, however, was its failure to achieve the ecumenical status of the caliphate. While there was only one caliph, with the occasional anticaliph, there were in fact many sultans in the Abode of Islam, and within their domains their own amirs waxed powerful on the feudal system of land grants. But if the sultan could not speak for Islam, and if the caliph had long since ceased to do so, others as a class were beginning to find their voice, the ulama, or scholars of the sharia (see II/4).

The dispersal of sultanic power is clearest in the case of the Saljuq Turks. Islamic (and Persian) notions of absolutism ran counter to the tradition of the steppe, where the khans shared power within a family of uncles, brothers, and sons. The head of the family, the sultan on whom the caliph bestowed title and insignia, was not slow perhaps to grasp both the notion of absolute sovereignty and the principle of succession. But the hasty appointment of the sultan's son as the official heir did not guarantee the latter's peaceful or uncontested succession to his father in the face of the traditional claims of his brothers and uncles. The result was the frequent separation of Iraq from eastern Iran, various Turkish appanages in Syria, and, finally, an entirely independent Saljuq sultanate in Anatolia.

The Ottomans and a Universal Caliphate

The Abbasid caliph went down in the destruction of Baghdad by the Mongols in 1258. In Syria and Egypt, however, the Mamluk sultans—military slaves who promoted themselves to sovereignty in Egypt in 1250 and held it until they were unseated by the Ottomans in 1517—turned back the Mongol advance. In the sequel, they provided themselves with an Abbasid "survivor" of the Mongol debacle in Baghdad and so could claim to possess, no matter what later historians might think, a legitimate caliph of their own in Cairo.

Note: There were other survivors of, other debacles. The original Muslims invaders of Spain in the early seventh century were mixed Berber and Arab bands, and once they had stabilized Muslim control of at least central and southern Iberia, al-Andalus, as the Muslim territory was called, was ruled by a series of amirs, military men turned governors, and often rivals, who ruled in the name of the caliph in Damascus. In 750 the Umayyads of Damascus were overturned by a rival dynasty, the Abbasids, who engineered a wholesale massacre of the house of Umayya. There was a survivor, however, one Abd al-Rahman, who made his way, amid almost legendary travail, to Spain in 756. He seized power there and gradually unified the Muslim domains into a single amirate based in Cordoba. It was a brilliant time, and the greatest of the Spanish Umayyad line was Abd al-Rahman III (r. 912–961), who in 929 declared that henceforward he should be regarded not as amir but as caliph and commander of the faithful. There was a caliph in Baghdad, an Abbasid, but the gesture was not directed so much to Baghdad as to Abd al-Rahman's closer and far more dangerous enemies, the Fatimid Ismailis whose caliph-Imam ruled all of North Africa from Qairwan and who were contesting control of the Mediterranean with the Umayyads of Spain. The Spanish caliphate finally expired, without much remark, in 1031.

The Ottoman Turks were not so nice in their pretensions, perhaps, and when in 1517 they absorbed the Mamluk sultanate into their own burgeoning domains—they already possessed Anatolia and a good part of the Balkans—they simply asserted that the caliphate had been bequeathed to them. Thus the reigning member of the house of Osman was both sultan or padishah, the political sovereign of the Ottoman Empire, and caliph and commander of the faithful for the entire Muslim community, as they would claim to be for the next four hundred years.

Though the office continued and the caliph enjoyed a degree of spiritual *auctoritas*, already by the tenth century his political *potentia* (on the distinction, see I/7) was limited to what might be called the caliphal states in Iraq. By the next century even that had disappeared, and the only real power in the Abode of Islam rested in the hands of the various amirs who ruled, sometimes carefully in the caliph's name, at other times carelessly or defiantly not. Muslim theorists eventually made a place for this usurpation of power, as we have seen, under the rubric of the sultanate, but so strong was the notion of a single and universal umma that the traditionalists invariably spoke as if there were one sultan, the amir who executed the caliph's will, when actually there were many from Spain to India and beyond, and the will they executed was invariably their own.

Was the caliph a kind of Muslim pope? Even in his purely episcopal role, the bishop of Rome had, like the other bishops of Christendom, far more authority than his counterpart in Baghdad or Istanbul. Though a bishop's jurisdiction was limited to his see, he could speak out definitively on matters of faith and morals. But once the claim to primacy put forward by the bishop of Rome was accepted as such in the Western churches, the pope's jurisdiction became truly imperial, and from the eleventh century on, when the caliphs were yielding to their Turkish sultans, the popes were vindicating their claims to superiority over their own sultans, the emperors (see I/7). The Eastern Churches only fitfully, and usually under duress, accepted the papal claim to absolute primacy, but they recognized that the pope certainly spoke for Western Christendom.

Recognition of a universal caliphate was far more nominal. It was rejected in fact, at least in its embodiment in an Abbasid or Ottoman claimant, by the Umayyad caliphs in Cordoba, by the Ismailis in North Africa and Egypt, and by the Imami Safavids in Iran. And among the regimes that were Sunni, or even claimed direct linear descent from the Prophet—the so-called sharifs or sayyids—recognition of the caliph often included little more than the mention of his name in the Friday prayers. Foreign policy was not directed by, taxes were not sent to, nor was instruction requested or received from the vague eminence in Baghdad or Cairo or the caliph who lay all but concealed behind the sultan in Istanbul.

The End of the Caliphate

By the early twentieth century Turkish rule was probably the most long-lived and vigorous of all the political realities of Islam, ancient and accustomed enough, at any rate, for some Sunni Muslim theoreticians to continue to maintain the notion of Islam as a universal and undivided theocratic community ruled by a succession of single and unique "deputies" (khalifa) of the Prophet descended from the noble clan of the Quraysh. The caliph, in the later, more pragmatic understanding—the one still current in the opening decades of the twentieth century—might, however, be any Muslim ruler who ensured that the principles and law of Islam were upheld. The Ottoman sovereigns certainly qualified under those conditions, and if they arrogated to themselves some of the titles, regalia, and perquisites of the earlier "universal" caliphate, there was no great harm in that: it strengthened the institution by affirming it's, and Islam's, continuing connection with the glorious past. But the reality was understood by most Muslims, and the sovereign in Istanbul was invariably referred to not as "the caliph" but as "the sultan."

The name of caliph still had powerful associations, however—strong enough to tempt the Ottomans to invoke it on occasion, and in jurisdictions into which the theory did not quite stretch: to those Muslims, for example, who were once but no longer the political subjects of the Ottoman sultan, like the Muslims of North Africa or Egypt, or Muslims who had never been, like the millions of the Islamic confession on the Indian subcontinent and in East

Asia. This was the aspect of the caliphate that was clearly being tested with the Ottoman call for a holy war in 1916. The lack of response to the caliph's summons illustrates the limits that most Muslims placed on their understanding of the Ottoman caliphate.

The Ottomans' call to holy war was never answered, and the Muslims of North Africa and India remained truer to their colonial masters than to their putative pope in Istanbul. In 1918 the Ottoman Empire went down in defeat along with its German and Austro-Hungarian allies, but out of the debacle arose the new state that called itself the Turkish Republic. On 28 January 1920 the deputies to the Ottoman National Assembly moved from Istanbul to Ankara. There they signed the Turkish National Pact declaring themselves in permanent session until the independence of the fatherland and the caliphate should be guaranteed. Two years later, however, the matter appeared somewhat differently. On 31 October 1922, the primary political institution of the Ottoman and Muslim past, the sultanate, was abolished, and though the office of the caliph was left untouched, its divorce from the sultanate effectively stripped it of whatever powers it may have possessed. On 17 November the last sultan, Muhammad Wahid al-Din, fled on a British ship to Malta, and two days later his cousin Abd al-Majid was elected to the vacant caliphate to preside, with severely limited powers, over a new, laicized Islam. On 29 October 1923 the revolution was accomplished: the Turkish Republic was proclaimed.

The laicization process went even further, as many of the traditionalists feared. On 3 March 1924 the Turkish National Assembly abolished the caliphate itself, an office the Ottomans had held for 407 years, and finally on 9 April 1928 that same body abrogated Article 2 of the Ottoman Constitution: Islam was no longer the religion of the state. Abd al-Majid was informed of the decision regarding the caliphate on the evening of the same day it was taken, and was told that he should prepare to leave the country forthwith. The family immediately began to pack its belongings, which were loaded onto trucks. At five the next morning all was ready. Abd al-Majid and his son occupied one car, the women and their attendants a second, and the cortege, escorted by the chief of police and patrolmen on motorcycles, left Istanbul and then, shortly afterward, the country itself.

Iran as a Shiite State

The destiny of Sunni Islam rested for centuries in the hands of the Ottoman Turks, who extended the borders of the Abode of Islam deep into the Christian Balkans and even to the gates of Vienna. Where they had less success was against their own Muslim rivals in Iran.

The community that later came to rule Iran as a dynasty, the Safavids, began their career as a Sufi tariqa, or religious order (see II/9), founded by one Safi al-Din (d. 1334) in northwestern Iran. His order, Sunni in its doctrine and sentiments, spread widely over southeastern Turkey and northern Iraq and Iran, and under its fourth sheikh managed to carve out for itself an autonomous political territory in northwestern Iran. Thus, by the mid–fifteenth century, the Safavid tariqa had become a political entity as well as a Sufi association. More, it veered sharply in the direction of a Shiism of the extremist variety—its sheikh was beginning to be regarded as himself a manifestation of God.

In 1494 a sheikh named Ismail (d. 1524) assumed the leadership of the order and of the still modest Safavid state in northern Iran. Iran at that time was still overwhelmingly Sunni in its allegiances and ideology, although there were already important Shiite influences at places like Qom and Neyshabur, and there were growing Shiite tendencies in some of the other Sufi orders, including the Safavid tariqa. By Ismail's time there was little doubt where Safavid thinking was. As the Fatimid Ismailis had claimed for their leaders in their day, in his followers' eyes Ismail was the Twelver Imam now returned from his concealment, and his troops reportedly cried out, on entering battle, "There is no god but The God and Ismail is the Friend of God." Battle they did, for ten years (1499–1509), until in the end Ismail and the Safavids ruled most of Iran. Already in 1501 Ismail had proclaimed Shiism the official version of Islam in his new kingdom.

The Safavids early possessed political sovereignty, bought at the end of a sword, but their claim to religious legitimacy was considerably less certain. The house, which was likely Türkmen or Kurdish in origin, claimed to have descended from Ali by way of the seventh Imam, Musa al-Kazim. This of itself gave Ismail prestige but no religious authority, and his claim that he was the Imam was entertained by none but his own most favored entourage of warriors. Most of his followers, and the population generally, appear to have known little about Twelver Shiism to begin with, and the more learned Shiite ulama whom Ismail and his successors invited to Iran seemed little inclined to unmask the pretensions of their benefactors. For most of the population, it was a relatively easy transition from Sunni to Shiite Islam, involving little more than heaping praise on Ali—never difficult among even the most devout Sunnis—and obloquy on his enemies, notably the Umayyads, and, where circumstances dictated, on the first three caliphs, who had usurped Ali's rightful position at the head of the umma. The only religious resistance that might in fact be expected would likely come from the Sunni tariqas. Ismail took no chances: the Sufi orders were disbanded.

The planting of deeper Shiite roots into Iranian soil was the work of Shah Abbas (d. 1629). His predecessors had already begun to disassociate the regime's ideology from its extremist origins, and Shah Abbas established more formal ties to normative Twelver Shiism by inviting Shiite ulama elsewhere to come to Iran and founding for the first time Shiite madrasas for the formal education of native clergy. Shah Abbas directed most of his attention to Isfahan, but under the next dynasty to rule Iran, the Qajars (1794–1925), similar colleges were opened, again with state support, in Najaf (now in Iraq), Qom, and Mashhad, which remain the chief centers of Shiite learning. The shahs' own connection with the Imams, meanwhile, fell increasingly into the background.

The Safavid regime managed to survive until 1722 when Afghans from the east penetrated the crumbling kingdom and took Isfahan. By their demise the Safavids had, however, established in an overwhelmingly Sunni world an apparently irreversible Shiite state, not the first in the Middle East but certainly the most powerful, and bound by strong ties to Iranian national sentiments. Shiites have never constituted more than 10 to 15 percent of the Muslim population as a whole. They remain the overwhelming majority in Iran, but it is probable—it is to nobody's interest to count, or be counted, too accurately—that they also constitute more than half the Muslims in Iraq, Lebanon, and Bahrain and are a significant presence in Sunni Pakistan and multiconfessional India.

The Shiite Ulama and the State

Shiites have always stood somewhat apart from the state. As a potentially revolutionary minority within an overarching system of Sunni sovereignty, Shiites have tended for most of their history to regard "church" and "state," the Shiite community of (true) believers (muminun) and the Sunni caliphate of submitters (muslimun), as separate institutions. Tactically they might practice "dissembling" (taqiyya) toward the latter (see II/4), but in what concerned their religious practices, their instructors were the ulama, Shiism's lawyers. The Shiite ulama were, however, neither as numerous nor as well trained as their Sunni counterparts until the sixteenth century. While the Sunni ulama were being formally trained in the expanding madrasa system—itself possibly a derivative of an earlier Ismaili Shiite experiment in Cairo—the Shiite lawyer-clergy received their instruction somewhat haphazardly in an apprentice arrangement, novice by master, with little certifiable competence on the part of either. Under Shah Abbas, however, the madrasa system was introduced into what was by then a Shiite Iran and thereafter the Shiite ulama, often known as mullahs, grew rapidly in skill, power, and prestige.

From about 1600, then, the Shiite ulama, who claimed for themselves the "general representation" of the Hidden Imam, had the option of cooperating with the government, resisting, or disregarding it. In most cases they have done the latter, which is obviously the most prudent course in Sunni-dominated lands and even when the regime is "secular," as in most of the modern states that constitute what was once the Abode of Islam. In Safavid Iran in contrast, the newly invigorated ulama often dominated the government. Under their more secular successors, the Qajars and then the Pahlavis (r. 1925–1979), and particularly with the triumph of the "interpretationist" over the "transmissionist" wing among the ulama (see II/4), Iranian mullahs forcefully intervened in politics, especially from Iraq, where they were beyond government control, against the king and for constitutional reform in 1906, for example. The constitution that was finally adopted on that occasion recognized Twelver Shiism as the official religion of the Iranian state and appointed a board of five *mujtahids*, or "interpreters," to screen all new legislation for its agreement with the sharia, an arrangement never put into effect. In more recent times, the Shiite mullahs were the single most potent force in unseating the shah of Iran in 1979 and establishing an Islamic republic.

The Islamic Republic of Iran

Ayatollah Khomeini, the prominent Shiite mullah instrumental in overthrowing the shah of Iran in January 1979, returned home in triumph from his Paris exile in February of that year to begin the momentous task not merely of putting in place a new government but of constructing a new state. What sort of state he preferred Khomeini had already made clear in his *Governance of the Cleric* (*Velayat-e Faqih*), which had appeared in 1970. In a referendum of 30–31 March 1979, the people were given the stark choice: an Islamic republic, yes or no? The answer was an overwhelming "yes" and the Ayatollah proclaimed its establishment on 1 April of that year. At the end of the summer an assembly of experts, most of them from Khomeini's Islamic Republic Party, started work on a draft constitution, which was submitted to a popular referendum, again with a simple yes or no choice and again overwhelmingly approved by the electorate. The Islamic Republic was a reality.

Iran had had a constitution and some form of republican government since the Constitutional Revolution of 1906–1911, but this latest version, though it preserved some of the republican structure, was radically different. It was wrought to ensure that the rule of law would be the rule of the sharia (as understood by the Imami Shiites) and that governance would in fact be "governance of the cleric." The first principle is asserted in the preamble of the Constitution and often thereafter. "Legislation, which forms guidelines for the direction of society" must, the preamble dictates, "be based on the Quran and the sunna," and thus the Constitution is founded on "the fundaments of Islamic principles and guidelines." Article 2 ties state legislation to the sharia by describing legislation as a power reserved to God and acknowledging that revelation has a fundamental role in the promulgation of laws. Article 4 states that "all laws and regulations . . . must be based on Islamic principles." Article 72 forbids the parliament to pass laws that "contradict the principles and ordinances of the state religion and the land." The same restriction is imposed on local councils, whose resolutions must agree with

"Islamic principles." Article 170 makes it incumbent on judges to refuse to implement government resolutions and decrees when these "contravene Islamic laws and regulations."

The clearest statement of principle is contained in Article 2 of the Constitution:

1. There is only one God . . . who by right is ruler and lawgiver, and man must submit to his command.

2. Divine revelation has a role to play in the promulgation of the laws.

3. The resurrection plays an essential role in the process of man's development vis-à-vis God.

4. God's justice is inherent in his creation and his law.

5. The Imamate will provide the leadership and will play a fundamental role in the progress of the Islamic revolution.

6. Man is endowed with nobility and elevated dignity; his freedom entails responsibility before God.

The governance of the Imami Shiite clerics is guaranteed by the most striking feature of the structure of the new Islamic Republic: side by side with the traditional republican institutions of elected executive, legislative, and judicial officials runs a parallel line of clerics, most of them appointed, who exercise a quite literal guardianship over the acts and enactments of their elected counterparts. Thus the president is "shadowed" by a religious leader, the parliament by a council of guardians, and the civil courts by religious ones. The purpose of this second, shadow government in the Islamic Republic of Iran is perfectly clear. As Article 2 of the Constitution expresses it, by means of "continual *ijtihad* [interpretation] exercised by qualified jurists on the basis of the Quran and the sunna of those who are infallible [that is, the Imams](God's peace be upon them all), . . . justice as well as political, economic, social, and cultural independence and national solidarity will be achieved." That power is expressed chiefly in the appointed clerics' right to void any acts or legislation deemed contrary to the sharia.

An Early Modern Christian Theocracy: Reform Geneva

There have not been many attempts at establishing a thoroughly Christian theocracy of the type presently operating in Iran. One of the most striking and interesting occurred early in the Reformation. In the late Middle Ages, Geneva was a city-state ruled, like many others, by a prince-bishop, though in this case under the influence and control of the neighboring duchy of Savoy, a much larger state with extensive holdings in northern Italy and southern France. The Genevans would not have it so: they revolted against Savoy and declared their independence not only of the duchy but of their own prince-archbishop. It was an exceedingly bold move and succeeded only because of the backing of the powerful Swiss republic of Bern, which may have had its own designs on Geneva. In the end Geneva escaped both Savoy and Bern and was free to pursue its own course, which was to dismantle its civil and ecclesiastical administration. Swept up in Reform zeal, it chased from the city the clerics, monks, and nuns who had constituted not only the episcopal establishment but the educated elite. This was a major displacement, and to fill the void, the burghers of Geneva threw open their doors to like-minded reformers from elsewhere, particularly neighboring France.

Among those who thought the prospect interesting was the Frenchman John Calvin (d. 1564), already the author of the *Institutes*, a blueprint for a new Reformed Christian community. In 1536 he accepted an invitation to move to Geneva, lecture there, and assist in the city's reform. Two years later Calvin published his *Articles for the Goverance of the Church*. In it he set stringent norms for being admitted to participation in the Eucharist, now the Lord's Supper (see II/6). He further required that all citizens of Geneva make a profession of faith in the form of an oath; those who refused to do so were banished from the city's lands. Geneva was not yet ready for such a regime and Calvin was soon pressured out of the city. His followers eventually prevailed, however, and he returned in 1541 and enjoyed almost total control of Geneva for the next fourteen years—long enough for him and his immediate successor, Theodore Beza (d. 1605), to establish a distinct brand of Reform Christianity in that city. Theirs was a reform not merely in doctrine, which had been the chief aim of Luther and his followers, but of behavior and practice. The city became, in effect, a Christian theocracy.

In a set of laws he drew up for Geneva, Calvin set up four principal ministries: a body of pastors to preach the Word of God; of scholars to study that Word; of elders to supervise the Christian behavior of the citizens; and of deacons to administer charity, each governed collectively by its members. The pastors meeting in common constituted the Company, of which Calvin himself was Moderator, and governed the Genevan Church, while the elders and pastors in convention constituted the Consistory, whose function was to supervise and regulate the citizens' behavior. A series of regulations were published commanding obedience under pain of excommunication. Strict religious practice was enforced; dancing and games were prohibited. Fines were levied for nonattendance at Sunday church services—or not remaining through the sermon. Obstinate opponents of the Church were executed, most famously the Spaniard Michael Servetus, a refugee from the Inquisition whose denial of both the Trinity and the divinity of Christ was well beyond any definition of Christian orthodoxy. After an ecclesiastical trial in Geneva he was sentenced to be burned at the stake—Calvin himself had preferred more humane beheading—along with his book. In October 1553 the sentence was carried out and shortly thereafter Calvin received congratulatory letters from both the Lutheran and Catholic authorities.

The powers of the Consistory in particular appeared to some Genevans to be little better than the episcopal oppression they had earlier suffered, but a continuous influx of new Reformers from France—by 1560 they constituted half the city's population—solidified the revolution, and stood ready to export it elsewhere in the Reform world. Back in France, the movement eventually failed: in Scotland it took deep root under the leadership of John Knox (d. 1572)—though not in England, where Elizabeth was not prepared for the notion of collective leadership and preferred that her national church remain firmly episcopal. In Germany, Reform Christianity contested the claims of Lutheranism. Geneva thus became the Protestant Rome, a model of a Reform Christian commonwealth, an authoritative court of last resort for all who shared that ideal, and a potent propaganda mill whose presses cranked out an enormous stream of works on the Reform in Latin and the European vernaculars.

Lutheranism was essentially a local Reform phenomenon, supported by, and indebted to, the princes of a patchwork sixteenth-century Germany. It was Catholic in many of its institutions and firmly episcopal in its hierarchical organization. Bishops were responsible for doctrine, but Lutherans were willing to turn over at least some responsibility for actual control of behavior to the state. Calvinism, largely spread and maintained by refugees, was far more international in its scope and ambitions, and, unlike Lutheranism, believed that the regulation of behavior was and should remain the responsibility of the church, not in the person of a single leader, but collectively, in the manner embodied at Geneva by the Consistory.

Modern Iran differs from sixteenth-century Geneva in several important respects, not least of which is scale: one is a small city, the other a sprawling and populous modern nation-state. The Geneva revolution displaced one ecclesiastical regime by another, with the very important, even critical, assistance of outsiders. The Iranian revolutionaries were all homegrown, and they replaced a secular regime with a religious one. But the two revolutions worked toward very similar ends. Both attempted to install a collective leadership in place of an aggressively monarchical one and, more importantly, they both subscribed to the notion that the behavior of members of the polity should be overseen and regulated by clerics—that the church, if it was not quite the state, could ensure that the members of the political community performed God's will.

The Calvinists' conflict with the Lutherans over the surrender to the state of those supervisory and regulatory powers finds its echo in contemporary Islam in the clash of Calvinist perspectives of the Iranian Shiites with the more Lutheran views of the Saudis. The House of Saud, which is a kinship group and neither a clerisy nor a holy family, is in effect the state of which the Wahhabi ulama constitute the highly dependent church, and to which those clerics have surrendered the responsibility of seeing to it that the sharia is observed.

Finally, though the Genevans actively proselytized their brand of Christian living, their commonwealth was essentially a parochial enterprise. The goals of the Islamic Republic of Iran, in contrast, are clearly and explicitly international. The army, particularly its shadow regiments, the Revolutionary Guard, must take on itself "the burden of the ideological mission, that is, jihad, to spread the rule of God's law throughout the world." And although "God's law" prevails within Iran in its Imami Shiite version, the Constitution in Article 11 recognizes that "all Muslims belong to one umma" and states as one of the government's goals the reunification of all Muslims in that pristine community.

End Thoughts

MONOTHEISTS ARE BRED-IN-the-bone fanatics, an attitude they learned at the (allegorical) knee of the Creator, who was, as he himself noted, "a jealous God" who would brook no competitors or rivals and who required absolute fidelity of his followers. Little wonder, then, that when circumstances have permitted, Jews, Christians, and Muslims have shown zero tolerance of the various *goyim*, *ethne*, *pagani*, or *kafirun* who have surrounded them. The latter had to recognize the One True God or else be remitted to death or enslavement.

This does not seem familiar, or even true, to us. In the twenty-first century "circumstances" do not give free rein to such behavior, and most Jews, Christians, and Muslims would be horrified at the prospect of posing such an alternative to the pagan family up the street. In the first place, the law does not permit it—the law, that is, of the civil society that is the circumstance in which most of us now live. The separation of church (read: religious communities) and state, which is one of the primary characteristics of civil society, had bade the monotheists to hold their peace, though not their tongues: shouting is permitted, but bashing, or even encumbrance, will not do. In civil states, religion is not acceptable as a ground for violence, toward the individual, the group, or, indeed, another state: crusades are no longer just wars.

Even more fundamentally, freedom of conscience has come to be recognized as a basic human right by societies generally and even by the churches of the Jews and Christians. There too the freedom to be wrong has trumped even the need to be right. Like their condemnation of slavery, this is a recent and still incomplete development among the monotheists, particularly among the Christians who have always made belief and doctrine primary criteria for both community membership and a share in the Afterlife. The Christian evolution toward accepting the primacy of conscience over doctrine began with the Reformation, which in the name of conscience rejected important aspects of what had been until then traditional beliefs. It received another powerful impetus from the Enlightenment, which granted reason absolute priority over belief, and found its political fulfillment in the American and French

Revolutions' creation of a secular state where religion was a private and, from the state's perspective, decidedly secondary concern.

Religion as a private matter was a novel notion in the monotheist family. From the Torah to the Quran, religion, the convenient catchall term for belief, ritual, and behavior, was a way of life, not merely an aspect of life, or a "life-in-Christ," as Paul never tired of saying. Indeed, it remains so for many Jews, Christians, and Muslims, who must nevertheless conform to the dictates of a secular polity that sometimes sanctions religious practices—one may be validly married by a (state-certified) faith minister, for example—sometimes prohibits them—the church may not dissolve that same contract—and otherwise simply ignores the beliefs and practices of the religious communities.

Civics and Civility

Most Jews and Christians have long lived in civil societies, which have taught the monotheists to be—how else can one put it?—"civil" to one another, to refrain from religious persecution, repression, or even discrimination, all of which were once, in one form or another, built into their charters. Tolerance is principally a secular virtue and the monotheists were constrained to embrace it. The Jews did so eagerly, even greedily, since they were far more often the objects of intolerance than its perpetrators. The Christians, who were wearied not of persecuting the Jews but of killing each other, eventually acceded as well, though both at the price of seeing their values, their projects, and their concerns increasingly marginalized in the secular state.

Muslims have not had quite the same experience. By the beginning of the twentieth century the rapidly disintegrating provinces of the Ottoman Empire, which itself was struggling to decide whether it was a civil or a religious polity, began to reorganize themselves, most at the urging of their European colonial masters, into Western-style secular states, with their own somewhat mitigated but nonetheless genuine separation of church and state. The results are still broadly apparent in the Muslim world. Morocco, Tunisia, Egypt, Syria, Turkey, Iraq, and Indonesia, to name the most important, were and remain civil societies, where citizenship is a juridical rather than a religious matter and hence can be extended to all. State policy has increasingly narrowed the church's jurisdiction to matters of personal status, marriage, for example, sometimes divorce, and sometimes inheritances. Civics is taught in the public schools, Islam in the mosques and madrasas.

But the Muslim evolution from umma, that peculiarly Islamic society that is simultaneously the community of believers and a functioning polity, a church *and* a state in our parlance, into a purely civil society has been much slower, and more halting, than in its Jewish and Christian counterparts. For Muslims, the notion of a religious state has been far more organic and powerful than for their monotheist counterparts. The Prophet's own umma at Medina, which lasted a scant ten years, constitutes the Muslim version of a golden age. A return to "true" Judaism, in contrast, has long teetered between some secular (and often anticlerical) Zionist vision of David's kingdom and an orthodox (and often anti-Zionist) version of seventeenth- or eighteenth-century life within the pale. The State of Israel provides the clinical example. Christian fundamentalists from the Reformation to the present locate their utopian Christianity in the apostolic age, which, whatever its other virtues, was ostentatiously free of both the Papism and the Caesaropapism that followed Constantine's imperial Council of Nicaea.

The notion of a singular, unitary Islamic umma—the Medina and early caliphal model—is reviving in the face of the twentieth century's version of a Muslim civil polity. And although that Abode of Islam model and its ideology are clearly contrary to the notion of a particular nation-state, the Islamists who embrace the former seem willing to countenance, at least as an interim stage, an Islamic state whose authenticity is validated by its promotion of the sharia as the law of the land but whose legitimacy is rendered problematic by its national character. Such have been created on a republican model in Iran, on a monarchical one in Saudi Arabia, for a time by the Taliban in Afghanistan, fitfully in Pakistan and the Sudan, and idiosyncratically in Libya. In all these instances, purists turn their eyes from "state" and dwell instead on the qualifier "Islamic."

Capital and Other Crimes

Whatever the monotheists lack in tolerance, they make up in conviction. God is not only jealous; he is also absolute in power and absolute in will. In the Torah and the Quran that divine will prescribes, with what seems to be a lavish hand, capital punishment, mutilation, stoning, and flogging in this life for those who would disobey his commandments, and, as it came to be believed, even more horrible torments in the life to come. God himself would presumably tend to the punishments beyond the tomb, but the exaction of divine justice here below rested on more pragmatic grounds. Where the church had judicial powers to execute those sentences, as in ancient Israel and the Islamic umma, such penalties for deviation were feasible, but when the faith community's political power disappeared (or passed into the hands of a secular state), those penalties were mitigated or commuted, although they forever remain, like all God's Words, "on the Books." In the reverse scenario, once Christianity consummated its uneasy fourth-century marriage with the Roman Empire, the Christian Church, which early on could do no more than show deviants the door, was then able to entertain more serious punishments for the heretic, the apostate, and the infidel. Without some form of the Roman state or its successors to wield the sword or put the torch to the pyre, the Christian Church could not have entertained thoughts of either the Crusade or the auto-de-fé.

Making Jews

Nowhere is the monotheists' conviction more visible perhaps than in their attempts to impose their beliefs, by persuasion or by force, on others who do not share them. There are nuances here, of course. Jews are remarkable in that they worshiped what they came to understand was the universal God, who apparently thought in as tribal a manner as they did—"Abraham and his descendants" speaks to kinship, not conviction—and reserved his command-ments, and the rewards for their observance, uniquely for the Benei Israel. God's universal reign would of course manifest itself in the End Time; mean-while the goyim could eat, drink, and fornicate as they would. The thought was somewhat troubling to the rabbis, and out of that unease came the notion of the Noahide Commandments, which were not a watered-down version of the Torah for the goyim but rather a more general (and more primitive) code for humankind sent down before the Mosaic dispensation was given to the Israelites.

Israelites and Jews have made only sporadic, short-lived efforts to persuade (and occasionally coerce) others to worship the One True God—but not from any lack of conviction that they were pursuing the true, the only, path. One reason others have not been more generally invited to join them is the com-munity's underlying tribal nature, which God Himself decreed. Kinship groups—the Benei Israel have identified themselves, loosely and at times uneasily, as such—can assimilate "aliens" only with difficulty and rarely with enthusiasm. That inability led to the separation of the Christians, whose wholesale "ingathering of the Gentiles" was unacceptable in numbers and manner to their fellow Jews, and the experience obviously deepened the Jewish reluctance to go out and seek non-Israelite converts to the Chosen People. The Christians, for their part, wrenchingly lost their tribal identifica-tion (which Jesus never did) and in the end embraced their own rather unex-pected success as a mission to the Gentiles. "Go, then, to all nations," Jesus is made to say at the end of Matthew's Gospel, "and make them my disciples" (Matt. 28:19). His followers never ceased to follow his advice. Christianity has been from the outset a universalist and missionary religion, and enormous resources in wealth and personnel have been expended on carrying the Gospel to all who would listen and, not infrequently, to many who would not.

Making Christians

After Constantine's conversion, the Christian mission to convert the pagans became a joint enterprise of the Church and the Roman Empire. Paganism and its rituals were criminalized by imperial law, and in 529, the emperor Justinian, who launched pagan-hunting expeditions into the Near Eastern outback, shut down both the last functioning pagan temple in the empire, in Upper Egypt, and the intellectual heart of pagan Hellenism, the Platonic Academy in Athens. Christian missionaries, meanwhile, many of them from the Church's monastic communities, pushed beyond the imperial frontiers. They clambered over Hadrian's wall in Britain to evangelize the Picts, sailed the Irish Sea to convert the wild Celts on the thither shore, and crossed the Rhine and the Danube to bring first the Germanic tribes and then the Slavs into the Christian fold. Eastern Christians, merchants and monks, traveled the silk routes eastward to China and India and planted the cross there.

New worlds discovered meant new worlds to be conquered both for Christ and for the king. Jesuits, Dominicans, and Franciscans rode Portuguese and Spanish men-of-war to the farthest realms of Asia and America, where the banner of the faith and the crown were planted, often on the same stanchion. With the Reformation and the Enlightenment that followed, Christians began to turn to the perhaps less fruitful but certainly equally satisfying task of converting one another to a particular confessional version of the faith. The overseas ventures among the heathen continued, but now without government subsidy or support, though churches' role in the progress of colonialism should not be discounted. And increasingly the evangelizing Christians encountered their other missionary rivals for the souls of the pagans, the Muslims.

Making Muslims

Muhammad was a missionary: his primary goal was to convert the pagans of Mecca to the cult of the One True God. While at Medina, and with the growing success of his mission, he turned from conversion to catechesis, the instruction of those who were already Muslims, and his followers took up the missionary task in his stead. Christian missionaries began by working within the Roman Empire, then followed in the military's tracks as the empire's borders expanded, and outran the emperor's troops in their zeal to carry the Word to the unredeemed. In Islam, the troops *were* the missionaries: monk and conquistador were one.

Submitting meant accepting the Muslims' political sovereignty and, for pagans, submitting, without preliminaries, to the absolute sovereignty of the Muslims' God. Christians and Jews, however, and latterly the Zoroastrians, who together soon constituted the overwhelming majority of the vanquished peoples, had only to accept the conqueror's political authority since they already worshiped, however imperfectly, the True God who was Allah. Thus the Abode of Islam expanded politically, and as it grew, it had within it large numbers of protected People of the Book who could not be coerced but could certainly be converted. And they were: not all, but most of the Jews and Christians of the Abode of Islam, at first slowly and then more rapidly, became Muslims. It was conversion from within, effected not by Muslim proselytizing but by Muslim example and Muslim inducements. The process went on as long as the Abode of Islam's political borders expanded, and, when they no longer did, after nearly a thousand years, other Muslims, mainly Sufis, went abroad to preach God's Word among the people to the east. To the west lay only Christians and Jews, who showed themselves little inclined to convert if they were not Muslim subjects—as little as Muslims did except when they were under Christian sovereignty.

A Crucial Difference

Muslims and Christians differ in one crucial regard. Muslims knew about Christianity, from the Quran initially and from the many Christians who lived in their midst. Christians had the same kind of enlightening contacts with Muslims, in Spain, for example, or Sicily. But Muslims had little sense or understanding of Christendom, whereas Christians were relatively well informed, and increasingly interested, in the Abode of Islam. Even as the Muslims were taking Jerusalem in the 630s, Latin Christian pilgrims were there, observing them and their ways. A steady stream of European pilgrims continued to pass through the Muslims lands of the Middle East before, during, and after the Crusades, observing, noting, and often publishing their reflections on what they had seen. In the twelfth and thirteenth centuries Italian and Spanish merchants, and the occasional missionary, began to show up in the port cities of North Africa, and from the sixteenth century onward European trading companies had branches in the Middle East. At the tail end of the eighteenth century Napoleon landed his grenadiers and his orientalists in Egypt, followed in the nineteenth by missionaries.

This knowledge of the state of Muslim affairs, however defective its content and polemical its intent, led to aggressive schemes for reconquering the Islamic lands and, of greater concern here, effecting conversion. In ecclesiastical circles plans for such a project began to be hatched in the twelfth century. They led to the Latin translation of the Quran and related Islamic writings for the instruction of missionaries. In the first decades of the fourteenth century a decree of the Council of Vienne (1311–1312) established centers for teaching Arabic, "for propagating the saving faith among the heathen," at the Roman curia and the universities of Paris, Oxford, Bologna, and Salamanca. There, Latin translations of Muslim philosophers were already curricular commonplaces. No such interest or plan arose in Marrakech, Cairo, or Damascus, no place in the madrasa for courses in Latin or Romance. Muslims remained, even during and after the European Crusades, uninterested and ignorant of the People of the Book beyond the borders of the Abode of Islam.

Index